Women's Poetry Index

Women's Poetry Index

by Patricia A. Guy

ORYX PRESS
1985

The rare Arabian Oryx is believed to have inspired the myth of the unicorn. This desert antelope became virtually extinct in the early 1960s. At that time several groups of international conservationists arranged to have 9 animals sent to the Phoenix Zoo to be the nucleus of a captive breeding herd. Today the Oryx population is over 400 and herds have been returned to reserves in Israel, Jordan, and Oman.

Copyright © 1985 by The Oryx Press
2214 North Central at Encanto
Phoenix, Arizona 85004-1483

Published simultaneously in Canada

Printed and Bound in the United States of America

 The paper used in this publication meets the minimum requirements of American National Standard for Information Science—Permanence of Paper for Printed Library Materials, ANSI Z39.48, 1984.

Library of Congress Cataloging in Publication Data

Guy, Patricia A.
  Women's poetry index.

  Bibliography: p.
  1. Poetry—Women authors—Indexes.   I. Title.
PN1024.G89   1985   016.8081   84-42816
ISBN 0-89774-173-0

Table of Contents

Acknowledgements   vii

Introduction   ix

User's Guide   xi

Anthologies   xiii

Poet Index   1

Title Index   57

First Line Index   93

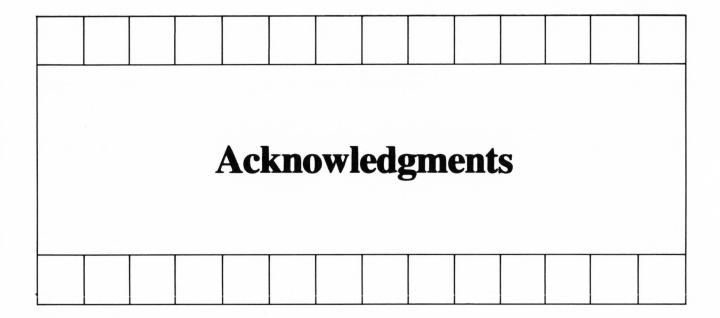

Acknowledgments

This index was not a solitary endeavor. Many helped!

During the formative stages of the project, Carole Leita (Reference Librarian and Women's Collection Specialist, Berkeley Public Library) reviewed the index proposal, including the organization of the index and the form and content of the entries. Her comments and enthusiasm remained with me throughout my work.

Joan Ariel (Women's Studies Librarian, University of California at Irvine); Ellen Broidy (Coordinator of Library Education Services, University of California at Irvine); Diane Davenport (Supervising Reference Librarian, Berkeley Public Library); Frances E. Kendall (Consultant on Multicultural Education and Racial Issues); and Neel Parikh (Coordinator of Children's Services, San Francisco Public Library) suggested anthologies. Their expertise in women's literature helped ensure that important anthologies were collected for the index.

Mama Bears and A Woman's Place, women's bookstores in Oakland, California, were indispensable as resources for identifying and acquiring the majority of the anthologies indexed.

Some collections were no longer available for purchase, and Catherine Sylvia (Bay Area Library and Information System) arranged library loans for these.

Sayre Van Young (author, editor, and Reference Librarian at Berkeley Public Library) provided invaluable assistance with the text portions.

Important all along the way, friends and family offered encouragement and understanding, even when it meant tolerating erratic visits, few phone calls, and fewer letters. Thank you all more than I can ever tell you!

Finally, I want to thank Neel Parikh, good friend and companion, who has provided useful advice, quiet time, and an atmosphere of interest and support from the project's inception.

Patricia A. Guy

Introduction

The publishing of women's poetry has reached a notable level of achievement. Since anthologies come into being only when enough of a literature has been published to allow selection, it is noteworthy that for the first time in history there are sufficient anthologies of women's poetry to warrant an index. Had this index been attempted six years ago, over half of the collections included here would have been missing, still unpublished. Now, and at an accelerating rate, new anthologies are coming forth. It is, indeed, a time to pause, to take note, and to celebrate!

This index covers 51 anthologies, each of which was compiled for specific and varied reasons. Some anthologies bring unknown, non-English poets to our attention or present new poets or poets known by only a small audience; others concentrate on particular ethnic contributions or provide women's studies courses with useful collections of women's literature. There is little duplication in the poetry selected, which shows the special care and unique purpose behind the compiling of each. Over and over, the editors of these anthologies have demonstrated high levels of scholarship, judgment, and determination to offer collections that break new ground and extend what is available.

Several basic principles guided the selection of the anthologies for this index. First, the books had to be reasonably available, either for purchase or through libraries. The user of an index is helped very little by finding that a poem is contained in an out-of-print collection owned by only a smattering of libraries or is in some other way not accessible. Second, the collections had to represent the full range of women's anthologies available, including multiethnic and non-English works in translation. Some collections were chosen which, while they are not exclusively poetry an-thologies, do contain a substantial amount of poetry. Finally, anthologies indexed in *Granger's Index to Poetry* are not included.

Why produce an index limited to women's anthologies? There are some compelling reasons. There is little access to women's poetry through indexes. *Granger's Index to Poetry,* the major reference work, covers some outstanding anthologies of women's poetry; however, the women's collections comprise only 5 percent of the anthologies covered in the most recent edition. Further, the small presses and the university and trade publishers who may have taken financial chances to produce the anthologies indexed here deserve not only gratitude for taking risks, but they also should be supported by making these and future anthologies increasingly marketable. Libraries, a major market, are more likely to acquire anthologies that are or will be indexed than those that are not.

While constructed in the standard format for a poetry index, this index adds several new features: (1) The bibliography includes an indicator that biographical information is contained in the text of an anthology when this is so. Given the dearth of biographical detail on many women poets, even the scant amount sometimes given in these collections is more than exists elsewhere. (2) Library of Congress and ISBN numbers have been added to most bibliographic entries to make searching these collections more efficient in bibliographic databases. (3) In Part 3, the First Lines Index, inclusion of more than the first line is given when the first line is too brief to permit poem identification.

With use, other refinements should become apparent. Meanwhile, may this index help the user find the poet and the poem, the end reason for a work of this kind, after all.

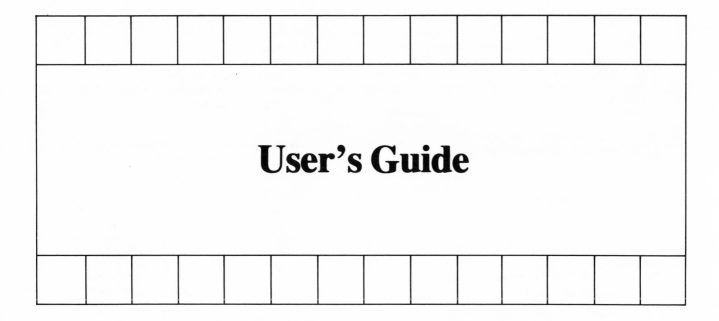

User's Guide

The arrangement of the index and the content of the entries follow common form in poetry indexing.* Variations exist for certain circumstances. These are shown with examples.

PART 1, POET INDEX

The main entry for each poem is found in this portion of the index. Each entry contains the poet's name, birth and death date (if known), poem title, anthology acronym (see ''Anthologies'' for key), and page number(s). When applicable, the following additional information is provided, indicated by format:

1. When the poem has no title, the first line of the poem is given in parentheses as a means of identification.

   Example:
   Yamakawa Tomiko (1879–1909)
   untitled. (I leave all the scarlet flowers). WPJ, 67.

2. When the title is really a subtitle of a larger poetical work, the subtitle is shown in indentation.

   Example:
   Rukeyser, Muriel (1913–1980)
   Searching/not searching. WAW, 240–45.
   For Dolci. WAW, 241.

---

*Because of the wide variety of nationalities reflected in the poets' names, alphabetization of their names in Part 1 is in a letter-by-letter sequence. The poem titles, however, and first lines are arranged in word-by-word order.

3. When the poem is published in the original language and in translation, the original title is shown in parentheses.

   Example:
   Pizarnik, Alejandra (1936–1972)
   I ask silence. (Pido el silencio). OTT, 238–39.

4. When the entire poem does not appear in an anthology, but only an excerpt, this is shown in parentheses following the page numbers of the anthology or anthologies listed.

   Examples:
   Grahn, Judy (1940–
   A woman is talking to death. APO, 99–103. (excerpts). LPO, 73–80. (excerpts). NET, 44–46. (excerpts).

   Loy, Mina (1882–1966)
   Parturition. SOW, 96–98; 100–02. (excerpts). WSO, 254–57.

In the Loy entry above ''Parturition'' is published in excerpts in SOW (*Seasons of Woman*), but it is published in its entirety in WSO (*The World Split Open*).

PART 2, TITLE INDEX

While most of these entries are straightforward references to the poet main entries, qualifications are added when variations occur.

1. When the entire poem does not appear in the anthology, but only an excerpt, this is shown in parentheses following the title.

   Example:
   In the Jerusalem Hills. (excerpt). **Leah Goldberg.**

2. When the title is really a subtitle of a larger work, the larger work is shown in parentheses.

   Example:
   Chorus. (The tragedie of Mariam, the faire queene of Jewry). **Elizabeth Tanfield Carey, Lady.**

3. When the parentheses come *before* the first period in the title, the words in parentheses are part of the title.

   Example:
   Gertrude Ederle swims the channel (August 6, 1926). **Mary Winfrey.**

4. For complete identification of nondistinctive titles, see Part 1, Poet Index. The Title Index makes no distinctions.

   Example:
   Sonnet. **Edna St. Vincent Millay.**

PART 3, FIRST LINE INDEX

The basic entry contains the first line, the poet, and the title of the poem. Exceptions are shown with examples.

1. When the first line is insufficient in length to provide adequate identification, the second line (and sometimes subsequent lines) is added, separated from the first line by a slash.

   Example:
   Ask me not/If now I write poems **Yosano Akiko.** Tangled hair.

2. Alphabetization is by the first line *only*, regardless of the addition of subsequent lines.

   Example:
   Now/the polar nights/startle the **Veronica Porembacu.** White bears.
   Now a whole year has waxed and waned and whitened **Isabel C. Clarke.** Anniversary of the Great Retreat.

3. To provide better coverage of poems, all first lines of subsections of poems have been included in the First Line Index.

   Example:
   Elegant replaced by delicate and tender, delicate and **Gertrude Stein.** Patriarchal poetry.
   Their origin and their history patriarchal poetry their **Gertrude Stein.** Patriarchal poetry.

4. When, however, a first line is the first line of a titled subsection to a larger work, the larger title is shown in parentheses at the end of the entry.

   Example:
   Initially glimpsing/an ivory pharoah figure **Barbara Guest.** Clouet of silks. (Quilts).

5. To the extent possible, an attempt was made to preserve unusual spacing in first lines.

   Example:
   You of the eternal truths   O great queen of queens **Enheduanna.** Inanna exalted.

CROSS-REFERENCES

Poets are cross-referenced from all possible constructions of their names if there is the slightest possibility for confusion. And, because of the differences in translations for bilingual titles and first lines, when a poem appears in more than one anthology and has variations in language, one translation has been selected, and cross-references are made to the selected translation.

Anthologies

AAA   *Alone amid All this Noise: A Collection of Women's Poetry.* Ann Reit, ed. New York: Four Winds Press, 1976. 118 p. 75-38705. 0-590-07359-1.

AOW   **Anthology of Women Poets.* Pamela Victorine, ed. Berkeley, CA: Dremen, 1971. 86 p.

APO   **Amazon Poetry: An Anthology of Lesbian Poetry.* Elly Bulkin and Joan Larkin, eds. Brooklyn: Out & Out Books, 1975. 109 p. 0-918314-07-0.

BAA   **Burning Air and a Clear Mind: Contemporary Israeli Women Poets.* Myra Glazer, ed. Athens, OH: Ohio University Press, 1981. 134 p. 80-22487 0-8214-0572-1; 0-8214-0617-5(pbk.).

BAR   **Bread and Roses: An Anthology of Nineteenth- and Twentieth-Century Poetry by Women Writers.* Diana Scott, ed. London: Virago, 1982. 282 p. 0-86068-235-8.

BAW   **By a Woman Writt: Literature from Six Centuries by and about Women.* Joan Goulianos, ed. Indianapolis, IN: Bobbs-Merrill, 1973; Baltimore, MD: Penguin Books, 1974. 379 p. 72-80810. 0-14-003786-1(Penguin).

BLS   *Black Sister: Poetry by Black American Women, 1746-1980.* Erlene Stetson, ed. Bloomington, IN: Indiana University Press, 1981. 312 p. 80-8847. 0-253-30512-8; 0-253-20268-X(pbk.).

BTS   **Breaking the Silences: An Anthology of 20th Century Poetry by Cuban Women.* Margaret Randall, trans. and ed. Vancouver, BC: Pulp Press Book Publishers, 1982. 293 p. 0-88978-106-0.

BTT   **Before Their Time: Six Writers of the Eighteenth Century.* Katharine M. Rogers, ed. New York: Ungar, 1979. 156 p. 78-20942. 0-8044-2742-9; 0-8044-6746-3(pbk.).

BWO   **By Woman: An Anthology of Literature.* Linda Heinlein Kirschner and Marcia McClintock Folsom, eds. Boston: Houghton Mifflin, 1976. 478 p. 74-30887. 0-395-20500-X.

CAM   **Cameos: 12 Small Press Women Poets.* Felice Newman, ed. Trumansburg, NY: Crossing Press, 1978. 167 p. 78-16033. 0-89594-010-8; 0-89594-011-6(pbk.).

CGW   **Contemporary Greek Women Poets.* Eleni Fourtouni, trans. and ed. New Haven, CT: Thelphini Press, 1978. 74 p. 82-155960.

CNF   **Confirmation: An Anthology of African American Women.* Amiri Baraka and Amina Baraka, eds. New York: Quill, 1983. 418 p. 82-21425. 0-688-01580-8; 0-688-01582-4(pbk.).

EOU   **Extended Outlooks: The Iowa Review Collection of Contemporary Women Writers.* Jane Cooper, et al, eds. New York: Macmillan, 1981. 381p. 82-12858. 0-02-528080-5; 0-02-049690-7 (Collier, pbk.).

FIR   **Fireflight: Three Latin American Poets.* Elsie Alvarado de Ricord, Lucha Corpi, and Concha Michel. Catherine Rodríguez-Nieto, trans. Kensington, CA: Oyez, 1976. 109p. 0-685-73658-X.

FYP   **Four Young Lady Poets.* New York: Totem Press, 1962. Unnumbered pages. 62-17666.

FYW   **Four Young Women: Poems, by Jessica Tarahata Hagedorn and Others.* Kenneth Rexroth, ed. New York: McGraw-Hill, 1973. 148 p. 72-10091. 0-07-073844-0.

---

*The asterisk (*) before the title means that the anthology contains biographical information on the poets in the collection.

HFE *Hard Feelings: Fiction and Poetry from Spare Rib*. Alison Fell, ed. London: Women's Press, 1979. 217 p. 80-488874. 0-7043-3838-6(pbk.).

HGI *Home Girls: A Black Feminist Anthology*. Barbara Smith, ed. New York: Kitchen Table: Women of Color Press, 1983. 377 p. 0-913175-02-1.

HOF *A House of Good Proportion: Images of Women in Literature*. Michele Murray, ed. New York: Simon and Schuster, 1973. 379 p. 72-93509. 0-671-21471-3; 0-671-21472-1(pbk.).

IAT *I Am the Fire of Time: The Voices of Native American Women*. Jane B. Katz, ed. New York: Dutton, 1977. 77-79801. 201 p. 0-525-47475-7.

IHO *In Her Own Image: Women Working in the Arts*. Elaine Hedges and Ingrid Wendt, eds. Old Westbury, NY: Feminist Press, 1980. 308 p. 79-17024. 0-912670-73-8; 0-912670-62-2(pbk.); 0-07-020439-X(McGraw-Hill, pbk.).

IWL-1 *Images of Women in Literature*. Mary Anne Ferguson, ed. Boston: Houghton Mifflin, 1973. 437 p. 72-4394. 0-395-13906-6.

IWL-2 *Images of Women in Literature*. Mary Anne Ferguson, ed. 2nd ed. Boston: Houghton Mifflin, 1977. 486 p. 76-13098. 0-395-24481-1.

IWL-3 *Images of Women in Literature*. Mary Anne Ferguson, ed. 3rd ed. Boston: Houghton Mifflin, 1981. 565 p. 80-82761. 0-395-29113-5.

KTF *Keeping the Faith: Writings by Contemporary Black American Women*. Pat Crutchfield Exum, ed. Greenwich, CT: Fawcett Publications, Inc., 1974. 288 p. 74-20743.

LAW *Latin American Women Writers: Yesterday and Today: Selected Proceedings from the Conference on Women Writers from Latin America, March 15-16, 1975*. 199 p. Sponsored by the Latin American Literary Review; Yvette E. Miller and Charles M. Tatum, eds. Pittsburgh, PA: Latin American Literary Review, 1977. 78-106724.

LPO *Lesbian Poetry: An Anthology*. Elly Bulkin and Joan Larkin, eds. Watertown, MA: Persephone Press, 1981. 297 p. 81-2607. 0-930436-08-3.

NET *Networks: An Anthology of San Francisco Bay Area Women Poets*. Carol A. Simone, ed. Palo Alto, CA: Vortex Editions, 1979. 140 p. 79-64273.

OTT *Open to the Sun: A Bilingual Anthology of Latin-American Women Poets*. Nora Jacquez Wieser, ed. Van Nuys, CA: Perivale Press, 1979. 279 p. 78-78126. 0-912288-16-7.

OVO *The Other Voice: Twentieth-Century Women's Poetry in Translation*. Joanna Bankier, et al., eds. New York: Norton, 1976. 218p. 76-45349. 0-393-04416-5; 0-393-04421-1(pbk.).

OWO *Ordinary Women: An Anthology of Poetry by New York City Women*. Sara Miles, et al, eds. New York: Ordinary Women Books, 1978. 135 p. 78-848.

SBB *Sturdy Black Bridges: Visions of Black Women in Literature*. Roseann P. Bell, Bettye J. Parker, and Beverly Guy-Sheftall, eds. Garden City, NY: Anchor Press/Doubleday, 1979. 422 p. 77-16898. 0-385-13347-2.

SOW *Seasons of Woman: Song, Poetry, Ritual, Prayer, Myth, Story*. Penelope Washbourn, ed. San Francisco: Harper & Row, 1979. 176 p. 79-273. 0-06-069258-8.

SUM *Scars upon My Heart: Women's Poetry and Verse of the First World War*. Catherine Reilly, ed. London: Virago, 1981. 144 p. 81-193380. 0-86068-226-9.

TBC *This Bridge Called My Back: Writings by Radical Women of Color*. Cherrie Moraga and Gloria Anzaldua, eds. Watertown, MA: Persephone Press, 1981. 261 p. 81-168894. 0-930436-10-5.

TIW *This Is Women's Work: An Anthology of Prose and Poetry*. Susan Efros, ed. San Francisco: Panjandrum Press, 1974. 147 p. 74-19118. 0-915572-02-8.

TPA *Touch Papers*. Judith Kazantzis, Michèle Roberts, and Michelene Wandor. London; New York: Allison & Busby, 1982. 96 p. 82-176531. 0-85031-476-3; 0-85031-477-1(pbk.).

TRP *Three Russian Poets: Margarita Aliger, Yunna Moritz, and Bella Akhmadulina*. Elaine Feinstein, trans. and ed. Manchester, England: Carcanet, 1979. 80 p. 79-319024. 0-85635-227-6.

TRW *Three Russian Women Poets*. Anna Akhmatova, Marina Tsvetayeva, and Bella Akhmadulina. Trumansburg, NY: Crossing Press, 1983. 109 p. 83-14436. 0-89594-121-X; 0-89594-120-1(pbk.).

TWO *The Third Woman: Minority Women Writers of the United States*. Dexter Fisher, ed. Boston: Houghton Mifflin, 1980. 594 p. 79-87863. 0-395-27707-8.

WAD *Without Adam: The Femina Anthology of Poetry*. Joan Murray Simpson, ed. London: Femina, 1968. 208 p. 68-143849.

WAI *Who Am I This Time?: Female Portraits in British and American Literature*. Carol Pearson and Katherine Pope, eds. New York: McGraw-Hill, 1976. 305 p. 75-29130. 0-07-049032-5.

WAW *Woman as Writer*. Jeannette L. Webber and Joan Grumman, eds. Boston: Houghton Mifflin, 1978. 451 p. 77-74379. 0-395-26088-4.

WPC *Women Poets of China*. Kenneth Rexroth and Chung Ling, trans. and eds. New York: New Directions, 1982. 150 p. 81-18698. 0-8112-0821-4. (Previously published as *The Orchid Boat: Women Poets of China*. Kenneth Rexroth and Chung Ling, trans. and eds. New York: McGraw-Hill, 1972. 72-6791. 0-07-073744-4.).

WPE *Woman Poet: The East*. Elaine Dallman, et al, eds. Reno, NV: Women-In-Literature, 1981. 123 p. 81-69793. 0-935634-03-7; 0-935634-02-9(pbk.).

WPJ   *Women Poets of Japan*. Kenneth Rexroth and
      Ikuko Atsumi, trans. and eds. New York:
      New Directions, 1982. 81-18693.
      0-8112-0820-6. (Previously published as *The
      Burning Heart*. Kenneth Rexroth and Ikuko
      Atsumi, trans. and eds. New York: Seabury
      Press, 1977. 184 p. 77-1833. 0-8164-9318-9.)
WPO   *Women Poets of the World*. Joanna Bankier and
      Deirdre Lashgari, eds. New York: Macmillan,
      1983. 442 p. 82-7794. 0-02-305720-3.
WPW   **Woman Poet: The West*. Elaine Dallman, et al, eds.
      Reno, NV: Women-In-Literature, 1980.

100 p. 79-55988. 0-935634-01-0;
0-935634-00-2 (pbk.).
WSO   **The World Split Open: Four Centuries of Women
      Poets in England and America, 1552-1950*. Louise
      Bernikow, ed. New York: Vintage Books, 1974.
      346 p. 74-8582. 0-394-71072-X.
WWO   **Women Working: An Anthology of Stories and
      Poems*. Nancy Hoffman and Florence Howe, eds.
      Old Westbury, NY: Feminist Press, 1979. 271 p.
      78-4636. 0-07-020431-4.

Women's
Poetry Index

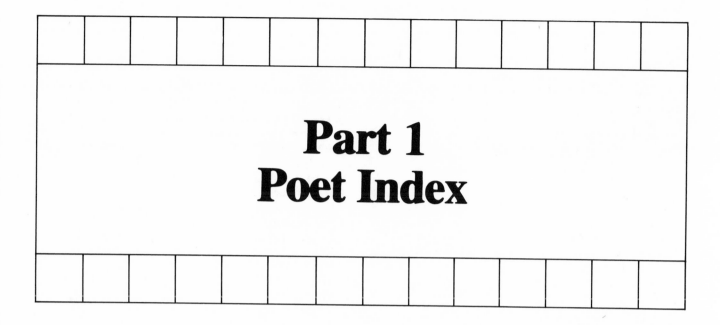

Part 1
Poet Index

Abbe, Cate
Khmer woman. NET, 70.
Abi Ya'qub al-Ansari, Maryam. *See* **Maryam bint Abi Ya'qub al-Ansari.**
Abu Khalid, Fawziyya (1955–
Mother's inheritance. WPO, 107–08.
Abutsu-Ni (1209–1283)
untitled. (Who knows/that in the depth of the ravine).
WPJ, 45.
Acosta, Teresa Palma. *See* **Palma Acosta, Teresa.**
Ada
Lines. BLS, 20–21.
Lines, suggested on reading 'An appeal to Christian Women of the South,' by A. E. Grimké. BLS, 17–19.
To the memory of J. Horace Kimball. BLS, 21–22.
untitled. (Oh, when this earthly tenement). BLS, 19–20.
Adam, Helen (1909–
I love my love. WPO, 266–69.
Adams, Anna
Her dancing days. BAR, 149–50.
Unrecorded speech. BAR, 148–49.
Adams, Jeanette
for my mamma and hers. KTF, 51–52.
missed you. KTF, 50–51.
on the first day of summer in the twenty fifth year of our lives. KTF, 52–53.
Portrait. KTF, 49.

Adawiyya, Rabi'a al-. *See* **Rabi'a al-Adawiyya.**
Adcock, Fluer (1934–
Tigers. WAD, 124–25.
Adnan, Etel (1925–
The Beirut—Hell Express. WPO. 102–05. (excerpt).
The enemy's testament. OV, 159–60.
Afif, Fatimah
Tanka. CNF, 47.
Aguirre, Mirta (1912–1980)
All may come. (Todo puede venir). BTS, 48–51.
Certainty. (Certidumbre). BTS, 50–53.
Poem of profound truth. (Poema de la verdad profunda). BTS, 46–49.
This road. (Este camino). BTS, 46–47.
Ahmad al-Qurtubiyya, 'Aisha bint. *See* **'Aisha bint Ahmad al-Qurtubiyya.**
Ai (1947–
The anniversary. TWO, 544.
The country midwife: a day. TWO, 544.
Twenty-year marriage. TWO, 543.
Aidoo, Ama Ata (1942–
Cornfields in Accra. WPO, 295–98.
'Aisha bint Ahmad al-Qurtubiyya (late 10th century)
untitled. (I am a lioness). WPO, 97.
Ait Attik, Mririda. *See* **n'Ait Attik, Mririda.**
Akazome Emon (?–1027)
untitled. (I can no longer tell dream from reality). WPJ, 23.
untitled. (I, who cut off my sorrows). WPJ, 24. WPO, 39.
untitled. (In my heart's depth). WPJ, 23. WPO, 39.
untitled. (It would have been better that I slept). WPJ, 24.
Åkesson, Sonja (1926–1977)
Ears. WPO, 252–53.
Evening walk. WPO, 251–52.
The marital problem I. OVO, 85–86.

Akhmadulina, Bella (1937–
  At night. TRW, 84.
  Automat with sparkling water. TRW, 87.
  Autumn. OVO, 104.
  A bad spring. TRP, 49–51.
  Bartholomew's night. TRW, 101–02.
  Black brook. TRW, 83.
  Chapters from a poem. TRP, 75–79.
  December. TRW, 97.
  A dream. BWO, 361.
  Fever. TRP, 55–59.
  Fifteen boys, or perhaps even more. WPO, 223–24.
  For how many years. TRP, 64.
  Goodbye. TRW, 98.
  How do I differ from a woman with a flower. TRW, 86.
  I swear. TRP, 60–61.
  I thought: you're my enemy. TRW, 88.
  The last day I live in a strange house. TRW, 96.
  Laughing, exulting and rebellious. TRW, 95.
  Music lessons. TRP, 53–54.
  Muteness. TRW, 99.
  Night. TRP, 62–63.
  Rain. TRP, 65–74. (excerpts).
  The rain sounds like a dombra. TRW, 94.
  Silence. OVO, 104–05.
  Snowless February. TRW, 103–05.
  To sleep. TRW, 100.
  Winter. TRP, 52. TRW, 91.
  Winter day. TRW, 92–93.
  You were sleeping. TRP, 80.
  Your window is on the eastern side. TRW, 89–90.
  Zhaleyka. TRW, 85.
Akhmatova, Anna (1889–1966)
  And after we damned each other. TRW, 23.
  Deception. TRW, 24–26.
  Everything is plundered. WPO, 219.
  How can you stare out at the Neva. TRW, 30.
  I pray to the light in the window. TRW, 21.
  In a shattered mirror. TRW, 36.
  In intimacy there's a secret place. TRW, 31. WPO, 220.
  In the evening. BWO, 333.
  In the high stars are all the souls. TRW, 38.
  It's all been taken away. TRW, 33.
  July 1914. WPO, 219.
  Like a white stone in the depths of a well. TRW, 32.
  Memory of the sun faints in my heart. TRW, 27.
  Memory's voice. TRW, 29.
  Northern elegy. TRW, 37. (excerpt).
  On a white night. TRW, 28.
  Requiem 1935–1940. OVO, 135–38. (excerpts).
  They never thought. TRW, 34.
  This room in which I lie sick. TRW, 40.
  Two poems. TRW, 22.
  Voronezh. TRW, 35.
  When the moon floats. TRW, 39.
  The white bird. AAA, 59.
  You are always new. AAA, 58.

Akiko, Baba. *See* **Baba Akiko.**
Akiko, Yosano. *See* **Yosano Akiko.**
Akjartoq (fl.c. 1920)
  An old woman's song. SOW, 154. WPO. 417–18.
al-Adawiyya, Rabi'a. *See* **Rabi'a al-Adawiyya.**
al-Ansari, Maryam bint Abi Ya'qub. *See* **Maryam bint Abi Ya'qub al-Ansari.**
Aleshire, Joan (1938–
  Exhibition of women artists (1790–1900). IHO, 57.
al-Hajj, Hafsa. *See* **Hafsa bint al-Hajj.**
Aliger, Margarita (1918–
  For a man on his way. TRP, 19–21. (excerpts).
  For Neruda. TRP, 31.
  Great expectations. TRP, 22–23.
  House in Meudon. TRP, 28–30.
  If everything. TRP, 27.
  Much too happy. TRP, 32.
  My lips are salt. TRP, 24.
  To the portrait of Lermontov. TRP, 26.
  Two. TRP, 25.
Alisjahbana, Samiati (1930–
  Quiet water. AAA, 90.
al-Khansa, Tumadir. *See* **Khansa, Tumadir, al-** (filed under Khansa).
Allah, Fareedah
  CINDERELLA. BLS, 167–69.
  Funky football. BLS, 170–72.
  The generation gap. BLS, 174–75.
  HUSH, HONEY. BLS, 164–67.
  Lawd, dese colored chillum. BLS, 175–76.
  You made it rain. BLS, 173–74.
Allegra, Donna (1953–
  Before I dress and soar again. HGI, 166–67.
  A rape poem for men. LPO, 255–57.
  When people ask. LPO, 257–59.
Allen, Marian
  The raiders. SUM, 1.
  The wind on the downs. SUM, 1–2.
Allen, Paula Gunn (1939–
  Beloved women. LPO, 65–66.
  Catching one clear thought alive. TWO, 128–29. WPO, 428–29.
  Creation story. LPO, 63–64.
  Diné. IAT, 154–55.
  Grandmother. TWO, 126.
  Madonna of the hills. LPO, 60.
  Medicine song. TWO, 129–30.
    The dead spider. TWO, 130.
    The duck-billed god. TWO, 130.
    Lament. TWO, 130.
    Shadow Way. TWO, 129.
  Moonshot: 1969. TWO, 127–28.
  Powwow '79, Durango. LPO, 64–65.
  Riding the thunder. LPO, 61–63.
  Wool season. IAT, 105–06. LPO, 60–61.
Allison, Dorothy (1949–
  Boston, Massachusetts. LPO, 202–03.

al-Malā'ika, Nažik. *See* **Malā'ika, Nažik, al-** (filed under Malā'ikah).

Alment, Alice
    On a picture by Smith Haldy. WAD, 129–30.

Alonso, Digdora (1921–
    Radio photo. (Radiofoto). BTS, 58–59.
    Two poems for my granddaughter. (Dos poemes para mi nieta). BTS, 56–57.
    untitled. (While the astronomer). (Mientras el astronómo). BTS, 58–59.

al-Qurtubiyya, 'Aisha bint Ahmad. *See* **'Aisha bint Ahmad al-Qurtubiyya.**

Alta (1942–
    Susie. TIW, 57.
    untitled. (we would rather lie alone). TIW, 57.
    untitled. (you, in yr levi jacket,). TIW, 55–56.

Alvarado de Ricord, Elsie
    As required by law. (Como manda la ley). FIR, 32–37.
    Interior dawn. (Alba interior). FIR, 12–13.
    A letter. (Una carta). FIR, 38–41.
    On the birth of a child. (En el advenimiento del hijo). FIR, 14–17.
    Passengers in transit. (Pasajeros en transito). FIR, 20–31.
    When your mouth said goodbye. (Cuando tu boca dijo adios). FIR, 18–19.

Ama, Fayola Kamaria
    for "Mamie." CNF, 48–49.

Ambapali (4th century B.C.)
    untitled. (Black and glossy as a bee and curled was my hair;). WPO, 53.

Amini, Johari M. *See* **Kunjufu, Johari M.**

Amiri, Akhtar
    I am a woman. WPO, 85–87. (excerpt).

Amrita Pritam. *See* **Pritam, Amrita.**

Anderson, Barbara
    There and here. EOU, 1.

Anderson, Lilian M.
    Leave in 1917. SUM, 3–5.

Andresen, Sophia de Mello Breyner (1919–
    Listen. OVO, 101.
    The small square. WPO, 258–59.
    Sonnet to Eurydice. OVO, 14.
    The young girl and the beach. WPO, 259.

Angelou, Maya (1928–
    My Arkansas. BLS, 266.
    On diverse deviations. BLS, 267.
    Phenomenal woman. TWO, 287–88.
    Sepia fashion show. BLS, 267.
    Still I rise. BLS, 265–66.
    Woman me. BLS, 264.

Anghelaki-Rooke, Katerina (1939–
    The body is the Victory and the Defeat of dreams. WPO, 255–56.
    Diogenes. OVO, 178–80.
    Magdalen the great mammal. CGW, 42–45.
    My mama and satan. CGW, 36–41.

Anne Finch, Countess of Winchilsea. *See* **Finch, Anne, Countess of Winchilsea.**

Anonymous
    The abortion. SOW, 83–84.
    The assembly of ladies. WAI, 154–55.
    Bride the aid-woman. SOW, 95.
    the choice. OVO, 45.
    Corn grinding song. IAT, 17.
    Dream song of a woman. IAT, 54–55.
    The good-looking boy. SOW, 23.
    Grandmother's prayer while presenting an infant to the sun. IAT, 7.
    The Hako. IAT, 15. (excerpt).
    Hard times cotton mill girls. WSO, 300–01.
    Hard times in the mill. WSO, 301.
    He stared at me. AAA, 32.
    I dream. IAT, 193.
    A joyful mother of children. SOW, 126.
    Love song. SOW, 61.
    Love-charm song. IAT, 49. OVO, 62.
    Love-making. SOW, 71.
    The Lowell factory girl. WSO, 302–04.
    Lullaby. IAT, 10.
    The lullaby of the snow. SOW, 118–19.
    Men's impotence. SOW, 68–69.
    The mother. SOW, 35–36.
    My love has departed. OVO, 62.
    On the slope of Hua mountain. SOW, 69. WPC, 11.
    Owl woman's death song. IAT, 59.
    Poem for Jacqueline Hill. BAR, 273–78.
    Serenade. AAA, 32.
    Song for a girl on her first menstruation. OVO, 40.
    Song for a young girl's puberty ceremony. OVO, 39.
    Song for bringing a child into the world. OVO, 44.
    Song for the newborn. SOW, 104–05.
    Song of a girl journeying to the country of the dead. OVO, 132.
    Song of a woman in labor. OVO, 43.
    A song of the dice. WPC, 56.
    Song of the old woman. OVO, 51. SOW, 156.
    Song to earth mother. IAT, 50–51.
    Songs of divorce. IAT, 48.
    To the tune "I paint my lips red." WPC, 43.
    To the tune "Picking mulberries." MPC, 44.
    To the tune "Red embroidered shoes." WPC, 54.
    Waiting for mother. SOW, 108.
    Warpath song. AAA, 33.
    The weaver's lamentation. SOW, 148–49.
    When I think of him. OVO, 63.
    Why should I be jealous. OVO, 62.
    The widow's song. IAT, 60, 62.
    The wife's lament. (modern version by Ann Stanford). WAI, 106–07.
    Wind song. AAA, 33.
    The wiping moss from the ruins. SOW, 110–11.
    A woman's song, about men. AAA, 34. OVO, 72.
    A woman's song for her drowned brother. IAT, 64.
    Women Transport Corps. WPO, 28.
    You may go on the warpath. AAA, 33.
    untitled. (Aj-ja-japa-pe). SOW, 10–11.

untitled. (Alas, alas, O Goddess, what misfortune has brought me here?). SOW, 139.

untitled. (Alas, that I should die,). SOW, 159–60.

untitled. (All Igbo come and see that my). SOW, 102.

untitled. (Ayii, Ayii, Ayii,). SOW, 62.

untitled. (The bed on which we used to sit). SOW, 36.

untitled. (Before me/when I look into the mirror). WPJ, 137.

untitled. (Between Awajishima and Suma). WPJ, 139.

untitled. (The bird that saw sings). SOW, 129–30.

untitled. (The bright sunbeams/Shoot down upon). SOW, 162.

untitled. (Clanged the keys on the table;). SOW, 30.

untitled. (come to thy beloved one). SOW, 59–60.

untitled. (The dance of the greased women). SOW, 65–67.

untitled. (Dark young pine, at the center of the earth). SOW, 19–21.

untitled. (Dearest, I know that thy body is but transitory; that). SOW, 73.

untitled. (Digging with my finger, parrot). SOW, 50–51.

untitled. (Don't give me food). SOW, 63.

untitled. (Don't scold me, grannie). SOW, 90.

untitled. (Ejaja-eja.). SOW, 132–33.

untitled. (Fine clothes have come for you). SOW, 49–50.

untitled. (For twelve years I worshipped Siva, and what is my reward?). SOW, 46.

untitled. (From the dream where we made love). WPJ, 138.

untitled. (From the heart of Earth, by means of yellow pollen). SOW, 94–95.

untitled. (From the Isle of Awaji). WPJ, 139.

untitled. (Give a seat to your visitor). SOW, 79.

untitled. (Give me my little hoe). SOW, 28.

untitled. (He who was wont to give me beautiful things, the son of Noworb,). SOW, 127.

untitled. (The heavy sobs which rise up and choke me). WPJ, 137.

untitled. (heye neye yana). SOW, 14–15.

untitled. (His teeth are white as curds). SOW, 56.

untitled. (I am about to sing this song of yours,). SOW, 18.

untitled. (I bathe thy palms/In showers of wine,). SOW, xiv–xvi.

untitled. (I come to White Painted Woman,). SOW, 18.

untitled. (I got up and opened the shoji). WPJ, 139.

untitled. (I have painted my eyes,). SOW, 75.

untitled. (I have prepared the hibachi). WPJ, 137.

untitled. (I know not whether thou has been absent:). SOW, 75.

untitled. (I searched,/I looked, but did not find.). SOW, 24–26.

untitled. (If the arms and the legs of the lover). SOW, 55.

untitled. (In the house with the tortoise chair). SOW, 91.

untitled. (It is that, in fact, that first among others, He). SOW, 92.

untitled. (It is that, when she has given birth to a child, as soon). SOW, 3.

untitled. (It is time that my mother comes home!). SOW, 119–20.

untitled. (Kangiak, while you take me for a fool,). SOW, 81.

untitled. (Listen I am just like/the cuckoo down the hillside). WPJ, 138.

untitled. (The loves of a little while ago). WPJ, 137.

untitled. (Men, divide into two groops oo). SOW, 26–27.

untitled. (My fathers,/Our Sun Father). IAT, 63.

untitled. (My little son/Where have they hidden you?). SOW, 117.

untitled. (Oh,/I am thinking). IAT, 32. SOW, 67.

untitled. (O Faithless thorn). SOW, 36.

untitled. (Oh, golden flower opened up). SOW, 78–79.

untitled. (O Mother, do not again give me a woman's birth). SOW, 87.

untitled. (O Ukko, god on high, come look here,). SOW, 99–100.

untitled. (O woman with child, it was good you gave birth.). SOW, 105–06.

untitled. (Of the [seven] and seven mother-wombs, seven). SOW, 95–96.

untitled. (Old age has come, my head is shaking). SOW, 157.

untitled. (Raja, my heart is mad for you). SOW, 56–57.

untitled. (Ri rina rina wo ri ri nawo rina). SOW, 48.

untitled. (She is graceful/My young darling). SOW, 28.

untitled. (She is very beautiful). SOW, 151.

untitled. (She says these words, made this remark:). SOW, 92–93.

untitled. (She was unloaded and delivered to us, glory be!). SOW, 2.

untitled. (The sky is covered with darkness,). SOW, 31.

untitled. (The tears gush from my eyes,). SOW, 72.

untitled. (Then . . . she (Ninmah) made into a woman who). SOW, 81.

untitled. (There was a small woman called G,). WSO, 146–47.

untitled. (This is the truth, my lover:). SOW, 12.

untitled. (Thy mother is the Great Wild Cow, living in Nekheb,). SOW, 108.

untitled. (Tonight as I sleep alone). WPJ, 137.

untitled. (The water from the little fall doth shine). SOW, 80.

untitled. (What difference does it make/What other people say). WPJ, 138.

untitled. (When a person has died the men bring their little drums.). SOW, 148.

untitled. (When I pour sake/for the man I love). WPJ, 138.

untitled. (When it's the man I love). WPJ, 137.

untitled. (When I've got the blues). WPJ, 138.

untitled. (When the child in your womb). SOW, 109–10.

untitled. (When the rain is raining,). SOW, 100.

untitled. (White Painted Woman has reached middle age by means of it,). SOW, 150–51.

untitled. (White Painted Woman's power emerges,). SOW, 18.

untitled. (Who is going to Rai Ratanpur and who is going to Drug?). SOW, 49.

untitled. (Yes my child come do the birth dance). SOW, 79.

untitled. (You and me/we live inside an egg). WPJ, 138.

untitled. (You have started out on the good earth;). SOW, 18.

untitled. (You thatched the roof with leaf and branch). SOW, 50.

untitled. (Young men there are in plenty,). SOW, 126.

Anryŭ Suharu (1923–
untitled. (When, with breaking heart,). WPJ, 73.

Ansari, Maryam bint Abi Ya'qub al-. *See* **Maryam bint Abi Ya'qub al-Ansari.**

an tSaoi, Máire Mhac. *See* **Mhac an tSaoi, Máire.**

Anzaldúa, Gloria (1946–
Three women in the closet. (Tres Mujeres en el Gabinete). LPO, 172–73.
  Contemporary goddess. (Diosa contemporanea). LPO, 172–73.
  The servant goddess. (La diosa sirvienta). LPO, 173.
  The woman. (La mujer). LPO, 172.

Apfel, Shulamit (1948–
Bedouin woman. BAA, 15.
A big woman screams out her guts. BAA, 14.
Mad Rosalinde. BAA, 16.

Appleton, Sarah (1930–
Book of my hunger, book of the earth. EOU, 3–6. (excerpts).

Araújo, Virginia de
Letter to Connie in the Maine woods. NET, 89–92.
Wild nights. NET, 88.

Armantrout, Rae (1947–
Extremities. NET, 124.
Generation. NET, 125.

Armitage, Jennifer
To our daughter. BAR, 204–05.

Armstrong, Frankie
The Collier lass. BAR, 184–85.
Month of January. BAR, 183.
Out of the darkness. BAR, 182.
Women of my land. BAR, 185–86.

Arrowsmith, Pat (1930–
Christmas story (1980). BAR, 249–51.
Political activist living alone. BAR, 243–44.

Asbaje, Juana de. *See* **Juana de Asbaje.**

Aslan, Odette
untitled. (I discover you in bits and pieces). OVO, 69.

Asphodel
Full moon in Malta. BAR, 212–13.
On the pilgrim's way in Kent, as it leads to the Coldrum Stones. BAR, 256–57.
Winter solstice—for Frank. BAR, 262.

Astra
Bloody pause. BAR, 251–52.
Daughters. BAR, 215.
Now or never. BAR, 223–24.
too late. HFE, 68–69.

Astrea. *See* **Behn, Aphra.**

Atimantiyar (c. 3rd century)
untitled. (Nowhere, not among the warriors at their festival,). WPO, 54.

Atsumi Ikuko (1940–
Different dimensions. WPJ, 128.
The ring. WPJ, 127.

Attik, Mririda n'Ait. *See* **Mririda n'Ait Attik.**

Atwood, Margaret (1939–
Against still life. WAW, 418–19.
Circle—Mud poems. IWL-3, 317. (excerpt).
Eden is a zoo. BWO, 362.
More and more. AAA, 98. WAW, 419–20.
You refuse to own. WAW, 417.
untitled. (At first I was given centuries). WAW, 416. WPO, 350–51.

Auerbach, Bethami (1949–
The search for the perfect rye bread. IHO, 58–60.

Augustine, Jane
After Yeats. WPE, 71.
I help my mother move out of her old house in the country. WPE, 71–72.

Augustini, Delmira (1886–1914)
Another race. (Otra estirpe). OTT, 24–25.
Unspeakable. (Lo inefable). OTT, 30–31.
Vision. (Visión). OTT, 26–29. WPO, 305–07.

Auvaiyar (c. 3rd century)
untitled. (Shall I charge like a bull). WPO, 54–55.
untitled. (You stand and hold the post of my small house,). WPO, 55.

Avellaneda, Gertrudis Gómez de. *See* **Gómez de Avellaneda, Gertrudis.**

Axiote, Melpo
The homestead. CGW, 22–28.

B

Baba Akiko (1928–
untitled. (In the autumn when words sound). WPJ, 74.
untitled. (Punished in the moment of love). WPJ, 75.
untitled. (Since I don't know my mother,). WPJ, 74.

Bacelo, Nancy (1933–
In a very, very quiet voice. (Muy bajito). OTT, 214–15.
It's still early. (Todavía es temprano). OTT, 220–21.
untitled. (From you from me painted dwellers). (De vos de mí teñidos habitantes). OTT, 216–17.
untitled. (I surprise myself in places). (Me sorprendo en lugares). OTT, 218–19.
untitled. (I'm not interested in facts). (No me interesan los datos). OTT, 212–13.

Bachmann, Ingeborg (1926–1973)

The respite. WPO, 242.
Songs in flight. WPO, 243–44. (excerpts).
Backberger, Barbro (1932–
I'm taking off. OVO, 64.
Bai, Mira. *See* **Mira Bai.**
Baldwin, Marjorie
The nature lesson. WAD, 50–51.
Banks, Barbara
Valediction. KTF, 54.
Banus, Maria (1914–
Wedding. OVO, 75.
Baraka, Amina (1934–
Haiti. CNF, 71.
I wanna make freedom. CNF, 72–73.
Sortin-out. CNF, 73–75.
Soweto song. CNF, 70.
Barba, Sharon (1943–
Dykes in the garden. APO, 64. LPO, 128.
Siblings. APO, 62–63. LPO, 126–27.
Barnard, Anne Lindsay, Lady (1750–1825)
Auld Robin Gray. WAI, 125–26.
Barnard, Mary (1909–
The gorge. WPW, 35.
Journey. WPW, 34.
The pump. WPW, 35.
Real estate. WPW, 34.
The Rock of Levkas. WPW, 35.
Static. WPW, 34.
Barnes, Jo
Clinic day. BAR, 241–42.
Barrington, Judith
Poems. HFE, 147–49.
Barrington, Pauline
'Education.' SUM, 6.
Barros, Silvia (1939–
untitled. (The ears of doves are tender). (Son tiernos los oídos de las palomas). LAW, 167.
untitled. (When you guess why the eyelid falls). (Cuando adivinas el por qué cae el parpado). LAW, 166.
Bass, Ellen (1947–
September 7. APO, 20–21.
Women of the baths. APO, 21.
You do not know the breaking through. IHO, 161–62.
untitled. (Vaginas of women, all the clusters). NET, 126.
Bates, Myrtle
From the sidelines. KTF, 57.
Tears. KTF, 55.
There should be time. KTF, 56–57.
Battcock, Marjorie
The refugee. WSO, 183–84.
Battin, Wendy
Letters from three women. EOU, 9–10.
The lives we invite to flower among us flower beyond us. EOU, 11–12.
Baumfree, Isabella. *See* **Truth, Sojourner.**
Beatrice, Countess of Dia. *See* **Beatritz de Dia.**
Beatritz de Dia (late 12th century)
I'll sing, although I'm loath to make this plea. AAA, 12–13.

untitled. (Handsome friend, charming and kind,). WPO, 157.
untitled. (My true love makes me happy). WPO, 156–57.
Beausoleil, Laura (1948–
Dance mad. TIW, 96.
Living where you are. TIW, 93.
Tonight. TIW, 94–95.
Welcome home from Vietnam. TIW, 92.
Beauveau, Marie-Françoise-Catherine de, La Marquise de Boufflers. *See* **Marie-Françoise-Catherine de Beauveau, La Marquise de Boufflers.**
Becker, Robin (1951–
The landing. APO, 36–38. LPO, 232–34.
Dorothy Bradford's dream. APO, 38. LPO, 234.
Bedford, Madeline Ida
Munition wages. SUM, 7–8.
The parson's job. SUM, 8–9.
Behn, Aphra (c. 1640–1689)
The Cabal at Nickey Nackeys. WSO, 69.
The defiance. AAA, 25.
The disappointment. BAW, 89–94. WAI, 67–70. WSO, 72–76.
The lucky chance. Song. WPO, 179–80.
Sir Patient Fancy. WPO, 180. (excerpt).
Song. (*Pan*, grant that I may . . .). BAW, 88.
Song: A thousand martyrs I have made. WSO, 70.
Song: As the inamour'd Thirsis lay. WAD, 111.
Song: Love arm'd. BAW, 87–88. BWO, 313. WSO, 69–70.
Song: The willing mistress. BAW, 88–89. WSO, 77–78.
To Alexis in answer to his poem against fruition. BAW, 97–98. WSO, 71–72.
To Lysander, on some verses he writ, and asking more for his heart than 'twas worth. BAW, 94–96. WAD, 112–13.
To the fair Clarinda, who made love to me, imagin'd more than woman. BAW, 96–97. WSO, 77.
When maidens are young. AAA, 26.
Bell, Maud Anna
From a trench. SUM, 10–11.
Bellerby, Frances (1899–1975)
It is not likely now. WAD, 137–38.
Belli, Gioconda (1947–
The mundane. (Cotidiano). OTT, 122–23.
Bellinger, Cindy
Children and other reasons. WPW, 89–90.
Beneyto, Maria (1925–
Nocturne in the women's prison. WPO. 261–62.
Bennett, Gwendolyn B. (1902–
Advice. BLS, 75.
Fantasy. BLS, 72.
Hatred. BLS, 73.
Heritage. BLS, 77.
Secret. BLS, 74–75.
Song. BLS, 73–74.
To a dark girl. BLS, 76.
To usward. BLS, 76–77.
Berenguer, Amanda
Communications. (Comunicaciones). OTT, 160–63.

The fire advances (second version). (El incendio se propaga). OTT, 174.
Housework. WPO, 308.
Housework. (Tarea doméstica). OTT, 164–65.
Poema cinético (third version). OTT, 175.
Solemn inventory. (Inventario solemne). OTT, 168–71.
The sunset on the sea Saturday the 4th of March, 1972. (Poniente sobre el mar del Sabado 4 de Marzo de 1972). OTT, 172–73.
The two times table. (Tabla del dos). OTT, 166–67.
Bergé, Carol (1928–
all wars. FYP.
Another view into love. HOF, 103–04.
farewell. FYP.
the friends, a celebration. FYP.
letter from point lobos. FYP.
moss, like cauls. FYP.
of roots and sources. FYP.
paris musée de cluny. FYP.
scene. FYP.
tessa's song. FYP.
Bernadine, Sister
The sermon (Revelations). KTF, 58–60.
Berssenbrugge, Mei-Mei (1947–
Chronicle. TWO, 561–62.
Ghost. TWO, 560.
Old man let's go fishing in the yellow reeds of the bay. TWO, 560–61.
Spring Street bar. WPO, 392.
Bertken, Suster. *See* **Jacobs, Bertha (Suster Bertken).**
Bey, Brenda Connor-
The dancer. CNF, 80–81.
Martha. CNF, 78–79.
Pretending. CNF, 76–78.
Bingen, Hildegard von. *See* **Hildegard von Bingen.**
Bird, Bessie Calhoun (1906–
Proof. BLS, 83–84.
Bird, Dolly (1950–
Can I say. IAT, 131–33. WPO, 426–28.
Return to the home we made. IAT, 99–103.
Birtha, Becky (1948–
Maria de Las Rosas. HGI, 177–78.
The woman in Buffalo is given to waiting. EOU, 13–14.
untitled. (At 20, I began to know). LPO, 195.
Bishop, Bobbie (1944–
Love poem. APO, 56–57.
untitled. (grandmother's little feet). LPO, 135.
Bissert, Ellen Marie (1947–
Farewell. APO, 29. LPO, 192.
Groves II. APO, 28. LPO, 191.
ode to my true nature. LPO, 192–93.
A romance. APO, 28. LPO, 191.
Bita, Lili (1935–
The barbarian. CGW, 31.
The blood criminal. CGW, 33.
Portrait. CGW, 30.
Womb. CGW, 32.
Blackford, Anne
Family script. EOU, 21–24.

Blackwomon, Julie (1943–
Revolutionary blues. LPO, 132.
Blanco, Yolanda (1954–
IT'S RAINING. (LLUEVE). OTT, 126–27.
Blandiana, Ana (1942–
The couple. WPO, 228–29.
I have the right. OVO, 47.
Blaustein, Rachel. *See* **Rachel.**
Bloch, Alice (1947–
Six years. LPO. 186–87.
Bloch, Chana
Magnificat. NET, 23.
Blomfield, Adelaide
Attics. WPW, 92–93.
Blumstein, Rachel. *See* **Rachel.**
Bobes, Marilyn (1955–
Chronicle of a morning in 1976. (Chrónica de una mañana del año 1976). BTS, 282–85.
Elvira. (Elvira). BTS, 280–83.
Notes on Gertrudis Gómez de Avellaneda. (Apuntes sobre Gertrudis Gómez de Avellaneda). BTS, 286–87.
Old ideas speaking. (Hablan los viejos conceptos). BTS, 280–81.
Pitiful role. (Triste oficio). BTS, 280–81.
Praise of future. (Elogio del futuro). BTS, 284–85.
War dispatch. (Parte de guerra). BTS, 282–83.
Boethel, Martha
Falling South. EOU, 25–26.
Bogan, Louise (1897–1970)
The meeting. BWO, 341.
Roman fountain. WPO, 361.
Boleyn, Anne (c. 1507–1536)
Defiled is my name full sore. WAI, 63.
Bomford, Nora
Drafts. SUM, 12.
Boodson, Alison (1925–
I do not want to be your weeping woman. WSO, 176–77.
Booth, Barbara Wolf
In the shallows. IAT, 83.
Boswell, D. *See* **Tonks, Rosemary.**
Boucher, Sandy (1936–
Copy clerk - North American Aviation. TIW, 97.
Three nights on Hoffman Street. TIW, 98.
Boufflers, La Marquise de. *See* **Marie-Françoise-Catherine de Beauveau, La Marquise de Boufflers.**
Boumi-Pappas, Rita (1906–
Artemis. CGW, 18.
Erasmina. CGW, 19.
Krinio. CGW, 17.
Maria R. CGW, 16.
Box, Muriel (1905–
The price of love. WAD, 116–17.
R.I.P. WAD, 189–90.
Boyd, Melba Joyce (1950–
Beer drops. BLS, 285–86.
Sundown sigh. SBB, 357–58.
Sunflowers and Saturdays. BLS, 281–82.
Why? BLS, 283–84.

Boye, Karin (1900–1941)
A sword. OVO, 38. WPO, 250.

Boyle, Kay (1903–
The invitation in it. NET, 60–61.

Bradley, Katherine. *See* **Field, Michael.**

Bradstreet, Anne (1612–1672)
Before the birth of one of her children. SOW, 51–52. WPO, 352. WSO, 192–93.
Contemplations. WPO, 352–53. (excerpts).
The flesh and the spirit. WSO, 189–92.
In honour of that high and mighty Princess Queen Elizabeth of happy memory. WSO, 194–97.
A letter to her husband, absent on public employment. WAD, 111–12. WAI, 123–24.
The prologue. IHO, 93–94. WSO, 188–89.
Some verses upon the burning of our house July 10th, 1666. WSO, 193–94.
To my dear and loving husband. AAA, 22. BWO, 285.

Branch, Anna Hempstead (1875–1937)
The monk in the kitchen. WSO, 241–45.
Sonnets from a lock box. (XIV, XXV, XXXI). WSO, 245–46.

Braverman, Kate Ellen (1950–
Details. CAM, 47–48.
Job interview. CAM, 51–53.
Lies. CAM, 49–50.
My husband who is not my husband. CAM, 46.
Picking up your mail. CAM, 48–49.
7 P.M. CAM, 43.
Soon. CAM, 53–54.
Tracks (after reading Blaise Cendrars). CAM, 54–58.
Weekend man. CAM, 44–45.

Brenner, Summer (1945–
Childless mothers. NET, 25.
Letter to an unborn daughter. NET, 24.

Breyner Andresen, Sophia de Mello. *See* **Andresen, Sophia de Mello Breyner.**

Bridges, Shirley
So few sleep soundly. WAD, 133–34.

Bristowe, Sybil
Over the top. SUM, 13.

Brittain, Vera (1896–1970)
The lament of the demobilised. SUM, 14.
Perhaps—. SUM, 14–15.
To my brother. SUM, 15.
We shall come no more. WAD. 158–59.

Brodine, Karen (1947–
Making the difference. LPO, 188–90.
The receptionist is by definition. LPO, 188.

Brontë, Anne (1820–1849)
The captive dove. WAI, 44–45.
Lines composed in a wood on a windy day. WAD, 59–60.

Brontë, Charlotte (1816–1855)
Evening solace. WSO, 105–06.
On the death of Anne Brontë. SOW, 139–40.
What does she dream of? WAD, 59.

Brontë, Emily (1818–1848)
Ah! why, because the dazzling sun. BAR, 41–42.
D.G.C. to J.A. BAR, 44.

Death, that struck when I was most confiding. WSO, 102–03.
High waving heather. WAD, 60.
I saw thee, child, one summer's day. WSO, 96–98.
Light up thy halls! 'Tis closing day. WSO, 98–99.
The linnet in the rocky dells. BAR, 49.
No coward soul is mine. BAR, 43. WSO, 103–04.
O thy bright eyes must answer now. BAR, 40–41.
Remembrance. BAR, 48. BWO, 320–21. WSO, 101–02.
Riches I hold in light esteem. WAI. 268–69.
Shall earth no more inspire thee? WAD, 61.
Silent is the House. BAR, 45–47. WAD, 134–35.
Stanzas. SOW, 158. WSO, 104–05.
There let thy bleeding branch atone. WSO, 100.
To imagination. WSO, 100–01.
Upon her soothing breast. WSO, 99.

Brooks, Gwendolyn (1917–
The Anniad. BLS, 102–11.
Appendix to the Anniad: leaves from a loose-leaf war diary. BLS, 111.
The bean eaters. BLS, 101.
Beverly Hills, Chicago. BWO, 348–49.
The birth in a narrow room. BLS, 102. SOW, 106. WSO, 329.
Bronzeville woman in a red hat. TWO, 252–54. WAW, 261–63.
The empty woman. AAA, 81.
Jessie Mitchell's mother. WAW, 261.
kitchenette building. TWO, 251. WSO, 329–30.
The mother. BLS, 100–01. IWL-1, 137–38. IWL-3, 85–86. SOW, 122–23. WSO, 328–29.
the old-marrieds. TWO, 251–52.
Primer for Blacks. CNF, 82–83.
Riot. KTF, 60–65.
A song in the front yard. AAA, 80.
To those of my sisters who kept their naturals. CNF, 84–85.
What shall I give my children? TWO, 252.
When you have forgotten Sunday: the love story. WPO, 377–78.

Broumas, Olga (1949–
Amazon twins. LPO, 206–07.
Artemis. IWL-3, 499–500. LPO, 207–08.
Epithalmion. EOU, 29–30.
the knife & the bread. LPO, 204–06.
Mornings remembering last nights. EOU, 27–28.
Of fruit whose black seed fire. WPW, 29–30.
  Breaking camp. WPW, 30.
  Deja vu. WPW, 29.
  Fools. WPW, 29.
  Lament. WPW, 30.
  Separation. WPW, 30.
Sleeping beauty. LPO, 209–11.
Sometimes, as a child. LPO, 208–09.
untitled. (With the clear/plastic speculum, transparent). LPO, 211–12.

Brown, Dorothy Ann
Later, to Jean-Pierre. TIW, 117.

Brown, Rita Mae (1944–
  Sappho's reply. APO, 43. LPO, 136.
Brown, Rosellen (1939–
  The Famous Writers School opens its arms in the next best
    thing to welcome. WWO, 193–95.
Brown, Wilmette (1946–
  Bushpaths. LPO, 181.
  Voices from the diaspora home. LPO, 182–83.
Browne, L. E. Morgan-. *See* **Morgan-Browne, L. E.**
Browning, Elizabeth Barrett (1806–1861)
  Aurora Leigh. BAR, 59–65. (excerpts). WPO, 197.
    (excerpts).
  Bianca among the nightingales. BAR, 65–69.
  The cry of the children. WSO, 118–22.
  A curse for a nation. WPO, 197–201. WSO, 114–16.
    (excerpt).
    The curse. WPO, 199–201. WSO, 114–16.
    Prologue. WPO, 197–99.
  Hiram Powers' "Greek Slave." WSO, 123.
  A man's requirements. WSO, 116–18.
  The romance of the swan's nest. WAD, 152–55.
  The runaway slave at Pilgrim's Point. BAR, 50–58.
  Sonnets from the Portuguese.
    I. (I thought once how Theocritus had sung). WSO,
      112.
    V. (I lift my heavy heart up solemnly,). WSO, 112.
    XIII. (And wilt thou have me fashion into speech).
      BAR, 58–59.
    XIV. (If thou must love me, let it be for nought). AAA,
      35. BWO, 318.
    XVII. (My poet, thou canst touch on all the notes).
      BAR, 59.
    XXII. (When our two souls stand up erect and strong,).
      WSO, 112–13.
    XXXV. (If I leave all for thee, wilt thou exchange).
      BWO, 318.
    XLIII. (How do I love thee? Let me count the ways.).
      BWO, 319.
    To George Sand. IHO, 226. WAI, 207–08. WSO, 113–
      14.
      A desire. IHO, 226. WAI, 207–08. WSO, 113.
      A recognition. IHO, 226. WAI, 208. WSO, 113–14.
  A true dream. WSO, 108–11.
Bunting, Karen (1938–
  her immaculate house. NET, 72.
  the neighbor women. NET, 73.
Burge, Maureen
  The diet. BAR, 242–43.
  Disillusion. BAR, 245.
Burgos, Julia de. *See* **de Burgos, Julia.**
Burroughs, Margaret Goss (1917–
  Black pride. BLS, 118–20.
  Everybody but me. BLS, 121–22.
  Only in this way. BLS, 120–21.
  To soulfolk. BLS, 118.
Burt, Della (1944–
  A little girl's dream world. BLS, 162–63.
  On the death of Lisa Lyman. BLS, 163.

Spirit flowers. BLS, 161–62.
Butcher, Grace (1934–
  After the quarrel. TIW, 68.
  Images. TIW, 66.
  My name in lights. TIW, 67–68.
  The runner wonders. TIW, 69.
  State mental hospital, 5 PM, summer. TIW, 70.

C

C.A.L.T.
  Y.M.C.A. SUM, 108–09.
Calhoun, Susan Kennedy
  Mission Street bus. TIW, 89.
  The orgy. TIW, 90–91.
Campbell, Janet (1947–
  Aaron Nicholas, almost ten. TWO, 108.
  Desmet, Idaho, March 1969. TWO, 107.
  On a Catholic childhood. TWO, 106–07.
Cannan, May Wedderburn (1893–1973)
  Lamplight. SUM, 16.
  Love, 1916. SUM, 19.
  Rouen. SUM, 17–18.
  'Since they have died.' SUM. 19.
Canter, Ruthe D. (1950–
  The resemblance. APO, 95. LPO, 215.
Cárdenas, Margarita Cota. *See* **Cota-Cárdenas, Margarita.**
Carenza (fl. c.1150–1250)
  Tenson. (Co-written by Iselda). WPO, 155–56.
Carey, Elizabeth Tanfield, Lady (c. 1585–1639)
  Chorus. (The tragedie of Mariam, the faire queene of
    Jewry). WAI, 117–18.
Carrier, Constance (1908–
  Seminary. BWO, 271.
  Two, remembered. EOU, 31.
Carrillo, Jo
  And when you leave, take your pictures with you. TBC,
    63–64.
  Beyond the Cliffs of Abiquiu. TBC, 65–67.
Carter, Charlotte
  Days and nights before winter. OWO, 15–19.
  This is to be told in the manner of . . . OWO, 20–22.
Cary, Alice (1820–1871)
  The bridal veil. IWL-3, 52–53.
Casal, Lourdes (1936–1981)
  Conversation at the Bridgeport train station with an old
    man who speaks Spanish. (Conversacion en la esta-
    cion de trenes de Bridgeport con un anciano que habla
    Espanol). BTS, 126–27.
  I live in Cuba. (Vivo en Cuba). BTS, 130–31.

Now I know. (Ahora sé). BTS, 130–31.
Profile of my city. (Perfil de mi cuidad). BTS, 126–29.
Casanova-Sanchez, Olga (1947–
The girl who is always with me. (Niña que siempre va
    conmigo). LAW, 188–89.
Neither from before nor ever. (Ni de antes ni de nunca).
    LAW, 187–88.
Cassian, Nina (1924–
The blood. WPO, 230
The Kiwi bird. OVO, 36–37.
Lady of miracles. WPO, 229–30.
A man. OVO, 140.
Castellanos, Rosario (1925–1974)
Chess. (Ajedrez). OTT, 136–37.
Dawn. (Amanecer). OTT, 134–35.
Elegy. (Elegía). OTT, 130–31.
Foreign woman. WPO, 321–23.
Learning about things. (Lecciones de cosas). OTT, 142–
    47.
Meditation on the brink. (Meditación en el umbral). OTT,
    140–41.
Someone else. (El otro). OTT, 132–33.
Speaking of Gabriel. (Se habla de Gabriel). OTT, 138–39.
Useless day. WPO, 321.
Castillejo, Irene Claremont de
The last years. SOW, 149–50.
Castillo, Ana (1953–
A Christmas carol: c.1976. TWO, 389–90.
Napa, California. TWO, 386–89. WPO, 395–96. (excerpt).
    Dedicado al Sr. Chávez, Sept. 1975. TWO, 386–87.
    WPO, 395–96.
    1975. TWO, 387–89.
Our tongue was Nahuatl. TWO, 390–92.
Castro, Rosalía de (1837–1885)
I love you . . . Why do you hate me? AAA, 40.
They say that the plants do not speak. AAA, 41. WPO,
    208–09.
Cavendish, Margaret, Duchess of Newcastle (1623–1673)
Song. (The convent of pleasure). WAI, 27.
The soul's garment. BWO, 312.
untitled. (O do not grieve, Dear Heart, nor shed a tear,).
    AAA, 22.
Cerrutti, Georgette
Raining the water. APO, 25–27.
Cervantes, Lorna Dee (1954–
Beneath the shadow of the freeway. TWO, 378–81.
Heritage. TWO, 304.
Para un revolucionario. TWO, 381–83.
Poem for the young white man who asked me how I, an
    intelligent, well-read person, could believe in the war
    between the races. WPO, 397–99.
Refugee ship. TWO, 381.
The woman in my notebook. WPO, 399–400.
Chacón Nardi, Rafaela (1926–
Amelia's color. (Color de Amelia). BTS, 86–87.
Mountain girl. (Nina de monte adentro). BTS, 86–87.
Words South. (Palabras al Sur). BTS, 86–89.
Zoia. (Zoia). BTS, 88–91.

Chalfi, Raquel
Like a field waiting. BAA, 61.
Lunatics. BAA, 62.
Tel Aviv beach, Winter '74. BAA, 65.
Tiger-lily. BAA, 63–64.
A witch cracking up. BAA, 67.
A witch without a cover. BAA, 66.
Chamberlain, Brenda (1912–
Lament. WPO, 269–70.
Chang, Diana (1934–
Allergory. TWO, 430.
Cannibalism. TWO, 527. WPO, 393.
On seeing my great-aunt in a funeral parlor. BWO, 359.
Rhythms. TWO, 525–26.
Still life. TWO, 527.
What Matisse is after. TWO, 526.
Chang Chi (c.768–c.830)
A faithful wife. SOW, 43.
Chang Wên-chi (9th century)
The bamboo shaded pool. WPC, 25.
Chao, Pan. *See* **Pan Chao.**
Chao Luan-luan (8th century)
Cloud hairdress. WPC, 29.
Creamy breasts. WPC, 30.
Red sandalwood mouth. WPC, 27.
Slender fingers. WPC, 26.
Willow eyebrows. WPC, 28.
Chaudhari, Kirti (1935–
Inertia. WPO, 60.
Chedid, Andrée (1921–
The future and the ancestor. WPO, 99–100.
Cheng Min (c.1924–
The drought. OVO, 145.
Evening rendezvous. WPC, 89.
Student. WPC, 90–91.
Chester, Laura (1949–
Bees inside me. NET, 120–21.
Chi, Chang. *See* **Chang Chi.**
Chiang, Fay (1952–
chinatown. OWO, 29–30.
choreopoem I. OWO, 24–25.
choreopoem IV; 1935/chinatown. OWO, 25–26.
choreopoem VI. OWO, 26. (excerpt).
impressions. OWO, 27–28.
it was as if. TWO, 550–53.
Chie, Shindō. *See* **Shindō Chie.**
Chieh-yü, Pan. *See* **Pan Chieh-yü**
Ch'ien T'ao (early 11th century)
Written at a party where my lord gave away a thousand
    bolts of silk. AAA, 9, WPC, 34.
Chigetsu-Ni, Kawai. *See* **Kawai Chigetsu-Ni.**
Chimako, Tada. *See* **Tada Chimako.**
Chin, Ch'iu. *See* **Ch'iu Chin.**
Chine-Jo. (late 17th century)
untitled. (The fireflies' light.). WPJ, 52.
Ch'ing-chao, Li. *See* **Li Ch'ing-chao.**
Ch'ing-hui, Wang. *See* **Wang Ch'ing-hui.**
Ch'ing-tsêng, Yü. *See* **Yü Ch'ing-tsêng.**

Chino Masako (1880–1946)
    untitled. (I shall hide myself). WPJ, 68.
Chio, Nakamura. *See* **Nakamura Chio.**
Ch'iu Chin (c. 1879–1907)
    A call to action. WPC, 80.
    A letter to Lady T'ao Ch'iu, to the tune "Walking through the sedges." WPC, 81.
    To the tune "The Narcissus by the river." WPC, 82.
    To the tune "The river is red." WPC, 83.
Ch'iung, Hsüeh. *See* **Hsüeh Ch'iung.**
Chiyojo. *See* **Fukuda Chiyo-Ni.**
Chiyo-Ni, Fukuda. *See* **Fukuda Chiyo-Ni.**
Christine de Pisan (1363–c. 1430)
    Christine to her son. AAA, 15.
    untitled. (Fountain of tears, river of grief). WPO, 160–61.
    untitled. (Marriage is a lovely thing). SOW, 40. WPO, 160.
Chrystos
    Ceremony for completing a poetry reading. TBC, 191–92.
    Give me back. TBC, 197.
    He saw. TBC, 18–19.
    I walk in the history of my people. TBC, 57.
Chü, Li. *See* **Li Chü.**
Chu, Mêng. *See* **Mêng Chu.**
Chu Chung-hsien (15th century)
    To the tune "A branch of bamboo." WPC, 55.
Chudleigh, Mary Lee, Lady. *See* **Lee, Mary (Lady Chudleigh).**
Chuilleanain, Eilean ni. *See* **ni Chuilleanain, Eilean.**
Chu Miao-tuan. *See* **Chu Chung-hsien.**
Chung, Frances C.
    Cantonese opera at Sun Sing Theater. OWO, 32.
    Chinese dentist. OWO, 34.
    Guatemala. OWO, 33.
    Piropos de la chinita. OWO, 34.
    recuerdos de la chinita en Guatemala. OWO, 32.
    untitled. (he was growing old). OWO, 35.
    untitled. (a memory of ivory chopsticks). OWO, 34.
    untitled. (No one uses words such as). OWO, 35.
    untitled. (they want me to settle down). OWO, 36.
    untitled. (Walking along the Bowery, can't). OWO, 35.
Chung-hsien, Chu. *See* **Chu Chung-hsien.**
Chung Ling (1945–
    Dusk on the veranda by Lake Mendota Summer 1968. WPC, 113.
    The fall of moon lady before the landing of Apollo X. WPC, 114–15.
    On the melting lake. WPC, 116.
    Song of rootless people. WPC, 117.
    Visiting. WPC, 118.
Chuo Wên-chün (c. 178–117 B. C.)
    A song of white hair. SOW, 44. WPC, 2.
Chu Shu-chên (early 12th century)
    Playing all a summer's day by the lake, to the tune "Clear bright joy." WPC, 48.
    Plum blossoms. WPC, 47.
    Spring joy. WPC, 45.
    Spring night, to the tune "Panning gold." WPC, 46.

Claremont de Castillejo, Irene. *See* **Castillejo, Irene Claremont de.**
Clark, Naomi (1932–
    Magdalene. NET, 71.
Clarke, Cheryl (1947–
    Freedom flesh. LPO, 185.
    Palm-reading. LPO, 184.
Clarke, Isabel C.
    Anniversary of the Great Retreat. SUM, 20.
Clausen, Jan (1950–
    A Christmas letter. APO, 50–52.
    dialectics. LPO, 218–24.
        (Assata on trial in New Jersey). LPO, 219.
        (reading Plath's *Letters Home*; rereading *Ariel*). LPO, 221–22.
        (the road). LPO, 220.
        (upstate poetry tour). LPO, 222.
    grandma. CAM, 153.
    the kitchen window. CAM, 154–59.
    likeness. APO, 47. LPO, 216.
    Poem on the occasion of not receiving the Academy of American Poets' Walt Whitman Award for an outstanding first manuscript of poetry. CAM, 159–61.
    Scenario. CAM, 150.
    A sense of reality. APO, 48–50.
    SESTINA, WINCHELL'S DONUT HOUSE. LPO, 216–17.
    the transplant. CAM, 152.
    Upstate. CAM, 151.
    Waking at the bottom of the dark. CAM, 150–51.
Clavijo, Uva A.
    Declaration. (Declaracion). BTS, 25, 31–32.
Clerbout, Marguerite
    Matinal. OVO, 103.
    Spring in the woods. OVO, 102.
Cliff, Michelle (1946–
    Obsolete geography. LPO, 174–78.
    Travel notes. EOU, 32–35.
Clifford, Carrie Williams (1882–1958)
    The black draftee from Dixie. BLS, 82–83.
Clifton, Lucille (1936–
    apology (to the panthers). KTF, 67–68.
    being property once myself. KTF, 66.
    for her. CNF, 87.
    the kind of man he is. KTF, 68.
    later i'll say. KTF, 66–67.
    The lost baby poems. BLS, 247, SOW, 121.
    Miss Rosie. BLS, 248, IWL-1, 434. IWL-3, 480.
    morning mirror. CNF, 88
    my dream about being white. CNF, 87.
    My Mama moved among the days. BLS, 248.
    Turning. IHO, 174.
Clinton, Michelle T.
    Debra. HGI, 13–14.
    For strong women. HGI, 325–27.
Cluer, Elisabeth
    The last enemy. WAD, 166.

Coatsworth, Elizabeth (1893–
The empresses. AAA, 70.
Cobb, Alice S. (1942–
Angela Davis, BLS, 147.
The searching. BLS, 146–47.
Coghill, Mary
Knowing. BAR, 208.
Cohen, Shlomit (1946–
Aphrodite. BAA, 25.
Drawing of a woman. BAA, 27.
The impossible is no hindrance. BAA, 24.
So abruptly. BAA, 23.
Struggling at the kill. BAA, 26.
Wife of Kohelet. BAA, 22.
Coignard, Gabrielle de (d. 1594)
Prayer, WPO, 176.
Colbert, Alison (1949–
The white worm. LPO, 196–98.
Cole, Margaret Postgate (1893–1980)
Afterwards. SUM, 21–22.
The falling leaves. SUM, 21.
Praematuri. SUM, 22.
The veteran. SUM, 22–23.
Coleman, Willie M.
Among the things that use to be. HGI, 221–22.
Coleridge, Mary Elizabeth (1861–1907)
A clever woman. BAN, 103.
Eyes. WSO, 138.
Horror. WSO, 139–40.
Mortal combat. WSO, 138.
The other side of a mirror. WSO, 137.
Regina. WSO, 139.
The white women. BAN, 104–05.
The witch. BAN, 103–04. WAI, 45–46. WSO, 138–39.
Collins, Anne (fl. 1653)
Song (I). WSO, 65–66.
Song (II). WSO, 66–67.
The soul's home. WSO, 66.
Collins, Martha (1940–
Homecoming. IWL-1, 440–42. IWL-3, 486–88.
Collins, Mary Gabrielle
Women at munition making. SUM, 24.
Colonna, Vittoria (1490–1547)
untitled. (As a hungry fledgling, who sees and hears). WPO, 172.
untitled. (When the Orient is lit by the great light). WPO, 172.
Compiuta Donzella (13th century)
untitled. (In the season when the world leafs and flowers, joy grows for all). AAA, 14.
untitled. (To leave the world/serve God). WPO, 157–58.
Connor-Bey, Brenda. *See* **Bey, Brenda Connor-.**
Cook, Eliza (1818–1889)
My old straw hat. BAR, 37–39.
The old arm-chair. BAR, 36.
Cooke, Rose Terry (1827–1892)
Arachne. WAI, 209.
Cook-Lynn, Elizabeth (1930–
Contradiction. TWO, 104.

History of Unchi. TWO, 105.
Some of my best friends. TWO, 105.
Cooper, Edith. *See* **Field, Michael.**
Corbin, Alice (1881–1949)
Fallen. SUM, 25.
Corinna (late 6th and early 5th centuries B.C.)
untitled. (I disapprove even of eloquent). WPO, 143.
untitled. (To the white-mantled maidens). WPO, 143.
Cornford, Frances (1886–1960)
For M. S. singing *Fruhlingsglaube* in 1945. BAR, 134.
In the backs. BAR, 133.
Inscription for a wayside spring. BAR, 135.
Ode on the whole duty of parents. WAD, 21.
The scholar. BAR, 134–35.
She warns him. AAA, 57
Summer beach. BAR, 133–34.
Corpi, Lucha (1945–
Absence. (Ausencia). FIR, 70–71.
The crystal bridge. (Puente de cristal). FIR, 60–63.
Dark romance. WPO, 324–25.
Doña Mariquita. FIR, 52–55.
For an attempted suicide of the 20th century. (A una suicida del siglo XX). FIR, 50–51.
Marina. FIR, 76–83. OVO, 154–56.
The devil's daughter. OVO, 155.
The devil's daughter. (La hija del diablo). FIR, 80–81.
Marina mother. OVO, 154.
Marina mother. (Marina madre). FIR, 76–77.
Marina virgin. OVO, 154–55.
Marina virgin. (Marina virgen). FIR, 78–79.
She (Marina distant). OVO, 155–56.
She (Marina distant). (Ella [Marina ausente]). FIR, 82–83.
Mexico. FIR, 48–49.
Movement. (Movimiento). FIR, 56–59.
Our worlds. (Nuestros mundos). FIR, 66–67.
Passion without a name. (Pasion sin nombre). FIR, 64–65.
Premonition. (Presentimiento). FIR, 74–75.
Rain. (Lluvia). FIR, 68–69.
Short history. (Breve historia). FIR, 72–73.
untitled. (Like the seed that waits). (Como la semilla en espera). FIR, 46–47.
Cortez, Jayne (1936–
Big fine woman from Ruleville. CNF, 94–95.
For the brave young students in Soweto. CNF, 95–97.
Grinding vibrato. BLS, 160–61.
In the morning. BLS, 157–59.
Orange chiffon. BLS, 153.
Orisha. BLS, 151–52.
Phraseology. BLS, 152.
Rape. CNF, 89–90.
So many feathers. BLS, 155–57.
Solo. KTF, 69–70.
There it is. CNF, 90–92.
Under the edge of february. BLS, 153–54.
You know. CNF, 92–94.
Coss, Clare (1935–
Emma. LPO, 36–37.
She is an older person now. LPO, 37–39.

Cota-Cárdenas, Margarita (1941–
  Gullible. (Creidisimas). TWO, 399–400.
  Spelling out the cosmos. (Deletreando al cosmos). TWO, 398–99.
Courtot, Martha (1941–
  untitled. (i am a woman in ice/melting). APO, 33. LPO, 98.
Cowdery. Mae V. (1910–
  I sit and wait for beauty. BLS, 93–94.
Cox, Ida (1889–1968)
  Wild women blues. WSO, 278–79.
Crapsey, Adelaide (1878–1914)
  Blossoming plum and cherry. WSO, 249.
  Expenses. WSO, 248.
  The lonely death. WSO, 248.
  Niagara. WSO, 247.
  Susanna and the elders. IWL-3, 207. WSO, 247.
  To an unfaithful lover. WSO, 249.
  Trapped. WSO, 247.
  Triad. WSO, 247.
  Witch. WSO, 248.
Creighton, Jane (1952–
  Ceres in an open field. LPO, 241.
Crosby, Ranice Henderson
  Waitresses. WWO, 41.
Crow, Mary
  The heat in Medellin. WPW, 64–65.
  Montserrate. WPW, 64.
  My barrow stones. WPW, 65.
  Not volcanoes, not minerals. WPW, 65–66.
Cruz, Juana Inés de la (Sister). *See* **Inés de la Cruz, Juana (Sister).**
Cumbo, Kattie M. (1938–
  Black sister. BLS, 135–36.
  Ceremony. BLS, 137–38.
  Domestics. BLS, 135.
  I'm a dreamer. BLS, 137.
  The morning after . . . love. BLS, 136.
  Nocturnal sounds. BLS, 134–35.
Cumming, Patricia (1932–
  Further notes for the alumni bulletin. BWO, 357–58.
  Midsummer. WWO, 145–46.
Cunard, Nancy (1896–1965)
  Zeppelins. SUM, 26.
Cuza Malé, Belkis (1942–
  Faust. (Fausto). OTT, 232–33.
  Oh, my Rimbaud. (Oh, mi Rimbaud). OTT, 228–29.
  The Photogenic ones. (Los fotogénicos). OTT, 224–25.
  The shrew who married God. (Mujer brava que casó con Dios). OTT, 230–31.
  The stepsisters. (Las cenicientas). OTT, 226–27.
  They're making a girl for the age. (Están haciendo una muchacha para la epoca). OTT, 234–35.

D. H. *See* **Doolittle, Hilda.**
Dahlen, Beverly (1934–
  D. NET. 50–51.
  For Darlene Tower. NET, 49.
  Gesture. NET, 51.
Daibu, Kenrei Mon-in Ukyō no. *See* **Kenrei Mon-in Ukyō no Daibu.**
Daini no Sanmi. (10th–11th centuries)
  untitled. (From Mt. Arima,/over the bamboo plains of Ina,). WPJ, 27.
D'Alessandro, Pat
  Sunday morning ritual. NET, 100.
Dallman, Elaine
  Later. WPW, 73.
  A parallel cut of air. WPW, 73.
Daniels, Gabrielle
  Millicent Fredericks. TBC, 76–78.
Danielson, Anita Endrezze. *See* **Endrezze-Danielson, Anita.**
Danner, Margaret (1915–
  At home in Dakar. BLS, 133–34.
  A grandson is a hoticeberg. BLS, 131–32.
  The rhetoric of Langston Hughes. BLS, 133.
  Women's lib. SBB, 356.
Dannstedt, Anna Rydstedt. *See* **Rydstedt-Dannstedt, Anna.**
Daryush, Elizabeth (1887–1976)
  Children of wealth in your warm nursery. WSO, 168.
  Flanders Fields. SUM, 27.
  For a survivor of the Mesopotamian Campaign. SUM, 27.
  Song: Ah, this is not enough, I cry—. WSO, 167.
  Subalterns. SUM, 28.
  This is the sword. WSO, 168.
  Unknown warrior. SUM, 28.
  You must break through old thought. WSO, 167.
Das, Kamala (1934–
  An introduction. WPO, 61–62.
da Sousa, Noémia. *See* **Sousa, Noémia da.**
Dávila, Ángela María (1944–
  I want for my name . . . AAA, 103.
Davis, Catherine (1924–
  SHE. IWL-1, 128–30. IWL-3, 112–14.
Davis, Helene (1945–
  Affair. IWL-1, 230. IWL-2, 265. IWL-3, 253.
Davis, Thadious M. (1944–
  Asante sana, Te Te. BLS, 280.
  Double take at Relais de l'Espadon. BLS, 277–78.
  "Honeysuckle was the saddest odor of all, I think." BLS, 279–80.
  It's all the same. BLS, 276.
  Remembering Fannie Lou Hamer. BLS, 277.
de Araújo, Virginia. *See* **Araújo, Virginia de.**

de Asbaje, Juana. *See* Juana de Asbaje.
de Avellaneda, Gertrudis Gómez. *See* Gómez de Avellaneda, Gertrudis.
de Beauveau, Marie-Françoise-Catherine, La Marquise de Boufflers. *See* Marie-Françoise-Catherine de Beauveau, La Marquise de Boufflers.
Deborah (c. 1200 B. C.)
  Song of Deborah. WPO, 128–29.
de Burgos, Julia (1914–1953)
  To Julia de Burgos. OVO, 15.
de Castillejo, Irene Claremont. *See* Castillejo, Irene Claremont de.
de Castro, Rosalía. *See* Castro, Rosalía de.
de Coignard, Gabrielle. *See* Coignard, Gabrielle de.
de Dia, Beatritz. *See* Beatritz de Dia.
de France, Marie. *See* Marie de France.
DeFrees, Madeline (1919–
  Extended outlook. EOU, 49.
  Gold ring triad. WPW, 40.
  Hanging the pictures. EOU, 48.
  Keeping up with the signs. WPW, 39.
  Lecture under the moose. WPW, 39–40.
  Slow-motion elegy for Kathy King. WPW, 40–41.
  Standing by on the third day. WPW, 39.
de Guillet, Pernette. *See* Guillet, Pernette de.
de Hoyos, Angela. *See* Hoyos, Angela de.
de Ibarbourou, Juana. *See* Ibarbourou, Juana de.
de Jesús, Teresa. *See* Jesús, Teresa de.
Delany, Clarissa Scott (1901–1927)
  Joy, SOW, 71.
de la Riva, Osa Hidalgo. *See* Hidalgo-de la Riva, Osa.
de Longchamps, Joanne (1923–
  The glassblower. WPW, 54.
del Río, Zaida (1954–
  untitled. (Between your life and mine, there's a fresh air). (Entre tu vida y la mía, hay un aire fresco). BTS, 272–73.
  untitled. (Classic heritage/the window open on all the rooftops). (Herencia clásica/la ventana abierta a los tejados). BTS, 276–77.
  untitled. (Grandpa:/Any day now you'll go off with your). (Abuelo:/Cualquier día de estos te nos irás con tus injertos). BTS, 274–75.
  untitled. (I inherited this anger from my lunches). (Heredé de mis almuerzos esta cólera). BTS, 272–73.
  untitled. (José, big brother.) (José, hermano mayor). BTS, 272–75.
  untitled. (Waiting for you now). (Ahora que te espero) BTS, 274–77.
de Mello Breyner Andresen, Sophia. *See* Andresen, Sophia de Mello Breyner.
Den Sute-Jo (1633–1698)
  untitled. (On the road through the clouds/Is there a short cut). WPJ, 50.
  untitled. (A snowy morning/Everywhere II, II, II two, two, two. WPJ, 50.
de Pescara, Marquise. *See* Colonna, Vittoria.
de Pisan, Christine. *See* Christine de Pisan.

de Rodríguez, Magdalena. *See* Rodríguez, Magdalena de.
Derricotte, Toi (1941–
  The damned. HGI, 6–7.
  For a godchild, Regina, on the occasion of her first love. HGI, 3–5.
  Hester's song. HGI, 8–9.
  Natural birth. EOU, 63–68. (excerpts).
    Maternity. EOU, 65.
    November. EOU, 63–65.
    Transition. EOU, 65–68.
  The testimony of Sister Maureen. WPE, 59–61.
Desbordes-Valmore, Marceline (1786–1859)
  The roses of Saadi. WPO, 202.
Desnoues, Lucienne (1921–
  First things. WPO, 263–64.
Deutsch, Babette (1895–1983)
  A bull. WSO, 292.
  Epistle to Prometheus. (VIII). WSO, 292–97.
  Lioness asleep. WSO, 291.
  Moving. AAA, 68–69.
  Natural law. BWO, 209.
  Niké at the Metropolitan. WSO, 291.
  Petrograd. WSO, 290–91.
De Veaux, Alexis (1948–
  . . . And then she said. CNF, 98–99.
  French doors: a vignette. CNF, 99–100.
  Madeleine's dreads. EOU, 62.
  The sisters. HGI, 10–12.
  The woman who lives in the botanical gardens. CNF, 101–02.
de Vinck, Catherine (1923–
  Venus—Aghia Sophia. HOF, 37.
Dhomhnaill, Nuala ní. *See* ní Dhomhnaill, Nuala.
Dia, Beatritz de. *See* Beatritz de Dia.
Dickinson, Emily (1830–1886)
  77. (I never hear the word "escape"). AAA, 38.
  199. (I'm "wife"—I've finished that—). AAA, 38. SOW, 32–33.
  214. (I taste a liquor never brewed—). WAD, 95–96.
  216. (Safe in their Alabaster Chambers—). WAD, 192.
  241. (I like a look of Agony,). BWO, 323.
  249. (Wild Nights—Wild Nights!). SOW, 55.
  254. ("Hope" is the thing with feathers—). WAD, 141–42.
  312. (Her—"last Poems"—). WSO, 209–10.
  315. (He fumbles at your soul). WSO, 206–07.
  324. (Some keep the Sabbath going to Church—). IHO, 100.
  363. (I went to thank Her—). WSO, 210.
  384. (No Rack can torture me—). WSO, 206.
  389. (There's been a Death, in the Opposite House,). BWO, 325.
  410. (The first Day's Night had come—). WPO, 355.
  441. (This is my letter to the World). BWO, 323. IHO, 229.
  465. (I heard a Fly buzz—when I died—). BWO, 326.
  508. (I'm ceded—I've stopped being Theirs—). IHO, 101. WPO, 353–54. WSO, 207.

520. (I started Early—Took my Dog—). WAI, 85–86.

579. (I had been hungry, all the Years—). HOF, 107.

593. (I think I was enchanted). IHO, 228–29. WSO, 208–09.

605. (The Spider holds a Silver Ball). WPO, 355.

613. (They shut me up in Prose—). IHO, 101.

652. (A Prison gets to be a friend—). IWL-3, 415–16.

657. (I dwell in Possibility—). IHO, 102.

709. (Publication—is the Auction). WSO, 210.

732. (She rose to His Requirement—dropt). AAA, 39. IHO, 102.

754. (My Life had stood—a Loaded Gun—). WPO, 354.

1072. (Title divine—is mine!). WSO, 207–08.

1583. (Witchcraft was hung, in History,). WSO, 208.

Dimoula, Kiki
Mark of recognition. CGW, 48–49.
Standstill. CGW, 52.
Talking to myself. CGW, 51.
Tied down. CGW, 50.

Dine, Carol
Babysitter. APO, 92–93.

di Prima, Diane (1934–
Brass furnace going out: song, after an abortion. NET, 94–99.

Dircks, Helen
After Bourlon Wood. SUM, 29.
London in war. SUM, 30.

Ditlevsen, Tove (1918–1976)
Divorce 1. OVO, 87–88.
Divorce 3. OVO, 88–90.
Self portrait 1. OVO, 27–28.
Self portrait 2. OVO, 28–29.
Self portrait 4. WPO, 246–47.

Ditmas, Monica
Annunciation. WAD, 175–76.

Dixon, Elizabeth
Ranmore. WAD, 54–55.

Djabali, Leila (1933–
For my torturer, Lieutenant D_____. WPO, 283.

Dmitrova, Blaga (1922–
To my father. OVO, 25.

Dobell, Eva (1867–1963)
Gramophone tunes. SUM, 31–32.
Night duty. SUM, 32–33.
Pluck. SUM, 31.

Dobson, Rosemary (1920–
Azay-le-rideau. WAD, 103–04.
Country press. WAD, 48–49.
The mirror. WAD, 165.

do Espirito Santo, Alda. *See* **Espirito Santo, Alda do.**

Donzella, Compiuta. *See* **Compiuta Donzella.**

Doolittle, Hilda (1886–1961)
Eurydice. (I). WSO, 269.
The flowering of the rod. (V). WAD, 142–43.
Helen. WSO, 268–69.
Helios and Athene. EOU, 150–54.
Love that I bear. HOF, 105.
The mysteries remain. WPO, 356.
The pear tree. BWO, 329.
The walls do not fall. (I, XLIII). WSO, 270–72.

Dorcey, Mary
First love. BAR, 219–21.
Sea flower. BAR, 207.

Dorman, Sonya (1924–
Two poets on the way to the palace. WPE, 35.
Whodunit. WPE, 35.

Dropkin, Celia (1888–1956)
Poem. AAA, 60. OVO, 66.

Droste-Hülshoff, Annette von (1797–1848)
On the tower. WPO, 202–03.

Dubé, Janet
Autobiography. BAR, 247–48.
So to tell the truth. BAR, 248–49.

Duchess of Newcastle. *See* **Cavendish, Margaret, Duchess of Newcastle.**

du Cille, Ann (1949–
from the bone, the blood, the rib, KTF, 72–74.
Lady in waiting. KTF, 71.
Song. KTF, 70–71.

Dufferin, Lady. *See* **Selina, Helen (Lady Dufferin).**

Dunbar-Nelson, Alice Ruth Moore (1875–1935)
I sit and sew. BLS, 65–66. WPO, 374–75. WSO, 260–61.
Music. BLS, 67.
Snow in October. BLS, 66.
Sonnett. (I had no thought of violets of late,). BLS, 65.

Dunmore, Helen
If no revolution come. HFE, 130–31.
The Polish husband. HFE, 132–33.

Dunn, Ann
untitled. (Come here/Come over here). AOW, 1.
untitled. (In misery buds music-words,). AOW, 2.
untitled. (Sick I am and tired of this everyone). AOW, 3.
untitled. (When he was a prince and I was a frog). AOW, 4.

Durham, Sukey
The crossing. APO, 94.

Duyn, Mona Van. *See* **Van Duyn, Mona.**

Dyak, Miriam (1946–
April 6. CAM, 22.
Dying. CAM, 25–30. (excerpts).
Forbidden sweets. CAM, 24.
January 23, 1976   the axe. CAM, 21.
On having to go round the circle and state our philoso-
      phies. CAM, 20.
Three. CAM, 23.
Winter solstice 1975. CAM, 21.

Dyer, Katherine (fl. 1641)
Epitaph on the monument of Sir William Dyer at Colm-
      worth, 1641. AAA, 23.

E

Easton, Y. W.
The welcome. CNF, 103–04.

Eden, Helen Parry (1885–
  A volunteer. SUM, 34.
Eersel, Eugenie
  Ada. OWO, 39.
  First communion picture. OWO, 38.
  For my number one younger sister. OWO, 38.
  4 A.M. OWO, 40.
  The plantation. OWO, 41.
  Shells. OWO, 42.
Efros, Lynda
  untitled. (Provincetown/The night). TIW, 100.
  untitled. (So we were reading poems). TIW, 99.
Efros, Susan (1947–
  An expression. TIW, 118–19.
  Her rooms. TIW, 120.
  Kaiser Hospital trilogy: three women at the mercy of
      unknown gods. TIW, 121–22.
  Not quite making it. TIW, 123.
  The process of dissolution. TIW, 119.
Eifuku, Empress
  untitled. (We dressed each other/Hurrying to say fare-
      well). WPO, 40.
Elise, Marie. *See* **Marie-Elise.**
Elisha, Gavriela (1954–
  Where do these steps lead? BAA, 18–19.
Elizabeth I, Queen of England (1533–1603)
  The doubt of future foes. WSO, 51–52.
  On monsieur's departure. WAD, 107. WSO, 52.
  When I was fair and young. AAA, 20.
Elliot, Gabrielle
  Pierrot goes to war. SUM, 35.
Ellis, Melanie (1957–
  Feel the coming rains. IAT, 115.
Elmy, Elizabeth Wolstenholme-. *See* **Wolstenholme-
      Elmy, Elizabeth.**
Emanuel, Lynn
  Silence. She is six years old. EOU, 77.
  The sleeping. EOU, 76.
Emon, Akazome. *See* **Akazome Emon.**
Endrezze-Danielson, Anita (1952–
  The belly dancer's song. TWO, 119.
  Making adjustments. TWO, 121.
  Shaman/Bear. TWO, 120–21.
  Still life. TWO, 120.
Engel, Kathy
  In my father's cabin. EOU, 78–79.
The English Sappho. *See* **Philips, Katherine.**
Enheduanna (c. 2300 B.C.)
  Inanna exalted. WPO, 114–17. (excerpts).
Enomoto Seifu-Jo (1731–1814)
  untitled. (Everyone is asleep). WPJ, 56.
Erinna (c. 354 B.C.)
  The distaff. SOW, 23–24. WPO, 144–45.
Espirito Santo, Alda do (1926–
  Far from the beach. OVO, 148–49.
  Where are the men seized in this wind of madness? WPO,
      284–86.
Esteves, Sandra Maria
  A Julia y a mi. OWO, 47–48.

  Ahora. OWO, 45.
  For Tulani. OWO, 44–45.
  POR TI, BRO. OWO, 46.
  Visiting. OWO, 45.
E'tesami, Parvin (1910–1941)
  To his father on praising the honest life of the peasant.
      WPO, 77.
Evans, Jo Ann Hall. *See* **Hall-Evans, Jo Ann.**
Evans, Mari (1923–
  The alarm clock. BWO, 353.
  . . . And the old women gathered (The Gospel Singers).
      BLS, 146.
  Daufuskie (Four movements). BLS, 142.
  early in the mornin. CNF, 108–09.
  The Friday ladies of the pay envelope. TWO, 260.
  A good assassination should be quiet. TWO, 261.
  The great Civil Rights Law (A.D. 1964). KTF, 75–76.
  How will you call me, brother. BLS, 144–45.
  I am a black woman. CNF, 105–06. KTF, 74–75. TWO,
      259–60.
  Jake. BLS, 143.
  Janis. BLS, 144.
  The people gather. BLS, 143.
  The 7:25 trolley. SBB, 338.
  Speak the truth to the people. CNF, 107–08.
  Where have you gone. CNF, 106.
Exum, Pat Crutchfield
  3 serendipitous poems. KTF, 77–79.
Eybers, Elisabeth (1915–
  Narrative. AAA, 77.

F

Fabio, Sarah Webster (1928–1979)
  All day we've longed for night. BLS, 141.
  Back into the garden. BLS, 139.
  To turn from love. BLS, 140.
Fainlight, Ruth (1931–
  Another full moon. BAR, 155.
  The other. BAR, 155–56.
Farjeon, Eleanor (1881–1965)
  Easter Monday. SUM, 36.
  The girl with the ball. WAD, 94–95.
  'Now that you too.' SUM, 37.
  Peace. SUM, 36–37.
Farrokhzād, Forūgh (1935–1967)
  I feel sorry for the garden. OVO, 141–44.
  Mechanical doll. OVO, 30–32.
  O realm bejewelled. WPO, 77–81.
  Someone like no one else. WPO, 82–84.
  A window. OVO, 21–23.

Fauset, Jessie Redmon (1888–1961)
Oriflamme. BLS, 64.
Touché. BLS, 63–64.
Fei-fei, Shao. *See* **Shao Fei-fei.**
Fein, Cheri
The earliest days. TIW, 133.
Rape at Progresso: a critical study. TIW, 134.
Rock bottom nourishment. TIW, 135–36.
Feinstein, Elaine (1930–
Calliope in the labour ward. BAR, 151.
Coastline. BAR, 153–54.
June. BAR, 152–53.
The magic apple tree. BAR, 154.
The medium. BAR, 151–52.
Patience. BAR, 152.
Fell, Alison
Significant fevers. BAR, 234–37.
Feria, Lina de (1945–
Kinfolk. (La parentela). BTS, 180–87.
Papers for a man's retirement. (Documentos para la jubila-
ción de un humbre). BTS, 192–93. (excerpt).
Stalingrad. (Stalingrado). BTS, 192–95.
Wet your fingers. (Humedece tus dedos). BTS, 186–91.
Fernández, Teresita (1930–
Every day that I love you. (Cada día que te amo). BTS,
102–03.
A fallen needle . . . (Una aguja caída . . .). BTS, 102–03.
I escape. (Me escapo). BTS, 104–05.
Our mother America. (América madre nuestra). BTS,
104–07.
Rag doll (a song). (Muneca de trapo [una canción]). BTS,
106–09.
Ugly things (a song). (Lo feo [una canción]). B̄TS, 106–07
Ferreira, María Eugenia Vaz. *See* **Vaz Ferreira, María
Eugenia.**
Fiamengo, Marya
In praise of old women. WPO, 348–50.
Field, Michael (1846–1914)
And on my eyes dark sleep by night. WAD, 109.
Possession. WAD, 99.
Second thoughts. WAD, 110.
Fields, Julia (1938–
Big momma. KTF, 80–81.
The Policeman. KTF, 82–83.
Seizin. KTF, 79–80.
Finch, Anne, Countess of Winchilsea (1661–1720)
Adam pos'd. WSO, 83.
The answer. WSO, 84–85.
The apology. BAW, 73.
Ardelia to melancholy. BAW, 74–75.
Ardelia's answer to Ephelia. BTT, 9–16. WSO, 85–91.
The bird and the arras. BTT, 16.
Clarinda's indifference at parting with her beauty. BAW,
79–80. SOW, 152–53. WAI, 158.
The consolation. BAW, 75. BTT, 5.
The introduction. BAW, 71–73. BTT, 3–4. WPO, 181–
82.
Jealousie is the rage of a man. BAW, 82.
A letter to Dafnis, April 2, 1685. BAW, 76. BTT, 5–6.

The loss. BTT, 4–5.
Melinda on an insippid beauty. WSO, 83.
A nocturnal reverie. BAW, 83–85. BTT, 22–23. WAD,
57–58. WSO, 81–83.
On myselfe. BAW, 75–76.
A song. (The nymph, in vain, bestows her pains,). BTT,
17.
A song. ('Tis strange, this Heart within my breast,).
BAW, 81–82. BTT, 17. BWO, 315.
To Mr. F. now Earl of W. BAW, 76–79. BTT, 6–9.
To the nightingale. BAW, 82–83. BTT, 21.
The unequal fetters. BAW, 81–82. BTT, 18. WAI, 124–
25.
The young rat and his dam, the cock and the cat. BTT,
18–20.
Finch, Vivienne
Green ice. BAR, 168–69.
Inertia. BAR, 170–71.
Flynn, Desirée
The collector. BAR, 257–58.
From the rain forest. BAR, 253–54.
Forché, Carolyn (1950–
Because one is always forgotten. EOU, 85.
Endurance. EOU, 83–84.
Expatriate. EOU, 82.
Message. EOU, 86.
Poem for Maya. EOU, 81.
Selective service. EOU, 87.
Ford, S. Gertrude
'A fight to a finish.' SUM, 38
Nature in war-time. SUM, 38.
The tenth Armistice Day. SUM, 38–39.
Fordham, Mary Weston (fl. 1897)
The coming woman. WAI, 281.
Forman, Elizabeth Chandler
The three lads. SUM, 40.
Forman, Joan
For Sally. WAD, 25–26.
Forsyth, Helen
Dichotomy. WAD, 116.
Forten, Charlotte L. (1839–1914)
A parting hymn. BLS, 22–23.
Poem. BLS, 23.
To W. L. G. on reading his 'Chosen Queen.' BLS, 24.
Fourtouni, Eleni
Child's memory. CGW, 62–63.
Eurynome. CGW, 64–65.
Homecoming. CGW, 70.
I have no poem for you father. CGW, 71–72.
In a dream. CGW, 67.
Lament. CGW, 68–69.
Monovacia. CGW, 74.
Pappouli. CGW, 66.
Parting. CGW, 73.
Frame, Janet (1925–
Vacant possession. AAA, 83.
France, Marie de. *See* **Marie de France.**
Francisco, Nia (1952–
Friday noon feelings. TWO, 101.

Iridescent child. TWO, 98–100.
She-bear. TWO, 98.
Tomorrow noon. TWO, 100–01.
Fraser, Kathleen (1937–
Agnes. NET, 83–86.
Casuist, Etc. WPW, 51.
The fault. TIW, 126.
Improvisation on lines by Spicer, No. 2. TIW, 131–32.
Joan Brown, about her painting. WPW, 51.
Poem in which my legs are accepted. IHO, 177–79.
The stranger. TIW, 129–30.
What you need. TIW, 127–28.
Friis, Irene
Mother, child. AOW, 5.
No walls. AOW, 6.
Frym, Gloria (1947–
Secrets. NET, 69.
Voodoo. NET, 68.
Fu, Tu. *See* **Tu Fu.**
Fuertes, Gloria (1920–
I write poems. WPO, 259–60.
I've never got anything. OVO, 16.
Love which frees. WPO, 260–61.
Now. OVO, 16–17.
We're OK. WPO, 260.
Fukao Sumako (1893–1974)
Bright house. WPJ, 88.
Fukuda Chiyo-Ni (1703–1775)
On her child's death. AAA, 29.
To her husband, at the wedding. AAA, 29.
untitled. ("Cuckoo!"/"Cuckoo!"). WPJ, 53.
untitled. (I forgot that my lips/were rouged,). WPJ, 54.
untitled. (My hunter of dragonflies,). WPJ, 53.
untitled. (See! The gleam/on my fishing line). WPJ, 54.
Fukui Hisako (1929–
Now is the time. WPJ, 104.
Fukunaka Tomoko (1928–
It's not the same. WPJ, 102–03.
Fuller, Jean Overton (1915–
Mask and essence. WAD, 135.
To a young man on his thirtieth birthday. WAD, 26.
Fumiko, Hayashi. *See* **Hayashi Fumiko.**
Furse, Jill (1915–1944)
Gloria in excelsis. WAD, 98.
The hare is vanished. WAD, 98–99.
Futabako, Mitsui. *See* **Mitsui Futabako.**

G

Gallagher, Tess (1943–
Each bird walking. EOU, 97–98.
In that time when it was not the fashion. WPW, 96–97.

Painted steps. WPW, 96.
Gandersheim, Hroswitha von. *See* **Hroswitha von Gandersheim.**
García Marruz, Fina (1923–
At the death of Martin Luther King. (En la muerte de Martin Lutero King). BTS, 68–69.
How rudely you speak to me. (Con que lenguaje tan rudo me hablas). BTS, 66–67.
I too am now among the others. (Ya yo también estoy entre los otros). BTS, 64–65.
Oedipus. (Edipo). BTS, 66–67.
This page too. (También esta página). BTS, 64–65.
You too. (También tú). BTS, 66–67.
Gard, Lillian
Her 'allowance'! SUM, 41.
Gardner, Isabella (1915–1981)
At a summer hotel. IWL-1, 127. IWL-3, 111.
Garitano, Rita (1939–
Morning at Salt River Day School. WPW, 31.
Gayles, Gloria
Cracked. SBB, 361–62.
Parade. SBB, 365–66.
Sometimes as women only. SBB, 363–64.
Genser, Cynthia Kraman (1950–
Club 82: Lisa. OWO, 54–59.
Hootchie Kootchie man. OWO, 51–52.
72 hours: Yom Kippur. OWO, 53.
Under the sword. OWO, 50.
Gensler, Kinereth
The border. WPE, 67–68.
Gernand, Jill (1947–
girl talk. NET, 52.
Lenore. NET, 52.
untitled. (what I think when I see). NET, 52.
Gershon, Karen (1923–
On planting a tree. WAD, 144–45.
Scene at evening. WAD, 107–08.
Gibbs, Joan
Internal geography - Part One. EOU, 99–100.
Gidlow, Elsa (1898–
Cunts have faces: dialogue among rumpled sheets. LPO, 4.
For the goddess too well known. LPO, 3.
untitled. (You say I am mysterious.). APO, 74.
Gilbert, Celia
At the ball. WPE, 53.
The stone maiden. WPE, 53.
Gilbert, Mary, Sister. *See* **DeFrees, Madeline.**
Gilbert, Sandra M.
Daguerreotype: lace maker. NET, 87.
The dream kitchen. WPW, 36–37.
The love sequence. EOU, 101–08.
   The cure. EOU, 106–08.
   The love sickness. EOU, 106.
   The one he loves. EOU, 105.
   You discover you're in love with the dead prince. EOU, 103–04.
   You fall. EOU, 101–02.
   You meet the real dream mother-in-law. EOU, 102–03.

The twelve dancing princesses. WPW, 37.
Winterpoem. WPW, 36.
Gilbert, Virginia (1946–
Awakening, in a church. CAM, 64.
The drought. CAM, 64–66.
Impressions at dawn. CAM, 63.
Leaving, the sepulcre city. CAM, 68–74.
Outside the Kampongs, at the market, waiting. CAM, 63.
The ritual. CAM, 66–67.
Two poems: in commemoration of a friend's happiness.
    CAM, 62.
untitled. (Somewhere/under my sleep/I am awake,).
    CAM, 74.
Gilchrist, Ellen
Clanking to Byzantium. EOU, 123–24.
Gill, Frances
Gulls. WAD, 73.
The pennywhistle man. WAD, 28.
Gilman, Charlotte Perkins (1860–1935)
The anti-suffragists. WSO, 224–26.
The prophets. WSO, 226.
She walketh veiled and sleeping. WSO, 224.
Gio (12th century)
untitled. (The sprouting grass waiting for spring,). WPJ,
    38.
Gioseffi, Daniela (1941–
Birth dance, belly dancer. SOW, 57–59.
Giovanni, Nikki (1943–
Atrocities. KTF, 83–84.
For Saundra. WAW, 191.
Knoxville, Tennessee. BLS, 237.
Legacies. AAA, 99. TWO, 266.
Mothers. AAA, 100–01.
Mother's habits. BLS, 236–37.
Nikki-Rosa. BLS, 233–34. BWO, 56.
Poem for Aretha. WWO, 42–45.
Poetry. WAW, 191–92.
Revolutionary dreams. WAW, 431.
They clapped. TWO, 265–66. WPO, 380–82.
The women gather. SBB, 340–41.
Women poem. BLS, 234–36. WAW, 430–31.
Gippius, Zinaida (1869–1945)
She. WPO, 211–12.
Gitterman, Heidi
The experiment. TIW, 32–34.
Poem for my father. TIW, 35–36.
Glazer, Myra
Recognition. BAA, 90.
Santa Caterina. BAA, 92.
Godden, Rumer (1907–
Michaelmas daisies. WAD, 53–54.
Goldberg, Leah (1911–1970)
The eighth part (at least) of everything. BAA, 7.
From my mother's home. BAA, 2.
Heavenly Jerusalem, Jerusalem of the earth. BAA, 9–10.
Hill excursion. BAA, 5–6.
Illuminations 2. OVO, 109.
In the Jerusalem Hills. BAA, 4. (excerpt).
Last brightness. OVO, 109.

A look at a bee. BAA, 11–12. WPO, 129–30.
On myself I. OVO, 12.
That poem I didn't write. BAA, 8.
Golden, Bernette
Paying dues. KTF, 85–86.
Gomez, Magdalena
Dream medley. OWO, 63–64.
For my lover, the artist. OWO, 62.
He got me the first time. OWO, 62.
One of too many. OWO, 61.
Rookie dyke T.V. toddler. OWO, 65.
Gómez de Avellaneda, Gertrudis (1814–1873)
On leaving Cuba, her native land. WPO, 305.
Gonzales, Sylvia Alicia (1943–
Chicana evolution. NET, 112–17. TWO, 418–26.
    Genesis and the original sin. NET, 112–14. TWO,
        418–21.
    In search of the messiahs of nativism. NET, 114–16.
        TWO, 421–22.
    Rebirth according to the New Testament. (Renacimi-
        ento segun el Nuevo Testamento). TWO, 422–26.
    Renacimiento segun el Nuevo Testamento. NET,
        116–17.
González, Milagros (1944–
First dialogue. (Diálogo primero). BTS, 170–77.
I am America's child . . . (De América soy hijo . . .). BTS,
    168–71. (excerpt).
Mother light, mother wind. (Madre luz, madre viento).
    BTS, 166–69.
Gorbanevskaya, Natalya (1936–
untitled. (And there is nothing at all—neither fear,).
    OVO, 71.
untitled. (The cricket sings on Twelfth-night,). OVO, 108.
untitled. (In the bird scream and whistle,). OVO, 167.
untitled. (Love, love! What nonsense it is,). WPO, 222.
Gordon, Rebecca (1952–
When I was a fat woman. LPO, 242–43.
Goren, Judith
The planting. AOW, 7.
Gotlieb, Phyllis
Paradigm. SOW, 133–34.
Gotō Miyoko (1898–
untitled. (Gay colors flow/down streets that swirl). WPJ,
    71.
untitled. (I listen to the pulse of a life). WPJ, 71.
Graham, Jorie
To a friend going blind. EOU, 125–26.
Graham, Muriel Elsie
The battle of the swamps. SUM, 42–43.
The lark above the trenches. SUM, 42.
Grahn, Judy (1940–
The common woman. LPO, 67–69. WPO, 369.
    (excerpts).
    Carol, in the park, chewing on straws. LPO, 67–68.
        WPO, 369.
    Ella, in a square apron, along Highway 80. LPO, 67.
    Vera, from my childhood. LPO, 68–69.
Confrontations with the devil in the form of love. NET,
    46. (excerpt).

Guidacci, Margherita (1921–
  At night. WPO, 256–57.
Guillén, Lygia
  A sadness which already knew me. (Una tristeza que ya
    me conocia). OTT, 114–15.
Guillet, Pernette de (1520–1545)
  Not that I wish to take the liberty. WPO, 174.
Gunning, Sarah Ogan (1910–
  Dreadful memories. WSO, 308.
  I hate the company bosses. WSO, 306–08.
  Old southern town. WSO, 309.
Gurney, Diana
  The fallen. SUM, 45.

H. D. *See* **Doolittle, Hilda.**
Hacker, Marilyn (1942–
  Feeling and form. WPE, 119–20.
  Home, and I've. LPO, 103–04.
  Peterborough. LPO, 105–06.
  Up from D. C. LPO, 102–03.
Hadas, Pamela White (1946–
  Queen charming. EOU, 164–66.
Hafsa bint al-Hajj (d. 1184)
  untitled. (Shall I come there, or you here?). WPO, 99.
Hagedorn, Jessica Tarahata (1949–
  Autobiography part one: Manila to San Francisco. FYW,
    3–8.
  Autobiography part two: rock and roll. FYW, 9–11.
  Birthday poem for Gregory Reeves. FYW, 14–15.
  The Blue Swan Cafe. FYW, 23–25.
  Canto de Nada/Para ti, M'wandishi. FYW, 41–43. NET,
    55–56.
  The death of Anna May Wong. FYW, 12–13.
  Dream war. FYW, 19.
  Epic eulogy for boy and girl who almost killed each other
    with aspirin for love and homosexuality and pregnan-
    cy's sake. FYW, 38–39.
  Filipino boogie. FYW, 16–18.
  Fillmore Street poems: August, 1967. FYW, 27–28.
  For Bruce who's on smack: May 31, 1967. FYW, 36–37.
  The fundamental man. FYW, 29.
  Letter to Rafael: 1966. FYW, 34–35.
  Listen. WPO, 388.
  Love poem from an unfaithful lady. FYW, 20–21.
  A plaster and plexiglas creation. FYW, 32–33.
  Poem for Rene Crevel. FYW, 30–31.
  Rock and roll. FYW, 22.
  A script: beauty is the beginning of terror . . . FYW, 40.
  Sometimes you look like lady day. NET, 53–54. TWO,
    534–35.

  Song for my father. TWO, 536–39.
  2. FYW, 26.
Hajj, Hafsa bint al-. *See* **Hafsa bint al-Hajj.**
Hales, Madge
  September. WAD, 52–53.
Hall-Evans, Jo Ann (1934–
  Cape Coast Castle revisited. BLS, 191.
  SEDUCTION. BLS, 192.
Hamblin, Angela
  Sensitivity. HFE, 114–16.
Hamill, Janet
  Belladonna. OWO, 76–77.
  The big sleep. OWO, 81–82.
  In my taboo. OWO, 80.
  The pyramid of the musicians. OWO, 78–79.
  SUBTERRANEOUS/Subterraneus. OWO, 75.
Hamilton, Cicely (1872–1952)
  The march of the women. BAN, 114.
  Non-combatant. SUM, 46.
Hamilton, Helen
  The ghouls. SUM, 47.
  The Jingo-woman. SUM, 47–49.
  The romancing poet. SUM, 49–50.
al-Hansa. *See* **al-Khansa, Tumadir** (filed under Khansa).
Hanscombe, Gillian E.
  Jezebel: her progress. BAR, 246–47. (excerpt).
    Jesus People. BAR, 246–47.
Han Ts'ui-p'in (9th century)
  A poem written on a floating red leaf. AAA, 7. WPC, 24.
Harakavy, Chedva (1941–
  At night, she sees voices. BAA, 42.
  It was gentle. BAA, 43.
  Talk to me, talk to me. BAA, 45.
  Whenever the snakes come. BAA, 44.
Hargreaves, Armitage
  Present tense. WAD, 162–63.
Harjoy, Joy (1951–
  ''Are you still there.'' TWO, 89–90.
  The black room. WPW, 49.
  Call it fear. WPW, 49–50.
  Conversations between here and home. TWO, 90.
  There was a dance, sweetheart. TWO, 88–89.
  Watching crow, looking south towards the Manzano
    Mountains. TWO, 90–91.
Harper, Frances Ellen Watkins (1825–1911)
  An appeal to my countrywomen. BLS, 31–32.
  The crocuses. BLS, 33–34.
  Deliverance. WPO, 373–74.
  A double standard. BLS, 26–27. WSO, 212–14.
  Learning to read. BLS, 29–30.
  Let the light enter. WSO, 215.
  She's free! BLS, 32–33.
  the slave mother. WSO, 214–15.
  Vashti. BLS, 27–29.
Harris, Emily Katherine
  Cabal. AOW, 18.
  I do not like it here. AOW, 19.
  Inform me. AOW, 21.
  Thee to a dead mountain. AOW, 20.

Harris, Jana (1947–
Elaina Elaina I almost got killed. NET, 26–27.
Glitter box. NET, 29–30.
I canned them pears and I canned them pears. NET, 28.
Poem for a stranger. TIW, 113–14.
Running scared. TIW, 109–12.
Harrison, Ada M.
New Year, 1916. SUM, 51.
Hartmann, Anna
Sleeping with Franz Kafka. AOW, 22–25.
Hartnoll, Phyllis (1906–
A death abroad. WAD, 188.
Hashimoto Takako (1899–1963)
untitled. (Towards the starry sky,). WPJ, 81.
Hatshepsut (ruled 1503–1482 B.C.)
The Obelisk inscriptions. WPO, 277–78. (excerpt).
Hatsui Shizue (1900–
untitled. (Scattered petals gather on the road,). WPJ, 72.
untitled. (Silently/time passes.). WPJ, 72.
Hawkins, Bobbie Louise
Mae, not to change . . . NET, 127.
Hayashi Fumiko (1904–1951)
The Lord Buddha. WPJ, 89.
Hebert, Anne (1916–
Eve. OVO, 9–11.
Landscape. OVO, 117–18.
Night. OVO, 117.
Wisdom has broken my arms. OVO, 81–82.
The wooden chamber. WPO, 347–48.
Hejinian, Lyn (1941–
The coffee drinkers answered ecstatically. NET, 122.
We are not forgetting the patience of the mad, their love of detail. NET, 123.
Hellerstein, Kathryn
For water, for air. NET, 108.
Hemans, Felicia (1793–1835)
Corinne at the capitol. BAR, 33–34.
To the poet Wordsworth. BAR, 34–35.
Hemschemeyer, Judith (1935–
Indulgence and accidents. EOU, 187–88.
Henderson, Mary H. J.
An incident. SUM, 52.
Henderson, Safiya
harlem/soweto. CNF, 134–35.
letter to my father . . . a solidarity long overdue. CNF, 135–40.
Portrait of a woman artist. CNF, 131–34.
Henderson, Sharon
Blue jean wearin women??? KTF, 87–88.
Henley, Patricia
Poem for Charley. WPW, 52.
Poem for Suzanne. WPW, 52–53.
To grave, to cradle. WPW, 52.
Herbert, Kathleen
The virgin capture. WAD, 72–73.
Herbert, Mary Sidney, Countess of Pembroke (1561–1621)
The dolefull lay of Clorinda. WSO, 55–58.
Psalm lii. (Tyrant, why swelst thou thus,). WSO, 54.

Psalm lvii. (Thy mercie Lord, Lord now thy mercie show,). WSO, 54.
Psalm lix. (Save me from such as me assaile,). WSO, 54.
Psalm lx. (Thy anger erst in field). WSO, 54.
Psalm lxvii. (God, on us thy mercy show,). WSO, 55.
Psalm lxxi. (Lord, on thee my trust is grounded:). WSO, 55.
Psalm lxxii. (Teach the kings sonne, who king hym selfe shall be,). WSO, 55.
Herbertson, Agnes Grozier
Airman, R.F.C. SUM, 53.
The Seed-Merchant's son. SUM, 53–54.
Herrera, Georgina (1936–
Birth. (El parto). BTS, 114–15.
Introduction and apology. (Como presentacion, como disculpa). BTS, 116–19.
Reflections. (Reflexiones). BTS, 114–17.
Street of the women of the world. (Calle de las mujeres de la vida). BTS, 118–23.
The way we were. (Asi eramos). BTS, 122–23.
Herschel-Clarke, May
'For valour.' SUM, 55.
'Nothing to report.' SUM, 55.
Hershman, M. F. (1951–
Eyes. APO, 34.
Making love to Alice. APO, 35. LPO, 235.
Hershman, Marcie. *See* **Hershman, M. F.**
Herzberg, Judith (1934–
On the death of Sylvia Plath. WPO, 245.
Vocation. WPO, 244.
Hesketh, Phoebe (1909–
Epitaph. WAD, 120–21.
Rescue. WAD, 121–22.
The serpent. WAD, 161–62.
Hidalgo-de la Riva, Osa (1954–
She's. LPO, 260–61.
Hien Luong
Songs that cannot be silenced. OVO, 161–62.
Hildegard von Bingen (1098–1197)
untitled. (Like the honeycomb dropping honey). WPO, 154.
untitled. (O crimson blood/Which fell from that high place). WPO, 153–54.
Hill, Ellen Wise. *See* **Hill, Nellie.**
Hill, Nellie (1942–
My inheritance. NET, 22.
The poet learns to fly like an angel but gets nothing to eat. NET, 21.
Hill, Roberta (1947–
Conversation overheard on Tamalpais Road. TWO, 124–25.
Leap in the dark. TWO, 122–24. WPO, 419–22.
Hind bint Utba (early 7th century)
Fury against the Moslems at Uhud. WPO, 94–95.
Tambourine song for soldiers going into battle. WPO, 95.
Hind bint Uthatha (early 7th century)
To a hero dead at al-Safra. WPO, 95–96.
Hippius, Zinaida. *See* **Gippius, Zinaida.**
Hisajo, Sugita. *See* **Sugita Hisajo.**

Hisako, Fukui. *See* **Fukui Hisako.**
Ho, Lady (300 B.C.)
  A song of magpies. WPC, 1.
Hochman, Sandra (1936–
  The practical clown. AAA, 95.
Hodge, Barbara Vere
  The night-light. WAD, 129.
Hollingworth, Sherry
  untitled. (He came and he sat). AOW, 26.
  untitled. (We went and we had spice apple ale together).
    AOW, 27.
Hooley, Teresa (1888–1973)
  A war film. SUM, 56.
Hope, Akua Lezli
  August. CNF, 142–43.
  Avatar. OWO, 84.
  D & C. OWO, 86.
  Getting to know, or stepping out in an entirely different
    way. EOU, 189.
  Gowanus Canal (because you said look again). EOU, 190.
  His own maniac self. KTF, 90.
  Lament. CNF, 141–42.
  Lovesigns. KTF, 88–89.
  Music screams in the mind. KTF, 91.
  No one comes home to lonely women. WPE, 102.
  Ode. KTF, 89.
  1. CNF, 143–44. OWO, 87–88.
  To every birth its pain. OWO, 85.
  To sister for Mother. WPE, 103.
Hope, Lezli. *See* **Hope, Akua Lezli.**
Horikawa, Lady (12th century)
  untitled. (How long will it last?). WPJ, 41. WPO, 40.
Horovitz, Frances
  The messenger. BAR, 162–63.
  Moon. BAR, 163.
  The woman's dream. BAR, 161–62.
Horta, Maria Teresa (1937–
  Secret. OVO, 60.
Hoshino Tatsuko (1903–
  untitled. (O brightness/of peony's buds). WPJ, 83.
Ho Shuang-ch'ing (c.1712–?
  To the tune "A watered silk dress." SOW, 67. WPC, 66.
  To the tune "Washing silk in the stream." SOW, 43–44.
    WPC, 67.
Howard, Dorothy
  Eurydice. WAD, 101–02.
Howard, Mariah Britton
  reports. CNF, 145.
  solution #9 "to touch you." CNF, 147–49.
  a using. CNF, 145–47.
Howe, Julia Ward (1819–1910)
  The battle hymn of the Republic. WSO, 216–17.
  Furthermore. WSO, 217–18.
Howes, Barbara (1914–
  A point of view. WPE, 106.
  Shunpike. WPE, 106.
Hoyos, Angela de
  Below zero. LAW, 174. TWO, 394.

  Blues in the barrio. LAW, 174–75.
  Brindis: for the barrio. (Brindis: Por el barrio). LAW,
    173–74.
  The final laugh. TWO, 393.
  The final laugh. (La risa final). LAW, 170–71.
  The missing ingredient. TWO, 394.
  The missing ingredient. (El ingrediente ausente). LAW,
    169–70.
  Problems of etiquette. (Problemas de etiqueta). LAW,
    171–72.
  Who killed brown love? Law, 175.
Hroswitha von Gandersheim (935–?
  Paphnutius. WPO, 153. (excerpt).
Hsiang-lan, Ma. *See* **Ma Hsiang-lan.**
Hsiao-hsiao, Su. *See* **Su Hsiao-hsiao.**
Hsieh Wan-ying. *See* **Ping Hsin (Hsieh Wan-ying).**
Hsin, Ping. *See* **Ping Hsin (Hsieh Wan-ying).**
Hsiung Hung (1940–
  If you think with fire. WPC, 106.
  The pitcher. WPC, 101.
  Summer freezes here. WPC, 102.
  Thinking of someone. WPC, 107.
  To _____. WPC, 104.
  Who stops the dance? WPC, 105.
  Written in the sunset. OVO, 129. WPC, 103.
Hsüan-chi, Yü. *See* **Yü Hsüan-chi.**
Hsüeh Ch'iung (8th or 9th century)
  A song of Chin Men District. WPC, 23.
Hsüeh T'ao (768–831)
  The autumn brook. WPC, 21.
  An old poem to Yuan Chen. WPC, 22.
Hua Jui, Lady (10th century)
  The Emperor asks why my husband surrendered. WPC,
    31.
  Life in the Palace. WPC, 32–33.
Huang O (1498–1569)
  A farewell to a southern melody. WPC, 58.
  To the tune "The fall of a little wild goose." WPC, 57.
    WPO, 22–23.
  To the tune "A floating cloud crosses Enchanted Moun-
    tain." WPC, 59.
  To the tune "Plucking a cinnamon branch." WPC,
    62.
  To the tune "Red embroidered shoes. SOW, 62. WPC,
    61. WPO, 22.
  To the tune "Soaring clouds." SOW, 56. WPC, 60.
    WPO, 21–22.
Huch, Ricarda (1864–1947)
  Young girl. WPO, 203–04.
Hucklenbroich, Frankie (1939–
  Due process. APO, 84. LPO, 40–41.
  For all the lovers among us. APO, 85. LPO, 41.
  Genealogy. APO, 83. LPO, 40.
Huie, Helen Wong
  My mother's arms. OWO, 92.
  The odyssey. OWO, 93.
  untitled. (I don't want any more of your gentle abuse.)
    OWO, 91.

untitled. (I watched her go). OWO, 90.
untitled. (What do I want out of life?). OWO, 92.
Hull, Gloria T. (1944–
Poem. HGI, lvii.
Hung, Hsiung. *See* **Hsiung Hung.**
Hunter, Jacquelyn Furgus
Mis' Lou. SBB, 328–30.
Hunter, John, Mrs.
My mother bids me bind my hair. WAD, 114–15.
Hyman, Lateifa-Ramona Lahleet
Paraphernalia for a suicide: a revelation of life. CNF, 150–51.

I

Ibaragi Noriko (1926–
Dialogue. WPJ, 100.
What a little girl had on her mind. WPJ, 101.
Ibarbourou, Juana de (1897–1979)
Chronicle. (Crónica). OTT, 48–49.
Life-hook. WPO, 307.
Life-hook. (Vida-garfio). OTT, 46–47.
Ikuko, Atsumi. *See* **Atsumi Ikuko.**
Ilce, Ana (1945–
Table. (Mesa). OTT, 120–21.
Imaizumi Sogetsu-Ni (?–1804)
untitled. (How beautiful the Buddhist statues). WPJ, 58.
Ines de la Cruz, Juana (Sister) (1651–1695)
Foolish men. AAA, 26.
I can't hold you and I can't leave you. BWO, 314.
To her portrait. AAA, 27.
Inez, Colette (1931–
Reading da leaves. WPE, 32.
Ingrum, Adrienne
Friday the 13th Candlelight March. CNF, 158–61.
Loomit. CNF, 152–58.
Inoue Michiko
Get angry, Compass. WPJ, 106.
Iratsume, Kasa no. *See* **Kasa no Iratsume.**
Ise, Lady (c.935)
untitled. (As the first spring mists appear). WPJ, 18.
untitled. (Even in dreams/I do not want him to know). WPJ, 18.
untitled. (If I consider/My body like the fields). WPO, 38.
untitled. (Is it your command/that we must pass through this life,). WPJ, 17.
untitled. (Not even in dreams/Can I meet him any-more—). WPO, 37.
untitled. (Shall I come to see). WPJ, 18.
untitled. (Since ''the pillow knows all''). WPJ, 17. WPO, 37.

Ise Tayū (11th century)
On receiving the gift of a robe with a pattern of mingled plum blossoms and chrysanthemums. WPJ, 32.
untitled. (The clear water of the imperial pond). WPJ, 31.
untitled. (The farmer's clothes are soaked through and never dried,). WPJ, 30, WPO, 40.
untitled. (In Nara, the ancient capital,). WPJ, 30.
untitled. (It is already so late at night). WPJ, 31.
untitled. (Only the waning morning moon). WPJ, 32.
untitled. (Today is the anniversary of our parting). WPJ, 33.
untitled. (Unable to sleep,/I gaze at the flowers of the bush clover,). WPJ, 33.
Iselda (c.1150–1250)
Tenson. (Co-written by **Carenza**). WPO, 155–56.
Ishigaki Rin (1920–
Cocoon. WPO, 42.
Shellfish. WPJ, 96.
Walking-with-a-cane-pass. WPJ, 97.
untitled. (I don't know why, but my hand knew). WPJ, 98.
Islas, Maya (1947–
untitled. (I am in the euphoria of your white wings). (Estoy en la euforia de tus alas blancas). LAW, 178.
untitled. (Stone of embittered particles,). (Con tus golpes invisibles,). LAW, 177–78.
Isma'il of Syria, Rabi'a bint. *See* **Rabi'a bint Isma'il of Syria.**
Ismaili, Rashidah
Dialogue. CNF, 164–65.
Murderous intent with a deadly weapon. CNF, 162–63.
Struggle of class. CNF, 166–67.
Ita, Saint (480–570)
Jesukin. AAA, 3.
Ivimy, May
On a death in an old people's home. WAD, 186–88.
Izumi Shikibu (c.974–c.1030)
At the Sutra chanting of her dead daughter. WPJ, 28.
untitled. (Another cruel letter today.). WPJ, 28.
untitled. (I go out of darkness). WPO, 38.
untitled. (In the dusk the path/You used to come to me). WPO, 39.
untitled. (It is the time of rain and snow.). WPO, 39.
untitled. (Out of the darkness/on a dark path,). WPJ, 29.
untitled. (The pillow that knows all). WPJ, 29.
untitled. (Soon I shall cease to be.). WPJ, 29.

J

Jackowska, Nicki
Family outing—a celebration. BAR, 176–78.
The insect kitchen. BAR, 178–79.

The meeting. BAR, 180–81.
The sisters. BAR, 179–80.
Jackson, Helen Hunt (1830–1885)
Danger. WSO, 211.
Emigravit. WSO, 211–12.
Jackson, Mae (1946–
For the count. CNF, 168–69.
Just one in a series. KTF, 93.
My last feeling this way poem. CNF, 170–73.
Night. KTF, 92.
On learning. CNF, 169–70.
A POEM FOR ALL THE MENS IN THE WORLD. CNF, 169.
(To someone I met on 125th Street, 1966). KTF, 93–94.
Jackson, Molly (Aunt) (1880–1961)
I am a union woman. WSO, 305–06.
Jackson, Sara
The window. WAD, 156–57.
Jacobs, Bertha (Suster Bertken) (1427–1514)
A ditty. WPO, 161–62.
Janowitz, Phyllis
Mrs. Lucky. WPE, 80.
Jen Jui (?–1949)
Midnight. WPC, 119.
Jenkins, Christina
Sunday morning. BAR, 240–41.
Jenkins, Elinor
Dulce et decorum? SUM, 57.
Jennings, Elizabeth (1926–
The diamond cutter. WAD, 164.
Greek statues. WAD, 169–70.
Old woman. WAD, 183–84.
Jensen, Laura (1948–
Mouse. EOU, 191.
Whale. EOU, 192–93.
Jesse, F. Tennyson
De mortuis. WAD, 190.
Jesús, Teresa de
All of a sudden. WPO, 316–17.
They go by, go by, love, the days and the hours. WPO, 317.
Jircitano, Lois Bissell
Love, Grandma. IAT, 127–28.
Jitō, Empress (645–702)
On the death of the Emperor Temmu. (Even flaming fire). WPJ, 7.
On the death of the Emperor Temmu. (Over North Mountain). WPJ, 6.
The sudden appearance of cherry blossoms. WPJ, 6.
untitled. (The stars pass.). WPJ, 7.
Joan, Polly (1933–
Scarred. APO, 91.
Johansen, Marguerite
High-heeled boots. WAD, 23–24.
Johansson, Majken (1930–
Proportion poetry. OVO, 112–13.
Johnson, E. Pauline. *See* **Tekahionwake.**

Johnson, Esther (1681–1728)
To Dr. Swift on his birthday, 30th November 1721. AAA, 28.
Johnson, Georgia Douglas (1886–1966)
Celibacy. WSO, 264.
Cosmopolite. WSO, 265.
The heart of a woman. AAA, 56. BLS, 58. WSO, 263.
I want to die while you love me. BLS, 58.
My little dreams. BLS, 59.
A paradox. WSO, 264.
Smothered fires. BLS, 59.
The suppliant. AAA, 56. WSO, 264.
Johnson, Helene (1907–
Bottled. BLS, 78–79.
Magalu. BLS, 79–80.
The road. BLS, 80.
Summer matures. BLS, 81–82.
Trees at night. BLS, 81.
Johnson, Honor
Maxims. TIW, 82–83.
Jonas, Rosalie
Ballade des Belles Milatraisses; The Octoroon Ball, New Orleans, 1840–1850. BLS, 55–56.
Brother Baptis' on woman suffrage. BLS, 56.
Envoy-The convent, New Orleans 1840–1850. BLS, 56.
Jones, Gayl (1949–
Many die here. BLS, 210–11.
Salvation. KTF, 94.
Satori. BLS, 210.
3-31-70. (Journal). BLS, 205–09.
Tripart. BLS, 209.
Jones, Marté
A flame within. KTF, 95.
You are stolen kisses in my unsuspecting sleep. KTF, 96.
Jones, Patricia (1951–
14th St/new york. OWO, 96–97. (excerpts).
I done got so thirsty that my mouth waters at the thought of rain. BLS, 249–51. OWO, 101–03.
mi chinita poem. OWO, 99–100.
a no blues love poem. OWO, 95.
poem for david murray. OWO, 98.
sonnet/for pedro pietri. OWO, 103.
Why I like movies (for Charlotte). BLS, 251–52.
Jong, Erica (1941–
Dear Colette. WAW 188–89.
Jonker, Ingrid (1933–1965)
Dark stream. OVO, 116.
Don't sleep. WPO, 292.
I drift in the wind. WPO, 292–93.
Ladybird (a memory of my mother). OVO, 26.
Pregnant woman. OVO, 41–42.
Time of waiting in Amsterdam. OVO, 65.
When you laugh. WPO, 292.
Jordan, Anasa
Sweet Otis Suite. CNF, 177–79.
Jordan, June (1936–
Blue ribbons for the baby girl. CNF, 181.

From sea to shining sea. HGI, 223–29.
Getting down to get over. KTF, 99–105.
If you saw a Negro lady. TWO, 262–63.
In memoriam: Rev. Martin Luther King, Jr. (Part one).
    TWO, 263–64.
A last dialog on the left. CNF, 182.
No poem because time is not a name. KTF, 98–99.
ON THE REAL WORLD: Meditation #1. CNF, 180–81.
Oughta be a woman. HGI, xxvii.
Poem about a night out: Michael: good-bye for awhile.
    WPE, 84–85.
Poem for inaugural rose. WPE, 85.
Poem for Nana. BLS, 148–51.
Poem nr. 2 for inaugural rose. WPE, 85–86.
Poem: on my happy/matrimonial condition. KTF, 97.
Poem towards a final solution. CNF, 183–84.
Problems of translation: problems of language. EOU,
    194–97.
This is a poem about Vieques, Puerto Rico. WPE, 83–84.
Unemployment/monologue. WPO, 376–77.

Joseph, Jenny (1932–
Back to base. BAR, 159–60.
Dog body and cat mind. BAR, 157–58.
The lost continent. BAR, 157.
Rose in the afternoon. BAR, 158–59.

Joseph, Rosemary
Going north for Christmas. WAD, 159–60.

Juana de Asbaje (1651–1695)
untitled. (Green enravishment of human life,). WPO, 304.
untitled. (Stay, shade of my shy treasure! Oh, remain,).
    WPO, 304.

Juana de Ibarbourou. *See* **Ibarbourou, Juana de.**

Juhasz, Suzanne (1942–
Shimmering threads like hair. WPW, 32.
These women at thirty-five. WPW, 32–33.

Jui, Hua. *See* **Hua Jui, Lady.**

Jui, Jen. *See* **Jen Jui.**

Jung Tzu
My dressing mirror is a humpbacked cat. WPC, 92.

Junko, Nishi. *See* **Nishi Junko.**

Ka'b, Rábi'a bint. *See* **Rábi'a bint Ka'b.**

Kaccipettu Nannakaiyar (c.3rd century)
untitled. (My lover capable of terrible lies). WPO, 54.

Kaga no Chiyo. *See* **Fukuda Chiyo-Ni.**

Kamala Das. *See* **Das, Kamala.**

Kanai Mieko (1947–
In the town with cat-shaped maze. WPJ, 129–31.

Kanazawa, Teru (1950–
Aborting. OWO, 107.
Dumb patronage. OWO, 105. TWO, 530.
The look of success. TWO, 529.
Revolution. OWO, 106–07.
Song to my Nisei mother. OWO, 108–09.
untitled. (I see smiles). OWO, 109.
untitled. (Spittle washes my face,). OWO, 105.

Kaneko, Helen Aoki (1919–
Enigma. TWO, 554.
Upon seeing an etching. TWO, 555.
Wind. TWO, 554.

Kanoko, Okamoto. *See* **Okamoto Kanoko.**

Karibo, Minji
Superstition. WPO, 288–89.

Karle, Alice (1949–
''Darkness.'' FYW, 52.
Earthquake. FYW, 63.
Elizabeth. FYW, 53.
An epic (with renaissance flute). FYW, 60–62.
Liebfraumilch. FYW, 47.
A play. FYW, 57.
Song of Circles. FYW, 67–69.
Suicide. FYW, 49.
to Shannon and Kenneths. FYW, 50.
untitled. (The days and nights of the river). FYW, 55.
untitled. (Light floats through the edges). FYW, 64.
untitled. (The lines in your hand). FYW, 56.
untitled. (The room is one brown color). FYW, 58.
untitled. (Sideman/how many edges fill?). FYW, 51.
untitled. (Snowmountains/way to Aspen). FYW, 48.
untitled. (Some come in the window). FYW, 65–66.
untitled. (Spring trees grow heavy). FYW, 54.
untitled. (Steps   Steps/Spaces   inbetween   steps).
    FYW, 59.

Károlyi, Amy (1909–
The third house. OVO, 188–90. (excerpts).

Kasa no Iratsume (8th century)
untitled. (Evening comes and sorrow crowds my mind,).
    WPJ, 13.
untitled. (The Gods of heaven are irrational.). WPJ, 13.
untitled. (I dreamed I held/A sword against my flesh.).
    WPO, 36.
untitled. (To love somebody/Who doesn't love you).
    WPO, 36.
untitled. (When evening comes/sorrow overwhelms my
    mind.). WPJ, 13.

Kaschnitz, Marie Luise (1901–
Humility. WPO, 238–39.
Resurrection. WPO, 239.
Return to Frankfurt. OVO, 61. (excerpt).

Kassia (c.840)
Sticheron for Matins, Wednesday of Holy Week. WPO,
    152–53.
untitled. (Poverty? wealth? seek neither—). WPO, 152.
untitled. (Wealth covers sin—the poor). WPO, 152.
untitled. (A woman working hard and wisely). WPO, 152.

Katz, Jane (1954–
The palm-reading. AAA, 112.

Kaufman, Shirley (1923–
Abishag. EOU, 198–99.

Claims. EOU, 200–02. (excerpts).
His wife. BAA, 105.
Jerusalem notebook. BAA, 108–15.
Meron. BAA, 98–101.
Rebecca. BAA, 106–07.
The Western Wall. BAA, 102–03.

Kawai Chigetsu-Ni (1632–1736)
untitled. (Cats making love in the temple). WPJ, 49.
untitled. (Grasshoppers/Chirping in the sleeves). WPJ, 49.
WPO, 41.

Kaye, Melanie (1945–
Brooklyn 1956: The walls are full of noise. LPO, 149–50.
Trojan. LPO, 150–51.

Kazantzis, Judith
And in Richmond. TPA, 31.
Arachne. BAR, 213–14. TPA, 8–9.
At the National Gallery. TPA, 12.
Ava Gardner in the film *Earthquake*. TPA, 10–11.
the bath. HFE, 47.
Cinderella. TPA, 28–29.
The diving board. TPA, 14.
Fatima. TPA, 28.
Fire. TPA, 29.
For my daughter. TPA, 7.
The frightened flier goes north. BAR, 237–40. TPA, 31–33.
The horses of instruction, the tigers of wrath. TPA, 16.
In memory, 1978. BAR, 263.
Marginal. TPA, 26–27.
No war. TPA, 13.
A piece of business. TPA, 11.
Playing water polo in Angola in the words of an ex-South
African mercenary, 32 Battalion, reported Feb '81.
TPA, 17.
The Pope at Dublin Airport. TPA, 15.
Progenitor. TPA, 18–25
shout. HFE, 48.
soeurs du mal. TPA, 26.
Song for the new year. TPA, 30.
A woman making advances publicly. BAR, 252–53.
TPA, 8.

Kazue, Shinkawa. *See* **Shinkawa Kazue.**
Kazuko, Shiraishi. *See* **Shiraishi Kazuko.**

Keeler, Elizabeth
Again, flowering. CAM, 115.
Autumnal claque. CAM, 114.
The couple. CAM, 119.
Daughter's funeral dirge at a Saturday burial (Union
gravediggers quit at noon). CAM, 117–18.
The face in the camera. CAM, 118–19.
Inheritance. CAM, 116.
Light. CAM, 113.
Looking for light and finding the sea. CAM, 113.
The mountain in my head, its periodic loss. CAM, 116.
Of generations and being woman. CAM, 120.
Phantoms. CAM, 121.
Snow in Marin County! CAM, 115.
Visiting a son in Java. CAM, 118.

Kemble, Fanny (1809–1893)
A wish. BWO, 388.

Kenrei Mon-in Ukyō no Daibu (12th century)
untitled. (I was sure I would never get lost). WPJ, 37.
untitled. (The leaves of the bush clover rustle in the
wind.). WPJ, 37.
untitled. (My heart, like my clothing/is saturated with
your fragrance.). WPJ, 37.

Kenward, Jean (1920–
Moorhens. WAD, 68–69.
An old snapshot. AAA, 82.

Kenyon, Jane
Briefly it enters, and briefly speaks. EOU, 204.
Philosophy in warm weather. EOU, 203.
The pond at dusk. EOU, 205.

Keown, Anna Gordon (1899–1957)
Reported missing. SUM, 58.

Ker, Alice
untitled. (Newington Butts were lively,). WSO, 150.

Khaketla, Caroline N. M. (1918–
The white and the black. OVO, 151.

Khalid, Fawziyya Abu. *See* **Abu Khalid, Fawziyya.**

al-Khansa, Tumadir (575–646)
Elegy for her brother, Sakhr. WPO, 93.

Khatun, Padeshah. *See* **Padeshah Khatun.**

Khoury, Venus (1937–
untitled. (Backed up against time). OVO, 68.
untitled. (My father has big skin like a soldier's cape).
OVO, 24.
untitled. (Our walls were thick). OVO, 67.

Kibkarjuk (fl. c. 1920)
I'm a little woman who's happy to slave. IAT, 39–40.
Song of the rejected woman. IAT, 44–45. WPO, 416–17.

Kicknosway, Faye (1936–
Crystal. AOW, 28.
Gracie. AOW, 31–32.
Persona. AOW, 30.
Rapunzil. AOW, 29.
Spitting backward,. NET, 57.
untitled. (and what shall i be today, what). NET, 59.
untitled. (no legs.). NET, 58.

Kii, Lady (8th century)
untitled. (I know the reputation/of the idle ways). WPJ,
12. WPO, 35–36.

Kikusha-Ni, Tagami. *See* **Tagami Kikusha-Ni.**

Killigrew, Anne (1660–1685)
Upon the saying that my verses were made by another.
WSO, 79–81.

Kim, Willyce (1946–
A fistful of flowers for Vivian's kid. APO, 76–77.
Keeping still, mountain. LPO, 158.
A woman's tribal belt. APO, 78. LPO, 157.

Kingston, Maxine Hong (1940–
Absorption of rock. EOU, 207–08.
Restaurant. EOU, 206.

Kirsch, Sarah (1935–
Before the sun rises. OVO, 139.
Brief landing. OVO, 73–74.
Dandelions for chains. WPO, 241–42.

Kirti Chaudhari. *See* **Chaudhari, Kirti.**
Kiyoko, Nagase. *See* **Nagase Kiyoko.**

Kizer, Carolyn (1925–
  Amusing our daughters. BWO, 223.
  The first of June again. WAW, 275–76.
  Lines to accompany flowers for Eve (who took heroin, then sleeping pills and who lies in a New York hospital). WAW, 276–77.
  Pro femina: parts one, two, and three. WAW, 93–96.
  Singing aloud. WAW, 93.
  What the bones know. WAW, 277.
Klepfisz, Irena (1941–
  Conditions. APO, 69.
  Contexts. LPO, 90–93. WPE, 107–08.
  death camp. APO, 70. LPO, 83.
  The monkey house and other cages. LPO, 86–90. (excerpts).
  they did not build wings for them. APO, 67–68. LPO, 84–86.
  they're always curious. LPO, 83–84.
Kobayashi, Chris
  Oba-san. NET, 101–02.
Koestenbaum, Phyllis (1930–
  Blood journey. NET, 103–07.
  Friday. WPW, 63.
  Minor poem. WPW, 62.
Kolmar, Gertrud (1899–1943?)
  Out of the darkness. WPO, 237–38.
Komachi, Ono no. *See* **Ono no Komachi.**
Konopnicka, Maria (1842–1910)
  A vision. WPO, 208.
Koolish, Lynda
  Joseph's coat. NET, 110–11.
  my flesh is flesh. NET, 109.
Kopelke, Kendra
  Eager Street. EOU, 209–10.
Kōra Rumiko (1932–
  Woman. WPJ, 123.
Korina. *See* **Corinna.**
Korinna. *See* **Corinna.**
Kowalkowska, Ana (1948–
  Azteca IV. (Spanish and English). APO, 79–80. LPO, 159–61.
Koyū-Ni, Matsumoto. *See* **Matsumoto Koyū-Ni.**
Kozioł, Urszula (1935–
  Alarum. WPO, 227–28.
Krmpotic, Vesna (1932–
  A December forest. WPO, 230–31.
Kuan P'an-p'an (8th or 9th century)
  Mourning. WPC, 15.
Kuan Tao-shêng (1262–1319)
  Married love. SOW, 41. WPC, 53.
Kubatum (c. 2032 B.C.)
  Love song to King Shu-Suen. WPO, 118.
Kudaka, Geraldine (1951–
  i shoulda told you. TWO, 547–49.
  On writing Asian-American poetry. TWO, 545–47.
Kujō Takeko (1887–1928)
  untitled. (I do not consider myself worth counting,). WPJ, 69.

Kumin, Maxine (1925–
  Leaving my daughter's house. EOU, 211–12.
  The marriage. AAA, 84–85.
  May 10th. BWO, 356.
Kunjufu, Johari M. (1936–
  Ceremony. BLS, 192–94.
  The promise. BLS, 195. CNF, 51.
  Return. BLS, 194.
  Story for the remainder. CNF, 51–53.
  There is no title: only echoes. CNF, 50–51.

L

Labé, Louise (c. 1524–1566)
  The eighth sonnet. AAA, 19.
  Elegy. XXIII. (How does it help me if, with flawless art,). WPO, 175.
  Sonnet, XVIII. (Kiss me again, re-kiss and kiss me whole;). WPO, 175.
LaBombard, Joan
  August. WPW, 71.
  The covenant. WPW, 71.
  In the old city: Dubrovnik. WPW, 72.
Labra, Carilda Oliver. *See* **Oliver Labra, Carilda.**
Labriola, Gina
  Orgy (that is, vegetable market, at Sarno). WPO, 257–58.
Laing, Dilys (1906–1960)
  The double goer. BAW, 325–26. BWO, 87–88.
  Ego. BAW, 328.
  Except ye become. . . . WSO, 323–24.
  Let them ask their husbands. BAW, 327.
  The little girls. BAW, 326–27.
  Lot's daughter. BAW, 327–28.
  Ocean fable. WSO, 324–25.
  Prayer of an ovulating female. BAW, 329–30. SOW, 80.
  Private entry in the diary of a female parent. BAW, 328–29. SOW, 112. WAI, 138.
  Sonnet to a sister in error. BAW, 329.
  Ten leagues beyond the wide world's end. WSO, 324.
  Venus petrified. BAW, 324–25.
  Veterans. BAW, 328.
  Villanelle. BAW, 323–24.
Lal Ded, Lalleswari. *See* **Lalleswari (Lalla).**
Lalla, Lalleswari. *See* **Lalleswari (Lalla).**
Lalleswari (Lalla) (14th century)
  untitled. (Good repute is water carried in a sieve.). WPO, 58.
  untitled. (I set forth hopeful—cotton-blossom Lal.). WPO, 58.
  untitled. (With my breath I cut my way through the six forests). WPO, 58.

Lance, Jeanne
New Jersey. AOW, 33.
The skin trade. AOW, 34–36.
Landsman, Frances
Advice. HFE, 198.
Frustration. HFE, 198.
Tampax. HFE, 197.
Lane, Pinkie Gordon (1939–
Migration. BLS, 231–32.
Nocturne. BLS, 233.
On being head of the English department. BLS, 228–29.
Sexual privacy of women on welfare. BLS, 230–31.
When you read this poem (for citizens opposed to [book]
censorship, Baton Rouge). BLS, 229–30.
Who is my brother? BLS, 232.
Langfield, Angela
The chariot. WAD, 167–68.
Lan Ling (1946–
The arrival. WPC, 109.
Beyond silence. WPC, 110.
A melody. WPC, 108.
The white color of nearness. WPC, 111. (excerpt).
Lanyon, Carla Lanyon (1906–1971)
The dunce. WAD, 22–23.
To my godson. WAD, 25.
Lapidus, Jacqueline (1941–
Caution. APO, 88.
Coming out. LPO, 99.
I Ching. APO, 89.
untitled. (If I had a child/by everyone I love). APO, 90.
Larcom, Lucy (1824–1893)
Weaving. IHO, 39–41. WSO, 200–02.
la Riva, Osa Hidalgo-de. *See* **Hidalgo-de la Riva, Osa.**
Larkin, Joan
Blood. LPO, 52.
Cow's skull with calico roses. WPE, 54–55.
Native tongue. LPO, 52–53.
Notations—the F Train. LPO, 48–51.
Rhyme of my inheritance. LPO, 44–45.
Sleeping on the left side. WPE, 54.
Some unsaid things. APO, 55. LPO, 46.
Song. APO, 53. LPO, 43–44.
Stop. APO, 54. LPO, 47–48.
''Vagina'' sonnet. LPO, 45.
Lars, Claudia (1899–1974)
Evocation of Gabriela Mistral. (Evocación de Gabriela
Mistral). OTT, 80–83.
Letters written when night grows. (Cartas escritas cuando
crece la noche). OTT, 64–79. (excerpts).
Lasker-Schuler, Else (1869–1945)
A love song. OVO, 57.
My people. WPO, 235.
Over shining shingle. AAA, 45.
The Shulamite. OVO, 168.
The voices of Eden. OVO, 52–53.
Lateiner, Bonnie
The word. NET, 67.
Latimore, Jewel C. *See* **Kunjufu, Johari M.**

Lauterbach, Ann
The yellow linen dress: a sequence. WPE, 104–05.
Lavant, Christine (1915–
Buy us a little grain. WPO, 240.
Do not ask. WPO, 240.
Lawrence, Margery (?–1969)
The lost army. SUM, 59.
Transport of wounded in Mesopotamia, 1917. SUM, 59–
60.
Lazarus, Emma (1849–1887)
Echoes. WSO, 220.
The new colossus. WSO, 219.
Venus of the Louvre. WSO, 219.
Leamon, Marlene
Upstairs. EOU, 213–14.
Lee, Audrey
The maudlin mist of morning. KTF, 106.
Nostalgia. KTF, 106–07.
Lee, Mary (Lady Chudleigh) (1656–1710)
To the ladies. WAI, 159. WPO, 180–81.
lee, mary hope
on not bein. TBC, 9–11.
Lefkowitz, Roberta (1941–
Scrawl. NET, 41–43.
Lenngren, Anna Maria (1754–1817)
The portraits. WPO, 193–95.
Lerman, Eleanor (1952–
The community of women causes an operation. APO, 44.
LPO, 240.
Finally I see your skin. APO, 45. LPO, 240.
Letts, Winifred M. (1882–1971)
Casualty. SUM, 61.
The deserter. SUM, 61–62.
Screens. SUM, 62–63.
What reward? SUM, 63.
Levertov, Denise (1923–
Abel's bride. WAW, 271.
About marriage. WAW, 272–73.
Bedtime. WAI, 139.
Come into animal presence. WAD, 65.
Hypocrite women. WAW, 273–74.
In mind. BWO, 84.
Life at war. WAW, 271–72.
Lonely man. WAD, 40–41.
O taste and see. WAW, 274.
Song to Ishtar. WAI, 241.
Stepping westward. HOF, 174–75. IWL-1, 438–39.
IWL-3, 484–85.
Woman alone. WPO, 362–63.
Levi, Jan Heller
A sequence for my mother. EOU, 215–19.
After her death. EOU, 217–19.
Formal feeling. EOU, 215–16.
My father's wedding. EOU, 216–17.
Levine, Molly Myerowitz
First tooth. BAA, 75.
Safed and I. BAA, 71–73.
A song to your blood. BAA, 74.

Levy, Amy
Xantippe. BAR, 100–02.
Lewis, Eiluned
Flowering current. WAD, 130.
Lewis, Fanchon
Love poem to the earth. TIW, 77–78.
Thermodynamics II. TIW, 76.
Lewis, Janet (1889–
The Anasazi woman. NET, 34–35.
Girl help. WSO, 299.
Helen grown old. WSO, 298.
Helen, the sad queen. WSO, 298–99.
Liadain (7th century)
untitled. (Gain without gladness/Is in the bargain I have
struck;). WPO, 151.
Li Ch'ing-chao (1084–1151)
Happy and tipsy, to the tune "A dream song." WPC, 38.
Poem to the tune of "Tsui hua yin." WPO, 20.
Poem to the tune of 'Yi chian mei." WPO, 20.
The sorrow of departure, to the tune "Butterflies love
flowers." WPC, 39.
Spring ends, to the tune "Spring in Wu-ling." WPC, 40.
To the short tune "The Magnolias." WPC, 36.
To the tune "A hilly garden." WPC, 37.
To the tune "Eternal happiness." WPC, 42.
To the tune "The honor of a fisherman." WPC, 41.
Li Chu
Harvesting wheat for the public share. OVO, 163. WPC,
120.
Lignell, Kathleen
To say whose side you're on. WPE, 109.
Lim, Genny
The only language she knows. NET, 93.
Wonder woman. TBC, 25–26.
Lim, Shirley Geok-Lin (1944–
Christmas in exile. TWO, 531–32.
I would like. TWO, 533.
Modern secrets. TWO, 531.
Potions. TWO, 532.
Lima, Chelly (1957–
Ballad by one who doesn't want to make love blindly.
(Balada de quien no quiere hacer el amoe a tientas).
BTS, 290–93.
Reservoir at night. (Nocturo del aljibe). BTS, 290–91.
Lincoln, Abbey (Aminata Moseka) (1930–
I am the weaver. CNF, 185–86.
In the middle. CNF, 188.
A name change. CNF, 189–90.
On being high. CNF, 187–88.
Lindsay, Olive E.
Despair. SUM, 64.
Ling, Chung. *See* **Chung Ling.**
Ling, Lan. *See* **Lan Ling.**
Ling, Lin. *See* **Lin Ling.**
Ling-hui, Pao. *See* **Pao Ling-hui.**
Lin Ling (1935–
Cloud dissects itself. WPC, 94.
Footpaths cross in the rice field. WPC, 95.
Sinking. WPC, 93.

Vague apprehension, to a gambler. WPC, 96.
Woman wall. WPC, 97.
Livesay, Dorothy (1909–
After grief. SOW, 140–41.
Aging. SOW, 155–56.
Breathing. SOW, 153.
Grandmother. SOW, 142.
One way conversation. SOW, 64–65.
Parenthood. SOW, 123.
Widow. SOW, 146.
Livesay, Florence Randal (1874–1953)
Gold ladies. AAA, 46.
Li Yeh (8th century)
A greeting to Lu Hung-Chien. WPC, 16.
Loden, Rachel
Mother. TIW, 26–27.
What the sirens sang. TIW, 29–31.
'When you become that cold sullen creature man.' TIW,
31.
Loftin, Elouise
Sunni's unveiling. KTF, 109–10.
Woman. KTF, 108.
Longchamps, Joanne de. *See* **de Longchamps, Joanne.**
Lorde, Audre (1934–
Between ourselves. LPO, 27–29. WPO, 382–83.
Black mother woman. LPO, 24.
Chain. BLS, 199–201.
Coal. BLS, 198.
Conversation in crisis. TWO, 278.
Equinox. LPO, 22–23.
The evening news. WPE, 13–14.
Harriet. BLS, 202–03.
Love poem. APO, 24. LPO, 23–24.
Morning is a time for miracles. WPE, 14.
Naturally. BLS, 203–04.
NEED: a chorale of Black women's voices. CNF, 191–97.
LPO, 31–35.
October. WPE, 13.
125th Street and Abomey. LPO, 26.
Paperweight. TWO, 279.
A poem for women in rage. EOU, 220–22.
Power. APO, 23–24. LPO, 29–30.
Rites of passage. KTF, 107.
Rooming houses are old women. TWO, 280.
Solstice. SBB, 375–76.
Summer oracle. BLS, 201–02.
To my daughter the junkie on a train. APO, 22. LPO, 25.
The woman thing. BLS, 204–05.
Louise, Esther
enough. CNF, 198.
for us. CNF, 201.
it's all in the name. CNF, 199.
running to gone. CNF, 200.
tokens for "t." CNF, 201–02.
Loving, Okoyo
Ritual. SBB, 355.
Lowell, Amy (1874–1925)
Convalescence. SUM, 65.
A decade. AAA, 47.

Meeting-house Hill. WAD, 151–52.
Patterns. BWO, 301–04.
Venus transiens. WSO, 227–28.
Witch-woman. WSO, 228–32.
Lowell, Maria White (1821–1853)
An opium fantasy. WSO, 203–04.
Loy, Mina (1882–1966)
Crab-angel. WSO, 259.
Love songs.
    IV. (Evolution fall foul of/Sexual equality). WSO, 258.
    V. (Shuttle-cock and battle-door). WSO, 258.
    VI. (Let Joy go solace-winged). WSO, 259.
Parturition. SOW, 96–98; 100–02. (excerpts). WSO, 254–57.
Loynaz, Dulce María (1902–
Eternity. (Eternidad). BTS, 38–39.
The harp. (Arpa). BTS, 38–41.
Premonition. (Premonición). BTS, 40–41.
The traveller. (Viajero). BTS, 40–41.
Water games. (Juegos de agua). BTS, 40–43.
Luan-luan, Chao. *See* **Chao Luan-luan.**
Lucero, Judy
I speak in an illusion. TWO, 396.
Jail-life walk. TWO, 395.
Lucero-Trujillo, Marcela Christine
The advent of my death. TWO, 405–06.
"Machismo is part of our culture." TWO, 401–02.
THE MUSICOS FROM CAPULÍN. TWO, 404–05.
No more cookies, please. TWO, 402–03.
Roseville, Minn., U.S.A. Two, 403–04.
untitled. (Lit major learned in "isms"). TWO, 401.
Ludwig, Paula (1900–1974)
To the dark god. BWO, 343.
Luong, Hien. *See* **Hien Luong.**
Lynch, Annette (1922–
Gratitude. AAA, 83.
Lynd, Sylvia (1888–1952)
The question. WAD, 136–37.
Lynn, Elizabeth Cook. *See* **Cook-Lynn, Elizabeth.**
Lyon, Lilian Bowes (1895–1949)
Helen meditates before her portrait as a woman. WSO, 175.
Leda. WSO, 175.
Northumbrian farm. WAD, 46–47.
A shepherd's coat. WSO, 175–76.

M.C.R.
untitled. (Before I came to Holloway,). WSO, 148–49.
Mabuza, Lindiwe
Summer 1970. WPO, 290–91.

McCalla, Deidre
Billy de Lye. HGI, 270–71.
Macaulay, F. E. M.
The women's Marseillaise. BAN, 113.
Macaulay, Rose (1889–1958)
Picnic. SUM, 66–67.
The shadow. SUM, 67–68.
McClaurin, Irma (1945–
I, Woman. BLS, 197.
The mask. BLS, 195–96.
To a gone era (My college days - class of '73). BLS, 196–97.
McCombs, Judith
Advice to the photographers of atrocities. AOW, 37–38.
Games mammals play. AOW, 40–41.
Horse and rider. AOW, 39.
McCray, Chirlane
I used to think. HGI, 57–59.
McDaniel, Judith (1943–
November passage. LPO, 129–31.
Snow in April. WPE, 81.
When mother died, rows of cans. WPE, 81.
Macdonald, Cynthia
The mosiac hunchback. WPE, 56–57.
My familiar lover. EOU, 234–35.
Remains—Stratigraphy: WPE. 58.
The river Honey Queen Bess. EOU, 232–33.
Macdonald, Nina
Sing a song of War-time. SUM, 69.
MacDonald, Susan
the application. AOW, 43.
Seamstress. NET, 74.
son, AOW, 42.
untitled. (I am the woman moving into your life). NET, 75.
McElroy, Colleen J. (1935–
Caledonia. BLS, 288–89.
Catacombs: dream poem number one. WPW, 70.
Dancing with the fifth horseman. TWO, 268–70.
Defining it for Vanessa. TWO, 267–68.
Flight. WPW, 69.
Looking for a country under its original name. BLS, 290–91.
Morning in Argentina. WPW, 69–70.
Ruth. BLS, 286–88.
When poets dream. WPW, 70.
Where iguanas still live. TWO, 271–72.
A woman's song. BLS, 291–93.
McGinley, Phyllis (1905–1978)
The adversary. AAA, 71.
Ballroom dancing class. WAD, 84–86.
The 5:32. BWO, 284
Portrait of a girl with comic book. BWO, 55.
Macgoye, Marjorie Oludhe
For Miriam. WPO, 293–95.
McGrath, Kristina
Sequence from blue to blue. WPE, 97–98.
    The afternoon in May. WPE, 97–98.
    August. WPE, 98.

By July. WPE, 98.
The hour in April. WPE, 97.
The nights in June. WPE, 98.
McHugh, Heather.
On faith. EOU, 236.
Mackey, Mary
In Indiana. NET, 36.
McMahon, Lynne
Asthma. EOU, 237.
McMichael, Michelle. *See* **Zimele-Keita, Nzadi.**
McPherson, Sandra (1943–
Utanikki, August 1978. EOU, 238–39.
Macuilxochitl (1435–late 15th century)
Battle song. WPO, 414–15.
Madgett, Naomi Long (1923–
Black woman. BLS, 130–31. TWO, 256.
Deacon Morgan. BLS, 127.
Exits and entrances. BLS, 128.
Midway. BLS, 128–29.
New day. BLS, 130.
Nomen. BLS, 129.
Offspring. TWO, 255.
Writing a poem. TWO, 256.
Magdeburg, Mechthild von. *See* **Mechthild von Magdeburg.**
Mahadeviyakka (12th century)
untitled. (Like/treasure hidden in the ground). WPO, 57.
untitled. (O brother, why do you talk/to this woman,).
WPO, 57.
Mahsati (12th century)
untitled. (Better to live as a rogue and a bum,). WPO, 73.
untitled. (Gone are the games we played all night,). WPO,
73–74.
untitled. (Good-looking, I'll never stoop for you). WPO,
74.
untitled. (I knew like a song your vows weren't strong,).
WPO, 73.
untitled. (Unless you can dance through a common bar).
WPO, 73.
Ma Hsiang-lan (16th century)
Waterlilies. WPC, 63.
Maines, Rachel
almost newyork. CAM, 91.
Finders keepers. CAM, 92–93.
RSVP. CAM, 93–94.
Schrafft's Third Avenue and East 57th Street. CAM, 91.
Textile women: (Lowell, Lawrence, Fall River,
Amoskeag, Gastonia, Marion, Columbia, Oneita).
CAM, 90.
2-15-43/2-15-76. CAM, 94–95.
the tyer-in. CAM, 95.
the union educator. CAM, 92.
Máire Mhac an tSaoi. *See* **Mhac an tSaoi, Máire.**
Maisun, Lady (c.650)
She scorns her husband the Caliph. AAA, 4.
Makhfi (Zibu'n-Nisa) (1639–1703)
untitled. (The beauty of the Friend it was that taught me).
WPO, 59–60.

Maksimovic, Desanka (1898–
For all Mary Magdalenes. WPO, 232.
al-Malā'ika, Nāzik (1923–
Elegy for a woman of no importance. OVO, 153.
Jamila. WPO, 101–02.
Malangatana, Valente
To the anxious mother. SOW, 2–3.
Malé, Belkis Cuza. *See* **Cuza Malé, Belkis.**
Manner, Eeva-Liisa (1921–
Cambrian. OVO, 185–87. (excerpts).
And so the oracles. OVO, 186–87.
Apathy. OVO, 185.
The lunar games. WPO, 247–48.
untitled. (The skin like burnt glass or). OVO, 119–20.
Mansour, Joyce (1928–
North express, WPO, 263.
untitled. (Yesterday evening I saw your corpse). WPO,
262–63.
Mar, Laureen (1953–
Chinatown 1. TWO, 522.
Chinatown 2. TWO, 523–24.
Chinatown 4. TWO, 524.
My Mother, who came from China, where she never saw
snow. TWO, 521–22. WPO, 385–86.
Marcus, Adrianne
Alone, we dream as gods. TIW, 139–41.
The child of earthquake country. WPW, 57.
Grey: the madness. WPW, 57–58.
In defense of circuses. TIW, 142.
It's Buffalo, Boise, or Boston this time. WPW, 58.
Lady, sister: for Janis Joplin. TIW, 141.
Letter from an exile. WPW, 59.
''To count a million objects, even in 12 years, one cannot
spend much time on each one.'' WPW, 58.
Wedding poem. TIW, 142.
The woman in the next room. TIW, 143.
Margaret, Duchess of Newcastle. *See* **Cavendish, Margaret, Duchess of Newcastle.**
Margarido, Manuela (1926–
You who occupy our land. WPO, 284.
Margolin, Anna (1887–1952)
Years. OVO, 19.
Marie de France (1155–1190)
Chartivel. WPO, 158–59. (excerpt).
Would I might go far over sea. AAA, 11.
Marie-Elise (1950–
Definition, WAW, 440.
Diapering this poem. WAW, 441.
Gemini. WAW, 441–42.
prose/poem Written after overhearing a conversation on a
Greyhound bus just outside of Oxnard, California.
WAW, 442–43.
Touching a friend. WAW, 443.
Marie-Françoise-Catherine de Beauveau, La Marquise de Boufflers (1711–1786)
Air: Sentir avec ardeur. AAA, 30. WPO, 192.
Markman, Stephanie
The rime of the ancient feminist. BAR, 268–71. (excerpt).

Marlowe, Marion
The trout. WAD, 76.
Marquise de Boufflers. *See* **Marie-Françoise-Catherine de Beauveau, La Marquise de Boufflers.**
Marquise de Pescara. *See* **Colonna, Vittoria.**
Marruz, Fina García. *See* **García Marruz, Fina.**
Marx, Erica (1909–
Speeding ship. WAD, 122–23.
Mary, Queen of Scots (1542–1587)
Prayer before execution. AAA, 21.
Maryam bint Abi Ya'qub al-Ansari (early 11th century)
untitled. (What can you expect). WPO, 99.
Mary Gilbert, Sister. *See* **DeFrees, Madeline.**
Mary Lee (Lady Chudleigh). *See* **Lee, Mary (Lady Chudleigh).**
Masako, Chino. *See* **Chino Masako.**
Masako, Takiguchi. *See* **Takiguchi Masako.**
Ma Shou-chen. *See* **Ma Hsiang-lan.**
Mastin, Florence Ripley (1896–
At the movies. SUM, 70.
Mastoraki, Jenny (1949–
How did it happen? CGW, 55.
How I managed to square the circle of dreams in the shape of a window at the top of the stairs in a tenement house. CGW, 56–59.
Birth. CGW, 57.
Marble busts. CGW, 58.
The poet. CGW, 56.
Theorem. CGW, 59.
untitled. (The day's gone/and you're left with a telephone coin). CGW, 60.
untitled. (This silence I've nurtured). CGW, 54.
Matsumoto Koyū-Ni (18th century)
untitled. (At Ichiyiama/Boating on Lake Nio). WPJ, 57.
Mattei, Olga Elena (1933–
untitled. (December thirty first). (Diciembre treinta y uno). OTT, 202–03.
untitled. (Do you remember,/your face in the soup,). (¿Recuerdas,/tu cara entre la sopa,). OTT, 200–01.
untitled. (I am a bourgeois wife). Yo soy una señora burguesa). OTT, 196–99.
untitled. (I am here/seated in this place). (Yo soy aquí/sentada en este sitio). OTT, 206–09.
untitled. (Pairs/of soda crackers/part). (Las galletas de soda/pareadas/se parten). OTT, 204–05.
Matveyeva, Novella (1934–
The eggplants have pins and needles. WPO, 222–23.
Mayes, Frances
Epitaph. NET, 37.
Nesting dolls. NET, 39.
Voice. NET, 38.
Mayfield, Suellen
Baking bread. AOW, 44.
Mayrocker, Friederike (1924–
Patron of flawless serpent beauty. WPO, 241.

M'buzi, Malkia
Lament. CNF, 218.
Tree women quest for sun . . . CNF, 219–20.
Mealy, Rosemari
A love poem to an African freedom fighter. CNF, 221–22.
New chapters for our history. CNF, 223–29.
untitled. CNF, 222.
Mechthild von Magdeburg (1210–1294)
Love flows from God. WPO, 154.
untitled. (Here too the Spirit shafts/Such heavenly floods of light). WPO, 154–55.
Mégroz, Phyllis
The crystal tree. WAD, 100.
Mehri (Mihru'n-Nisa of Herat) (c. 1404–1447)
Coming across. WPO, 75.
Meireles, Cecilia (1901–1964)
Absolute sea. (Mar absoluto). OTT, 86–93.
Ballad of the ten casino dancers. OVO, 48–49.
Song. WPO, 312–13.
Mello Breyner Andresen, Sophia de. *See* **Andresen, Sophia de Mello Breyner.**
Melnikoff, Pamela
The lighthouse at Acre. WAD, 138–40.
Meneghetti, Cristina (1948–
untitled. (the form small form). (la forma pequeña forma). OTT, 268–69.
untitled. (I need you/here and now). (te necesito/aquí y ahora). OTT, 272–73.
untitled. (the last chapter of a maturity). (último capítulo de una madurez). OTT, 270–71.
untitled. (they were nebulous visitors). (eran borrosos visitantes). OTT, 266–67.
untitled. (the utter form of giving form to thought). (la forma de dar forma al pensamiento). OTT, 264–65.
Meneses, Vidaluz (1944–
Warnings. (Advertencias). OTT, 118–19.
When I married. (Cuando yo me case). OTT, 116–17.
Mêng Chu (3rd century)
Spring song. SOW, 63. WPC, 8.
Mew, Charlotte (1869–1928)
Again. WSO, 157.
The Cenotaph. SUM, 71.
Domus caedet arborem. WSO, 156–57.
Fame. BAN, 116–17. WSO, 156.
The farmer's bride. BWO, 283–84. WAI, 137–38.
Here lies a prisoner. WSO, 157.
June, 1915. SUM, 72.
Madeleine in church. WAD, 118–19. (excerpt).
May, 1915. SUM, 72.
On the road to the sea. BAN, 115–16.
The quiet house. BAN, 118–19.
Rooms. WSO, 157–58.
Smile, death. WPO, 209–10.
The trees are down. BAN, 117–18. WPO, 210–11.
Meynell, Alice (1847–1922)
Easter night. BAN, 121. WSO, 142–43.

A father of women: ad sororem E. B. BAN, 122. WSO, 143–44.

In sleep. BAN, 121.

In time of war. SUM, 73. WSO, 145.

Maternity. SOW, 104. WAI, 134. WSO, 142.

Parentage. WSO, 141.

Regrets. WAD, 119–20.

Saint Catherine of Siena. WSO, 141–42.

Summer in England, 1914. BAN, 120. SUM, 73–74.

The Sunderland children. WSO, 144.

To conscripts. WSO, 145.

Meynell, Viola (1888–1956)

Sympathy. WAD, 119.

Mhac an tSaoi, Máire (1922–

The first shoe. OVO, 46.

Michel, Concha (1899–

Genesis. FIR, 95–109.

In the vital process (1964). (En proceso vital [1964]). FIR, 90–93.

Only a second (1940). (Solo un segundo[1940]). FIR, 86–89.

Michiko, Inoue. *See* **Inoue Michiko.**

Michitsuna, Mother of (10th century)

untitled. (Is our love over?). WPJ, 26.

untitled. (Sighing, sleeping alone all night,). WPJ, 26.

untitled. (Whenever the wind blows). WPJ, 26.

Middlebrook, Diane

Two poems. NET, 82.

One woman looking at another. NET, 82.

You, seated near a lamp. NET, 82.

Mieko, Kanai. *See* **Kanai Mieko.**

Mihru'n-Nisa of Herat. *See* **Mehri (Mihru'n-Nisa of Herat).**

Mikajo, Yagi. *See* **Yagi Mikajo.**

Miles, Josephine (1911–

Afternoon walk. EOU, 240.

Demeanor. WPW, 16.

Denial. WSO, 321.

Figure. WPW, 16.

Fund raising. WPW, 16.

Government injunction restraining Harlem Cosmetic Co. NET, 40. WSO, 322.

Nadirs. WPW, 17.

Nine o'clock show. NET, 40.

Noon. WPW, 17.

Players. WSO, 321–22.

Readers. WPW, 17.

Ride. BWO, 346.

Trip. WPW, 15.

Why we are late. WPW, 15.

Miles, Sara

Calling on the live wire. OWO, 116.

Contrary ways to make fire. OWO, 111.

Doing time. EOU, 241–42.

for Cynthia. OWO, 114.

for Nancy. OWO, 112.

More. WPE, 111.

Native dancer. WPE, 110–11.

Portrait in available light. OWO, 117.

Rosas de la tarde. OWO, 113.

Talking about it. WPE, 111–12.

Through the weather. OWO, 115.

Millay, Edna St. Vincent (1892–1950)

An ancient gesture. BWO, 210. WAD, 37–38.

Conscientious objector. WPO, 358.

The courage that my mother had. AAA, 65.

Sonnets.

XIX. (And you as well must die, belovèd dust,). WAI, 89.

XXXI. (Oh, oh, you will be sorry for that word!). WSO, 287.

XLI. (I, being born a woman and distressed). WSO, 287.

LXVII. (Upon this marble bust that is not I). BWO, 387.

XCV. (Women have loved before as I love now;). AAA, 64.

CXXVI. (Thou famished grave, I will not fill thee yet,). WAD, 191.

Miller, Jane

5 a.m. WPE, 30.

Lightning storm. WPE, 29.

The long fingers of 1956. WPE, 31.

6 a.m. WPE, 30.

Miller, May (1918–

Death is not master. TWO, 257.

Gift from Kenya. BLS, 112.

Not that far. BLS, 113–17.

Canary Islands. BLS, 113.

Egypt. BLS, 114–15.

Gibraltar. BLS, 114.

Greece. BLS, 116.

The Holy Land. BLS, 115.

Italy. BLS, 116–17.

Madeira. BLS, 117.

Portugal. BLS, 113–14.

Rhodes. BLS, 115.

Spain. BLS, 114.

The trip back. BLS, 117.

Tunisia. BLS, 114.

Turkey. BLS, 115.

Yugoslavia. BLS, 116.

Place in the morning. TWO, 258.

The scream. TWO, 258.

Miller, Vassar (1924–

First intimation. EOU, 243.

Min, Cheng. *See* **Cheng Min.**

Minamoto no Toshitaka, The daughter of (12th century)

untitled. (For the sake of a night of a little sleep). WPJ, 42.

Mines, Stephanie (1944–

My own impression. NET, 118.

Take the skin off the mama. NET, 118–19.

Minnie, Memphis (1900–
Me and my chauffeur blues. WSO, 279–80.

Minty, Judith
Meditation on friendship: getting lost in the woods with Deena—Jamesville, NY. EOU, 244–45.

Mira Bai (1498–1547)
untitled. (O King, I know you gave me poison.). WPO, 58–59.
untitled. (Wake up, dear boy that holds the flute!). WPO, 59.

Miriam, Rivka
Flute. BAA, 86.
In that green field. BAA, 87.

Mirikitani, Janice
Attack the water. TWO, 541–42.
Sing with your body. TWO, 540–41. WPO, 391–92.

Mistral, Gabriela (1889–1957)
Bread. WPO, 314–15.
Bread. (PAN). OTT, 58–61.
Dear little man. AAA, 62.
Death sonnets. (Los Sonetos de la Muerte). OTT, 52–57.
Intimate. BWO, 334–35.
Rocking. AAA, 61.
Sister. OVO, 152.
Stranger. OVO, 157.

Mitchell, Charlotte
May Day. WAD, 86–88.

Mitchell, Lorna
The hermaphrodite's song. BAR, 265–67.

Mitchell, Ruth Comfort (1882–1953)
He went for a soldier. SUM, 75–76.

Mitsuhashi Takajo (1899–1972)
untitled. (The hair ornament of the sun/has sunk). WPJ, 80.
untitled. (O bird's singing!). WPJ, 80.

Mitsui Futabako (1919–
Grazing. WPJ, 95.

Miyoko, Gotō. *See* **Gotō Miyoko.**

Moffett, Judith (1942–
"Cambridge University Swimming Club/no public access to river." WPE, 36–38.
Key West (Triple ballade with enjambed refrain, plus envoy). EOU, 246–49.

Mollison, Jean (1918–
untitled. (Do you remember now the night that we,). LPO, 6.
untitled. (It seems unlikely that we'll talk again). LPO, 6.

Molodowsky, Kadia (1894–
God of Mercy. WPO, 359–60.
Song of the Sabbath. WPO, 358–59.
Women songs I. OVO, 18.

Mon-in Ukyō no Daibu, Kenrei. *See* **Kenrei Mon-in Ukyō no Daibu.**

Monroe, Harriet (1861–1936)
On the porch. SUM, 77–78.

Montagu, Mary Wortley, Lady (1689–1762)
An answer to a love-letter. WSO, 94–95.
In answer to a lady who advised retirement. WSO, 95.
Saturday: the small pox. WAI, 71–73.
Verses addressed to the imitator of the first satire of the second book of Horace. WSO, 92–94.

Moore, Honor (1945–
Abundance and scarcity. WPE, 114–15.
First time: 1950. LPO, 152–53.
In Mrs. N's palace. EOU, 250–51.
Poem: for the beginning. LPO, 153–54. WPE, 113–14.

Moore, Marianne (1887–1972)
Marriage. WSO, 313–20.
The mind is an enchanting thing. WPO, 356–57.
Silence. AAA, 55. BWO, 336.
What are years? WAD, 145–46.

Moore, Rosalie (1910–
Near Cologne: 1212. WPW, 25–26.
The phone. WPW, 25.

Moore, Virginia (1903–
Avowal. WSO, 165.
"In dejection near Naples." WSO, 165–66.
Not an apology. WSO, 166.

Moraff, Barbara (1940–
you, phoebusapollo. FYP.
untitled. (and tom, the existentialiste, drives, off, in his). FYP.
untitled. (i hear a mandolin). FYP.
untitled. (in a hospital room from a halfclosed eye from a half). FYP.
untitled. (Let us suppose the mind/to be a reversible teakettle). FYP.
untitled. (the river for the poem). FYP.
untitled. (ships in deep water). FYP.
untitled. (the wild wind whoops birds   shoots bulls of milk whoops). FYP.

Moraga, Cherríe (1952–
For amber. LPO, 251–52.
For the color of my mother. LPO, 249–50. TBC, 12–13.
Like I am to no one. LPO, 246–47.
The welder. TBC, 219–20.
You upset the whole system of this place. LPO, 248–49.

Morejón, Nancy (1944–
Apple tree in Oakland. (Un manzano de Oakland). BTS, 146–47.
Black woman (Mujer Negra). BTS, 150–53.
Bricklayer's fable. (Fabula de albañil). BTS, 142–43.
In praise of dialectics. (Elogio de la dialéctica). BTS, 146–49.
The reason for poetry. WPO, 325–26.
Woman in a tobacco factory. (Obrera del tabaco). BTS, 144–45.

Moreno, Victoria (1957–
en público. TWO, 397.
La Llorona, Crying Lady of the Creekbeds, 483 years old, and aging. TWO, 319–20.

Morgan, Natasha
He said: Mostly I feel like a tractor. HFE, 173.
The nets. HFE, 172.

Morgan, Robin (1941–
Documentary. WPE, 26–28.
Lunch hour. WPE, 28.
Morgan-Browne, L. E.
The purple, white and green. BAN, 109–10.
Moritz, Yunna (1937–
Autumn morning frost. TRP, 43–44.
The bell. TRP, 46.
In memory of Francois Rabelais. TRP, 37–38.
In twilight. TRP, 36.
Midday in Gantiadi. TRP, 35.
Midnight cold. TRP, 42.
Now we'll go. TRP, 45.
Poems for her sick mother. TRP, 39–41. (excerpts).
Morton, Katharine
untitled. (degeneration was the way backwards). AOW, 47.
untitled. (the flow of sound breaks even from the minds of/artists). AOW, 45.
untitled. (no more wondering   when the grass was taller than). AOW, 46.
Moseka, Aminata. *See* **Lincoln, Abbey (Aminata Moseka).**
Mririda n'Ait Attik (fl. 1940)
Azouou. WPO, 279–80.
Mririda. WPO, 280–81.
Msham, Mwana Kupona (c. 1810–1860)
Poem to her daughter. WPO, 278–79. (excerpt).
Mueller, Lisel (1924–
Fracture. EOU, 253.
A nude by Edward Hopper. IHO, 175–76.
Stone soup. EOU, 252.
Murasaki Shikibu (c. 978–1031)
The tale of the Genji. WPJ, 22. (excerpts). WPO, 38. (excerpts).
untitled. (From the North send a message). WPJ, 21.
untitled. (I feel of others' affairs). WPJ, 21.
untitled. (This life of ours would not cause you sorrow). WPJ, 21.
Murillo, Rosario (1951–
On account of the picture. (Por culpa del retrato). OTT, 124–25.
Murray, Michele (1934–1974)
At sixteen. IHO, 110.
Coming to self. IWL-3, 447.
The woman who lives inside the world. HOF, 367–70.
Murray, Pauli (1910–
Dark testament. BLS, 84–92.
Inquietude. BLS, 92.
Song. BLS, 93.
Musafir, Safiya bint. *See* **Safiya bint Musafir.**
Muske, Carol (1945–
Chapter one. WPE, 33.
Fairy tale. EOU, 254.
Special delivery to Curtis: the future of the world. WPE, 34.

N

Nagase Kiyoko (1906–
Mother. WPJ, 90.
Nagy, Ágnes Nemes (1922–
Ikhnaton's night. OVO, 191–93.
Nahem, Rachel
Elegy for my mad mother. AOW, 49–50.
End. AOW, 48.
n'Ait Attik, Mririda (fl. 1940–1945)
The abandoned. OVO, 93–94.
The second wife. OVO, 92–93.
Sister. OVO, 92.
Nakamura Chio (1913–
A diary without dates. WPJ, 91.
Nakamura Teijo (1900–
untitled. (The season of changing clothes). WPJ, 82.
Nameroff, Rochelle
Eucalyptus grave. TIW, 39–40.
Invocation. TIW, 37–38.
Machine. TIW, 41–42.
The welcome. TIW, 40.
Nannakaiyar, Kaccipettu. *See* **Kaccipettu Nannakaiyar.**
Napier, Felicity
Houseplant. BAR, 229–30.
Nardi, Rafaela Chacón. *See* **Chacón Nardi, Rafaela.**
Nāzik al-Mala'ikah. *See* **Mala'ikah, Nāzik al-.**
Negri, Ada (1870–1945)
Tonight. OVO, 110.
Nelson, Alice Ruth Moore Dunbar. *See* **Dunbar-Nelson, Alice Ruth Moore.**
Nesbit, Edith (1858–1924)
The fields of Flanders. SUM, 79.
Spring in war-time. SUM, 79–80.
Newcastle, Duchess of. *See* **Cavendish, Margaret, Duchess of Newcastle.**
Newman, Felice (1956–
Rites of spring. APO, 58–59.
Sister. LPO, 262.
Newton, Eileen
Last leave. SUM, 81.
Revision. SUM, 81–82.
Ngatho, Stella (1953–
Footpath. WPO, 289–90.
ni Chuilleanain, Eilean (1942–
Swineherd. WPO, 265.
Wash. WPO, 265.
Nickerson, Sheila
In the alley: June. WPW, 61.
ní Dhomhnaill, Nuala (1952–
Móir hatching. OVO, 35.

Nieh Shêng-ch'iung (Sung Dynasty)
Farewell to Li, to the tune "A partridge sky." WPC, 49.
Nishi Junko
Remorse came slowly. WPJ, 133.
Revolution. WPJ, 132.
Noailles, Anna de (1876–1933)
Poem on azure. WPO, 204–05.
Noda, Barbara (1953–
Strawberries. LPO, 253.
Noriko, Ibaragi. *See* **Ibaragi Noriko.**
Norman, Rosemary
Cabbage. BAR, 223.
My son and I. BAR, 222.
North, Susan (1940–
After ten years. CAM, 80–81.
Ascent. CAM, 86.
Aunt Lenore at forty-five. CAM, 84.
Farmers' almanac, or a guide to loving. CAM, 83.
For Michael. CAM, 81–82.
It isn't that you don't understand. CAM, 78.
Poem for her thirty-fifth birthday. CAM, 85.
Small poem for Michael. CAM, 84.
There is a point. CAM, 77.
The truth of the matter in Coolidge, Arizona. CAM, 79.
When your husband goes to prison. CAM, 79–80.
Norton, Caroline (1808–1876)
I do not love thee. WAD, 113–14.
Norton, Eleanour (1881–
In a restaurant, 1917. SUM, 83.
Norvig, Gerda S.
Even before the mirror Myra. EOU, 255.
Hand fantasy. EOU, 256.
Nottingham, Pat
Carnevale. KTF, 110–11.
Entries: 13. KTF, 111–12.
Entries: 14. KTF, 112.
Entries: 15. KTF, 112.
Entries: 21. KTF, 113.
Nukada, Princess (7th century)
When the Emperor Tenji ordered Fujiwara Kamatari to
judge between the beauty of cherry blossoms and the
red autumn leaves on the hills, Princess Nukada gave
judgment with this poem. WPJ, 5.
untitled. (As we pass through the field of purple herbs).
WPJ, 4.
untitled. (At Nigitazu we wait for the moon). WPJ, 3.
untitled. (Does that bird/think of bygone times).
WPJ, 4.
untitled. (Longing for you,/loving you,). WPJ, 3.
Nuraini, Siti (c. 1960–
A woman. AAA, 105.

O, Huang. *See* **Huang O.**
Obi, Dorothy S.
Winds of Africa. WPO, 288.
Oden, Gloria C. (1923–
This child is the mother. BLS, 123–27.
Odio, Eunice (1922–1974)
Dawn's territory. (Territorio del Alba). OTT, 150–51.
(excerpt).
Portraits of the heart. (Retratos del corazón). OTT, 152–
57.
Ogawa, Pelorhankhe. *See* **Ai.**
Ó Hehir, Diana
Alicia's dream: entering Knossos. WPW, 27.
Breaking the lid of night. WPW, 28.
Casualty in Mexico City. WPW, 27–28.
Final anatomy. EOU, 257.
Okamoto Kanoko (1889–1939)
untitled. (All day long having/buried himself/in the
peonies,). WPJ, 70.
Olds, Sharon
History: 13. EOU, 259.
Homage. WPE, 99.
The house of fecundity. EOU, 262–63.
The meal. EOU, 261.
The mole. WPE, 99.
Pilot captured by the Japanese, 1942. EOU, 258.
Sex without love. EOU, 264.
The takers. EOU, 260.
Oliver, Mary
The grandmothers. SOW, 141. WAD, 27.
No voyage. WAD, 36.
Oliver, Merrill
The birthmark. EOU, 265.
Oliver Labra, Carilda (1924–
Elegy for Mercedes. (Elegía por Mercedes). BTS,
78–81.
Last conversation with Rolando Escardó. (Ultima con-
versación con Rolando Escardó). BTS, 72–73.
Naked and forever. (Desnudo y para siempre). BTS, 72–
77.
Verses for Anna. (Versos para Ana). BTS, 76–79.
Oman, Carola (1897–1978)
Ambulance train 30. SUM, 84.
Brussels, 1919. SUM, 84–85.

Ōme Shūshiki (1668–1725)
  untitled. (Be careful! Be careful!). WPJ, 51.
O'Neill, Moira (1874–1965)
  A bud in the frost. WAD, 115–16.
Ono no Komachi (9th century)
  untitled. (Although I come to you constantly). WPJ, 15.
  untitled. (The colors of the flowers fade). WPJ, 16.
  untitled. (Doesn't he realize/that I am not). WPJ, 14.
    WPO, 36.
  untitled. (He does not come.). WPJ, 15.
  untitled. (I fell asleep thinking of him,). WPJ, 14.
  untitled. (If it were real/Perhaps I'd understand it;). WPO,
    37.
  untitled. (In the daytime/I can cope with them,). WPJ, 15.
  untitled. (No moon, no chance to meet;). WPO, 37.
  untitled. (Since I've felt this pain). WPO, 37.
  untitled. (Without changing color/in the emptiness). WPJ,
    16.
Oren, Miriam
  About her & about him. BAA, 79.
  At least. BAA, 78.
  When she was no longer. BAA, 80.
Orient, Betsy
  The divorce. AOW, 52–53.
  The proposition. AOW, 51.
Orinda. *See* Philips, Katherine.
O'Rourke, May (1898–
  The minority: 1917. SUM, 86.
Orozco, Olga (1920–
  Jonah's lament. (Lamento de Jonás). OTT, 100–03.
  Noica. OTT, 98–99.
  "Olga Orozco." OTT, 96–97.
  Sphinxes inclined to be. (Esfinges suelen ser). OTT, 104–
    07. WPO, 310–12.
Orr, Emily
  A recruit from the slums. SUM, 87.
Ossandón, Francisca
  Games of earth and light. (Los Juegos de la tierra y de la
    luz). OTT, 192–93. (excerpt).
  untitled. (Shadows dressed in silence). (Sombras revesti-
    das de silencio). OTT, 188–89.
  untitled. (The unfurling of bark). (Despliegue de cor-
    tezas). OTT, 190–91.
Otomo no Sakanoe (8th century)
  Envoy. AAA, 5.
  Sent from the capital to her elder daughter. AAA, 5.
    WPO, 35.
  untitled. (I gave the jewel away to its owner.). WPJ, 9.
  untitled. (I swore not to love you,). WPJ, 8.
  untitled. (My heart, thinking/"How beautiful he is").
    AAA, 6.
  untitled. (My love hurts me because you cannot know
    it—). WPJ, 9.
  untitled. (The orange tree/we planted in my garden). WPJ,
    8.
  untitled. (You say, "I will come."). AAA, 6.
Otomo no Sakanoe no Iratsume. *See* Otomo no Sakanoe.

Owen, Maureen
  Cubism. AOW, 57.
  How to get by. AOW, 55–56.
  Silk-screen. AOW, 54.
Owens, Rochelle (1936–
  Hera Hera Hera. FYP.
  Loon lord and master O jack pollock. FYP.
  The name, the haunch. FYP.
  O supreme Domine. FYP.
  Penobscot bird. FYP.
  Split a passionflower. FYP.
  Up up on the disorders of the hairs. FYP.
  A verse on the 50th day. FYP.

Padeshah Khatun (14th century)
  Sovereign queen. WPO, 74.
Pai Wei (1902–
  Madrid. WPC, 88.
Pallottini, Renata
  Message. WPO, 313–14.
Palma Acosta, Teresa
  My mother pieced quilts. WPO, 393–95.
Pamela Victorine
  Menses: a seasonal. AOW, 76–77.
  untitled. (The snowdeer licking salt). AOW, 78.
Pan Chao (c.45–c.115)
  Needle and thread. WPO, 15.
Pan Chieh-yü (1st century B.C.)
  A song of grief. WPC, 3.
Pankhurst, Sylvia (1882–1960)
  In lofty scorn. WSO, 151–52.
  The mothers. SOW, 88. WSO, 151.
P'an-p'an, Kuan. *See* Kuan P'an-p'an.
Pao Ling-hui (5th century)
  After one of the 19 famous Han poems. WPC, 13.
Parker, Dorothy (1893–1967)
  The little old lady in lavender silk. SOW, 54.
  Résumé. BWO, 340.
  Song of perfect propriety. AAA, 66–67.
  Ultimatum. WAD, 89.
Parker, Pat (1944–
  For Willyce. APO, 73. LPO, 138.
  From the cavities of bones. BLS, 238. LPO, 137.
  I followed a path. BLS, 239.
  A small contradiction. LPO, 137–38.
  Sunday. APO, 71–72.
  There is a woman in this town. BLS, 240–42.
  Where will you be? HGI, 209–13. LPO, 144–48.
  untitled. (Movement in Black). LPO, 139–44.

Parra, Violeta (1917–1967)
Goddamn the empty sky. OVO, 95–97.
Parun, Vesna (1922–
A return to the tree of time. WPO, 231.
Parvin, Betty
Gulls aground. WAD, 74.
Passavant, Elise
Thoughts on the unicorn. WAD, 71–72.
Pastan, Linda (1932–
Emily Dickinson. IHO, 235.
In the middle of a life. EOU, 269–70.
One blue flag. EOU, 268.
To my son, approaching 11. AAA, 92.
Patten, Mary
Mother. APO, 46.
Peck, Rita
Fish market. WAD, 75–76.
Pedrick, Jean
Hats. WWO, 139.
Peirse, Juanita (1897–
Lament for a dictator. WSO, 182–83.
Pembroke, Countess of. *See* **Herbert, Mary Sidney, Countess of Pembroke.**
Pereira, Teresinha
Austin: foreign city. (Austin: ciudad ajena). LAW, 179–80.
News from my town. (Noticias de mi pueblo). LAW, 180–81.
Pescara, Marquise de. *See* **Colonna, Vittoria.**
Peterson, Marsha
Some pieces I lost. AOW, 58.
Petröczi, Kata Szidónia (1662–1708)
Swift floods. WPO, 177–78.
Philips, Katherine (1631–1664)
Against love. WSO, 62–63.
An answer to another persuading a lady to marriage. WSO, 63.
Orinda to Lucasia. WSO, 60.
Orinda upon little Hector Philips. WSO, 59–60.
Parting with Lucasia: a song. WSO, 61–62.
To my excellent Lucasia, on our friendship. WPO, 178–79. WSO, 61.
Upon the double murther of King Charles I, in answer to a libellous copy of rimes by Vavasor Powell. WSO, 64.
Pierce, Edith Lovejoy (1904–
Pattern. AAA, 71.
Piercy, Marge (1936–
All clear. TIW, 19.
Barbie doll. IWL-1, 323.
The consumer, TIW, 23.
Gracious goodness. TIW, 22.
Homage to Lucille, Dr. Lord-Heinstein. EOU, 278–79.
Images emerging. TIW, 20.
Laocoön is the name of the figure. EOU, 280.
Looking at quilts. IHO, 35–36.
Night fight. WPE, 70.
Seedlings in the mail. TIW, 21.
Shadows of the burning. WPE, 69–70.

Simple-song. AAA, 107.
16/53. TIW, 24.
To be of use. WWO, 263.
The total influence or outcome of the matter: THE SUN. WPO, 367–69.
Unlearning to not speak. IWL-3, 448–49.
Ping Hsin (Hsieh Wan-ying). (1902–
For the record (given to my little brother). WPC, 85.
Multitudinous stars and spring waters. OVO, 130–31. (excerpts). WPC, 86–87. (excerpts).
Receiving Buddha. OVO, 171.
Remembering. WPC, 84.
The spring waters. WPO, 26. (excerpts).
The stars. WPO, 26. (excerpts).
Piper, Linda (1949–
Missionaries in the jungle. BLS, 184.
Sweet Ethel. BLS, 183–84.
Pisan, Christine de. *See* **Christine de Pisan.**
Pitter, Ruth (1897–
The Irish patriarch. WSO, 171.
The lost tribe. WPO, 270.
Maternal love triumphant or, song of the virtuous female spider. WSO, 172–74.
The old woman. WSO, 169–70.
The sparrow's skull. WSO, 170–71.
The swan bathing. WAD, 66–67.
To J. S. Collis. WSO, 170.
The unicorn. WAD, 100–01.
Vision of the cuckoo. WAD, 76–77.
Pixner, Stef (1945–
A day in the life . . . BAR, 230–32.
Pizarnik, Alejandra (1936–1972)
Abodes. (Moradas). OTT, 242–43.
Before. (Antes). OTT, 240–41.
Clock. (Reloj). OTT, 256–57.
Dusk. (Crepúsculo). OTT, 248–49.
The great words. (Las grandes palabras). OTT, 252–53.
Green paradise. (Verde paraiso). OTT, 246–47.
I ask silence. (Pido el silencio). OTT, 238–39.
Lovers. (Amantes). OTT, 244–45.
Party. (Fiesta). OTT, 258–59.
Sorceries. (Sortilegios). OTT, 260–61.
To name you. (Nombrarte). OTT, 250–51.
Useless frontiers. (Fronteras inútiles). OTT, 254–55.
Plath, Sylvia (1932–1963)
Childless woman. AAA, 91.
The jailor. IWL-1, 90–91. IWL-3, 62–63.
Kindness. HOF, 242–43. WAW, 356.
Lady Lazarus. WAW, 356–58.
Mirror. BWO, 86.
The moon and the yew tree. WAD, 131. WPO, 365–66.
Morning song. BWO, 225. WAW, 355.
Mushrooms. WPO, 366–67.
Poppies in October. WAW, 355.
Tulips. WAD, 33–35.
Plato, Ann
The natives of America. BLS, 43–45.
Reflections, written on visiting the grave of a venerated friend. BLS, 46–47.

To the first of August. BLS, 45–46.
Ponsot, Marie
  Half-life: copies to all concerned. WPE, 40.
  Late. WPE, 43–44.
  On the country sleep of Susanne K. Langer. WPE, 44.
  "Sois sage o ma douleur." WPE, 40–42.
Pope, Jessie (–1941)
  The call. SUM, 88.
  The Nut's birthday. SUM, 88–89.
  Socks. SUM, 89–90.
  War girls. SUM, 90.
Portal, Magda (1901–
  Woman. WPO, 318–19.
Porter, Margaret
  inflation. CNF, 264.
  Sugarman. CNF, 262–63.
  when i rite. CNF, 263–64.
Porumbacu, Veronica (1921–1977)
  White bears. OVO, 175.
  With a ring. OVO, 122.
Posamentier, Evelyn (1951–
  The gun is back. NET, 66.
  I bring roses. NEW, 65.
  Immigration. NET, 62–64.
Pozzi, Antonia (1912–1938)
  Awakening. OVO, 121.
  Canzonetta. OVO, 125–26.
  Landing. OVO, 172.
Pratt, Minnie Bruce (1946–
  Oconeechee Mountain. LPO, 162.
  Rape. LPO, 162–64.
  The segregated heart. LPO, 167–71.
    First home. LPO, 167–68.
    Second home. LPO, 168–69.
    Third home. LPO, 170–71.
  The sound of one fork. LPO, 164–66.
  untitled. (My mother loves women.). LPO, 166–67.
Praxilla (c.450 B.C.)
  Of the sensual world. AAA, 2. WPO, 144.
  untitled. (Girl of the lovely glance, looking out through
    the). WPO, 144.
Pridgett, Gertrude. *See* **Rainey, Gertrude "Ma."**
Prima, Diane di. *See* **di Prima, Diane.**
Pritam, Amrita (1919–
  The annunciation. WPO, 62–65.
  The breadwinner. OVO, 83–84.

Qorratu'l-Ayn (Umm-i Salma) (1814–1852)
  He the beloved. WPO, 75–76. (excerpt).
Quilter, Inez
  'Sall.' SUM, 91.

Qurtubiyya, 'Aisha bint Ahmad al-. *See* **'Aisha bint Ahmad al-Qurtubiyya.**

Raab, Esther (1899–
  Folk tune. BAA, 119.
  My poor raging sisters. BAA, 121.
  A serenade for two poplars. BAA, 118.
  Today I am modest. BAA, 120.
Rabi'a al-Adawiyya (712–810)
  Two prayers. WPO, 97.
Rabi'a bint Isma'il of Syria (d.755)
  Sufi quatrain. WPO, 96.
Rábi'a bint Ka'b (12th century)
  A curse. AAA, 10.
Rabi'a of Balkh (10th century)
  untitled. (My wish for you/that God should make your
    love). WPO, 73.
Rachel (1890–1931)
  Dawn. AAA, 63.
  His wife. WPO, 130.
Rachel, Naomi
  The very rose. WPW, 91.
  William Carlos Williams' buddy. WPW, 91.
Raine, Kathleen (1908–
  The clue. WSO, 180–81.
  Images. WAD, 166–67.
  Invocation. WSO, 178.
  Maternal grief. SOW, 129. WSO, 178–79.
  The phythoness. WSO, 180.
  Statues. WAD, 170–71.
  Storm. WSO, 179–80.
  The transit of the gods. WSO, 179.
Rainey, Gertrude "Ma" (1886–1939)
  Don't fish in my sea. WSO, 274–75.
  Sweet rough man. WSO, 275.
Randall, Celia
  Harvest. WAD, 48.
Ratcliffe, Dorothy Una (1894–1967)
  Remembrance day in the dales. SUM, 92.
Ravikovitch, Dahlia (1936–
  Clockwork doll. OVO, 50.
  The dress. BAA, 32–33.
  Hills of salt. WPO, 134–35.
  How Hong Kong was destroyed. OVO, 182–84.
  The Marionette. BAA, 34–35.
  Memory. BAA, 39.
  The noise of the waters. BAA, 37.
  On the road at night there stands the man. WPO, 134.
  Portrait. OVO, 33–34.
  Pride. BAA, 40. OVO, 124.
  Time caught in a net. BAA, 38.

Ray, Henrietta Cordelia (c. 1861–1916)
  Antigone and Oedipus. BLS, 40–41.
  The dawn of love. BLS, 39–40.
  Idyl: sunrise. BLS, 37–38.
  Idyl: sunset. BLS, 38.
  Milton. BLS, 39.
  Robert G. Shaw. BLS, 37.
  To my father. BLS, 38–39.
Raymond, Monica
  Self-criticism. EOU, 281.
Read, Sylvia
  The dark rider. WAD, 184–85.
  Pictures. WAD, 93–94.
Reese, Lizette Woodworth (1856–1935)
  A flower of mullein. WSO, 222.
  I never talk of hunger. WSO, 223.
  The second wife. WSO, 222–23.
Replansky, Naomi
  A good day's work. WWO, 5–6.
  I met my Solitude. BAR, 255.
  In the sea of tears. BAR, 260.
Rich, Adrienne (1929–
  Diving into the wreck. IWL-3, 496–98.
  For Ethel Rosenberg. EOU, 286–90.
  Ghazals: Homage to Ghalib. HOF, 104. (excerpt).
  Integrity. EOU, 293–94.
  Living in sin. WAW, 310.
  Mother-in-law. EOU, 291–92.
  Night-pieces: for a child. IWL-1, 125–26. IWL-2, 121.
      (excerpt).
    The crib. IWL-1, 125. IWL-2, 121.
    Her waking. IWL-1, 125–26.
  Phantasia for Elvira Shatayev. APO, 41–42. LPO, 9–11.
      WWO, 260–62.
  Photographs of an unmade bed. WAW, 311–12.
  Planetarium. AAA, 88–89.
  Prospective immigrants please note. IHO, 160.
  Re-forming the crystal. APO, 39–40.
  Sisters. SOW, 136.
  To Judith, taking leave. LPO, 7–9.
  Transcendental etude. LPO, 16–20.
  Transit. LPO, 20–21.
  Translations. WAW, 313. WPO, 364–65.
  Two songs. WAW, 310–11.
  White night. WAW, 314.
  A woman dead in her forties. LPO, 11–15.
  A woman mourned by daughters. BWO, 242. SOW, 137–
      38.
  Women. SOW, 136–37.
  Your small hands. IHO, 299–300.
Rich, Vera
  The bronze of Poseidon. WAD, 168–69.
Ridge, Lola (1873–1941)
  Amy Lowell. WSO, 252.
  Palestine. WSO, 252.
  Russian women. WSO, 253.
  Spires. WSO, 252.

Ridler, Anne (1912–
  A dream observed. WSO, 181–82.
  The gaze. WAD, 181.
  A matter of life and death. WAD, 177–78. (excerpt).
Rie, Yoshiyuki. *See* **Yoshiyuki Rie.**
Rihaku
  The River-merchant's wife: a letter. SOW, 41–42.
Rin, Ishigaki. *See* **Ishigaki Rin.**
Río, Zaida del. *See* **del Río, Zaida.**
Ríos, Soleida (1950–
  Autumn rains. (Agua de otoño). BTS, 258–61.
  The clown. (Payaso). BTS, 256–59.
  Difficult hour. (Hora difícil). BTS, 252–53.
  I also sing of myself. (También me canto). BTS,
      254–57.
  Of the Sierra. (De la Sierra). BTS, 252–55.
Riva, Osa Hidalgo-de la. *See* **Hidalgo-de la Riva, Osa.**
Rivera, Eliana
  Identification card. (Cédula de indentidad). BTS, 24, 31.
Rivera, Marina (1942–
  Chon. TWO, 409.
  Even. TWO, 408.
  Station. TWO, 407–08.
Roberts, Elizabeth Madox (1885–1941)
  Cold fear. BWO, 328.
Roberts, Lynette
  Poem from Llanbyri. WAD, 56–57.
Roberts, Michèle
  after my grandmother's death. TPA, 51.
  after seeing *Walkabout*. TPA, 44–45.
  and so it all goes on. TPA, 41.
  busy Lizzie. TPA, 40.
  city limited. TPA, 56.
  hangover. TPA, 37.
  he is merely socially inept. TPA, 43.
  in the bar. TPA, 38.
  Irish prisoners of war. TPA, 50.
  lament for my grandmother on the day of the winter
      solstice. TPA, 52–53.
  Leeds weekend. TPA, 49.
  levelling with death. TPA, 60.
  madwoman at Rodmell. BAR, 226. TPA, 48.
  Magnificat. BAR, 221–22. TPA, 46.
  masochism one. TPA, 39.
  masochism two/man of iron. TPA, 39.
  New England, 1980. TPA, 47.
  Out of chaos out of order out. BAR, 232–33.
  persephone descends to the underworld. TPA, 62–63.
  poem on midsummer's day. TPA, 54.
  poem on St. Valentine's Day. TPA, 58.
  poem on the day of the autumn equinox. TPA, 55.
  poem on the day of the spring equinox. TPA, 53–54.
  rite de passage. TPA, 59.
  The Sibyl's song. BAR, 205.
  to a male intellectual. TPA, 45.
  whose death at easter (on the train between London and
      Leeds). TPA, 61.

winter sacrament. TPA, 57.
the woman who wanted to be a hero. TPA, 42.

Roberts, Ursula (1887–
The Cenotaph. SUM, 93–94.

Robles, Mireya
untitled. (Let us ask fear to be silent). (Pidámosle silencio al miedo). LAW, 183–84.
untitled. (When the hours are only being filled). (Cuando sólo se llenan las horas). LAW, 183.

Rodgers, Carolyn M. (1942–
Aunt Dolly. CNF, 313–14.
Folk. CNF, 314.
It is deep. SBB, 377–78.
Jesus was crucified or: it must be deep (an epic pome). BLS, 180–82.
Mannessahs. CNF, 312.
Masquerade. BLS, 178–80.
Poem for some Black women. BLS, 176–78.
Portrait. AAA, 108–09.
Touch. Poem 5. CNF, 313.
Touch. Poem 4. CNF, 312.
U name this one. BLS, 183.
Wimmin. CNF, 315.

Rodríguez, Magdalena de
June 10. WPO, 320–21.

Rodríguez, Reina María (1952–
Adam. (Adán). BTS, 264–65.
From my guard post watching the world. (Desde mi guardia de mirar al mundo). BTS, 266–67.
Neighborhood in the breast. (El barrio del pecho). BTS, 264–65.
Now, at the hour of our life. (Ahora, que es la hora de nuestra vida). BTS, 266–69.
To Lumi Videla. (A Lumi Videla). BTS, 264–67.

Rogers, Sandra
Waiting for her man too long. CNF, 316.

Roland-Holst, Henriette (1869–1952)
Concerning the awakening of my soul. WPO, 207.
I looked for a sounding-board. WPO, 206.
Small paths. WPO, 207–08.

Rooke, Katerina Anghelaki-. *See* **Anghelaki-Rooke, Katerina.**

Rose, Harriet
Mellisandra. BAR, 264–65.
The succubus. BAR, 206–07.
The wedding coat. BAR, 271–73.

Rose, Wendy (1948–
For the White poets who would be Indian. TWO, 86–87.
How I came to be a graduate student. IAT, 167–68.
I expected my skin and my blood to ripen. TWO, 85–86. WPO, 423–24.
Long division: a tribal history. TWO, 2.
Lost copper. NET, 48.
Moon metals: inventing a new daughter. NET, 47.
Native American studies, University of California at Berkeley, 1975. IHO, 197.
Vanishing point: urban Indian. TWO, 87.

Rossetti, Christina (1830–1894)
Autumn. BAR, 78–79.
A birthday. BWO, 322.
A bitter resurrection. WSO, 134.
Dream-land. BAR, 74–75.
Echo. WSO, 125.
Eve. WAI, 129–31.
Goblin market. BAR, 70–74. (excerpts).
The hope I dreamed of. AAA, 37.
In an artist's studio. WSO, 125.
Introspective. WSO, 135.
Is this the end? WSO, 135–36.
Monna Innominata: a sonnet of sonnets. AAA, 36. (excerpt). WSO, 126–34.
My dream. BAR, 75–76.
Rest. WAD, 190–91.
A royal princess. BAR, 80–84.
Song. WSO, 124.
A soul. WPO, 201.
Winter: my secret. BAR, 77.
The world. WSO, 126.

Roth, Hemda
Four ways of writing one poem. BAA, 96.
A young deer/dust. BAA, 94–95.

Rouil, Marie-Thérèsa
Childhood. AAA, 106.

Rukeyser, Muriel (1913–1980)
Ann Burlak. BAW, 364–68. WSO, 330–35.
Effort at speech between two people. BWO, 115–16.
Kathe Kollwitz. BAW, 373–78. IHO, 263–68.
  Self-portrait. BAW, 377–78. IHO, 267–68.
  Song: the calling-up. BAW, 377. IHO, 266.
More of a corpse than a woman. BWO, 270.
Mortal girl. WAI, 95–96.
Nine poems for the unborn child. BAW, 368–72. SOW, 90–91. (V & VIII).
Night feeding. BAW, 372–73. SOW, 109.
The poem as mask. BAW, 379. WAW, 52.
Rondel. SOW, 151.
Searching/not searching. WAW, 240–45. WPO, 361–62. (excerpt).
  The Artist as social critic. WAW, 243.
  Brecht's Galileo. WAW, 241–42.
  Concrete. WAW, 241.
  The floor of ocean. WAW, 242–43.
  For Dolci. WAW, 241.
  Miriam: the Red Sea. WAW, 240–41.
  Not searching. WAW, 243–44.
  The president and the laser bomb. WAW, 243.
  The question. WAW, 244–45. WPO, 361–62.
  Reading the Kieu. WAW, 242.
Wherever. IHO, 301.
Who in one lifetime. BAW, 363. WAW, 52.
Woman as market. BAW, 373.

Rumiko, Kōra. *See* **Kōra Rumiko.**

Rushin, Donna Kate
The Black back-ups. HGI, 60–63.

The Black Goddess. HGI, 328–30.

The bridge poem. TBC, xxi-xxii.

The tired poem: last letter from a typical unemployed Black professional woman. HGI, 255–59.

Rydstedt-Dannstedt, Anna (1928–

This thing only. OVO, 13.

Sabaroff, Nina

untitled. (My cat doesn't mind I'm a lesbian). APO, 75.

Sabina, Maria (1894–

Shaman. WPO, 415–16.

Sachiko, Yoshihara. *See* **Yoshihara Sachiko.**

Sachs, Nelly (1891–1969)

But look. OVO, 176–77.

Chorus of the rescued. WPO, 236.

In the blue distance. OVO, 176.

Sackville, Margaret (1881–1963)

A memory. SUM, 95.

Sacrament. SUM, 95–96.

Sackville-West, Victoria (1892–1962)

Full moon. WAD, 94.

The land. WAD, 45–46. (excerpt).

Saffarzadeh, Tahereh

Birthplace. WPO, 84–85.

Safiya bint Musafir (7th century)

At the Badr Trench. WPO, 94.

Sagami, Lady (11th century)

untitled. (There is no night/when the lightning does not flash,). WPJ, 34.

untitled. (With hate and misery/my sleeves are never dry.). WPJ, 34.

Sakanoe, Otomo no. *See* **Otomo no Sakanoe.**

Salado, Minerva (1944–

The city. (La ciudad). BTS, 156–59.

Nela. (Nela). BTS, 162–63.

The news. (La noticia). BTS, 158–59.

Old woman in the park. (Anciana en el parque). BTS, 156–57.

Special report for International Women's Day. (Reportaje especial por el Día Internacional de la Mujer). BTS, 160–61.

Villages cities. (Aldeas cuidades). BTS, 158–61.

Saldaña, Excilia (1946–

Autobiography. (Autobiografía). BTS, 200–03. (excerpt).

Fish - bird. (Pez - pájaro). BTS, 202–03.

Obba (a patakin). (Obba [un patakin]). BTS, 202–14.

Salfeld, Denise

Ballad of the handsome man. WAD, 29.

Salih, Saniya (1939–

Exile. OVO, 158.

Salma, Umm-i. *See* **Qorratu'l-Ayn (Umm-i Salma).**

Sampter, Jessie (1883–1938)

Kadia the young mother speaks. AAA, 49.

Sanchez, Carol Lee

The emergence no. 1. NET, 33.

Sanchez, Magaly (1940–

Almost love. (Casi el amor). BTS, 136–37.

Among the hours. (Entre las horas). BTS, 134–37.

Confusion. (Confusión). BTS, 134–35.

End of the first act: ovation for Théroigne de Mericourt. (Fin del primer acto: ovación por Théroigne de Mericourt). BTS, 138–39.

He forgets me. (Se olvida de mí). BTS, 136–37.

Woman waiting in the park. (Mujer que espera en el parque). BTS, 134–35.

Sanchez, Olga Casanova. *See* **Casanova-Sanchez, Olga.**

Sanchez, Sonia (1934–

Kwa mama zetu waliotuzaa. CNF, 327–29.

Malcolm. KTF, 113–14.

Memorial. BLS, 242–45.

 bobby hutton. BLS, 243–44.

 rev pimps. BLS, 244–45.

 The supremes-cuz they dead. BLS, 242–43.

Old words. CNF, 322–25.

personal letter no. 2. AAA, 94.

Poem at thirty. BLS, 245–46.

A poem for Sterling Brown. CNF, 317–18.

Present. CNF, 325–26. WPO, 379–80.

Small comment. KTF, 115.

Summer words for a sister addict. BLS, 246.

10:15 A.M.-April 27, 1969. SBB, 342.

Sanmi, Daini no. *See* **Daini no Sanmi.**

Sanson, Mariana (1918–

untitled. (I didn't hear the door/slam when it closed.). (No he oído el golpe/que ha dado mi puerta). OTT, 110–11.

untitled. (When God was/folding up the sky). (Cuando Dios estaba/doblando el cielo). OTT, 112–13.

Santo, Alda do Espirito. *See* **Espirito Santo, Alda do.**

Sapphire

New York City tonight. LPO, 226–31.

untitled. (She hated the rain. Never could figure out what people be). LPO, 225–26.

Sappho (fl. 600 B.C.)

Andromeda, what now? AAA, 1.

Bridesmaids' carol. SOW, 30.

Bridesmaids' carol I. SOW, 45.

Headdress. AAA, 2.

Lament for a maidenhead. SOW, 34.

Ode to Aphrodite. WAD, 157–58.

Sleep, darling. BWO, 226. SOW, 114.

To an uneducated woman. AAA, 1.

A woman's plea. AAA, 1.

untitled. (Come to me from Crete to this holy temple,). WPO, 142.

untitled. (I ask you, sir, to/Stand face to face). BWO, 105.

untitled. (Like the very gods in my sight is he who). WPO, 142.

untitled. (Now, while we dance/Come here to us). SOW, 22.

untitled. (Some there are who say that the fairest thing seen). WPO, 143.

untitled. (Tell everyone/Now, today, I shall). BWO, 309.

untitled. (This way, that way/I do not know). BWO, 105.

untitled. (We shall enjoy it/As for him who finds). BWO, 309.

untitled. (When the Cretan maidens/Dancing up the full moon). SOW, 34–35.

untitled. (Why hast thou left me? Whither fled,). SOW, 34.

Sarton, May (1912–
After four years. AAA, 74–75.
In time like air. BWO, 346–47.
Joy in Provence. IWL-3, 501–02.
The muse as Medusa. APO, 30. LPO, 5.
My father's death. AAA, 76.

Sa'udi, Mona (1945–
untitled. (How do I enter the silence of stones). WPO, 109.
untitled. (When the loneliness of the tomb went down into the marketplace). WPO, 109.
untitled. (Why don't I write in the language of air? master a new). WPO, 109.

Saunders, Lesley
Mothers of sons. BAR, 216–19.

Saunders, Ruby C. *See* **Allah, Fareedah.**

Saxe, Susan (1949–
Notes from the first year. LPO, 199–201.
I argue my case. LPO, 200–01.
Patience. LPO, 199.
Questionnaire. LPO, 199–200.

Schaeffer, Susan Fromberg (1941–
For Judy Garland. AOW, 59–61.
The hills. AOW, 62.
Housewife. AOW, 63–64.

Schaye, Margriet
My fat Mama. AOW, 68.
An old witch's warning to a young man in love. AOW, 66–67.
Recollected in tranquility. AOW, 69–70.
untitled. (Life moves slowly through me). AOW, 65.

Schuler, Else Lasker. *See* **Lasker-Schuler, Else.**

Schweik, Susan
The short order cook in the mountains. EOU, 300–01.

Scott, Aimee Byng (–1953)
July 1st, 1916. SUM, 97.

Scott, Barbara Noel
Stillbirth. WAD, 178–79.
The wild poppies. WAD, 52.

Scott, Diana
Lucy taking birth. BAR, 211–12.
Prayer for the little daughter between death and burial. BAR, 260–61.
Winter solstice poem. BAR, 258–59.

Scott, Griselda
Joseph and the magi. WAD, 30.

Scovell, E. J.
Child waking. WAD, 182–83.

Seifu-Jo, Enomoto. *See* **Enomoto Seifu-Jo.**

Sei Shōnagon. (10th century)
untitled. (Since our relations/are like the crumbling). WPJ, 25.

Selina, Helen (Lady Dufferin) (1807–1867)
The charming woman. WAD, 89–91.

Senesh, Hannah (1921–1944)
One-two-three. WPO, 131.

Sexton, Anne (1928–1974)
The black art. WAW, 116.
Consorting with angels. HOF, 272–73.
Frenzy. WAW, 117.
Her kind. AAA, 86. WPO, 363–64.
Little girl, my string bean, my lovely woman. BWO, 219–22.
Live. WAW, 299–301.
Oysters. AAA, 87.
Said the poet to the analyst. WAW, 116.
Unknown girl in the maternity ward. WAD, 179–81.

Shange, Ntozake (1948–
cypress. (dancin is the movement of oceans/). TWO, 218–82.
cypress. (miz fitzhugh/it's gotta be done by). TWO, 283–84.
cypress. (wrist/ arial moroe took her into). TWO, 285.
Dark phrases. BLS, 270–72.
Frank Albert & Viola Benzena Owens. BLS, 273–76.
jonestown or the disco. WPE, 74–75.
Nappy edges (A cross country sojourn). BLS, 268–69.
No more love poems #1. BLS, 272–73.
sassafrass. (down to the wharf/ there waz always). TWO, 282–83.
sassafrass. (sick folks/ n spells that so n so's). TWO, 285–86.
sassafrass. (they called the 'jump-up'/ or the mambo/). TWO, 284.
With no immediate cause. IWL-3, 314–16.
untitled. (somebody almost walked off wid alla my stuff). WPO, 383–85.

Shao Fei-fei (17th century)
A letter. WPC, 64.

Shaw, Maxine (1945–
Damaris. CAM, 145.
For Billie Holiday and Janis Joplin. CAM, 146–47.
For Mrs. W., who would not be black, white or other. CAM, 142–43.
Going back to school. CAM, 143.
Issue. CAM, 144.
Tengo Puerto Rico en mi Corazón. CAM, 138–39.

Shelley, Martha (1943–
The tree of begats. APO, 60–61. LPO, 133–34.

Shêng-ch'iung, Nieh. *See* **Nieh Shêng-ch'iung.**

Shenhav, Chaya
Four. BAA, 30.

Sherman, Susan (1939–
Amerika. LPO, 57–59.
Because words do not suffice. LPO, 54.
Lilith of the Wildwood, of the Fair Places. APO, 31–32.
LPO, 54–56.
Love poem/for a capricorn. LPO, 56.
Sherwin, Judith Johnson (1936–
Miranda's birthspell. WPE, 23–25.
Shikibu, Izumi. *See* **Izumi Shikibu.**
Shikibu, Murasaki. *See* **Murasaki Shikibu.**
Shikishi, Princess (–1201)
untitled. (I slept in the past,). WPJ, 36.
untitled. (Life, like a thread piercing through jewels,).
WPJ, 36.
Shindō Chie (1920–
Space. WPJ, 99.
Shinkawa Kazue (1929–
An event which makes no news. WPJ, 105.
Shiraishi Kazuko (1931–
The anniversary of Samansa's death. WPJ, 108.
A Chinese Ulysses. WPJ, 112–14.
I fire at the face of the country where I was born. WPJ,
110–11.
The man root. WPJ, 115–17. WPO, 43–45.
untitled. ("On the roof of the beer garden,). WPJ, 109.
Shirome (10th century)
untitled. (If I were only sure/I could live as long as I
wanted to,). WPJ, 19.
Shizue, Hatsui. *See* **Hatsui Shizue.**
Shizuka (12th century)
untitled. (How I long for the man who climbed Mt.
Yoshino). WPJ, 40.
Shneurson, Zelda. *See* **Zelda.**
Shore, Jane
Basic training. EOU, 302.
High holy days. EOU, 303–05.
Shou-chen, Ma. *See* **Ma Hsiang-lan.**
Shove, Fredegond (1889–1949)
The new ghost. WAD, 192–93.
Shuang-ch'ing, Ho. *See* **Ho Shuang-ch'ing.**
Shu-chên, Chu. *See* **Chu Shu-chên.**
Shunzei's daughter (c.1171–c.1252)
untitled. (As the season changes,). WPJ, 44.
untitled. (How can I blame the cherry blossoms). WPJ,
43.
untitled. (It is unreasonable to ask my tears). WPJ, 44.
untitled. (The wind blows through/the little hut in the rice
field). WPJ, 43.
Shūshiki, Ōme. *See* **Ōme Shūshiki.**
Shuttle, Penelope
Early pregnancy. BAR, 166.
Expectant mother. BAR, 167.
Gone is the sleepgiver. BAR, 164.
Locale. BAR, 164–65.
Maritimes. BAR, 165–66.
Śilabhattarika (between 700 and 1050)
untitled. (He who stole my virginity/is the same man/I am
married to). WPO, 56.

Silko, Leslie Marmon (1948–
Toe'osh: A Laguna coyote story. TWO, 93–95.
Where mountain lion lay down with deer. IAT, 165.
TWO, 92–93. WPO, 422.
Silverman, Esther (1948–
South Bronx girl. LPO, 194.
Silverstrini, Rota (1941–
The fish tank. OWO, 119–20.
Kaleidoscope. OWO, 121.
Pieces of echoes. LPO, 95–97. OWO, 122–23.
Unfinished. LPO, 94–95.
Simmons, Judy Dothard
Equal opportunity. CNF, 331–32.
Linseed oil and dreams. CNF, 332.
Minority. CNF, 330.
Simone, Carol
At thirty. NET, 80.
I come up smiling. NET, 76.
Linda, come down. NET, 77–79.
Simpson, Joan Murray
Le bonheur. WAD, 38–39.
St. Marks, midnight. WAD, 132.
Sinason, Valerie
In the beginning. BAR, 228–29.
The renaming. BAR, 203–04.
Will you come out now? BAR, 224–25.
Sinclair, May (1865–1946)
Field ambulance in retreat. SUM, 98–99.
Sirotkin, Jeanne
Debutante. TIW, 87.
A love poem. TIW, 87.
Tarantella. TIW, 84.
To, from, for and about Detroit. TIW, 85–86.
Untitled. TIW, 88.
Sisay, Femi (1933–
Yon pastures green. AAA, 93.
Sitwell, Edith (1887–1964)
Anne Boleyn's song. WSO, 159–60.
The dancers. SUM, 100.
Heart and mind. WAD, 96–97.
Mary Stuart to James Bothwell. WSO, 160–62.
Still falls the Rain. BWO, 330–31.
The swans. WAD, 97–98.
Skeeter, Sharyn Jeanne
Self. KTF, 116.
Summer street. KTF, 116–17.
Smith, Ann (1930–
untitled. (Desire makes you/beautiful). OVO, 58.
Smith, Barbara (1946–
The bowl. WWO, 137–38.
Theft. LPO, 179–80.
Smith, Bessie (1898–1937)
Dirty no gooder blues. WSO, 276–77.
Young woman's blues. WSO, 277–78.
Smith, Charlotte (1749–1806)
Thirty-eight. WPO, 195–96.
Smith, Cicily Fox (–1954)
The convalescent. SUM, 101.

Smith, Margery
Prize-fighter. WAD, 163–64.
Smith, Stevie (1902–1971)
Anger's freeing power. WAD, 140–41.
Childe Rolandine. BAR, 138–39.
The dedicated dancing bull and the water maid. WAD, 84.
The galloping cat. BAR, 139–41.
I rode with my darling . . . BAR, 136–37.
My hat. BAR, 137–38. WAD, 83.
The river god. BAR, 136.
Smolensky, Stephanie
I told you when we started this relationship what to expect.
HFE, 97–101.
Södergran, Edith (1892–1923)
Love. OVO, 70.
Pain. WPO, 249–50.
Violet twilights. WPO, 248–49.
We women. WPO, 248.
Sogetsu-ni, Imaizumi. *See* **Imaizumi Sogetsu-Ni.**
Sohappy, Liz
Once again. IAT, 152–53.
Solís, Cleva (1926–
January moon. (Luna de Enero). BTS, 94–97.
The road. (Camino). BTS, 94–95.
The traveller. (Caminante). BTS, 94–95.
Sorrells, Helen
To a child born in time of small war. SOW, 130–31.
Sousa, Noémia da (1927–
Appeal. WPO, 286–87.
Our voice. OVO, 146–47.
Southwick, Marcia
Doors opening here, and there. EOU, 306–08.
Spafford, Roswell
Song of the diner waitress. NET, 31.
Song of the woman painted hot and cold. NET, 32.
Spear, Roberta
Fishes at Saint-Jean: Chagall, 1949. EOU, 309–13.
Speght, Rachel (fl. 1617–1621)
The dream. WAI, 155–57.
Spencer, Anne (1882–1975)
At the carnival. BLS, 68–69. WSO, 266–67.
Before the Feast of Shushan. BLS, 69–70.
Lady, Lady. BLS, 72.
Letter to my sister. AAA, 48. BLS, 70–71. WSO, 265–66.
Substitution. BLS, 71.
Speyer, Leonora (1872–1956)
The ladder. WSO, 250.
Salome. WSO, 250.
Witch! WSO, 251.
Spires, Elizabeth
Days. EOU, 314–15.
Spivack, Kathleen (1938–
Humanitarian. WPE, 73.
Spurr, Rita
The white horse. WAD, 136.
Ssu, Tuo. *See* **Tuo Ssu.**
Stamp, Catriona
Rebirth. BAR, 209–10.

Stampa, Gaspara (1523–1554)
Hunger. WPO, 173.
untitled. (Deeply repentant of my sinful ways). WPO, 174.
untitled. (I am now so weary with waiting,). WPO, 173.
untitled. (O wicked tyrant, send me back my heart,).
AAA, 18.
Stanford, Ann (1916–
Composing the garden. WPW, 77–81.
Crisis. WPW, 81.
The descent. IWL-3, 503–04.
The fountain. WPW, 77.
Going to sleep. WPW, 81.
The Trojan women. IWL-1, 211–13. (excerpt).
Cassandra's wedding song. IWL-1, 211–13.
The wife's lament. (modern version of anonymous poem).
WAI, 106–07.
Stanier, Maida
Freshmen. WAD, 91.
Hiawatha's pancake. WAD, 92–93.
Stanley-Wrench, Margaret
Hinterland. WAD, 151.
In the radiotherapy unit. WAD, 35–36.
A visitation. WAD, 65–66.
Stein, Dona
Carol's house. CAM, 107.
For F.J.L. (May 7, 1919 - May 2, 1972). CAM, 104.
In the year of the tiger. CAM, 104–05.
Lady and the wolf. CAM, 100.
Map (for Matthew). CAM, 106.
Night garden, with ladies. CAM, 99.
Putting Mother by. CAM, 103.
van Gogh painting his way out of the asylum. CAM, 100–01.
Visiting M. at the Happy Valley Nursing Home. CAM, 102.
Stein, Gertrude (1874–1946)
Patriarchal poetry. WSO, 233–41.
A sonnet. WSO, 237–38.
Stepto, Michele
her song. AOW, 73.
I will work with my hands I will not work with my hands.
AOW, 71–72.
Sternburg, Janet
At my house. OWO, 125.
The facts of life. OWO, 128–29.
My mother's breakfront. OWO, 129.
Vitalie. OWO, 126–28.
Stevens, Wendy (1953–
The hymns my mother sang. APO, 96. LPO, 254.
Stevenson, Anne (1933–
From an asylum: Kathy Chattle to her mother, Ruth Arbeiter. BAR, 142–47.
The mother. AAA, 93.
Stewart, Pamela (1946–
Postcard. EOU, 317.
Stone, Isabel. *See* **Truth, Sojourner.**
Stone, Ruth (1915–
Poetry. EOU, 322.
Secondhand coat. EOU, 321.

What can you do? EOU, 318–19.

When the furnace goes on in a California tract house. EOU, 320.

Stopes, Marie Carmichael (1880–1958)

Night on the shore. SUM, 102–03.

Storni, Alfonsina (1892–1938)

Ancestral weight. (Peso ancestral). OTT, 34–35. WPO, 308–09.

Dog and sea. OVO, 173.

I'm going to sleep. (Voy a dormir). OTT, 42–43.

It may be. OVO, 20.

The lost caress. (La Caricia perdida). OTT, 36–37.

Pain. WPO, 309–10.

The park in winter. (Plaza en invierno). OTT, 40–41.

She who understands. AAA, 66.

They've come. WPO, 309.

They've come. (Han venido). OTT, 38–39.

Stoutenburg, Adrien

Icarus on wheels. WPW, 67.

Memory album. WPW, 68.

Riding Hood, updated. WPW, 67–68.

River boat. WPW, 68.

Strickland, Stephanie

How we love now. EOU, 331–32.

Love that gives us ourselves. EOU, 333.

Strome, Celia Watson

Nr. 19. WPE, 79.

Nr. 6. WPE, 78.

Nr. 10. WPE, 78–79.

Nr. 12. WPE, 79.

Strongin, Lynn (1939–

Sayre (Woman professor). APO, 97. LPO, 42.

Strozzi, Barbara Torelli. *See* **Torelli-Strozzi, Barbara.**

Struther, Jan (1901–1953)

Glamour. WAD, 104.

Stuart, Alice V.

Water lily on Loch Bran. WAD, 51.

Stuart, Muriel (–1967)

Forgotten dead, I salute you. SUM, 104–05.

Sugita Hisajo (1890–1946)

untitled. (Mending his broken *tabi*). WPJ, 79.

untitled. (O flower garment!). WPJ, 79.

Suharu, Anryū. *See* **Anryū Suharu.**

Su Hsiao-hsiao (5th century)

A song of Hsi-ling Lake. WPC, 12.

Sullivan, Jonny Kyoko

SAGIMUSUME: The white heron maiden. WPO, 390–91.

Sullivan, Nancy

For my Aunt Florence who when praying gives God not only her friends' names but also their addresses. EOU, 334–35.

Sulpicia (64 B.C.–8 A.D.)

untitled. (Love has come to me, the kind I am far more ashamed). SOW, 72.

Sumako, Fukao. *See* **Fukao Sumako.**

Sun Tao-hsüan (12th century)

To the tune "A dream song." WPC, 51.

Sun Yün-fêng (1764–1814)

On the road through Chang-Te. WPC, 68. WPO, 24.

Starting at dawn. WPC, 70.

The trail up Wu Gorge. WPC, 71.

Travelling in the mountains. WPC, 69.

Suruma, Lynn

Turning corners. SBB, 367.

Sute-Jo, Den. *See* **Den Sute-Jo.**

Sutherland, Millicent (1867–1955)

One night. SUM, 106–07.

Sutton, Lorraine (1949–

Your olive face. LPO, 213–14.

Suwō, Lady (11th century)

untitled. (Pillowed on your arm/only for the dream of a spring night,). AAA, 10. WPJ, 35.

Swander, Mary

Pears. EOU, 336–37.

Swarth, Hélène (1859–1941)

Candles. WPO, 205–06.

Ecstasy. WPO, 206.

Swenson, May (1919–

The centaur. BWO, 350–52. IHO, 103–05.

To confirm a thing. APO, 81–82.

Women. IWL-1, 80. IWL-3, 49–50.

Swift, Joan

Father. EOU, 339.

My grandmother's hair. EOU, 338.

1933. EOU, 341.

Pneumonia. EOU, 430.

Symons, Jean

Elegy. WAD, 39–40.

Szécsi, Margit (1928–

The death of Moses. OVO, 181.

Szerlip, Barbara (1949–

Ambassador's daughter. FYW, 86–87.

Breech. FYW, 88–89.

The crossing. FYW, 90.

The end of something. FYW, 80.

59: Huan/dispersion. FYW, 82–83.

Four short poems. FYW, 81.

Beehive. FYW, 81.

Lines upon waking. FYW, 81.

No hay Olvido. FYW, 81.

untitled. (the poet is a hunter of invisible beasts that die). FYW, 81.

How to determine your birthday upon waking in a strange place which is more than likely your own bed. FYW, 98.

Icarus to his father. FYW, 93–94.

Mute's definition Blind man's definition Deaf man's definition. FYW, 99–100.

Note to a hitchhiker who stayed for one day for Fernando. FYW, 74–75.

Nothing of innocence. FYW, 76–77.

Poem to an imaginary Japanese lover. FYW, 96–97.

Sweet revenge. FYW, 103.

This place. FYW, 84–85.

Who will finally say. FYW, 78–79.

zocalo. FYW, 91–92.
untitled. (Hang the children by/their buttons to the gate.). FYW, 95.
untitled. (. . . I would have tied my breasts in a black slip). FYW, 101–02.
untitled. (thumb/poet of misfortune). FYW, 104–05.
untitled. (your body is a wasteland). FYW, 73.

Szymborska, Wisława (1923–
Starvation camp near Jasło. WPO, 226.
The women of Rubens. WPO, 224–25.

T

Tada Chimako (1930–
Mirror. WPJ, 107.
Taeko, Tomioka. *See* **Tomioka Taeko.**
Tafolla, Carmen (1951–
Allí por La Calle San Luís. TWO, 411. WWO, 147.
Bailar . . . TWO, 410–11.
. . . Repeating chorus . . . TWO, 411.
San Antonio. TWO, 412.
Tagami Kikusha-Ni (1752–1826)
The wind from Mt. Fuji. WPJ, 59.
Taggard, Genevieve (1894–1948)
Everyday alchemy. WSO, 288.
Image. WSO, 289.
With child. SOW, 86. WSO, 289–90.
Takada Toshiko (1916–
The seacoast at Mera. WPJ, 92.
Takajo, Mitsuhashi. *See* **Mitsuhashi Takajo.**
Takako, Hashimoto. *See* **Hashimoto Takako.**
Takeko, Kujō. *See* **Kujō Takeko.**
Takiguchi Masako (1933–
Blue horse. WPJ, 94.
Slaughterhouse. WPJ, 93.
Tanenhaus, Beverly
First you tell him all your problems. CAM, 34–36.
My hair is black. CAM, 36–37.
Quasi-liberation in Upstate New York. CAM, 33–34.
Reunion. CAM, 38–39.
untitled. (She comes to beg.). CAM, 38.
untitled. (She tells you she is beautiful). CAM, 37.
T'ang Wan (12th century)
To the tune "The Phoenix Hairpin." WPC, 50. WPO, 21.
Tan Ying (1943–
Drinking the wind. WPC, 112. WPO, 27.
T'ao, Ch'ien. *See* **Chi'ien T'ao.**
T'ao, Hsüeh. *See* **Hsüeh T'ao.**
Tao-hsüan, Sun. *See* **Sun Tao-hsüan.**
Tao-shêng, Kuan. *See* **Kuan Tao-shêng.**
Tatsuko, Hoshino. *See* **Hoshino Tatsuko.**

Taylor, Rachel Annand (1876–
Art and women. WSO, 146.
Tayu, Ise. *See* **Ise Tayu.**
Tchernine, Odette
The leopard. WAD, 69–70.
Teague, Kathleen (1937–
The harmony of sirens. AOW, 75.
untitled. (I saw a picture of your embryo). AOW, 74.
Teasdale, Sara (1884–1933)
Advice to a girl. BWO, 406.
Central Park at dusk. AAA, 51. WSO, 282.
Effigy of a nun. WAD, 31. WSO, 281–82.
The old maid. AAA, 52.
The solitary. BWO, 379.
Spring in war-time. SUM, 110.
Strange victory. WSO, 282.
'There will come soft rains.' SUM, 110–11.
Teijo, Nakamura. *See* **Nakamura Teijo.**
Teish, Luisah
Hoodoo Moma. HGI, 336.
Tekahionwake (1869–1913)
"And he said, fight on." AAA, 44.
The cattle thief. WPO, 411–13.
Tepperman, Jean (1945–
Witch. WAI, 296–97.
Teresa of Ávila (1515–1582)
Bookmark. AAA, 17. WPO, 171.
If, Lord, thy love for me is strong. BWO, 311.
In the inmost recesses. WPO, 171.
Terry, Lucy (1730–1821)
Bars fight, August 28, 1746. BLS, 12.
Thanet, Lesbia
In time of war. SUM, 112.
Theodorou, Victoria
Galatia Kazanzaki. CGW, 12.
Nuyen Ti Soy. CGW, 14.
Old song. CGW, 13.
Picnic. CGW, 2–11.
Thompson, Alice. *See* **Meynell, Alice.**
Thompson, Clara Ann
His answer. BLS, 42.
Mrs. Johnson objects. BLS, 42–43.
Thompson, Phyllis
Rainwater. WPW, 74–75.
Tillyard, Aelfrida (1883–
Invitation au Festin. SUM, 113.
A letter from Ealing Broadway Station. SUM, 113–14.
Tinker, Carol (1940–
buddha's birthday. FYW, 129–30.
golden triangle. FYW, 113.
Hannya. FYW, 139–43. (excerpt).
Heron of oblivion. FYW, 112.
How can we end human suffering. FYW, 120–24.
Ishtar or the explosion on a shingle factory. FYW, 136–37.
lank pier. FYW, 118–19.
Naramasu. FYW, 110.
a smart & final iris. FYW, 116–17.

sunday parlor park freeway. FYW, 131–32.
thank you capitalism for the expanding universe. FYW, 133.
wet green hallelujahs. FYW, 111.
The young emerald, Evening Star. FYW, 144–45. (excerpt).
untitled. ("The bitter wormword shivers in the endless plains"). FYW, 125.
untitled. (I watch cypress/trees through the smoke). FYW, 135.
untitled. (it works so slow it/takes days and). FYW, 115.
untitled. (person who stole/landlady's wash left her). FYW, 128.
untitled. (Shiva/is dancing/in the fire). FYW, 126.
untitled. (struck and calm/i want what you want). FYW, 109.
untitled. (a thousand miles not a single). FYW, 138.
untitled. (the tissue went with/vision the integrity of). FYW, 114.
untitled. (yes, sam johnson,). FYW, 127.
untitled. (Zuni ring knocks/against steel). FYW, 134.
Tokunaga, Laura (1950–
Behind locked doors. TWO, 556–57.
Geography. TWO, 557–58.
Tiger year. TWO, 558–59.
Tomiko, Yamakawa. *See* **Yamakawa Tomiko.**
Tomioka Taeko (1935–
Girlfriend. WPJ, 124–25.
Life story. WPO, 46–48.
Living together. WPO, 48.
Please say something. WPO, 45–.
Tomoko, Fukunaka. *See* **Fukunaka Tomoko.**
Tonks, Rosemary
Story of a hotel room. WAD, 123.
Torelli-Strozzi, Barbara (c. 1475–1533)
On the murder of her husband. AAA, 16.
Torres, Albis (1947–
Caguayo. (Caguayo). BTS, 218–19.
Cocosi. (Cocosí). BTS, 218–21.
Coffee field dorm. (Albergue de los cafetales). BTS, 224–27.
The dead one. (Muerto). BTS, 220–23.
The visitor. (Visitante). BTS, 222–23.
Wood smoke. (El humo de madera). BTS, 222–25.
Torres, Teresa
Poem. OVO, 111.
Toshiko, Takada. *See* **Takada Toshiko.**
Toshitaka, Minamoto no, The daughter of. *See* **Minamoto no Toshitaka, The daughter of.**
Tóth, Judit (1936–
Dead embryos. WPO, 234–35.
To the newborn. WPO, 232–34.
Tovar, Inés Hernandez (1947–
Para Teresa. TWO, 414–16.
Para un viejito desconocido que aun conozco. TWO, 413–14.
To other women who were ugly once. TWO, 416–17.
Tree, Iris (1897–1968)
untitled. (And afterwards, when honour has made good,). SUM, 116.

untitled. (Of all who died in silence far away). SUM, 115.
Triem, Eve (1902–
Breaking a voodoo. EOU, 342.
Tripp, Karen. *See* **Gershon, Karen.**
Trotter, Alys Fane (1863–1962)
The hospital visitor. SUM, 117.
Trujillo, Marcela Christine Lucero. *See* **Lucero-Trujillo, Marcela Christine.**
Truth, Sojourner (1797–1883)
Ain't I a woman? BLS, 24–25.
Truvido, Gloria
My people are the poor. IAT, 172.
Ts'ai Yen (c. 162–c. 239)
Eighteen verses sung to a Tatar reed whistle. WPC, 4–7. (excerpts). WPO, 15–18.
The lamentation. SOW, 127–28. (excerpt).
Tsao, Wu. *See* **Wu Tsao.**
tSaoi, Máire Mhac an. *See* **Mhac an tSaoi, Máire.**
Tsê-t'ien, Wu. *See* **Wu Tsê-t'ien.**
Tsui, Kitty (1952–
the words of a woman who breathes fire: one. LPO, 244–45.
Ts'ui-p'in, Han. *See* **Han Ts'ui-p'in.**
Tsvetayeva, Marina (1892–1941)
Akhmatova. TRW, 46–47. (excerpts).
An attempt at jealousy. TRW, 76–77. WPO, 220–21.
Earthly name. TRW, 49.
Epitaph. OVO, 91. (excerpt).
Homesickness. TRW, 79–80.
I unsealed my veins: unstoppable. TRW, 78.
In praise of Aphrodite. HOF, 242.
A letter. BWO, 337. TRW, 50.
Poem of the end. BAR, 172–75. (excerpts). OVO, 76–80. (excerpts). TRW, 51–75.
The smell, smell, TRW, 48.
Verses about Moscow. TRW, 44. (excerpt).
Verses to Blok. TRW, 45. (excerpt).
We shall not escape hell. OVO, 54.
You, walking past me. TRW, 43.
Tuéni, Nadia (1935–1983)
untitled. (Of course/the sun is angry). OVO, 115.
untitled. (This evening/the night protecting me). OVO, 59.
Tu Fu (712–770)
Parting of a newly wedded couple. SOW, 46–48.
Washing and pounding clothes. SOW, 145.
Tuo Ssu (1939–
Night street. WPC, 100.
Sprout. WPC, 99.
Train. WPC, 98.
Tuqān, Fadwa (1917–
Behind bars. OVO, 150. (excerpts). WPO, 100–01. (excerpts).
1. (My mother's phantom hovers here). OVO, 150.
3. (From the ravine pours silent angry darkness). WPO, 100–01.
Turner, Alberta
A dictionary of common terms. EOU, 348–49. (excerpts).
Arch. EOU, 348.

Bliss. EOU, 348.
Die. EOU, 349.
Tussman, Malka Heifetz (1896–
Leaves. OVO, 106–07.
Spoil. OVO, 107.
Water without sound. OVO, 106.
Twichell, Chase
Franz, the world is abstract. EOU, 350–51.
Starkweather House. EOU, 352–53.
Tynan, Katharine (1861–1931)
The broken soldier. SUM, 118.
A girl's song. SUM, 118–19.
Joining the colours. SUM, 119.
Larks. WAD, 78.
Tzu, Jung. *See* **Jung Tzu.**
Tzu Yeh (3rd or 4th century)
untitled. (The bare branches tremble). WPC, 10. WPO, 19.
untitled. (I am the North Pole). WPC, 10.
untitled. (I cannot sleep/For the blaze of the full moon.).
SOW, 60. WPC, 9.
untitled. (I had not fastened my sash over my gown,).
SOW, 60–61. WPC, 9. WPO, 19.
untitled. (It is night again). SOW, 60. WPC, 9. WPO, 18.

Ukihashi (17th century)
untitled. (Whether I sit or lie). WPJ, 55. WPO, 41.
Ukon, Lady (10th century)
untitled. (I am forgotten now.). WPJ, 20.
Ukyō no Daibu, Kenrei Mon-in. *See* **Kenrie Mon-in Ukyō no Daibu.**
Ullman, Leslie (1947–
Running. EOU, 354–57.
Ulloa, Yolanda (1948–
Ita. (Ita). BTS, 240–43.
She went, she said, losing herself. (Se fue, dijimos, perdiendo). BTS, 238–41.
Short biography of a washerwoman. (Pequeña biografía de una lavandera). BTS, 238–39.
Umm-i Salma. *See* **Qorratu'l-Ayn (Umm-i Salma).**
Underhill, Evelyn (1875–1941)
Mountain flora. WAD, 143.
Utba, Hind bint. *See* **Hind bint Utba.**
Uthatha, Hind bint. *See* **Hind bint Uthatha.**
Uvavnuk (fl. c. 1920)
A woman shaman's song. IAT, 57. WPO, 418.

Vakalo, Eleni (1921–
untitled. (But there was/once/a time). WPO, 254–55.
Valdivia, Omara. *See* **Islas, Maya.**
Valentine, Jean
Sex. HOF, 101.
Van Duyn, Mona (1921–
The gardener to his god. BWO, 354.
Varela, Blanca (1926–
The captain. WPO, 319–20.
Madonna. OTT, 178–79.
Waltz of the Ángelus I. (Vals del Ángelus I). OTT, 182–83.
Waltz of the Ángelus II. (Vals del Ángelus II). OTT, 184–85.
untitled. (Perhaps in the spring). (Tal vez en primavera). OTT, 180–81.
Vaux, Molly
April. OWO, 135.
Farmer's news. OWO, 133.
February. OWO, 134–35.
January. OWO, 134.
Landing. OWO, 131.
March. OWO, 135.
Northern lights. OWO, 132.
On my birthday. OWO, 133.
Out on the water. OWO, 131.
Setting sail. OWO, 131.
Vaz Ferreira, María Eugenia (1875–1924)
The floating casket. (El ataúd flotante). OTT, 14–17.
A furtive glass. (Vaso furtivo). OTT, 18–19.
Posthumous story. (Historia póstuma). OTT, 12–13.
The vacuous rime. (La rima vacua). OTT, 20–21.
The voice of return. (Voz del retorno). OTT, 10–11.
Verne, Viviane
Kensington gardens. SUM, 120–21.
Vián, Enid (1948–
IV. (Keep that discourse, hummingbird brief,). (Guarda bajo el árbol hijo). BTS, 246–47.
In the mirror. (En el espejo). BTS, 248–49.
The river. (El río). BTS, 246–49.
X. (Full moon round/and the earth like a glass.). (La luna entera/redonda,/y la tierra como un vaso.). BTS, 246–47.
Vickridge, Alberta
In a V.A.D. pantry. SUM, 122.
Vidya (Vijjika) (c.659)
untitled. (I praise the disk of the rising sun,). WPO, 55.
untitled. (You are fortunate, dear friends, that you can tell). WPO, 55–56.

Vijja. *See* **Vidya (Vijjika).**
Vijjaka. *See* **Vidya (Vijjika).**
Vijjika, Vidya. *See* **Vidya (Vijjika).**
Villanueva, Alma (1944–
  untitled. (I was always fascinated/with lights then,).
    WPO, 396–97.
Vinograd, Julia
  Analysis. TIW, 74–75.
  Deal. TIW, 72.
  Downhill. TIW, 72.
  Morning. TIW, 73.
  Summer murder. TIW, 73.
Voigt, Ellen Bryant (1943–
  Farm wife. WWO, 144.
Volborth, Judith Ivaloo (1950–
  Black-Coat meets coyote (Three conversations of the ab-
    surd). TWO, 96–97.
  Three songs to mark the night. TWO, 97.
von Greiffenberg, Catharina Regina. *See* **Greiffenberg,**
    Catharina Regina von.
Vose, Julia
  untitled. (Moose in Mexico and little local deer). TIW,
    105.
Vuckovic, Isabelle
  Maturity. OVO, 123.

Waddington, Miriam (1917–
  Old women of Toronto. AAA, 79.
Wade, Cory
  Enough. NET, 81.
Wade, Grace
  The difference. TIW, 108.
  Lessons. TIW, 107.
Wakoski, Diane (1937–
  Belly dancer. IWL-1, 321–22.
  Black leather, because bumble bees look like it. FYP.
  The blackbird. AAA, 97.
  Cock fight under the magnolias. FYP.
  Journey. FYP.
  Largely because of coincidence and partly because of
    chance, I have taken up a new address at 47th Street
    and Avenue F. FYP.
    The brass coin. FYP.
    Dried flower under my pillow. FYP.
    The statue. FYP.
    We visit the gorilla at his 47th Street address. FYP.
  Medieval tapestry and questions. IHO, 37–38.
  Mill. FYP.
  My Chinese fairy tales for La Monte, who dislikes the
    obvious. FYP.

  My trouble. WAW, 165.
  No more soft talk. WAW, 386–87.
  On Barbara's shore. HOF, 175–77.
  The poem. WAW, 165.
  The starving vicuna. FYP.
  Thanking my mother for piano lessons. BWO, 432–35.
  The tightrope walker. FYP.
  To an autocrat. WAW, 388–89.
  W. Rings on her fingers & bells on her toes she shall have
    music wherever she goes. WAW, 389–91.
  With words (for Tony). WAW, 165–67.
Waldman, Anne (1945–
  Mother country. AAA, 104.
Waldrop, Rosmarie (1935–
  Confession to settle a curse. AAA, 110–11.
Walker, Alice (1944–
  Beyond what. IWL-3, 550.
  Burial. TWO, 294–96.
  Each one, pull one. CNF, 356–59.
  Early losses: a requiem. BLS, 223–28.
    Part I. BLS, 223–27.
    Part II: The child. BLS, 227–28.
  FAMILY OF. CNF, 354–56.
  I said to poetry. CNF, 353–54.
  I'm really very fond. CNF, 359–60.
  Once. BLS, 213–23.
  Representing the universe. CNF, 360.
  Revolutionary petunias. BLS, 212.
  Women. AAA, 102. TWO, 297. WPO, 376. WWO,
    202–03.
Walker, Annie Louisa (c. 1850–
  Song. AAA, 42–43.
Walker, Jeanne Murray
  For my daughter's twenty-first birthday. EOU, 366.
  The last migration: Amherst, Mass., Winter 1981. EOU,
    362–63.
  Making the painting. EOU, 360–61.
  Necessity. EOU, 365.
  Northern liberties. EOU, 364.
  Physics. EOU, 358–59.
Walker, Margaret (1915–
  Ballad of the Hoppy-Toad. BLS, 98–99.
  Childhood. BAW, 339. WPO, 375.
  Dark blood. BAW, 335–36. WSO, 326–27.
  FANFARE, CODA, AND FINALE. CNF, 372–73.
  FIVE BLACK MEN . . . and ten will save the city . . .
    CNF, 363–68.
  For Gwen—1969. TWO, 249–50.
  For Malcolm X. KTF, 117–18.
  For my people. BAW, 333–35. BWO, 413–15.
  Girl held without bail. BAW, 340. WWO, 201.
  I HEAR A RUMBLING . . . CNF, 369–71.
  I want to write. TWO, 249.
  Kissie Lee. BAW, 336–37. BLS, 95–96.
  Lineage. BAW, 336. BLS, 94. SBB, 339. WAI, 294–95.
    WSO, 326. WWO, 50.
  Long John Nelson and Sweetie Pie. BAW, 337–39.
  Micah. KTF, 120–21.
  Molly Means. BLS, 96–97.

MY TRUTH AND MY FLAME. CNF, 361.
Now. BAW, 341.
Prophets for a new day. KTF, 118–20.
Street demonstration. BAW, 340.
THIS IS MY CENTURY . . . Black synthesis of time.
    CNF, 361–63.
Whores. BAW, 339–40.

Wallach, Yona
again you slept with mr no man. BAA, 49–52.
All this so tasteless and threatening. BAA, 57.
Cradle song. BAA, 56.
I emptied. BAA, 54.
Lola. BAA, 53.
A terrible heart. BAA, 48.
Two gardens. BAA, 55.

Wallada (11th century)
To Ibn Zaidun. WPO, 98.

Wallbank, Susan
If I come. HFE, 57–58.
Why so many of them die. BAR, 230.

Walsh, Christina
Prayer to Isis. BAN, 111.
A woman to her lover. BAN, 111–12.

Walsh, Marnie
Poets/poems. TWO, 115–16.
Thomas Iron-Eyes. Born circa 1840. Died 1919, Rosebud
    Agency, S.D. TWO, 113–15. WPO, 424–26.
Vickie Loans-Arrow 1972. TWO, 116–18.

Walters, Anna Lee (1946–
Hartico. TWO, 110–12.
I have bowed before the sun. IAT, 190, 192. WPO, 429–30.
A teacher taught me. TWO, 109–10.

Wan, T'ang. *See* **T'ang Wan.**

Wandor, Michelene
American Margaret. TPA, 71.
'chick.' TPA, 77.
chocolate egg. TPA, 86–87.
Christmas, 1978. TPA, 84–85.
crafty. TPA, 87–88.
dream. TPA, 68.
fields. TPA, 78–79.
geography. TPA, 75.
hell. TPA, 73.
He-man. TPA, 68–69.
My mother's funeral in Waltham Abbey. TPA, 90–91.
office party 1981. TPA, 72–73.
Olive Schreiner. TPA, 91–92.
people, on a bad day. TPA, 70.
ritual. TPA, 76.
song of the ostrich. TPA, 93–94.
Tourist in Rumania. TPA, 67.
two poetry readings. TPA, 74.
Wonderland. TPA, 88–89.
untitled. (credence crawled over like/a rat). TPA, 83.
untitled. (crossed desires, the sun). TPA, 81.
untitled. (dark and who/can see properly and a waste).
    TPA, 79.
untitled. (lambs to the slaughter/sheep to the altar). TPA,
    82–83.

untitled. (ripping the skin off a dead rabbit). TPA, 80.
untitled. (thick ice/you/rib me). TPA, 69.

Wang Ch'ing-hui (13th century)
To the tune "The river is red." WPC, 52.

Wang Wei (17th century)
Seeking a mooring. WPC, 65. WPO, 23.

Wan-ying, Hsieh. *See* **Ping Hsin (Hsieh Wan-ying).**

Warmond, Ellen (1930–
Change of scene. OVO, 114.

Warner, Sylvia Townsend (1893–1978)
Elizabeth. BWO, 339.

The Watchless Orinda. *See* **Philips, Katherine.**

Waters, Chocolate (1949–
Father poem II. WPW, 56.
I feel so good I ain't written a fuckin' thing in a year.
    WPW, 55–56.

Webb, Mary (1881–1927)
Autumn, 1914. SUM, 123.
Fairy-led. WAD, 102–03.
Swallows. WAD, 79.

Webster, Augusta
A castaway. BAR, 95–98. (excerpt).
Medea in Athens. BAR, 99. (excerpt).

Wedgwood, M. Winifred
Christmas, 1916. SUM, 124–25.
The V.A.D. scullery-maid's song. SUM, 124.

Wei, Lady (11th century to 12th century)
To the tune "The Bodhisattva's barbaric headdress."
    WPC, 35.

Wei, Pai. *See* **Pai Wei.**
Wei, Wang. *See* **Wang Wei.**

Weil, Simone (1909–1943)
Illumination. OVO, 169.
Random thoughts on the love of God. OVO, 170. (excerpt).

Weiss, Ruth
Desert journal. Second day. TIW, 58.
There is no evil only restlessness! TIW, 59–62.
    Sixteenth Day. TIW, 60–62.

Wellesley, Dorothy (1891–1956)
Demeter in Sicily. WSO, 162–64.
Swannery. WAD, 67–68.

Welsh, Anne (1922–
Sight. WAD, 55–56.

Wên-chi, Chang. *See* **Chang Wên-chi.**
Wên-chün, Chuo. *See* **Chuo Wên-chün.**

Wendt, Ingrid (1944–
Dust. IHO, 130–33.

West, Kathleene
Striking out. WPW, 60.

Wheatley, Phillis (1753–1784)
Liberty and peace, a poem. BLS, 13. (excerpt).
On being brought from Africa to America. AAA, 31.
    BWO, 316. WSO, 198.
On imagination. BLS, 16–17.
On the death of a young lady of five years of age. WAI,
    29–30.
To a gentleman and lady on the death of the lady's brother
    and sister, and a child of the name Avis, aged one
    year. BLS, 14–15.

To S.M. a young African painter, on seeing his work. BLS, 15–16.
To the Right Honorable William, Earl of Dartmouth. WPO, 373. WSO, 198–99.

Whetham, Catherine Durning.
The poet and the butcher. SUM, 126.

Whitewing, Donna (1943–
August 24, 1963 - 1:00 a.m.: Omaha. IAT, 84.

Whitman, Ruth (1922–
Cutting the Jewish bride's hair. IWL-1, 81. IWL-3, 51.

Whitmell, Lucy
Christ in Flanders. SUM, 127–28.

Wickham, Anna (1884–1947)
Divorce. WSO, 153–54.
The economist. WSO, 154.
The fired pot. WAD, 37.
Gift to a jade. WSO, 153.
Inspiration. WSO, 155.
Meditation at Kew. AAA, 50.
Nervous prostration. WSO, 154.

Wieber, Wendy Brooks (1951–
One, The other, And. LPO, 236–39.
And. LPO, 238–39.
One. LPO, 236.
The other. LPO, 237–38.

Wiggins, Ella May (1889–1929)
All around the jailhouse. WSO, 310–11.
The mill mother's lament. WSO, 311.

Wilcox, Ella Wheeler (1850–1919)
Solitude. WSO, 221.

Wilkinson, Anne (1910–1961)
Boys and girls. SOW, 8–9.
Letter to my children. SOW, 115.
Summer acres. AAA, 72–73.

Wilkinson, Elena
Face: border. AOW, 80.
The logical mind of the martyr. AOW, 79.

Willard, Nancy (1936–
Bone poem. TIW, 146–47.
The graffiti poet. AAA, 96.
Night rising. TIW, 145.
The poet invites the moon for supper. TIW, 144.

Williams, Delores S.
Little girl talk. KTF, 121–22.

Williams, Lucy Ariel (1905–
Northboun'. BLS, 57.

Williams, Paulette. *See* **Shange, Ntozake.**

Williams, Regina
ASYLUM. CNF, 378–79.
For our life is a matter of faith. CNF, 379–80.
I AM NOT MY SISTER'S KEEPER: I AM MY SISTER. CNF, 381–82.

Williams, Sherley Anne (1944–
Any woman's blues. TWO, 289–90.
The collateral adjective. TWO, 290.
Driving wheel. BLS, 260–64.
first fable. BLS, 261–63.
first story.BLS, 260–61.

fourth life. BLS, 263–64.
second song. BLS, 261.
The Empress brand trim: Ruby reminisces. BLS, 253–54.
Generations. (Daddy/is a shadow on). TWO, 292.
Generations. (Mamma/is a silent movie). TWO, 291–92.
Generations. I. TWO, 292.
Generations. II. TWO, 293.
The house of desire. BLS, 255–60. CNF, 390–91. (excerpt).
the house of desire. BLS, 259–60.
the peacock poem. BLS, 257–58.
this city-light. BLS, 256–57. CNF, 390–91.
What is love if it is only known through words saying would be hard for me to leave you? BLS, 258–59.
The iconography of childhood. CNF, 383–86. (excerpt
a record for my friends. CNF, 388–90.
Say hello to John. BLS, 254–55. TWO, 291.
the wishon line. CNF, 392–93.
you were never miss brown to me. CNF, 386–87.

Willy, Margaret (1919–
Lament of Heloise. WAD, 117.

Wilson, Geraldine L.
OUR CHILDREN ARE OUR CHILDREN. CN 95.
REFUGEE MOTHER. CNF, 394.

Wilson, Margaret Adelaide
Gervais. SUM, 129.

Wilson, Marjorie
To Tony (aged 3). SUM, 130.

Wilson, Ramona C. (1945–
Eveningsong 2. TWO, 102.
Keeping hair. TWO, 103.

Winant, Fran (1943–
Dyke jacket. LPO, 120–25.
A sacred grove. BAR, 210–11.
To begin. BAR, 227–28.
Yesterday. APO, 65–66. LPO, 119–20

Winchilsea, Countess of. *See* **Finch, A Winchilsea.**

Winfrey, Mary.
at menopause. CAM, 15.
at the diagnostician's office. CAM,
Charlotte Corday/Marat (July 13, 1
the conditioning. CAM, 12.
Demeter's song. CAM, 16.
Gertrude Ederle swims the Chan CAM, 9–10.
hera of the locker room. CAM,
historical footnote. CAM, 12–
Kleis. CAM, 8.
meeting. CAM, 15.
thoughts about Clara Schum

Wingfield, Sheila (1906–
Envy. WAD, 47–48.

Wingrove, Edith Aubrey
untitled. (There's a stran 48.

Winters, Janet Lewis. *Se*

Witherby, Diana
The leafy day. WAD, 70.
Wittlinger, Ellen
In cahoots. WPE, 100–01.
Red. WPE, 101.
Someone you love. WPE, 101.
Waiting. WPE, 100.
Wolf, Naomi
Alice James. EOU, 367–68.
Wolfstenholme-Elmy, Elizabeth
Woman free. BAR, 106–08. (excerpts).
Wong, Helen. *See* **Huie, Helen Wong.**
Wong, Nellie (1934–
How a girl got her Chinese name. WPO, 386–87.
Toward a 44th birthday. EOU, 371.
When I was growing up. TBC, 7–8.
A woman at the window. EOU, 369–70.
Wood, Marguerite.
Rouen. WAD, 32–33.
Wood, Susan
Your story. EOU, 372.
Wood, Sybil
The civil servant is eaten too. TIW, 64.
Picnic. TIW, 65.
untitled. (Mornings/I'm pressed to elevators). TIW, 63.
Wood-Thompson, Susan (1942–
Fever. LPO, 100.
Territory. LPO, 100–01.
Wrench, Margaret Stanley. *See* **Stanley-Wrench, Margaret.**
Wright, Judith (1915–
Portrait. AAA, 78.
The surfer. WAD, 160–61.
The twins. WAD, 41.
Woman's song. WAD, 176.
Wu Tsao (c. 1800–
For the courtesan Ch'ing Lin. SOW, 70. WPC, 73. WPO, 24–25.
In the home of the scholar Wu Su-chiang from Hsin-An, I saw two psalteries of the late Sung General Hsieh Fang-tê. WPC, 77. WPO, 25–26.
Returning from Flower Law Mountain on a winter day, to the tune "Washing silk in the stream." WPC, 76.
To the tune "A dream song." WPC, 78.
To the tune "Flowers along the path through the field." WPC, 75.
To the tune "The joy of peace and brightness." WPC, 74.
To the tune "The pain of lovesickness." WPC, 72.
Wu Tsê-t'ien (624–705)
Love song of the Empress Wu. WPC, 14.
Wylie, Elinor (1885–1928)
The prophet. WSO, 285.
Down to earth. WAD, 146–48.
To a charitable hope. AAA, 53. WSO, 285.
Prophecy. WSO, 284.
Pretty words. (XII). (In our content, before the autumn came). WSO, 284.
O, Where? AAA, 54.

Xelina (1954–
Nightmare. TWO, 385.
Urban life. TWO, 384.
Witnesses. TWO, 385.

Yagi Mikajo (1924–
untitled. (The genitals of woods/in full bloom;). WPJ, 84.
untitled. (A marathon runner's legs/fan in and out.). WPJ, 84.
Yamada, Mitsuye (1923–
Camp notes. WPO, 389–90.
In the outhouse. WPO, 389–90.
On the bus. WPO, 389.
Yamakawa Tomiko (1879–1909)
untitled. (I leave all the scarlet flowers). WPJ, 67.
untitled. (The white roses I tried to braid in my hair). WPJ, 67.
Yañez, Mirta (1947–
Reminder. (Recordatorio). BTS, 232–33.
Springtime in Vietnam. (Primavera en Vietnam). BTS, 234–35.
The visits. (Las visitas). BTS, 230–33. (excerpts).
Ya'qub al-Ansari, Maryam bint Abi. *See* **Maryam bint Abi Ya'qub al-Ansari.**
Yeh, Li. *See* **Li Yeh.**
Yeh, Tzu. *See* **Tzu Yeh.**
Yen, Ts'ai. *See* **Ts'ai Yen.**
Ying, Tan. *See* **Tan Ying.**
Yokobue (12th century)
untitled. (How can I complain/that you have shaved your hair?). WPJ, 39.
Yosami, Wife of Hitomaro (8th century)
untitled. (Day after day I've longed for my husband,). WPJ, 10.
untitled. (We will never meet again face to face.). WPJ, 11.
untitled. (You tell me not to long for you.). WPJ, 10.
Yosano Akiko (1878–1942)
Labor pains. WPJ, 87.
Tangled hair. OVO, 127–28. (excerpts).
untitled. (As I am unhappy). WPO, 41.
untitled. (A bird comes/delicately as a little girl). WPJ, 64. WPO, 42.
untitled. (I can give myself to her). WPJ, 63. WPO, 42.

untitled. (I have the delusion/that you are with me). WPJ, 64.

untitled. (I remember the days/When the lily). WPJ, 64.

untitled. (Is it because you always hope, my heart,). WPJ, 65.

untitled. (Last autumn/The three of us tossed acorns). WPJ, 63.

untitled. (My heart is like the sun,). WPJ, 65.

untitled. (Purple butterflies/fly at night through my dreams.). WPJ, 65.

untitled. (She who carries/in her heart a love). WPJ, 66.

untitled. (Sweet and sad/like love overwhelmed). WPJ, 66.

untitled. (A wave of coldness). WPO, 41.

untitled. (Without a word/Without a demand). WPJ, 63.

Yoshihara Sachiko (1932–
Blasphemy. WPJ, 121.
Candle. WPJ, 118–19.
I forget. WPJ, 122.
Resurrection. WPJ, 120.

Yoshiyuki Rie (1939–
Sacrificial victim. WPJ, 126.

Young, Elise (1946–
untitled. (The First Separation). APO, 86–87. LPO, 155–56.

Yü Ch'ing-tsêng (19th century)
To the tune "Intoxicated with shadows of flowers." WPC, 79.

Yü Hsüan-chi (–870)
Advice to a neighbor girl. AAA, 8. WPC, 17.
Composed on the theme "Willows by the Riverside." WPO, 19.
Living in the summer mountains. WPC, 18.
On a visit to Ch'ung Chên Taoist temple I see in the South Hall the list of successful candidates in the Imperial examinations. WPC, 19.
Sending spring love to Tzu-an. WPC, 20.

Yün-fêng, Sun. *See* **Sun Yün-fêng.**

Yup, Paula (1957–
Opaque. TWO, 528.
Peace. TWO, 528.
Untitled. TWO, 528.

Yvonne
Aunt Martha: severance pay. TWO, 273–77.
1936. TWO, 275–77.
The tearing of the skin. WPE, 62–66.

Z

Zaldivar, Gladys
Hector floating in the night. (Hector flotando en la noche). LAW, 192–94.
Vagabond in the tower. (Vagamundo en la torre). LAW, 191–92.

Zaleski, Jan
In answer to what he said. TIW, 137.
With my velvet gun. TIW, 138.

Zarchi, Nurit
Furtively. BAA, 82.
Wild orchards. BAA, 83.

Zaturenska, Marya (1902–1982)
Song. (Life with her weary eyes,). BWO, 344.

Zavala, Iris (1936–
Escritura desatada. (Spanish and English). LAW, 199. (excerpt).
The great mammoth . . . (El gran mamut . . .). LAW, 196, 198.
Smile lie rockets . . . (Sonrisa mentira cohetes . . .). LAW, 197.

Zeb-un-Nissa (1639–1689)
Lament. AAA, 24.

Zelda (1914–
A black rose. BAA, 125.
The fine sand, the terrible sand. BAA, 132.
In the dry riverbed. BAA, 127.
The invisible Carmel. BAA, 133.
The light is my delight. BAA, 128–29.
The moon is teaching Bible. BAA, 124.
sound out your voices, morning prayers. BAA, 130–31.
Strange plant. BAA, 126.
Wicked neighbor. WPO, 131–33.
A woman who's arrived at a ripe old age. BAA, 134.

Zerbe, Evelyn Arcad
In memory of my Arab grandmother. WPO, 106–07.

Zibu'n-Nisa, Makhfi. *See* **Makhfi (Zibu'n-Nisa).**

Zier, Alison
Postage due. TIW, 124–25.

Zimele-Keita, Nzadi (Michelle McMichael)
Birds of paradise. CNF, 396–98.
once. CNF, 396.
Prayer. CNF, 397–98.
Wa-Ko-Da. CNF, 396–97.
long road rhythm. CNF, 398.
what we know. CNF, 399.

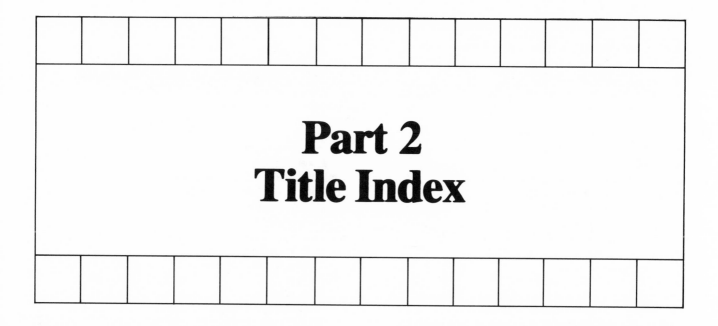

Part 2
Title Index

A Julia y a mi. **Sandra Maria Esteves.**
Aaron Nicholas, almost ten. **Janet Campbell.**
The abandoned. **Mririda n'Ait Attik.**
Abel's bride. **Denise Levertov.**
Abishag. **Shirley Kaufman.**
Abodes. **Alejandra Pizarnik.**
Aborting. **Teru Kanazawa.**
The abortion. **Anonymous.**
About her & about him. **Miriam Oren.**
About marriage. **Denise Levertov.**
Absence. **Lucha Corpi.**
Absolute sea. **Cecilia Meireles.**
Absorption of rock. **Maxine Hong Kingston.**
Abundance and scarcity. **Honor Moore.**
Ada. **Eugenie Eersel.**
Adam. **Reina María Rodríguez.**
Adam pos'd. **Anne Finch, Countess of Winchilsea.**
The advent of my death. **Marcela Christine Lucero-Trujillo.**
The adversary. **Phyllis McGinley.**
Advice. **Gwendolyn B. Bennett.**
Advice. **Frances Landsman.**
Advice to a girl. **Sara Teasdale.**
Advice to a neighbor girl. **Yü Hsüan-chi.**
Advice to the photographers of atrocities. **Judith McCombs.**
Affair. **Helene Davis.**
After Bourlon Wood. **Helen Dircks.**

After four years. **May Sarton.**
After grief. **Dorothy Livesay.**
After her death. (A sequence for my mother). **Jan Heller Levi.**
after my grandmother's death. **Michèle Roberts.**
After one of the 19 famous Han poems. **Pao Ling-hui.**
After seeing *Walkabout*. **Michèle Roberts.**
After ten years. **Susan North.**
After the quarrel. **Grace Butcher.**
After Yeats. **Jane Augustine.**
The afternoon in May. (Sequence from blue to blue). **Kristina McGrath.**
Afternoon walk. **Josephine Miles.**
Afterwards. **Margaret Postgate Cole.**
Again. **Charlotte Mew.**
Again, flowering. **Elizabeth Keeler.**
again you slept with mr no man. **Yona Wallach.**
Against love. **Katherine Philips.**
Against still life. **Margaret Atwood.**
Aging. **Dorothy Livesay.**
Agnes. **Kathleen Fraser.**
Ah! why, because the dazzling sun. **Emily Brontë.**
Ahora. **Sandra Maria Esteves.**
Ain't I a woman? **Sojourner Truth.**
Air: Sentir avec ardeur. **Marie-Françoise-Catherine de Beauveau, La Marquise de Boufflers.**
Airman, R. F. C. **Agnes Grozier Herbertson.**
Akhmatova. (excerpts). **Marina Tsvetayeva.**
The alarm clock. **Mari Evans**
Alarum. **Urszula Kozioł.**
Alice James. **Naomi Wolf.**
Alicia's dream: entering Knossos. **Diana Ó Hehir.**
All around the jailhouse. **Ella May Wiggins.**
All clear. **Marge Piercy.**

All day we've longed for night. **Sarah Webster Fabio.**
All may come. **Mirta Aguirre.**
All of a sudden. **Teresa de Jesús.**
All this so tasteless and threatening. **Yona Wallach.**
all wars. **Carol Bergé.**
Allegory. **Diana Chang.**
Allí por La Calle San Luís. **Carmen Tafolla.**
Almost love. **Magaly Sánchez.**
almost newyork. **Rachel Maines.**
Alone, we dream as gods. **Adrianne Marcus.**
Amazon twins. **Olga Broumas.**
Ambassador's daughter. **Barbara Szerlip.**
Ambulance train 30. **Carola Oman.**
Amelia's color. **Rafaela Chacón Nardi.**
American Margaret. **Michelene Wandor.**
Amerika. **Susan Sherman.**
Among the hours. **Magaly Sánchez.**
Among the things that use to be. **Willie M. Coleman.**
Amusing our daughters. **Carolyn Kizer.**
Amy Lowell. **Lola Ridge.**
Analysis. **Julia Vinograd.**
The Anasazi woman. **Janet Lewis.**
Ancestral weight. **Alfonsina Storni.**
An ancient gesture. **Edna St. Vincent Millay.**
And. (One, The other, And). **Wendy Brooks Wieber.**
And after we damned each other. **Anna Akhmatova.**
"And he said, fight on." **Tekahionwake.**
And in Richmond. **Judith Kazantzis.**
And on my eyes dark sleep by night. **Michael Field.**
and so it all goes on. **Michèle Roberts.**
And so the oracles. (Cambrian). **Eeva-Liisa Manner.**
. . . And the old women gathered (The Gospel Singers). **Mari Evans.**
. . . And then she said. **Alexis De Veaux.**
And when you leave, take your pictures with you. **Jo Carrillo.**
Andromeda, what now? **Sappho.**
Angela Davis. **Alice S. Cobb.**
Anger's freeing power. **Stevie Smith.**
Ann Burlak. **Muriel Rukeyser.**
Anne Boleyn's song. **Edith Sitwell.**
The Anniad. **Gwendolyn Brooks.**
The anniversary. **Ai.**
The anniversary of Samansa's death. **Shiraishi Kazuko.**
Anniversary of the Great Retreat. **Isabel C. Clarke.**
Annunciation. **Monica Ditmas.**
The annunciation. **Amrita Pritam.**
Another full moon. **Ruth Fainlight.**
Another race. **Delmira Augustini.**
Another view into love. **Carol Bergé.**
The answer. **Anne Finch, Countess of Winchilsea.**
An answer to a love-letter. **Mary Wortley Montagu, Lady.**
An answer to another persuading a lady to marriage. **Katherine Philips.**
Antigone and Oedipus. **Henrietta Cordelia Ray.**
The anti-suffragists. **Charlotte Perkins Gilman.**
Any woman's blues. **Sherley Anne Williams.**

Apathy. (Cambrian). **Eeva-Liisa Manner.**
Aphrodite. **Shlomit Cohen.**
The apology. **Anne Finch, Countess of Winchilsea.**
apology (to the panthers). **Lucille Clifton.**
Appeal. **Noémia da Sousa.**
An appeal to my countrywomen. **Frances Ellen Watkins Harper.**
Appendix to the Anniad: leaves from a loose-leaf war diary. **Gwendolyn Brooks.**
Apple tree in Oakland. **Nancy Morejón.**
the application. **Susan MacDonald.**
April. **Molly Vaux.**
April 6. **Miriam Dyak.**
Arachne. **Rose Terry Cooke.**
Arachne. **Judith Kazantzis.**
Arch. (A dictionary of common terms). **Alberta Turner.**
Ardelia to melancholy. **Anne Finch, Countess of Winchilsea.**
Ardelia's answer to Ephelia. **Anne Finch, Countess of Winchilsea.**
"Are you still there." **Joy Harjo.**
The arrival. **Lan Ling.**
Art and women. **Rachel Annand Taylor.**
Artemis. **Rita Boumi-Pappas.**
Artemis. **Olga Broumas.**
The artist as social critic. (Searching/not searching). **Muriel Rukeyser.**
As required by law. **Elsie Alvarado de Ricord.**
Asante sana, Te Te. **Thadious M. Davis.**
Ascent. **Susan North.**
(Assata on trial in New Jersey). (dialectics). **Jan Clausen.**
The assembly of ladies. **Anonymous.**
Asthma. **Lynne McMahon.**
ASYLUM. **Regina Williams.**
At a summer hotel. **Isabella Gardner.**
At April. **Angelina Weld Grimké.**
At home in Dakar. **Margaret Danner.**
At least. **Miriam Oren.**
at menopause. **Mary Winfrey.**
At my house. **Janet Sternburg.**
At night. **Bella Akhmadulina.**
At night. **Margherita Guidacci.**
At night, she sees voices. **Chedva Harakavy.**
At sixteen. **Michele Murray.**
At the Badr Trench. **Safiya bint Musafir.**
At the ball. **Celia Gilbert.**
At the carnival. **Anne Spencer.**
At the death of Martin Luther King. **Fina García Marruz.**
at the diagnostician's office. **Mary Winfrey.**
At the movies. **Florence Ripley Mastin.**
At the National Gallery. **Judith Kazantzis.**
At the sutra chanting of her dead daughter. **Izumi Shikibu.**
At thirty. **Carol Simone.**
Atrocities. **Nikki Giovanni.**
Attack the water. **Janice Mirikitani.**
An attempt at jealousy. **Marina Tsvetayeva.**
Attics. **Adelaide Blomfield.**
August. **Akua Lezli Hope.**

August. **Joan LaBombard.**
August. (Sequence from blue to blue). **Kristina McGrath.**
August 24, 1963—1:00 a.m.: Omaha. **Donna Whitewing.**
Auld Robin Gray. **Anne Lindsay Barnard, Lady.**
Aunt Dolly. **Carolyn M. Rodgers.**
Aunt Lenore at forty-five. **Susan North.**
Aunt Martha: severance pay. **Yvonne.**
Aurora Leigh. (excerpt). **Elizabeth Barrett Browning.**
Austin: foreign city. **Teresinha Pereira.**
Autobiography. **Janet Dubé.**
Autobiography. (excerpt). **Excilia Saldaña.**
Autobiography part one: Manila to San Francisco. **Jessica Tarahata Hagedorn.**
Autobiography part two: rock and roll. **Jessica Tarahata Hagedorn.**
Automat with sparkling water. **Bella Akhmadulina.**
Autumn. **Bella Akhmadulina.**
Autumn. **Christina Rosetti.**
The autumn brook. **Hsüeh T'ao.**
Autumn morning frost. **Yunna Moritz.**
Autumn, 1914. **Mary Webb.**
Autumn rains. **Soleida Ríos.**
Autumnal claque. **Elizabeth Keeler.**
Ava Gardner in the film *Earthquake*. **Judith Kazantzis.**
Avatar. **Akua Lezli Hope.**
Avowal. **Virginia Moore.**
Awakening. **Antonia Pozzi.**
Awakening, in a church. **Virginia Gilbert.**
Azay-le-rideau. **Rosemary Dobson.**
Azouou. **Mririda n'Ait Attik.**
Azteca IV. **Ana Kowalkowska.**

B

Babysitter. **Carol Dine.**
Back into the garden. **Sarah Webster Fabio.**
Back to base. **Jenny Joseph.**
A bad spring. **Bella Akhmadulina.**
Bailar . . . **Carmen Tafolla.**
The bairn. **Rosamund Greenwood.**
Baking bread. **Suellen Mayfield.**
Ballad by one who doesn't want to make love blindly. **Chelly Lima.**
Ballad of the handsome man. **Denise Salfeld.**
Ballad of the Hoppy-Toad. **Margaret Walker.**
Ballad of the ten casino dancers. **Cecília Meireles.**
Ballade des Belles Milatraisses; The Octoroon Ball, New Orleans, 1840–1850. **Rosalie Jonas.**
Ballroom dancing class. **Phyllis McGinley.**
The bamboo shaded pool. **Chang Wên-chi.**
A Barbadian true to life fantasy. **Lois Elaine Griffith.**

The barbarian. **Lili Bita.**
Barbie doll. **Marge Piercy.**
Bars fight, August 28, 1746. **Lucy Terry.**
Bartholomew's night. **Bella Akhmadulina.**
Basic training. **Jane Shore.**
the bath. **Judith Kazantzis.**
The battle hymn of the Republic. **Julia Ward Howe.**
The battle of the swamps. **Muriel Elsie Graham.**
Battle song. **Macuilxochitl.**
The bean eaters. **Gwendolyn Brooks.**
Because one is always forgotten. **Carolyn Forché.**
Because words do not suffice. **Susan Sherman.**
Bedouin woman. **Shulamit Apfel.**
Bedtime. **Denise Levertov.**
Beehive. (Four short poems). **Barbara Szerlip.**
Beer drops. **Melba Joyce Boyd.**
Bees inside me. **Laura Chester.**
Before. **Alejandra Pizarnik.**
Before I dress and soar again. **Donna Allegra.**
Before the birth of one of her children. **Anne Bradstreet.**
Before the Feast of Shushan. **Anne Spencer.**
Before the sun rises. **Sarah Kirsch.**
Before your waking. **Anna Gréki.**
Behind bars. (excerpts). **Fadwa Tuqān.**
Behind locked doors. **Laura Tokunaga.**
Being driven. **Alexandra Grilikhes.**
being property once myself. **Lucille Clifton.**
The Beirut—Hell Express. (excerpt). **Etel Adnan.**
The bell. **Yunna Moritz.**
Belladonna. **Janet Hamill.**
Belly dancer. **Diane Wakoski.**
The belly dancer's song. **Anita Endrezze-Danielson.**
Beloved women. **Paula Gunn Allen.**
Below zero. **Angela de Hoyos.**
Beneath the shadow of the freeway. **Lorna Dee Cervantes.**
Between ourselves. **Audre Lorde.**
Between what persons love may exist. (De arte honeste amandi). **Linda Gregerson.**
Beverly Hills, Chicago. **Gwendolyn Brooks.**
Beyond silence. **Lan Ling.**
Beyond the Cliffs of Abiquiu. **Jo Carrillo.**
Beyond what. **Alice Walker.**
Bianca among the nightingales. **Elizabeth Barrett Browning.**
Big fine woman from Ruleville. **Jayne Cortez.**
Big momma. **Julia Fields.**
The big sleep. **Janet Hamill.**
A big woman screams out her guts. **Shulamit Apfel.**
Billy de Lye. **Deidre McCalla.**
The bird and the arras. **Anne Finch, Countess of Winchilsea.**
Birds of paradise. **Nzadi Zimele-Keita (Michelle McMichael).**
Birth. **Georgina Herrera.**
Birth. (How I managed to square the circle of dreams in the shape of a window at the top of the stairs in a tenement house). **Jenny Mastoraki.**
Birth dance, belly dancer. **Daniela Gioseffi.**

The birth in a narrow room. **Gwendolyn Brooks.**
A birthday. **Christina Rossetti.**
Birthday poem for Gregory Reeves. **Jessica Tarahata Hagedorn.**
The birthmark. **Merrill Oliver.**
Birthplace. **Tahereh Saffarzadeh.**
A bitter resurrection. **Christina Rossetti.**
The black art. **Anne Sexton.**
The Black back-ups. **Donna Kate Rushin.**
Black brook. **Bella Akhmadulina.**
The black draftee from Dixie. **Carrie Williams Clifford.**
The Black Goddess. **Donna Kate Rushin.**
Black leather, because bumble bees look like it. **Diane Wakoski.**
Black mother woman. **Audre Lorde.**
Black pride. **Margaret Goss Burroughs.**
The black room. **Joy Harjo.**
A black rose. **Zelda.**
Black sister. **Kattie M. Cumbo.**
Black woman. **Naomi Long Madgett.**
Black woman. **Nancy Morejón.**
The blackbird. **Diane Wakoski.**
blackbirds over water. **Elizabeth Gross.**
Black-Coat meets coyote (Three conversations of the absurd). **Judith Ivaloo Volborth.**
Blasphemy. **Yoshihara Sachiko.**
Bliss. (A dictionary of common terms). **Alberta Turner.**
The blood. **Nina Cassian.**
Blood. **Joan Larkin.**
The blood criminal. **Lili Bita.**
Blood journey. **Phyllis Koestenbaum.**
Bloody pause. **Astra.**
Blossoming plum and cherry. **Adelaide Crapsey.**
Blue horse. **Takiguchi Masako.**
Blue jean wearin women??? **Sharon Henderson.**
Blue ribbons for the baby girl. **June Jordan.**
The Blue Swan Cafe. **Jessica Tarahata Hagedorn.**
Blues in the barrio. **Angela de Hoyos.**
bobby hutton. (Memorial). **Sonia Sanchez.**
The body is the Victory and the Defeat of dreams. **Katerina Anghelaki-Rooke.**
Bone poem. **Nancy Willard.**
Le bonheur. **Joan Murray Simpson.**
Book of my hunger, book of the earth. (excerpts). **Sarah Appleton.**
Bookmark. **Teresa of Ávila.**
The border. **Kinereth Gensler.**
Boston, Massachusetts. **Dorothy Allison.**
Bottled. **Helene Johnson.**
The bowl. **Barbara Smith.**
Boys and girls. **Anne Wilkinson.**
The brass coin. (Largely because of coincidence and partly because of chance, I have taken up a new address at 47th Street and Avenue F). **Diane Wakoski.**
Brass furnace going out: song, after an abortion. **Diane di Prima.**
Bread. **Gabriela Mistral.**
The breadwinner. **Amrita Pritam.**

Breaking a voodoo. **Eve Triem.**
Breaking camp. (Of fruit whose black seed fire). **Olga Broumas.**
Breaking the lid of night. **Diana Ó Hehir.**
Breathing. **Dorothy Livesay.**
Brecht's Galileo. (Searching/not searching). **Muriel Rukeyser.**
Breech. **Barbara Szerlip.**
Breviary. **Susan Griffin.**
Bricklayer's fable. **Nancy Morejón.**
The bridal veil. **Alice Cary.**
Bride the aid-woman. **Anonymous.**
Bridesmaids' carol. **Sappho.**
Bridesmaids' carol I. **Sappho.**
The bridge poem. **Donna Kate Rushin.**
Brief landing. **Sarah Kirsch.**
Briefly it enters, and briefly speaks. **Jane Kenyon.**
Bright house. **Fukao Sumako.**
Brindis: for the barrio. **Angela de Hoyos.**
The broken soldier. **Katharine Tynan.**
The bronze of Poseidon. **Vera Rich.**
Bronzeville woman in a red hat. **Gwendolyn Brooks.**
Brooklyn 1956: The walls are full of noise. **Melanie Kaye.**
Brother Baptis' on woman suffrage. **Rosalie Jonas.**
Brussels, 1919. **Carola Oman.**
A bud in the frost. **Moira O'Neill.**
buddha's birthday. **Carol Tinker.**
A bull. **Babette Deutsch.**
Burial. **Alice Walker.**
Bushpaths. **Wilmette Brown.**
busy Lizzie. **Michèle Roberts.**
But look. **Nelly Sachs.**
Buy us a little grain. **Christine Lavant.**
By July. (Sequence from blue to blue). **Kristina McGrath.**

Cabal. **Emily Katherine Harris.**
The cabal at Nickey Nackeys. **Aphra Behn.**
Cabbage. **Rosemary Norman.**
Caguayo. **Albis Torres.**
Caledonia. **Colleen J. McElroy.**
The call. **Jessie Pope.**
Call it fear. **Joy Harjo.**
A call to action. **Ch'iu Chin.**
Calling on the live wire. **Sara Miles.**
Calliope in the labour ward. **Elaine Feinstein.**
Cambrian. (excerpts). **Eeva-Liisa Manner.**
"Cambridge University Swimming Club/no public access to river." **Judith Moffett.**
Camp notes. (excerpts). **Mitsuye Yamada.**

Can I say. **Dolly Bird.**
Canary Islands. (Not that far). **May Miller.**
Candle. **Yoshihara Sachiko.**
Candles. **Hélène Swarth.**
Cannibalism. **Diana Chang.**
Canto de Nada/Para ti, M'wandishi. **Jessica Tarahata Hagedorn.**
Cantonese opera at Sun Sing Theater. **Frances C. Chung.**
Canzonetta. **Antonia Pozzi.**
Cape Coast Castle revisited. **Jo Ann Hall-Evans.**
The captain. **Blanca Varela.**
The captive dove. **Anne Brontë.**
Carnevale. **Pat Nottingham.**
Carol, in the park, chewing on straws. (The common woman). **Judy Grahn.**
Carol's house. **Dona Stein.**
Cassandra's wedding song. (The Trojan women). **Ann Stanford.**
A castaway. (excerpt). **Augusta Webster.**
Casualty. **Winifred M. Letts.**
Casualty in Mexico City. **Diana Ó Hehir.**
Casuist, Etc. **Kathleen Fraser.**
Catacombs: dream poem number one. **Colleen J. McElroy.**
Catching one clear thought alive. **Paula Gunn Allen.**
The cattle thief. **Tekahionwake.**
Caution. **Jacqueline Lapidus.**
Celibacy. **Georgia Douglas Johnson.**
The Cenotaph. **Charlotte Mew.**
The Cenotaph. **Ursula Roberts.**
The centaur. **May Swenson.**
Central Park at dusk. **Sara Teasdale.**
Ceremony. **Kattie M. Cumbo.**
Ceremony. **Johari M. Kunjufu.**
Ceremony for completing a poetry reading. **Chrystos.**
Ceres in an open field. **Jane Creighton.**
Certainty. **Mirta Aguirre.**
Chain. **Audre Lorde.**
Change of scene. **Ellen Warmond.**
Chapter one. **Carol Muske.**
Chapters from a poem. **Bella Akhmadulina.**
The chariot. **Angela Langfield.**
Charlotte Corday/Marat (July 13, 1793). **Mary Winfrey.**
The charming woman. **Helen Selina (Lady Dufferin).**
Chartivel. (excerpt). **Marie de France.**
Chess. **Rosario Castellanos.**
Chicana evolution. **Sylvia Alicia Gonzales.**
'chick.' **Michelene Wandor.**
The child. (Early losses: a requiem. Part II). **Alice Walker.**
The child of earthquake country. **Adrianne Marcus.**
Child waking. **E. J. Scovell.**
Childe Rolandine. **Stevie Smith.**
Childhood. **Marie-Thérèse Rouil.**
Childhood. **Margaret Walker.**
Childless mothers. **Summer Brenner.**
Childless woman. **Sylvia Plath.**
Children and other reasons. **Cindy Bellinger.**
Children of wealth in your warm nursery. **Elizabeth Daryush.**

Child's memory. **Eleni Fourtouni.**
Chile. **Susan Griffin.**
chinatown. **Fay Chiang.**
Chinatown 4. **Laureen Mar.**
Chinatown 1. **Laureen Mar.**
Chinatown 2. **Laureen Mar.**
Chinese dentist. **Frances C. Chung.**
A Chinese Ulysses. **Shiraishi Kazuko.**
chocolate egg. **Michelene Wandor.**
the choice. **Anonymous.**
Chon. **Marina Rivera.**
choreopoem IV; 1935/chinatown. **Fay Chiang.**
choreopoem I. **Fay Chiang.**
choreopoem VI. (excerpt). **Fay Chiang.**
Chorus. (The tragedie of Mariam, the faire queene of Jewry). **Elizabeth Tanfield Carey, Lady.**
Chorus of the rescued. **Nelly Sachs.**
Christ in Flanders. **Lucy Whitmell.**
Christine to her son. **Christine de Pisan.**
A Christmas carol: c. 1976. **Ana Castillo.**
Christmas in exile. **Shirley Geok-Lin Lim.**
A Christmas letter. **Jan Clausen.**
Christmas, 1978. **Michelene Wandor.**
Christmas, 1916. **M. Winifred Wedgwood.**
Christmas story (1980). **Pat Arrowsmith.**
Chronicle. **Mei-mei Berssenbrugge.**
Chronicle. **Juana de Ibarbourou.**
Chronicle of a morning in 1976. **Marilyn Bobes.**
CINDERELLA. **Fareedah Allah.**
Cinderella. **Judith Kazantzis.**
Circe—Mud poems. (excerpt). **Margaret Atwood.**
The city. **Minerva Salado.**
city limited. **Michèle Roberts.**
The civil servant is eaten too. **Sybil Wood.**
Claims. (excerpts). **Shirley Kaufman.**
Clanking to Byzantium. **Ellen Gilchrist.**
Clarinda's indifference at parting with her beauty. **Anne Finch, Countess of Winchilsea.**
A clever woman. **Mary Elizabeth Coleridge.**
Clinic day. **Jo Barnes.**
Clock. **Alejandra Pizarnik.**
Clockwork doll. **Dahlia Ravikovitch.**
Cloud dissects itself. **Lin Ling.**
Cloud hairdress. **Chao Luan-luan.**
Clouet of silks. (Quilts). **Barbara Guest.**
The clown. **Soleida Ríos.**
Club 82: Lisa. **Cynthia Kraman Genser.**
The clue. **Kathleen Raine.**
Coal. **Audre Lorde.**
Coastline. **Elaine Feinstein.**
Cock fight under the magnolias. **Diane Wakoski.**
Cocoon. **Ishigaki Rin.**
Cocosi. **Albis Torres.**
The coffee drinkers answered ecstatically. **Lyn Hejinian.**
Coffee field dorm. **Albis Torres.**
Cold fear. **Elizabeth Madox Roberts.**
The collateral adjective. **Sherley Anne Williams.**
The collector. **Desirée Flynn.**

The Collier lass. **Frankie Armstrong.**
Come into animal presence. **Denise Levertov.**
Coming across. **Mehri (Mihru'n-Nisa of Herat).**
Coming out. **Jacqueline Lapidus.**
Coming to self. **Michele Murray.**
The coming woman. **Mary Weston Fordham.**
The common woman. (excerpts). **Judy Grahn.**
Communications. **Amanda Berenguer.**
The community of women causes an operation. **Eleanor Lerman.**
Composed on the theme "Willows by the Riverside." **Yu Hsuan-chi.**
Composing the garden. **Ann Stanford.**
Concerning the awakening of my soul. **Henriette Roland-Holst.**
Concrete. (Searching/not searching). **Muriel Rukeyser.**
the conditioning. **Mary Winfrey.**
Conditions. **Irena Klepfisz.**
Confession to settle a curse. **Rosmarie Waldrop.**
Confrontations with the devil in the form of love. (excerpt). **Judy Grahn.**
Confusion. **Magaly Sánchez.**
Conscientious objector. **Edna St. Vincent Millay.**
The consolation. **Anne Finch, Countess of Winchilsea.**
Consorting with angels. **Anne Sexton.**
The consumer. **Marge Piercy.**
Contemplations. (excerpts). **Anne Bradstreet.**
Contemporary goddess. (Three women in the closet). **Gloria Anzaldúa.**
Contexts. **Irena Klepfisz.**
Contradiction. **Elizabeth Cook-Lynn.**
Contrary ways to make fire. **Sara Miles.**
Convalescence. **Amy Lowell.**
The convalescent. **Cicily Fox Smith.**
Conversation at the Bridgeport train station with an old man who speaks Spanish. **Lourdes Casal.**
Conversation in crisis. **Audre Lorde.**
Conversation overheard on Tamalpais Road. **Roberta Hill.**
Conversations between here and home. **Joy Harjo.**
Copy clerk—North American Aviation. **Sandy Boucher.**
Corinne at the capitol. **Felicia Hemans.**
Corn grinding song. **Anonymous.**
Cornfields in Accra. **Ama Ata Aidoo.**
Cosmopolite. **Georgia Douglas Johnson.**
"Couch of space." (Quilts). **Barbara Guest.**
The country midwife: a day. **Ai.**
Country press. **Rosemary Dobson.**
The couple. **Ana Blandiana.**
The couple. **Elizabeth Keeler.**
The courage that my mother had. **Edna St. Vincent Millay.**
The covenant. **Joan LaBombard.**
Cow's skull with calico roses. **Joan Larkin.**
Crab-angel. **Mina Loy.**
Cracked. **Gloria Gayles.**
Cradle song. **Yona Wallach.**
crafty. **Michelene Wandor.**
Creamy breasts. **Chao Luan-luan.**
Creation story. **Paula Gunn Allen.**

The crib. (Night-pieces: for a child). **Adrienne Rich.**
Crisis. **Ann Stanford.**
The crocuses. **Frances Ellen Watkins Harper.**
The crossing. **Sukey Durham.**
The crossing. **Barbara Szerlip.**
The cry of the children. **Elizabeth Barrett Browning.**
Crystal. **Faye Kicknosway.**
The crystal bridge. **Lucha Corpi.**
The crystal tree. **Phyllis Mégroz.**
Cubism. **Maureen Owen.**
Cunts have faces: dialogue among rumpled sheets. **Elsa Gidlow.**
The cure. (The love sequence). **Sandra M. Gilbert.**
The curse. (A curse for a nation). **Elizabeth Barrett Browning.**
A curse. **Rábi'a bint Ka'b.**
A curse for a nation. **Elizabeth Barrett Browning.**
Cutting the Jewish bride's hair. **Ruth Whitman.**
cypress. **Ntozake Shange.**

D. **Beverly Dahlen.**
D & C. **Akua Lezli Hope.**
D. G. C. to J. A. **Emily Brontë.**
Daguerreotype: lace maker. **Sandra M. Gilbert.**
Damaris. **Maxine Shaw.**
The damned. **Toi Derricotte.**
Dance mad. **Laura Beausoleil.**
The dance of the greased women. **Anonymous.**
The dancer. **Brenda Connor-Bey.**
The dancers. **Edith Sitwell.**
Dancing with the fifth horseman. **Colleen J. McElroy.**
Dandelions for chains. **Sarah Kirsch.**
Danger. **Helen Hunt Jackson.**
Dark blood. **Margaret Walker.**
Dark phrases. **Ntozake Shange.**
The dark rider. **Sylvia Read.**
Dark romance. **Lucha Corpi.**
Dark stream. **Ingrid Jonker.**
Dark testament. **Pauli Murray.**
"Darkness." **Alice Karle.**
Daufuski (Four movements). **Mari Evans.**
Daughters. **Astra.**
Daughter's funeral dirge at a Saturday burial (Union gravediggers quit at noon). **Elizabeth Keeler.**
Dawn. **Rosario Castellanos.**
Dawn. **Rachel.**
The dawn of love. **Henrietta Cordelia Ray.**
Dawn's territory. (excerpt). **Eunice Odio.**
A day in the life. . . **Stef Pixner.**

Days. **Elizabeth Spires.**

Days and nights before winter. **Charlotte Carter.**

De arte honeste amandi. **Linda Gregerson.**

De mortuis. **F. Tennyson Jesse.**

Deacon Morgan. **Naomi Long Madgett.**

Dead embryos. **Judit Tóth.**

The dead one. **Albis Torres.**

The dead spider. (Medicine song). **Paula Gunn Allen.**

Deal. **Julia Vinograd.**

Dear Colette. **Erica Jong.**

Dear little man. **Gabriela Mistral.**

A death abroad. **Phyllis Hartnoll.**

Death and disfiguration. (A woman is talking to death). **Judy Grahn.**

death camp. **Irene Klepfisz.**

Death is not master. **May Miller.**

The death of Anna May Wong. **Jessica Tarahata Hagedorn.**

The death of Moses. **Margit Szécsi.**

Death sonnets. **Gabriela Mistral.**

Death, that struck when I was most confiding. **Emily Brontë.**

Debra. **Michelle T. Clinton.**

Debutante. **Jeanne Sirotkin.**

A decade. **Amy Lowell.**

December. **Bella Akhmadulina.**

A December forest. **Vesna Krmpotic.**

Deception. **Anna Akhmatova.**

Declaration. **Uva A. Clavijo.**

Dedicado al Sr. Chávez, Sept. 1975. (Napa, California). **Ana Castillo.**

The dedicated dancing bull and the water maid. **Stevie Smith.**

Deer skull. **Susan Griffin.**

The defiance. **Aphra Behn.**

Defiled is my name full sore. **Anne Boleyn.**

Defining it for Vanessa. **Colleen J. McElroy.**

Definition. **Nikki Grimes.**

Definition. **Marie-Elise.**

Deja vu. (Of fruit whose black seed fire). **Olga Broumas.**

Deliverance. **Frances Harper.**

Demeanor. **Josephine Miles.**

Demeter in Sicily. **Dorothy Wellesley.**

Demeter's song. **Mary Winfrey.**

Denial. **Josephine Miles.**

The descent. **Ann Stanford.**

Desert journal. Second day. **Ruth Weiss.**

The deserter. **Winifred M. Letts.**

A desire. (To George Sand). **Elizabeth Barrett Browning.**

Desmet, Idaho, March 1969. **Janet Campbell.**

Despair. **Olive E. Lindsay.**

Details. **Kate Ellen Braverman.**

The devil's daughter. (Marina). **Lucha Corpi.**

dialectics. **Jan Clausen.**

Dialogue. **Ibaragi Noriko.**

Dialogue. **Rashidah Ismaili.**

The diamond cutter. **Elizabeth Jennings.**

Diapering this poem. **Marie-Elise.**

A diary without dates. **Nakamura Chio.**

Dichotomy. **Helen Forsyth.**

A dictionary of common terms. (excerpts). **Alberta Turner.**

Die. (A dictionary of common terms). **Alberta Turner.**

The diet. **Maureen Burge.**

The difference. **Grade Wade.**

Different dimensions. **Atsumi Ikuko.**

Difficult hour. **Soleida Ríos.**

Dine. **Paula Gunn Allen.**

Diogenes. **Katerina Anghelaki-Rooke.**

Dirty no gooder blues. **Bessie Smith.**

The disappointment. **Aphra Behn.**

Disillusion. **Maureen Burge.**

The distaff. **Erinna.**

A ditty. **Bertha Jacobs (Suster Bertken).**

The diving board. **Judith Kazantzis.**

Diving into the wreck. **Adrienne Rich.**

The divorce. **Betsy Orient.**

Divorce. **Anna Wickham.**

Divorce 1. **Tove Ditlevsen.**

Divorce 3. **Tove Ditlevsen.**

Do not ask. **Christine Lavant.**

Do women have souls? **Elizabeth Gross.**

Documentary. **Robin Morgan.**

Dog and sea. **Alfonsina Storni.**

Dog body and cat mind. **Jenny Joseph.**

Doing time. **Sara Miles.**

The dolefull lay of Clorinda. **Mary Sidney Herbert, Countess of Pembroke.**

Domestics. **Kattie M. Cumbo.**

Domus caedet arborem. **Charlotte Mew.**

Dona Mariquita. **Lucha Corpi.**

Don't fish in my sea. **Gertrude "Ma" Rainey.**

Don't sleep. **Ingrid Jonker.**

Doors opening here, and there. **Marie Southwick.**

Dorothy Bradford's dream. (The landing). **Robin Becker.**

The double goer. **Dilys Laing.**

A double standard. **Frances Ellen Watkins Harper.**

Double take at Relais de l'Espadon. **Thadious M. Davis.**

The doubt of future foes. **Elizabeth I, Queen of England.**

Downhill. **Julia Vinograd.**

Drafts. **Nora Bomford.**

Drawing of a woman. **Shlomit Cohen.**

Dreadful memories. **Sarah Ogan Gunning.**

A dream. **Bella Akhmadulina.**

The dream. **Rachel Speght.**

dream. **Michelene Wandor.**

The dream kitchen. **Sandra M. Gilbert.**

Dream medley. **Magdalena Gomez.**

A dream observed. **Anne Ridler.**

Dream song of a woman. **Anonymous.**

Dream war. **Jessica Tarahata Hagedorn.**

Dream-land. **Christina Rossetti.**

The dress. **Dahlia Ravikovitch.**

Dried flower under my pillow. (Largely because of coincidence and partly because of chance, I have taken up a new address at 47th Street and Avenue F). **Diane Wakoski.**

Drinking the wind. **Tan Ying.**
Driving wheel. **Sherley Anne Williams.**
The drought. **Cheng Min.**
The drought. **Virginia Gilbert.**
The duck-billed god. (Medicine song). **Paula Gunn Allen.**
Due process. **Frankie Hucklenbroich.**
Dulce et decorum? **Elinor Jenkins.**
Dumb patronage. **Teru Kanazawa.**
The dunce. **Carla Lanyon Lanyon.**
Dusk. **Alejandra Pizarnik.**
Dusk on the veranda by Lake Mendota Summer 1968.
    Chung Ling.
Dust. **Ingrid Wendt.**
Dying. (excerpts). **Miriam Dyak.**
Dyke jacket. **Fran Winant.**
Dykes in the garden. **Sharon Barba.**

Each bird walking. **Tess Gallagher.**
Each one, pull one. **Alice Walker.**
Eager Street. **Kendra Kopelke.**
The earliest days. **Cheri Fein.**
early in the mornin. **Mari Evans.**
Early losses: a requiem. **Alice Walker.**
Early pregnancy. **Penelope Shuttle.**
Ears. **Sonja Åkesson.**
Earthly name. **Marina Tsvetayeva.**
Earthquake. **Alice Karle.**
Easter Monday. **Eleanor Farjeon.**
Easter night. **Alice Meynell.**
Echo. **Christina Rossetti.**
Echoes. **Emma Lazarus.**
The economist. **Anna Wickham.**
Ecstasy. **Hélène Swarth.**
Eden is a zoo. **Margaret Atwood.**
'Education.' **Pauline Barrington.**
Effigy of a nun. **Sara Teasdale.**
Effort at speech between two people. **Muriel Rukeyser.**
The eggplants have pins and needles. **Novella Matveyeva.**
Ego. **Dilys Laing.**
Egypt. (Not that far). **May Miller.**
Eighteen verses sung to a Tatar reed whistle. (excerpts).
    Ts'ai Yen.
The eighth part (at least) of everything. **Leah Goldberg.**
The eighth sonnet. **Louise Labé.**
Elaina Elaina I almost got killed. **Jana Harris.**
Elegy. **Rosario Castellanos.**
Elegy. **Jean Symons.**
Elegy for a woman of no importance. **Nāzik al-Malā'ika.**
Elegy for her brother, Sakhr. **Tumadir al-Khansa.**

Elegy for Mercedes. **Carilda Oliver Labra.**
Elegy for my mad mother. **Rachel Nahem.**
Elegy XXIII. **Louise Labé.**
Elizabeth. **Alice Karle.**
Elizabeth. **Sylvia Townsend Warner.**
Ella, in a square apron, along Highway 80. (The common
    woman). **Judy Grahn.**
Elvira. **Marilyn Bobes.**
The emergence no. 1. **Carol Lee Sanchez.**
Emigravit. **Helen Hunt Jackson.**
Emily Dickinson. **Linda Pastan.**
Emma. **Clare Coss.**
The Emperor asks why my husband surrendered. **Hua Jui,
    Lady.**
The Empress brand trim: Ruby reminisces. **Sherley Anne
    Williams.**
The empresses. **Elizabeth Coatsworth.**
The empty woman. **Gwendolyn Brooks.**
En las internas entrañas. *See* In the inmost recesses.
en público. **Victoria Moreno.**
End. **Rachel Nahem.**
The end of something. **Barbara Szerlip.**
End of the first act: ovation for Théroigne de Mericourt.
    Magaly Sánchez.
Endurance. **Carolyn Forché.**
The enemy's testament. **Etel Adnan.**
Enigma. **Helen Aoki Kaneko.**
enough. **Esther Louise.**
Enough. **Cory Wade.**
Entries: 15. **Pat Nottingham.**
Entries: 14. **Pat Nottingham.**
Entries: 13. **Pat Nottingham.**
Entries: 21. **Pat Nottingham.**
Envoy. **Otomo no Sakanoe.**
Envoy - The convent, New Orleans 1840–1850. **Rosalie
    Jonas.**
Envy. **Sheila Wingfield.**
Epic eulogy for boy and girl who almost killed each other
    with aspirin for love and homosexuality and pregnan-
    cy's sake. **Jessica Tarahata Hagedorn.**
An epic (with renaissance flute). **Alice Karle.**
Epistle to Prometheus. **Babette Deutsch.**
Epitaph. **Phoebe Hesketh.**
Epitaph. **Frances Mayes.**
Epitaph. (excerpt). **Marina Tsvetayeva.**
Epitaph on the monument of Sir William Dyer at Colmworth,
    1641. **Katherine Dyer.**
Epithalmion. **Olga Broumas.**
Equal opportunity. **Judy Dothard Simmons.**
Equinox. **Audre Lorde.**
Erasmina. **Rita Boumi-Pappas.**
Escritura desatada. (excerpt). **Iris Zavala.**
Eternity. **Dulce María Loynaz.**
Eucalyptus grave. **Rochelle Nameroff.**
Eurydice. **Hilda Doolittle.**
Eurydice. **Dorothy Howard.**
Eurynome. **Eleni Fourtouni.**
Eve. **Anne Hébert.**

Eve. **Christina Rossetti.**
Even. **Marina Rivera.**
Even before the mirror Myra. **Gerda S. Norvig.**
The evening news. **Audre Lorde.**
Evening rendezvous. **Cheng Min.**
Evening solace. **Charlotte Brontë.**
Evening walk. **Sonja Åkesson.**
Eveningsong 2. **Ramona C. Wilson.**
An event which makes no news. **Shinkawa Kazue.**
Every day that I love you. **Teresita Fernández.**
Everybody but me. **Margaret Goss Burroughs.**
Everyday alchemy. **Genevieve Taggard.**
Everything is plundered. **Anna Akhmatova.**
Evocation of Gabriela Mistral. **Claudia Lars.**
Except ye become. . . . **Dilys Laing.**
Exhibition of women artists (1790–1900). **Joan Aleshire.**
Exile. **Saniya Sälih.**
Exits and entrances. **Naomi Long Madgett.**
Expatriate. **Carolyn Forché.**
Expectant mother. **Penelope Shuttle.**
Expenses. **Adelaide Crapsey.**
The experiment. **Heidi Gitterman.**
An expression. **Susan Efros.**
Extended outlook. **Madeline DeFrees.**
Extremities. **Rae Armantrout.**
Eyes. **Mary Elizabeth Coleridge.**
Eyes. **M. F. Hershman.**

F

Face: border. **Elena Wilkinson.**
The face in the camera. **Elizabeth Keeler.**
The facts of life. **Janet Sternburg.**
Fairy tale. **Carol Muske.**
Fairy-led. **Mary Webb.**
A faithful wife. **Chang Chi.**
The fall of moon lady before the landing of Apollo X. **Chung Ling.**
Fallen. **Alice Corbin.**
The fallen. **Diana Gurney.**
A fallen needle . . . **Teresita Fernández.**
The falling leaves. **Margaret Postgate Cole.**
Falling South. **Martha Boethel.**
False prophet. **Elinor Wylie.**
Fame. **Charlotte Mew.**
FAMILY OF. **Alice Walker.**
Family outing—a celebration. **Nicki Jackowska.**
Family script. **Anne Blackford.**
The Famous Writers School opens its arms in the next best thing to welcome. **Rosellen Brown.**
FANFARE, CODA, AND FINALE. **Margaret Walker.**

Fantasy. **Gwendolyn B. Bennett.**
Far from the beach. **Alda do Espírito Santo.**
farewell. **Carol Bergé.**
Farewell. **Ellen Marie Bissert.**
A farewell to a southern melody. **Huang O.**
Farewell to Li, to the tune "A partridge sky." **Nieh Shêng-ch'iung.**
Farm wife. **Ellen Bryant Voigt.**
Farmers' almanac, or a guide to loving. **Susan North.**
The farmer's bride. **Charlotte Mew.**
Farmer's news. **Molly Vaux.**
Father. **Joan Swift.**
A father of women: ad sororem E. B. **Alice Meynell.**
Father poem II. **Chocolate Waters.**
Fatima. **Judith Kazantzis.**
The fault. **Kathleen Fraser.**
Faust. **Belkis Cuza Malé.**
February. **Molly Vaux.**
Feel the coming rains. **Melanie Ellis.**
Feeling and form. **Marilyn Hacker.**
Feeling the goddess II. **Alexandra Grilikhes.**
Fever. **Bella Akhmadulina.**
Fever. **Susan Wood-Thompson.**
Field ambulance in retreat. **May Sinclair.**
fields. **Michelene Wandor.**
The fields of Flanders. **Edith Nesbit.**
Fifteen boys, or perhaps even more. **Bella Akhmadulina.**
59: Huan/dispersion. **Barbara Szerlip.**
'A fight to a finish.' **S. Gertrude Ford.**
Figure. **Josephine Miles.**
Filipino boogie. **Jessica Tarahata Hagedorn.**
Fillmore Street poems: August, 1967. **Jessica Tarahata Hagedorn.**
The film by the woman. **Alexandra Grilikhes.**
Final anatomy. **Diana Ó Hehir.**
The final laugh. **Angela de Hoyos.**
Finally I see your skin. **Eleanor Lerman.**
Finders keepers. **Rachel Maines.**
The fine sand, the terrible sand. **Zelda.**
Fire. **Judith Kazantzis.**
The fire advances. (second version). **Amanda Berenguer.**
Fire wind's song to Sundae (Loba). **Lois Elaine Griffith.**
The fired pot. **Anna Wickham.**
First communion picture. **Eugenie Eersel.**
First dialogue. **Milagros González.**
first fable. (Driving wheel). **Sherley Anne Williams.**
First home. (The segregated heart). **Minnie Bruce Pratt.**
First intimation. **Vassar Miller.**
First love. **Mary Dorcey.**
The first of June again. **Carolyn Kizer.**
The first shoe. **Máire Mhac an tSaoi.**
first story. (Driving wheel). **Sherley Anne Williams.**
First things. **Lucienne Desnoues.**
First time: 1950. **Honor Moore.**
First tooth. **Molly Myerowitz Levine.**
First you tell him all your problems. **Beverly Tanenhaus.**
Fish - bird. **Excilia Saldaña.**
Fish market. **Rita Peck.**

The fish tank. **Rota Silverstrini.**
Fishes at Saint-Jean: Chagall, 1949. **Roberta Spear.**
A fistful of flowers for Vivian's kid. **Willyce Kim.**
5 a.m. **Jane Miller.**
FIVE BLACK MEN . . . and ten will save the city . . .
    Margaret Walker.
The 5:32. **Phyllis McGinley.**
A flame within. **Marté Jones.**
Flanders Fields. **Elizabeth Daryush.**
The flesh and the spirit. **Anne Bradstreet.**
Flight. **Colleen J. McElroy.**
The floating casket. **María Eugenia Vaz Ferreira.**
The floor of ocean. (Searching/not searching). **Muriel
    Rukeyser.**
A flower of mullein. **Lizette Woodworth Reese.**
Flowering current. **Eiluned Lewis.**
The flowering of the rod. (excerpt). **Hilda Doolittle.**
Flute. **Rivka Miriam.**
Folk. **Carolyn M. Rodgers.**
Folk tune. **Esther Raab.**
Foolish men. **Juana Inés de la Cruz (Sister).**
Fools. (Of fruit whose black seed fire). **Olga Broumas.**
Footpath. **Stella Ngatho.**
Footpaths cross in the rice field. **Lin Ling.**
For a godchild, Regina, on the occasion of her first love. **Toi
    Derricotte.**
For a man on his way. (excerpts). **Margarita Aliger.**
For a survivor of the Mesopotamian Campaign. **Elizabeth
    Daryush.**
For all Mary Magdalenes. **Desanka Maksimovic.**
For all the homesick sunshine girls in spring. **Lois Elaine
    Griffith.**
For all the lovers among us. **Frankie Hucklenbroich.**
For amber. **Cherríe Moraga.**
For an attempted suicide of the 20th century. **Lucha Corpi.**
For Billie Holiday and Janis Joplin. **Maxine Shaw.**
For Bruce who's on smack: May 31, 1967. **Jessica Tarahata
    Hagedorn.**
for Cynthia. **Sara Miles.**
For Darlene Tower. **Beverly Dahlen.**
For Dolci. (Searching/not searching). **Muriel Rukeyser.**
For Ethel Rosenberg. **Adrienne Rich.**
For F. J. L. (May 7, 1919 - May 2, 1972). **Dona Stein.**
For Gwen—1969. **Margaret Walker.**
for her. **Lucille Clifton.**
For how many years. **Bella Akhmadulina.**
For Judy Garland. **Susan Fromberg Schaeffer.**
For M. S. singing *Fruhlingsglaube* in 1945. **Frances
    Cornford.**
For Malcolm X. **Margaret Walker.**
for "Mamie." **Fayola Kamaria Ama.**
For Michael. **Susan North.**
For Miriam. **Marjorie Oludhe Macgoye.**
For Mrs. W., who would not be Black, White or other.
    Maxine Shaw.
For my Aunt Florence who when praying gives God not only
    her friends' names but also their addresses. **Nancy
    Sullivan.**

For my daughter. **Judith Kazantzis.**
For my daughter's twenty-first birthday. **Jeanne Murray
    Walker.**
For my lover, the artist. **Magdalena Gomez.**
for my mamma and hers. **Jeanette Adams.**
For my number one younger sister. **Eugenie Eersel.**
For my people. **Margaret Walker.**
For my torturer, Lieutenant D_____. **Leila Djabali.**
for Nancy. **Sara Miles.**
For Neruda. **Margarita Aliger.**
For our life is a matter of faith. **Regina Williams.**
For Sally. **Joan Forman.**
For Saundra. **Nikki Giovanni.**
For strong women. **Michelle T. Clinton.**
For the brave young students in Soweto. **Jayne Cortez.**
For the candle light. **Angelina Weld Grimké.**
For the color of my mother. **Cherríe Moraga.**
For the count. **Mae Jackson.**
For the courtesan Ch'ing Lin. **Wu Tsao.**
For the goddess too well known. **Elsa Gidlow.**
For the record (given to my little brother). **Ping Hsin (Hsieh
    Wan-ying).**
For the white poets who would be Indian. **Wendy Rose.**
For Tulani. **Sandra Maria Esteves.**
for us. **Esther Louise.**
'For valour.' **May Herschel-Clarke.**
For water, for air. **Kathryn Hellerstein.**
For Willyce. **Pat Parker.**
Forbidden sweets. **Miriam Dyak.**
Foreign woman. **Rosario Castellanos.**
Forgotten dead, I salute you. **Muriel Stuart.**
Formal feeling. (A sequence for my mother). **Jan Heller
    Levi.**
The fountain. **Ann Stanford.**
Four. **Chaya Shenhav.**
IV. **Enid Vian.**
4 A.M. **Eugenie Eersel.**
Four short poems. **Barbara Szerlip.**
Four ways of writing one poem. **Hemda Roth.**
14th St/new york. (excerpts). **Patricia Jones.**
fourth life. (Driving wheel). **Sherley Anne Williams.**
Fracture. **Lisel Mueller.**
Fragments: mousetrap. **Nikki Grimes.**
Frank Albert & Viola Benzena Owens. **Ntozake Shange.**
Franz, the world is abstract. **Chase Twichell.**
Freedom flesh. **Cheryl Clarke.**
A freedom song for the Black woman. **Carole C.
    Gregory.**
French doors: a vignette. **Alexis De Veaux.**
Frenzy. **Anne Sexton.**
Freshmen. **Maida Stanier.**
Friday. **Phyllis Koestenbaum.**
The Friday ladies of the pay envelope. **Mari Evans.**
Friday noon feelings. **Nia Francisco.**
Friday the 13th Candlelight March. **Adrienne Ingrum.**
the friends, a celebration. **Carol Bergé.**
The frightened flier goes north. **Judith Kazantzis.**
From a trench. **Maud Anna Bell.**

From an asylum: Kathy Chattle to her mother, Ruth Arbeiter. **Anne Stevenson.**
From my guard post watching the world. **Reina María Rodríguez.**
From my mother's home. **Leah Goldberg.**
From sea to shining sea. **June Jordan.**
from the bone, the blood, the rib. **Ann du Cille.**
From the cavities of bones. **Pat Parker.**
From the rain forest. **Desirée Flynn.**
From the sidelines. **Myrtle Bates.**
From water mill. (Quilts). **Barbara Guest.**
Frustration. **Frances Landsman.**
Full moon. **Victoria Sackville-West.**
Full moon in Malta. **Asphodel.**
Fund raising. **Josephine Miles.**
The fundamental man. **Jessica Tarahata Hagedorn.**
A funeral plainsong from a younger woman to an older woman. **Judy Grahn.**
Funky football. **Fareedah Allah.**
Further notes for the alumni bulletin. **Patricia Cumming.**
Furthermore. **Julia Ward Howe.**
A furtive glass. **María Eugenia Vaz Ferreira.**
Furtively. **Nurit Zarchi.**
Fury against the Moslems at Uhud. **Hind bint Utba.**
The future and the ancestor. **Andrée Chedid.**

Galatia Kazanzaki. **Victoria Theodorou.**
The galloping cat. **Stevie Smith.**
Games mammals play. **Judith McCombs.**
Games of earth and light. (excerpt). **Francisca Ossandón.**
The gardener to his god. **Mona Van Duyn.**
The gaze. **Anne Ridler.**
Gemini. **Marie-Elise.**
Genealogy. **Frankie Hucklenbroich.**
Generation. **Rae Armantrout.**
The generation gap. **Fareedah Allah.**
Generations: (Daddy). **Sherley Anne Williams.**
Generations: (Mamma). **Sherley Anne Williams.**
Generations: I. **Sherley Anne Williams.**
Generations: II. **Sherley Anne Williams.**
Genesis. **Concha Michel.**
Genesis and the original sin. (Chicana evolution). **Sylvia Alicia Gonzales.**
Geography. **Laura Tokunaga.**
geography. **Michelene Wandor.**
Gertrude Ederle swims the Channel (August 6, 1926). **Mary Winfrey.**
Gervais. **Margaret Adelaide Wilson.**
Gesture. **Beverly Dahlen.**

Get angry, Compass. **Inoue Michiko.**
Getting down to get over. **June Jordan.**
Getting to know, or stepping out in an entirely different way. **Akua Lezli Hope.**
Ghazals: Homage to Ghalib. (excerpt). **Adrienne Rich.**
Ghost. **Mei-Mei Berssenbrugge.**
The ghouls. **Helen Hamilton.**
Gibraltar. (Not that far). **May Miller.**
The gift. **Rosamund Greenwood.**
Gift from Kenya. **May Miller.**
Gift to a jade. **Anna Wickham.**
Girl held without bail. **Margaret Walker.**
Girl help. **Janet Lewis.**
girl talk. **Jill Gernand.**
The girl who is always with me. **Olga Casanova-Sanchez.**
The girl with the ball. **Eleanor Farjeon.**
Girlfriend. **Tomioka Taeko.**
A girl's song. **Katharine Tynan.**
Give me back. **Chrystos.**
Glamour. **Jan Struther.**
The glassblower. **Joanne de Longchamps.**
Glitter box. **Jana Harris.**
Gloria in excelsis. **Jill Furse.**
Goblin market. (excerpts). **Christina Rossetti.**
God of Mercy. **Kadia Molodowsky.**
Goddamn the empty sky. **Violeta Parra.**
Going back to school. **Maxine Shaw.**
Going north for Christmas. **Rosemary Joseph.**
Going to sleep. **Ann Stanford.**
Gold ladies. **Florence Randal Livesay.**
Gold ring triad. **Madeline DeFrees.**
golden triangle. **Carol Tinker.**
Gone is the sleepgiver. **Penelope Shuttle.**
A good assassination should be quiet. **Mari Evans.**
A good day's work. **Naomi Replansky.**
Goodbye. **Bella Akhmadulina.**
The good-looking boy. **Anonymous.**
The gorge. **Mary Barnard.**
Government injunction restraining Harlem Cosmetic Co. **Josephine Miles.**
Gowanus Canal (because you said look again). **Akua Lezli Hope.**
Gracie. **Faye Kicknosway.**
Gracious goodness. **Marge Piercy.**
The graffiti poet. **Nancy Willard.**
Gramophone tunes. **Eva Dobell.**
grandma. **Jan Clausen.**
Grandmother. **Paula Gunn Allen.**
Grandmother. **Dorothy Livesay.**
The grandmothers. **Mary Oliver.**
Grandmother's prayer while presenting an infant to the sun. **Anonymous.**
A grandson is a hoticeberg. **Margaret Danner.**
Gratitude. **Annette Lynch.**
Grazing. **Mitsui Futabako.**
The great Civil Rights Law (A.D. 1964). **Mari Evans.**
Great expectations. **Margarita Aliger.**
The great mammoth . . . **Iris Zavala.**

The great words. **Alejandra Pizarnik.**
The Greater Friendship Baptist Church. **Carole C. Gregory.**
Greece. (Not that far). **May Miller.**
Greek statues. **Elizabeth Jennings.**
Green ice. **Vivienne Finch.**
Green paradise. **Alejandra Pizarnik.**
A greeting to Lu Hung-Chien. **Li Yeh.**
Grey: the madness. **Adrianne Marcus.**
Grinding vibrato. **Jayne Cortez.**
Groves II. **Ellen Marie Bissert.**
Guatemala. **Frances C. Chung.**
Gullible. **Margarita Cota-Cárdenas.**
Gulls. **Frances Gill.**
Gulls aground. **Betty Parvin.**
The gun is back. **Evelyn Posamentier.**

Haiti. **Amina Baraka.**
The Hako. (excerpt). **Anonymous.**
Half-life: copies to all concerned. **Marie Ponsot.**
Hand fantasy. **Gerda S. Norvig.**
Hanging the pictures. **Madeline DeFrees.**
hangover. **Michèle Roberts.**
Hannya. (excerpt). **Carol Tinker.**
Happy and tipsy, to the tune ''A dream song.''
    Li Ch'ing-chao.
Hard times cotton mill girls. **Anonymous.**
Hard times in the mill. **Anonymous.**
The hare is vanished. **Jill Furse.**
harlem/soweto. **Safiya Henderson.**
The harmony of sirens. **Kathleen Teague.**
The harp. **Dulce María Loynaz.**
Harriet. **Audre Lorde.**
Hartico. **Anna Lee Walters.**
Harvest. **Celia Randall.**
Harvesting wheat for the public share. **Li Chu.**
Hatred. **Gwendolyn B. Bennett.**
Hats. **Jean Pedrick.**
He forgets me. **Magaly Sánchez.**
He got me the first time. **Magdalena Gomez.**
he is merely socially inept. **Michèle Roberts.**
He said: Mostly I feel like a tractor. **Natasha Morgan.**
He saw. **Chrystos.**
He stared at me. **Anonymous.**
He the beloved. (excerpt). **Qorratu'l-Ayn
    (Umm-i Salma).**
He went for a soldier. **Ruth Comfort Mitchell.**
Headdress. **Sappho.**
Heart and mind. **Edith Sitwell.**
The heart of a woman. **Georgia Douglas Johnson.**

The heat in Medellin. **Mary Crow.**
Heavenly Jerusalem, Jerusalem of the earth. **Leah
    Goldberg.**
Hector floating in the night. **Gladys Zaldivar.**
Helen. **Hilda Doolittle.**
Helen grown old. **Janet Lewis.**
Helen meditates before her portrait as a woman. **Lilian
    Bowes Lyon.**
Helen, the sad queen. **Janet Lewis.**
hell. **Michelene Wandor.**
He-man. **Michelene Wandor.**
Her 'allowance'! **Lillian Gard.**
Her dancing days. **Anna Adams.**
her immaculate house. **Karen Bunting.**
Her kind. **Anne Sexton.**
Her rooms. **Susan Efros.**
her song. **Michele Stepto.**
Her waking. (Night-pieces: for a child). **Adrienne Rich.**
Hera Hera Hera. **Rochelle Owens.**
hera of the locker room. **Mary Winfrey.**
Here lies a prisoner. **Charlotte Mew.**
Heritage. **Gwendolyn B. Bennett.**
Heritage. **Lorna Dee Cervantes.**
The hermaphrodite's song. **Lorna Mitchell.**
Heron of oblivion. **Carol Tinker.**
Hester's song. **Toi Derricotte.**
Hey you death. (A woman is talking to death). **Judy Grahn.**
Hiawatha's pancake. **Maida Stanier.**
High holy days. **Jane Shore.**
High waving heather. **Emily Brontë.**
High-heeled boots. **Marguerite Johansen.**
Hill excursion. **Leah Goldberg.**
The hills. **Susan Fromberg Schaeffer.**
Hills of salt. **Dahlia Ravikovitch.**
Hinterland. **Margaret Stanley-Wrench.**
Hiram Powers' ''Greek Slave.'' **Elizabeth Barrett
    Browning.**
His answer. **Clara Ann Thompson.**
His own maniac self. **Akua Lezli Hope.**
His wife. **Shirley Kaufman.**
His wife. **Rachel.**
historical footnote. **Mary Winfrey.**
A history of lesbianism. **Judy Grahn.**
History of Unchi. **Elizabeth Cook-Lynn.**
History: 13. **Sharon Olds.**
The Holy Land. (Not that far). **May Miller.**
Homage. **Sharon Olds.**
Homage to Lucille, Dr. Lord-Heinstein. **Marge Piercy.**
Home, and I've. **Marilyn Hacker.**
Homecoming. **Martha Collins.**
Homecoming. **Eleni Fourtouni.**
Homesickness. **Marina Tsvetayeva.**
The homestead. **Melpo Axiote.**
''Honeysuckle was the saddest odor of all, I think.''
    Thadious M. Davis.
Hoodoo Moma. **Luisah Teish.**
Hootchie Kootchie man. **Cynthia Kraman Genser.**
The hope I dreamed of. **Christina Rossetti.**

Horror. **Mary Elizabeth Coleridge.**
Horse and rider. **Judith McCombs.**
The horses of instruction, the tigers of wrath. **Judith Kazantzis.**
The hospital visitor. **Alys Fane Trotter.**
The hour in April. (Sequence from blue to blue). **Kristina McGrath.**
House in Meudon. **Margarita Aliger.**
The house of desire. **Sherley Anne Williams.**
The house of fecundity. **Sharon Olds.**
Houseplant. **Felicity Napier.**
Housewife. **Susan Fromberg Schaeffer.**
Housework. **Amanda Berenguer.**
How a girl got her Chinese name. **Nellie Wong.**
How can we end human suffering. **Carol Tinker.**
How can you stare out at the Neva. **Anna Akhmatova.**
How did it happen? **Jenny Mastoraki.**
How do I differ from a woman with a flower. **Bella Akhmadulina.**
How Hong Kong was destroyed. **Dahlia Ravikovitch.**
How I came to be a graduate student. **Wendy Rose.**
How I managed to square the circle of dreams in the shape of a window at the top of the stairs in a tenement house. **Jenny Mastoraki.**
How love, when it has been acquired, may be kept. (De arte honeste amandi). **Linda Gregerson.**
How rudely you speak to me. **Fina García Marruz.**
How to determine your birthday upon waking in a strange place which is more than likely your own bed. **Barbara Szerlip.**
How to get by. **Maureen Owen.**
How we love now. **Stephanie Strickland.**
How will you call me, brother. **Mari Evans.**
Humanitarian. **Kathleen Spivack.**
Humility. **Marie Luise Kaschnitz.**
Hunger. **Gaspara Stampa.**
HUSH, HONEY. **Fareedah Allah.**
Hymn to earth. **Elinor Wylie.**
The hymns my mother sang. **Wendy Stevens.**
Hypocrite women. **Denise Levertov.**

I

I also sing of myself. **Soleida Ríos.**
I am a black woman. **Mari Evans.**
I am a union woman. **Molly (Aunt) Jackson.**
I am a woman. (excerpt). **Akhtar Amiri.**
I am America's child . . . (excerpt). **Milagros González.**
I AM NOT MY SISTER' KEEPER: I AM MY SISTER. **Regina Williams.**
I am the weaver. **Abbey Lincoln (Aminata Moseka).**

I argue my case. (Notes from the first year). **Susan Saxe.**
I ask silence. **Alejandra Pizarnik.**
I, Boudica. **Judy Grahn.**
I bring roses. **Evelyn Posamentier.**
I canned them pears and I canned them pears. **Jana Harris.**
I can't hold you and I can't leave you. **Juana Inés de la Cruz (Sister).**
I Ching. **Jacqueline Lapidus.**
I come up smiling. **Carol Simone.**
I do not like it here. **Emily Katherine Harris.**
I do not love thee. **Caroline Norton.**
I do not want to be your weeping woman. **Alison Boodson.**
I done got so thirsty that my mouth waters at the thought of rain. **Patricia Jones.**
I dream. **Anonymous.**
I drift in the wind. **Ingrid Jonker.**
I emptied. **Yona Wallach.**
I escape. **Teresita Fernández.**
I expected my skin and my blood to ripen. **Wendy Rose.**
I feel so good I ain't written a fuckin' thing in a year. **Chocolate Waters.**
I feel sorry for the garden. **Forūgh Farrokhzād.**
I fire at the face of the country where I was born. **Shiraishi Kazuko.**
I followed a path. **Pat Parker.**
I forget. **Yoshihara Sachiko.**
I hate the company bosses. **Sarah Ogan Gunning.**
I have bowed before the sun. **Anna Lee Walters.**
I have no poem for you father. **Eleni Fourtouni.**
I have the right. **Ana Blandiana.**
I HEAR A RUMBLING . . . **Margaret Walker.**
I help my mother move out of her old house in the country. **Jane Augustine.**
I like to think of Harriet Tubman. **Susan Griffin.**
I live in Cuba. **Lourdes Casal.**
I looked for a sounding-board. **Henriette Roland-Holst.**
I love my love. **Helen Adam.**
I love you . . . Why do you hate me? **Rosalía de Castro.**
I met my Solitude. **Naomi Replansky.**
I never talk of hunger. **Lizette Woodworth Reese.**
I pray to the light in the window. **Anna Akhmatova.**
I rode with my darling . . . **Stevie Smith.**
I said to poetry. **Alice Walker.**
I saw thee, child, one summer's day. **Emily Brontë.**
i shoulda told you. **Geraldine Kudaka.**
I sit and sew. **Alice Ruth Moore Dunbar-Nelson.**
I sit and wait for beauty. **Mae V. Cowdery.**
I speak in an illusion. **Judy Lucero.**
I swear. **Bella Akhmadulina.**
I thought: you're my enemy. **Bella Akhmadulina.**
I told you when we started this relationship what to expect. **Stephanie Smolensky.**
I too am now among the others. **Fina García Marruz.**
I unsealed my veins: unstoppable. **Marina Tsvetayeva.**
I used to think. **Chirlane McCray.**
I walk in the history of my people. **Chrystos.**
I wanna make freedom. **Amina Baraka.**
I want for my name . . . **Ángela María Dávila.**

I want to die while you love me. **Georgia Douglas Johnson.**
I want to write. **Margaret Walker.**
I will work with my hands I will not work with my hands.
    Michele Stepto.
I, woman. **Irma McClaurin.**
I would like. **Shirley Geok-Lin Lim.**
I write poems. **Gloria Fuertes.**
Icarus on wheels. **Adrien Stoutenburg.**
Icarus to his father. **Barbara Szerlip.**
The iconography of childhood. (excerpts). **Sherley Anne
    Williams.**
Identification card. **Eliana Rivera.**
Idyl: sunrise. **Henrietta Cordelia Ray.**
Idyl: sunset. **Henrietta Cordelia Ray.**
If everything. **Margarita Aliger.**
If I come. **Susan Wallbank.**
If, Lord, thy love for me is strong. **Teresa of Ávila.**
If no revolution come. **Helen Dunmore.**
If you saw a Negro lady. **June Jordan.**
If you think with fire. **Hsiung Hung.**
Ikhnaton's night. **Ágnes Nemes Nagy.**
I'll sing, although I'm loath to make this plea. **Beatritz de
    Dia.**
Illumination. **Simone Weil.**
Illuminations 2. **Leah Goldberg.**
I'm a dreamer. **Kattie M. Cumbo.**
I'm a little woman who's happy to slave. **Kibkarjuk.**
I'm going to sleep. **Alfonsina Storni.**
I'm really very fond. **Alice Walker.**
I'm taking off . . .   **Barbro Backberger.**
Image. **Genevieve Taggard.**
Images. **Grace Butcher.**
Images. **Kathleen Raine.**
Images emerging. **Marge Piercy.**
Immigration. **Evelyn Posamentier.**
The impossible is no hindrance. **Shlomit Cohen.**
impressions. **Fay Chiang.**
Impressions at dawn. **Virginia Gilbert.**
Improvisation on lines by Spicer, No. 2. **Kathleen Fraser.**
In a dream. **Eleni Fourtouni.**
In a restaurant, 1917. **Eleanour Norton.**
In a shattered mirror. **Anna Akhmatova.**
In a V. A. D. pantry. **Alberta Vickridge.**
In a very, very quiet voice. **Nancy Bacelo.**
In an artist's studio. **Christina Rossetti.**
In answer to a lady who advised retirement. **Mary Wortley
    Montagu, Lady.**
In answer to what he said. **Jan Zaleski.**
In cahoots. **Ellen Wittlinger.**
In defense of circuses. **Adrianne Marcus.**
"In dejection near Naples." **Virginia Moore.**
In honour of that high and mighty Princess Queen Elizabeth
    of happy memory. **Anne Bradstreet.**
In Indiana. **Mary Mackey.**
In intimacy there's a secret place. **Anna Akhmatova.**
In lofty scorn. **Sylvia Pankhurst.**
In memoriam: Rev. Martin Luther King, Jr. (Part one). **June
    Jordan.**

In memory, 1978. **Judith Kazantzis.**
In memory of Francois Rabelais. **Yunna Moritz.**
In memory of my Arab grandmother. **Evelyn Arcad Zerbe.**
In mind. **Denise Levertov.**
In Mrs. N's palace. **Honor Moore.**
In my father's cabin. **Kathy Engel.**
In my taboo. **Janet Hamill.**
In praise of Aphrodite. **Marine Tsvetayeva.**
In praise of dialectics. **Nancy Morejón.**
In praise of old women. **Marya Fiamengo.**
In search of the messiahs of nativism. (Chicana evolution).
    Sylvia Alicia Gonzales.
In sleep. **Alice Meynell.**
In that green field. **Rivka Miriam.**
In that time when it was not the fashion. **Tess Gallagher.**
In the alley: June. **Sheila Nickerson.**
In the backs. **Frances Cornford.**
in the bar. **Michèle Roberts.**
In the beginning. **Valerie Sinason.**
In the blue distance. **Nelly Sachs.**
In the dry riverbed. **Zelda.**
In the evening. **Anna Akhmatova.**
In the high stars are all the souls. **Anna Akhmatova.**
In the home of the scholar Wu Su-chiang from Hsin-An, I
    saw two psalteries of the late Sung General Hsieh Fang-
    tê. **Wu Tsao.**
In the inmost recesses. **Teresa of Ávila.**
In the Jerusalem Hills. (excerpt). **Leah Goldberg.**
In the middle. **Abbey Lincoln (Aminata Moseka).**
In the middle of a life. **Linda Pastan.**
In the mirror. **Enid Vián.**
In the morning. **Jayne Cortez.**
In the old city: Dubrovnik. **Joan LaBombard.**
In the outhouse. (Camp notes). **Mitsuye Yamada.**
In the radiotherapy unit. **Margaret Stanley-Wrench.**
In the sea of tears. **Naomi Replansky.**
In the shallows. **Barbara Wolf Booth.**
In the town with cat-shaped maze. **Kanai Mieko.**
In the vital process (1964). **Concha Michel.**
In the year of the tiger. **Dona Stein.**
In time like air. **May Sarton.**
In time of war. **Alice Meynell.**
In time of war. **Lesbia Thanet.**
In twilight. **Yunna Moritz.**
Inanna exalted. (excerpts). **Enheduanna.**
An incident. **Mary H. J. Henderson.**
Indications that one's love has returned. (De arte honeste
    amandi). **Linda Gregerson.**
Indulgence and accidents. **Judith Hemschemeyer.**
Inertia. **Kirti Chaudhari.**
Inertia. **Vivienne Finch.**
inflation. **Margaret Porter.**
Inform me. **Emily Katherine Harris.**
Inheritance. **Elizabeth Keeler.**
Inquietude. **Pauli Murray.**
Inscription for a wayside spring. **Frances Cornford.**
The insect kitchen. **Nicki Jackowska.**
Inspiration. **Anna Wickham.**

Integrity. **Adrienne Rich.**
Interior dawn. **Elsie Alvarado de Ricord.**
Internal geography - Part One. **Joan Gibbs.**
Intimate. **Gabriela Mistral.**
An introduction. **Kamala Das.**
The introduction. **Anne Finch, Countess of Winchilsea.**
Introduction and apology. **Georgina Herrera.**
Introspection. **Christina Rossetti.**
The invisible Carmel. **Zelda.**
Invitation au Festin. **Aelfrida Tillyard.**
The invitation in it. **Kay Boyle.**
Invocation. **Rochelle Nameroff.**
Invocation. **Kathleen Raine.**
Iridescent child. **Nia Francisco.**
The Irish patriarch. **Ruth Pitter.**
Irish prisoners of war. **Michèle Roberts.**
Is this the end? **Christina Rossetti.**
Isabel Rawsthorne standing in a street in Soho (the portrait by
    Frances Bacon). **Alexandra Grilikhes.**
Ishtar or the explosion in a shingle factory. **Carol Tinker.**
Issue. **Maxine Shaw.**
It is deep. **Carolyn M. Rodgers.**
It is not likely now. **Frances Bellerby.**
It isn't that you don't understand. **Susan North.**
It may be. **Alfonsina Storni.**
it was as if. **Fay Chiang.**
It was gentle. **Chedva Harakavy.**
Ita. **Yolanda Ulloa.**
Italy. (Not that far). **May Miller.**
It's all been taken away. **Anna Akhmatova.**
it's all in the name. **Esther Louise.**
It's all the same. **Thadious M. Davis.**
It's Buffalo, Boise, or Boston this time. **Adrianne Marcus.**
It's not the same. **Fukunaka Tomoko.**
IT'S RAINING. **Yolanda Blanco.**
It's still early. **Nancy Bacelo.**
I've never got anything. **Gloria Fuertes.**

J

Jail-life walk. **Judy Lucero.**
The jailor. **Sylvia Plath.**
Jake. **Mari Evans.**
Jamila. **Nāzik al-Malā'ika.**
Janis. **Mari Evans.**
January. **Molly Vaux.**
January moon. **Cleva Solís.**
January 23, 1976   the axe. **Miriam Dyak.**
Jealousie is the rage of a man. **Anne Finch, Countess of
    Winchilsea.**
Jerusalem notebook. **Shirley Kaufman.**

Jessie Mitchell's mother. **Gwendolyn Brooks.**
Jesukin. **Saint Ita.**
Jesus people. (Jezebel: her progress). **Gillian E.
    Hanscombe.**
Jesus was crucified or: it must be deep (an epic pome).
    Carolyn M. Rodgers.
Jezebel: her progress. (excerpt). **Gillian E. Hanscombe.**
The Jingo-woman. **Helen Hamilton.**
Joan Brown, about her painting. **Kathleen Fraser.**
Job interview. **Kate Ellen Braverman.**
Joining the colours. **Katharine Tynan.**
Jonah's lament. **Olga Orozco.**
jonestown or the disco. **Ntozake Shange.**
Joseph and the magi. **Griselda Scott.**
Joseph's coat. **Lynda Koolish.**
Journal. (excerpt). **Gayl Jones.**
Journey. **Mary Barnard.**
Journey. **Diane Wakoski.**
Joy. **Clarissa Scott Delany.**
Joy in Provence. **May Sarton.**
A joyful mother of children. **Anonymous.**
July 1st, 1916. **Aimee Byng Scott.**
July 1914. **Anna Akhmatova.**
June. **Elaine Feinstein.**
June, 1915. **Charlotte Mew.**
June 10. **Magdalena de Rodríguez.**
Just one in a series. **Mae Jackson.**
Juxtaposer. **Lois Elaine Griffith.**

K

Kadia the young mother speaks. **Jessie Sampter.**
Kaiser Hospital trilogy: three women at the mercy of
    unknown gods. **Susan Efros.**
Kaleidoscope. **Rota Silverstrini.**
Kathe Kollwitz. **Muriel Rukeyser.**
Keeping hair. **Ramona C. Wilson.**
Keeping still, mountain. **Willyce Kim.**
Keeping up with the signs. **Madeline DeFrees.**
Kensington gardens. **Viviane Verne.**
Key West (Triple ballade with enjambed refrain, plus en-
    voy). **Judith Moffett.**
Khmer woman. **Cate Abbe.**
the kind of man he is. **Lucille Clifton.**
Kindness. **Sylvia Plath.**
Kinfolk. **Lina de Feria.**
Kissie Lee. **Margaret Walker.**
the kitchen window. **Jan Clausen.**
kitchenette building. **Gwendolyn Brooks.**
The Kiwi bird. **Nina Cassian.**

Kleis. **Mary Winfrey.**
the knife & the bread. **Olga Broumas.**
Knowing. **Mary Coghill.**
Knoxville, Tennessee. **Nikki Giovanni.**
Krinio. **Rita Boumi-Pappas.**
Kwa mama zetu waliotuzaa. **Sonia Sanchez.**

L

Labor pains. **Yosano Akiko.**
The ladder. **Leonora Speyer.**
Lady and the wolf. **Dona Stein.**
Lady in waiting. **Ann du Cille.**
Lady, Lady. **Anne Spencer.**
Lady Lazarus. **Sylvia Plath.**
Lady of miracles. **Nina Cassian.**
Lady, sister: for Janis Joplin. **Adrianne Marcus.**
Ladybird (a memory of my mother). **Ingrid Jonker.**
Lament. (Medicine song). **Paula Gunn Allen.**
Lament. (Of fruit whose black seed fire). **Olga Broumas.**
Lament. **Brenda Chamberlain.**
Lament. **Eleni Fourtouni.**
Lament. **Akua Lezli Hope.**
Lament. **Malkia M'buzi.**
Lament. **Zeb-un-Nissa.**
Lament for a dictator. **Juanita Peirse.**
Lament for a maidenhead. **Sappho.**
lament for my grandmother on the day of the winter solstice.
      Michèle Roberts.
Lament of Heloise. **Margaret Willy.**
The lament of the demobilised. **Vera Brittain.**
The lamentation. (excerpt). **Ts'ai Yen.**
Lamplight. **May Wedderburn Cannan.**
The land. (excerpt). **Victoria Sackville-West.**
The landing. **Robin Becker.**
Landing. **Antonia Pozzi.**
Landing. **Molly Vaux.**
Landscape. **Anne Hébert.**
lank pier. **Carol Tinker.**
Laocoon is the name of the figure. **Marge Piercy.**
Largely because of coincidence and partly because of
      chance, I have taken up a new address at 47th Street and
      Avenue F. **Diane Wakoski.**
The lark above the trenches. **Muriel Elsie Graham.**
Larks. **Katharine Tynan.**
Last brightness. **Leah Goldberg.**
Last conversation with Rolando Escardó. **Carilda Oliver
      Labra.**
The last day I live in a strange house. **Bella Akhmadulina.**
A last dialog on the left. **June Jordan.**
The last enemy. **Elisabeth Cluer.**

Last leave. **Eileen Newton.**
The last migration: Amherst, Mass., Winter 1981. **Jeanne
      Murray Walker.**
The last years. **Irene Claremont de Castillejo.**
Late. **Marie Ponsot.**
Later. **Elaine Dallman.**
later i'll say. **Lucille Clifton.**
Later, to Jean-Pierre. **Dorothy Ann Brown.**
Laughing, exulting and rebellious. **Bella Akhmadulina.**
Lawd, dese colored chillum. **Fareedah Allah.**
The leafy day. **Diana Witherby.**
Leap in the dark. **Roberta Hill.**
Learning about things. **Rosario Castellanos.**
Learning to read. **Frances Ellen Watkins Harper.**
Leave in 1917. **Lilian M. Anderson.**
Leaves. **Malka Heifetz Tussman.**
Leaving my daughter's house. **Maxine Kumin.**
Leaving, the sepulcre city. **Virginia Gilbert.**
Lecture under the moose. **Madeline DeFrees.**
Leda. **Lilian Bowes Lyon.**
Leeds weekend. **Michèle Roberts.**
Legacies. **Nikki Giovanni.**
Lena Lime observes Ash Wednesday in New York City '77.
      Lois Elaine Griffith.
Lena Lime thinking she up close but being far away. **Lois
      Elaine Griffith.**
Lenore. **Jill Gernand.**
The leopard. **Odette Tchernine.**
Lessons. **Grace Wade.**
Let no charitable hope. **Elinor Wylie.**
Let the light enter. **Frances Ellen Watkins Harper.**
Let them ask their husbands. **Dilys Laing.**
A letter. **Elsie Alvarado de Ricord.**
A letter. **Shao Fei-fei.**
A letter. **Marina Tsvetayeva.**
Letter from an exile. **Adrianne Marcus.**
A letter from Ealing Broadway Station. **Aelfrida Tillyard.**
letter from point lobos. **Carol Bergé.**
Letter to an unborn daughter. **Summer Brenner.**
Letter to Connie in the Maine woods. **Virginia de Araújo.**
A letter to Dafnis April: 2d 1685. **Anne Finch, Countess of
      Winchilsea.**
A letter to her husband, absent on public employment. **Anne
      Bradstreet.**
A letter to Lady T'ao Ch'iu, to the tune "Walking through
      the sedges." **Ch'iu Chin.**
Letter to my children. **Anne Wilkinson.**
letter to my father . . . a solidarity long overdue. **Safiya
      Henderson.**
Letter to my sister. **Anne Spencer.**
Letter to Rafael: 1966. **Jessica Tarahata Hagedorn.**
Letters from three women. **Wendy Battin.**
Letters written when night grows. (excerpts). **Claudia Lars.**
levelling with death. **Michèle Roberts.**
Liberty and peace, a poem. (excerpt). **Phillis Wheatley.**
Liebfraumilch. **Alice Karle.**
Lies. **Kate Ellen Braverman.**
Life at war. **Denise Levertov.**

Life in the Palace. **Hua Jui, Lady.**
Life story. **Tomioka Taeko.**
Life-hook. **Juana de Ibarbourou.**
Light. **Elizabeth Keeler.**
The light is my delight. **Zelda.**
Light up thy halls! 'Tis closing day. **Emily Brontë.**
The lighthouse at Acre. **Pamela Melnikoff.**
Lightning storm. **Jane Miller.**
Like a field waiting. **Raquel Chalfi.**
Like a white stone in the depths of a well. **Anna Akhmatova.**
Like I am to no one. **Cherríe Moraga.**
likeness. **Jan Clausen.**
Lilith. **Linda Gregg.**
Lilith of the Wildwood, of the Fair Places. **Susan Sherman.**
Linda, come down. **Carol Simone.**
Lineage. **Margaret Walker.**
Lines. **Ada.**
Lines composed in a wood on a windy day. **Anne Brontë.**
Lines, suggested on reading 'An appeal to Christian women of the South,' by A. E. Grimké. **Ada.**
Lines to accompany flowers for Eve (who took heroin, then sleeping pills and who lies in a New York hospital). **Carolyn Kizer.**
Lines upon waking. (Four short poems). **Barbara Szerlip.**
The linnet in the rocky dells. **Emily Brontë.**
Linseed oil and dreams. **Judy Dothard Simmons.**
Lioness asleep. **Babette Deutsch.**
Listen. **Sophia de Mello Breyner Andresen.**
Listen. **Jessica Tarahata Hagedorn.**
Listening to the story of your life. **Alexandra Grilikhes.**
Little girl, my string bean, my lovely woman. **Anne Sexton.**
Little girl talk. **Delores S. Williams.**
The little girls. **Dilys Laing.**
A little girl's dream world. **Della Burt.**
The little old lady in lavender silk. **Dorothy Parker.**
Live. **Anne Sexton.**
The lives we invite to flower among us flower beyond us. **Wendy Battin.**
Living in sin. **Adrienne Rich.**
Living in the summer mountains. **Yü Hsüan-chi.**
Living together. **Tomioka Taeko.**
Living where you are. **Laura Beausoleil.**
La Llorona, Crying Lady of the Creekbeds, 483 years old, and aging. **Victoria Moreno.**
Locale. **Penelope Shuttle.**
The logical mind of the martyr. **Elena Wilkinson.**
Lola. **Yona Wallach.**
London in war. **Helen Dircks.**
The lonely death. **Adelaide Crapsey.**
Lonely man. **Denise Levertov.**
Long division: a tribal history. **Wendy Rose.**
The long fingers of 1956. **Jane Miller.**
Long John Nelson and Sweetie Pie. **Margaret Walker.**
long road rhythm. **Nzadi Zimele-Keita (Michelle McMichael).**

A look at a bee. **Leah Goldberg.**
The look of success. **Teru Kanazawa.**
Looking at quilts. **Marge Piercy.**
Looking for a country under its original name. **Colleen J. McElroy.**
Looking for light and finding the sea. **Elizabeth Keeler.**
Loomit. **Adrienne Ingrum.**
Loon lord and master O jack pollock. **Rochelle Owens.**
The Lord Buddha. **Hayashi Fumiko.**
The loss. **Anne Finch, Countess of Winchilsea.**
The lost army. **Margery Lawrence.**
The lost baby poem. **Lucille Clifton.**
The lost caress. **Alfonsina Storni.**
The lost continent. **Jenny Joseph.**
Lost copper. **Wendy Rose.**
The lost tribe. **Ruth Pitter.**
Lot's daughter. **Dilys Laing.**
Love. **Edith Södergran.**
Love flows from God. **Mechthild von Magdeburg.**
Love, Grandma. **Lois Bissell Jircitano.**
Love letter. **Carole C. Gregory.**
Love, 1916. **May Wedderburn Cannan.**
The love of nuns. (De arte honeste amandi). **Linda Gregerson.**
Love poem. **Bobbie Bishop.**
Love poem. **Audre Lorde.**
A love poem. **Jeanne Sirotkin.**
Love poem/for a capricorn. **Susan Sherman.**
Love poem from an unfaithful lady. **Jessica Tarahata Hagedorn.**
A love poem to an African freedom fighter. **Rosemari Mealy.**
Love poem to the earth. **Fanchon Lewis.**
The love sequence. **Sandra M. Gilbert.**
The love sickness. (The love sequence). **Sandra M. Gilbert.**
Love song. **Anonymous.**
A love song. **Else Lasker-Schüler.**
A love song of the Empress Wu. **Wu Tsê-t'ien.**
Love song to King Shu-Suen. **Kubatum.**
Love songs. **Mina Loy.**
Love that gives us ourselves. **Stephanie Strickland.**
Love that I bear. **Hilda Doolittle.**
Love which frees. **Gloria Fuertes.**
Love-charm song. **Anonymous.**
Love-making. **Anonymous.**
Lovers. **Alejandra Pizarnik.**
Lovesigns. **Akua Lezli Hope.**
The Lowell factory girl. **Anonymous.**
The lucky chance. Song. **Aphra Behn.**
Lucy taking birth. **Diana Scott.**
Lullaby. **Anonymous.**
The lullaby of the snow. **Anonymous.**
The lunar games. **Eeva-Liisa Manner.**
Lunatics. **Raquel Chalfi.**
Lunch hour. **Robin Morgan.**

Machine. **Rochelle Nameroff.**
"Machismo is part of our culture." **Marcela Christine Lucero-Trujillo.**
Mad Rosalinde. **Shulamit Apfel.**
Madeira. (Not that far). **May Miller.**
Madeleine in church. (excerpt). **Charlotte Mew.**
Madeleine's dreads. **Alexis De Veaux.**
Madonna. **Blanca Varela.**
Madonna of the hills. **Paula Gunn Allen.**
Madrid. **Pai Wei.**
madwoman at Rodmell. **Michèle Roberts.**
Mae, not to change . . . **Bobbie Louise Hawkins.**
Magalu. **Helene Johnson.**
Magdalen the great mammal. **Katerina Anghelaki-Rooke.**
Magdalene. **Naomi Clark.**
The magic apple tree. **Elaine Feinstein.**
Magnificat. **Chana Bloch.**
Magnificat. **Michèle Roberts.**
Making adjustments. **Anita Endrezze-Danielson.**
Making love to Alice. **M. F. Hershman.**
Making the difference. **Karen Brodine.**
Making the painting. **Jeanne Murray Walker.**
Malcolm. **Sonia Sanchez.**
A man. **Nina Cassian.**
The man root. **Shiraishi Kazuko.**
Mannessahs. **Carolyn M. Rodgers.**
A man's requirements. **Elizabeth Barrett Browning.**
Many die here. **Gayl Jones.**
Map (for Matthew). **Dona Stein.**
Marble busts. (How I managed to square the circle of dreams in the shape of a window at the top of the stairs in a tenement house). **Jenny Mastoraki.**
March. **Molly Vaux.**
The march of the women. **Cicely Hamilton.**
Marginal. **Judith Kazantzis.**
Maria de Las Rosas. **Becky Birtha.**
Maria R. **Rita Boumi-Pappas.**
Marina. **Lucha Corpi.**
Marina mother. (Marina). **Lucha Corpi.**
Marina virgin. (Marina). **Lucha Corpi.**
The marionette. **Dahlia Ravikovitch.**
The marital problem I. **Sonja Åkesson.**
Maritimes. **Penelope Shuttle.**
Mark of recognition. **Kiki Dimoula.**
The marriage. **Maxine Kumin.**
Marriage. **Marianne Moore.**
Married love. **Kuan Tao-shêng.**
Martha. **Brenda Connor-Bey.**
Mary Stuart to James Bothwell. **Edith Sitwell.**
The mask. **Irma McClaurin.**
Mask and essence. **Jean Overton Fuller.**

masochism one. **Michèle Roberts.**
masochism two/man of iron. **Michèle Roberts.**
Masquerade. **Carolyn M. Rodgers.**
Maternal grief. **Kathleen Raine.**
Maternal love triumphant or, song of the virtuous female spider. **Ruth Pitter.**
Maternity. (Natural birth). **Toi Derricotte.**
Maternity. **Alice Meynell.**
Matinal. **Marguerite Clerbout.**
A matter of life and death. (excerpt). **Anne Ridler.**
Maturity. **Isabelle Vuckovic.**
The maudlin mist of morning. **Audrey Lee.**
Maxims. **Honor Johnson.**
May Day. **Charlotte Mitchell.**
May, 1915. **Charlotte Mew.**
May 10th. **Maxine Kumin.**
Me and my chauffeur blues. **Memphis Minnie.**
The meal. **Sharon Olds.**
Mechanical doll. **Forūgh Farrokhzād.**
Medea in Athens. (excerpt). **Augusta Webster.**
Medicine song. **Paula Gunn Allen.**
Medieval. (Quilts). **Barbara Guest.**
Medieval tapestry and questions. **Diane Wakoski.**
Meditation at Kew. **Anna Wickham.**
Meditation on friendship: getting lost in the woods with Deena—Jamesville, NY. **Judith Minty.**
Meditation on the brink. **Rosario Castellanos.**
The medium. **Elaine Feinstein.**
The meeting. **Louise Bogan.**
The meeting. **Nicki Jackowska.**
meeting. **Mary Winfrey.**
Meeting-house Hill. **Amy Lowell.**
Melinda on an insippid beauty. **Anne Finch, Countess of Winchilsea.**
Mellisandra. **Harriet Rose.**
A melody. **Lan Ling.**
Memorial. **Sonia Sanchez.**
Memory. **Dahlia Ravikovitch.**
A memory. **Margaret Sackville.**
Memory album. **Adrien Stoutenburg.**
Memory of the sun faints in my heart. **Anna Akhmatova.**
Memory's voice. **Anna Akhmatova.**
Men's impotence. **Anonymous.**
Menses: a seasonal. **Pamela Victorine.**
Meron. **Shirley Kaufman.**
Message. **Carolyn Forché.**
Message. **Renata Pallottini.**
The messenger. **Frances Horovitz.**
Mexico. **Lucha Corpi.**
mi chinita poem. **Patricia Jones.**
Micah. **Margaret Walker.**
Michaelmas daisies. **Rumer Godden.**
Midday in Gantiadi. **Yunna Moritz.**
Midnight. **Jen Jui.**
Midnight cold. **Yunna Moritz.**
Midsummer. **Patricia Cumming.**
Midway. **Naomi Long Madgett.**
Migration. **Pinkie Gordon Lane.**

Mill. **Diane Wakoski.**
The mill mother's lament. **Ella May Wiggins.**
Millicent Fredericks. **Gabrielle Daniels.**
Milton. **Henrietta Cordelia Ray.**
The mind is an enchanting thing. **Marianne Moore.**
Minor poem. **Phyllis Koestenbaum.**
Minority. **Judy Dothard Simmons.**
The minority: 1917. **May O'Rourke.**
Miranda's birthspell. **Judith Johnson Sherwin.**
Miriam: the Red Sea. (Searching/not searching). **Muriel Rukeyser.**
The mirror. **Rosemary Dobson.**
Mirror. **Sylvia Plath.**
Mirror. **Tada Chimako.**
Mis' Lou. **Jacquelyn Furgus Hunter.**
Miss Rosie. **Lucille Clifton.**
missed you. **Jeanette Adams.**
The missing ingredient. **Angela de Hoyos.**
Mission Street bus. **Susan Kennedy Calhoun.**
Missionaries in the jungle. **Linda Piper.**
Mistress of the animals. **Alexandra Grilikhes.**
A mock interrogation. (A woman is talking to death). **Judy Grahn.**
Modern secrets. **Shirley Geok-Lin Lim.**
Móir hatching. **Nuala ní Dhomhnaill.**
The mole. **Sharon Olds.**
Molly Means. **Margaret Walker.**
A Mona Lisa. **Angelina Weld Grimké.**
The monk in the kitchen. **Anna Hempstead Branch.**
The monkey house and other cages. (excerpts). **Irena Klepfisz.**
Monna Innominata: a sonnet of sonnets. **Christina Rossetti.**
Monovacia. **Eleni Fourtouni.**
Month of January. **Frankie Armstrong.**
Montserrate. **Mary Crow.**
Moon. **Frances Horovitz.**
The moon and the yew tree. **Sylvia Plath.**
The moon is teaching Bible. **Zelda.**
Moon metals: inventing a new daughter. **Wendy Rose.**
Moonshot: 1969. **Paula Gunn Allen.**
Moorhens. **Jean Kenward.**
More. **Sara Miles.**
More and more. **Margaret Atwood.**
More of a corpse than a woman. **Muriel Rukeyser.**
Morning. **Julia Vinograd.**
The morning after . . . love. **Kattie M. Cumbo.**
Morning at Salt River Day School. **Rita Garitano.**
Morning in Argentina. **Colleen J. McElroy.**
Morning is a time for miracles. **Audre Lorde.**
morning mirror. **Lucille Clifton.**
Morning song. **Sylvia Plath.**
Mornings remembering last nights. **Olga Broumas.**
Mortal combat. **Mary Elizabeth Coleridge.**
Mortal girl. **Muriel Rukeyser.**
The mosiac hunchback. **Cynthia Macdonald.**
moss, like cauls. **Carol Bergé.**
The mother. **Anonymous.**
The mother. **Gwendolyn Brooks.**

Mother. **Rachel Loden.**
Mother. **Nagase Kiyoko.**
Mother. **Mary Patten.**
The mother. **Anne Stevenson.**
Mother, child. **Irene Friis.**
Mother country. **Anne Waldman.**
Mother light, mother wind. **Milagros González.**
Mother-in-law. **Adrienne Rich.**
Mothers. **Nikki Giovanni.**
The mothers. **Sylvia Pankhurst.**
Mother's habits. **Nikki Giovanni.**
Mother's inheritance. **Fawziyya Abu Khalid.**
Mothers of sons. **Lesley Saunders.**
Mountain flora. **Evelyn Underhill.**
Mountain girl. **Rafaela Chacón Nardi.**
The mountain in my head, its periodic loss. **Elizabeth Keeler.**
Mourning. **Kuan P'an-p'an.**
Mouse. **Laura Jensen.**
Movement. **Lucha Corpi.**
Moving. **Babette Deutsch.**
Mririda. **Mririda n'Ait Attik.**
Mrs. Johnson objects. **Clara Ann Thompson.**
Mrs. Lucky. **Phyllis Janowitz.**
Much too happy. **Margarita Aliger.**
Multitudinous stars and spring waters. (excerpts). **Ping Hsin (Hsieh Wan-ying).**
The mundane. **Gioconda Belli.**
Munition wages. **Madeline Ida Bedford.**
Murderous intent with a deadly weapon. **Rashidah Ismaili.**
The muse as Medusa. **May Sarton.**
The mushroom quilt from water mill. **Barbara Guest.**
Mushrooms. **Sylvia Plath.**
Music. **Alice Ruth Moore Dunbar-Nelson.**
Music lessons. **Bella Akhmadulina.**
Music screams in the mind. **Akua Lezli Hope.**
THE MUSICOS FROM CAPULÍN. **Marcela Christine Lucero-Trujillo.**
Muteness. **Bella Akhmadulina.**
Mute's definition Blind man's definition Deaf man's definition. **Barbara Szerlip.**
My Arkansas. **Maya Angelou.**
My barrow stones. **Mary Crow.**
My cat doesn't mind I'm a lesbian. **Nina Sabaroff.**
My Chinese fairy tales for La Monte, who dislikes the obvious. **Diane Wakoski.**
My dream. **Christina Rossetti.**
my dream about being white. **Lucille Clifton.**
My dressing mirror is a humpbacked cat. **Jung Tzu.**
My familiar lover. **Cynthia Macdonald.**
My fat Mama. **Margriet Schaye.**
My father's death. **May Sarton.**
My father's wedding. (A sequence for my mother). **Jan Heller Levi.**
my flesh is flesh. **Lynda Koolish.**
My grandmother's hair. **Joan Swift.**
My hair is black. **Beverly Tanenhaus.**
My hat. **Stevie Smith.**

My husband who is not my husband. **Kate Ellen Braverman.**
My inheritance. **Nellie Hill.**
My last feeling this way poem. **Mae Jackson.**
My lips are salt. **Margarita Aliger.**
My little dreams. **Georgia Douglas Johnson.**
My love has departed. **Anonymous.**
My mama and satan. **Katerina Anghelaki-Rooke.**
My Mama moved among the days. **Lucille Clifton.**
My mother bids me bind my hair. **Mrs. John Hunter.**
My mother pieced quilts. **Teresa Palma Acosta.**
My Mother who came from China, where she never saw snow. **Laureen Mar.**
My mother's arms. **Helen Wong Huie.**
My mother's breakfront. **Janet Sternburg.**
My mother's funeral in Waltham Abbey. **Michelene Wandor.**
My name in lights. **Grace Butcher.**
My old straw hat. **Eliza Cook.**
My own impression. **Stephanie Mines.**
My people. **Else Lasker-Schüler.**
My people are the poor. **Gloria Truvido.**
My poor raging sisters. **Esther Raab.**
My son and I. **Rosemary Norman.**
My trouble. **Diane Wakoski.**
MY TRUTH AND MY FLAME. **Margaret Walker.**
The mysteries remain. **Hilda Doolittle.**
Myth sight. **Lois Elaine Griffith.**

N

Nadirs. **Josephine Miles.**
Naked and forever. **Carilda Oliver Labra.**
A name change. **Abbey Lincoln (Aminata Moseka).**
The name, the haunch. **Rochelle Owens.**
Napa, California. **Ana Castillo.**
Nappy edges (A cross country sojourn). **Ntozake Shange.**
Naramasu. **Carol Tinker.**
Narrative. **Elisabeth Eybers.**
Native American studies, University of California at Berkeley, 1975. **Wendy Rose.**
Native dancer. **Sara Miles.**
Native tongue. **Joan Larkin.**
The natives of America. **Ann Plato.**
Natural birth. (excerpts). **Toi Derricotte.**
Natural law. **Babette Deutsch.**
Naturally. **Audre Lorde.**
Nature in war-time. **S. Gertrude Ford.**
The nature lesson. **Marjorie Baldwin.**
Near Cologne: 1212. **Rosalie Moore.**
Necessity. **Jeanne Murray Walker.**
NEED: A chorale of Black women's voices. **Audre Lorde.**
Needle and thread. **Pan Chao.**

the neighbor women. **Karen Bunting.**
Neighborhood in the breast. **Reina María Rodríguez.**
Neither from before nor ever. **Olga Casanova-Sanchez.**
Nela. **Minerva Salado.**
Nervous prostration. **Anna Wickham.**
Nesting dolls. **Frances Mayes.**
The nets. **Natasha Morgan.**
Never to look a hot comb in the teeth. *See* To those of my sisters who kept their naturals.
New chapters for our history. **Rosemari Mealy.**
The new colossus. **Emma Lazarus.**
New day. **Naomi Long Madgett.**
New England, 1980. **Michèle Roberts.**
The new ghost. **Fredegond Shove.**
New Jersey. **Jeanne Lance.**
The new Joan come out of the fire. (excerpts). **Barbara Gravelle.**
New York City tonight. **Sapphire.**
New York, 1916. **Ada M. Harrison.**
The news. **Minerva Salado.**
News from my town. **Teresinha Pereira.**
Niagara. **Adelaide Crapsey.**
Night. **Bella Akhmadulina.**
Night. **Anne Hébert.**
Night. **Mae Jackson.**
Night duty. **Eva Dobell.**
Night feeding. **Muriel Rukeyser.**
Night fight. **Marge Piercy.**
Night garden, with ladies. **Dona Stein.**
Night on the shore. **Marie Carmichael Stopes.**
Night rising. **Nancy Willard.**
Night street. **Tuo Ssu.**
The night-light. **Barbara Vere Hodge.**
Nightmare. **Xelina.**
Night-pieces: for a child. **Adrienne Rich.**
The nights in June. (Sequence from blue to blue). **Kristina McGrath.**
Niké at the Metropolitan. **Babette Deutsch.**
Nikki-Rosa. **Nikki Giovanni.**
Nine o'clock show. **Josephine Miles.**
Nine poems for the unborn child. **Muriel Rukeyser.**
1975. (Napa, California). **Ana Castillo.**
1936. (Aunt Martha: severance pay). **Yvonne.**
1933. **Joan Swift.**
a no blues love poem. **Patricia Jones.**
No coward soul is mine. **Emily Brontë.**
No hay Olvido. (Four short poems). **Barbara Szerlip.**
No more cookies, please. **Marcela Christine Lucero-Trujillo.**
No more love poems #1. **Ntozake Shange.**
No more soft talk. **Diane Wakoski.**
No one comes home to lonely women. **Akua Lezli Hope.**
No poem because time is not a name. **June Jordan.**
No voyage. **Mary Oliver.**
No walls. **Irene Friis.**
No war. **Judith Kazantzis.**
A nocturnal reverie. **Anne Finch, Countess of Winchilsea.**
Nocturnal sounds. **Kattie M. Cumbo.**
Nocturne. **Pinkie Gordon Lane.**

Nocturne in the women's prison. **Maria Beneyto.**
Noica. **Olga Orozco.**
The noise of the waters. **Dahlia Ravikovitch.**
Nomen. **Naomi Long Madgett.**
Non que je veuille ôter la liberté. *See* Not that I wish to take the liberty.
Non-combatant. **Cicely Hamilton.**
Noon. **Josephine Miles.**
North express. **Joyce Mansour.**
Northboun'. **Lucy Ariel Williams.**
Northern elegy. (excerpt). **Anna Akhmatova.**
Northern liberties. **Jeanne Murray Walker.**
Northern lights. **Molly Vaux.**
Northumbrian farm. **Lilian Bowes Lyon.**
Nostalgia. **Audrey Lee.**
Not an apology. **Virginia Moore.**
Not quite making it. **Susan Efros.**
Not searching. (Searching/not searching). **Muriel Rukeyser.**
Not that far. **May Miller.**
Not that I wish to take the liberty. **Pernette de Guillet.**
Not volcanoes, not minerals. **Mary Crow.**
Notations—the F Train. **Joan Larkin.**
Note to a hitchiker who stayed for one day for Fernando. **Barbara Szerlip.**
Notes from the first year. **Susan Saxe.**
Notes on Gertrudis Gómez de Avellaneda. **Marilyn Bobes.**
Nothing of innocence. **Barbara Szerlip.**
'Nothing to report.' **May Herschel-Clarke.**
November. (Natural birth). **Toi Derricotte.**
November passage. **Judith McDaniel.**
Now. **Gloria Fuertes.**
Now. **Margaret Walker.**
Now, at the hour of our life. **Reina María Rodríguez.**
Now I know. **Lourdes Casal.**
Now is the time. **Fukui Hisako.**
Now or never. **Astra.**
'Now that you too.' **Eleanor Farjeon.**
Now we'll go. **Yunna Moritz.**
A nude by Edward Hopper. **Lisel Mueller.**
Nr. 19. **Celia Watson Strome.**
No. 6. **Celia Watson Strome.**
Nr. 10. **Celia Watson Strome.**
Nr. 12. **Celia Watson Strome.**
The Nut's birthday. **Jessie Pope.**
Nuyen Ti Soy. **Victoria Theodorou.**

Oh, my Rimbaud. **Belkis Cuza Malé.**
O realm bejewelled. **Forūgh Farrokhzād.**

O supreme Domine. **Rochelle Owens.**
O taste and see. **Denise Levertov.**
O thy bright eyes must answer now. **Emily Brontë.**
Oba-san. **Chris Kobayashi.**
Obba (a patakin). **Excilia Saldaña.**
The Obelisk inscriptions. (excerpt). **Hatshepsut.**
Observation of a bee. *See* A look at a bee.
Obsolete geography. **Michelle Cliff.**
Ocean fable. **Dilys Laing.**
Oconeechee Mountain. **Minnie Bruce Pratt.**
October. **Audre Lorde.**
The Octoroon Ball. *See* Ballade des Belles Milatraisses; The Octoroon Ball, New Orleans, 1840–1850.
Ode. **Akua Lezli Hope.**
Ode on the whole duty of parents. **Frances Cornford.**
Ode to Aphrodite. **Sappho.**
ode to my true nature. **Ellen Marie Bissert.**
The odyssey. **Helen Wong Huie.**
Oedipus. **Fina García Marruz.**
Of fruit whose black seed fire. **Olga Broumas.**
Of generations and being woman. **Elizabeth Keeler.**
of roots and sources. **Carol Bergé.**
Of the sensual world. **Praxilla.**
Of the Sierra. **Soleida Ríos.**
office party 1981. **Michelene Wandor.**
Offspring. **Naomi Long Madgett.**
The old arm-chair. **Eliza Cook.**
Old ideas speaking. **Marilyn Bobes.**
The old maid. **Sara Teasdale.**
Old man let's go fishing in the yellow reeds of the bay. **Mei-Mei Berssenbrugge.**
An old poem to Yüan Chên. **Hsüeh T'ao.**
An old snapshot. **Jean Kenward.**
Old song. **Victoria Theodorou.**
Old southern town. **Sarah Ogan Gunning.**
An old witch's warning to a young man in love. **Margriet Schaye.**
Old woman. **Elizabeth Jennings.**
The old woman. **Ruth Pitter.**
Old woman in the park. **Minerva Salado.**
An old woman's song. **Akjartoq.**
Old women of Toronto. **Miriam Waddington.**
Old words. **Sonia Sanchez.**
the old-marrieds. **Gwendolyn Brooks.**
''Olga Orozco.'' **Olga Orozco.**
Olive Schreiner. **Michelene Wandor.**
On a Catholic childhood. **Janet Campbell.**
On a death in an old people's home. **May Ivimy.**
On a picture by Smith Haldy. **Alice Alment.**
On a visit to Ch'ung Chên Taoist Temple I see in the South Hall the list of successful candidates in the Imperial examinations. **Yü Hsüan-chi.**
On a white night. **Anna Akhmatova.**
On account of the picture. **Rosario Murillo.**
On Barbara's shore. **Diane Wakoski.**
On being brought from Africa to America. **Phillis Wheatley.**
On being head of the English department. **Pinkie Gordon Lane.**

On being high. **Abbey Lincoln (Aminata Moseka).**
On diverse deviations. **Maya Angelou.**
On faith. **Heather McHugh.**
On having to go round the circle and state our philosophies. **Miriam Dyak.**
On her child's death. **Fukuda Chiyo-Ni.**
On imagination. **Phillis Wheatley.**
On learning. **Mae Jackson.**
On leaving Cuba, her native land. **Gertrudis Gómez de Avellaneda.**
On monsieur's departure. **Elizabeth I, Queen of England.**
On my birthday. **Molly Vaux.**
On myself I. **Leah Goldberg.**
On myselfe. **Anne Finch, Countess of Winchilsea.**
on not bein. **mary hope lee.**
On planting a tree. **Karen Gershon.**
On receiving the gift of a robe with a pattern of mingled plum blossoms and chrysanthemums. **Ise Tayū.**
On seeing my great-aunt in a funeral parlor. **Diana Chang.**
On the birth of a child. **Elsie Alvarado de Ricord.**
On the bus. (Camp notes). **Mitsuye Yamada.**
On the country sleep of Susanne K. Langer. **Marie Ponsot.**
On the death of a young lady of five years of age. **Phillis Wheatley.**
On the death of Anne Bronte. **Charlotte Bronte.**
On the death of Lisa Lyman. **Della Burt.**
On the death of Sylvia Plath. **Judith Herzberg.**
On the death of the Emperor Temmu. (Even flaming fire). **Empress Jitō.**
On the death of the Emperior Temmu. (Over North Mountain). **Empress Jitō.**
on the first day of summer in the twenty fifth year of our lives. **Jeanette Adams.**
On the melting lake. **Chung Ling.**
On the murder of her husband. **Barbara Torelli-Strozzi.**
On the pilgrim's way in Kent, as it leads to the Coldrum Stones. **Asphodel.**
On the porch. **Harriet Monroe.**
ON THE REAL WORLD: Meditation #1. **June Jordan.**
On the road at night there stands the man. **Dahlia Ravikovitch.**
On the road through Chang-Te. **Sun Yün-fêng.**
On the road to the sea. **Charlotte Mew.**
On the slope of Hua mountain. **Anonymous.**
On the tower. **Annette von Droste-Hülshoff.**
On writing Asian-American poetry. **Geraldine Kudaka.**
Once. **Alice Walker.**
once. (Birds of paradise). **Nzadi Zimele-Keita (Michelle McMichael).**
Once again. **Liz Sohappy.**
1. **Akua Lezli Hope.**
One. (One, The other, And). **Wendy Brooks Wieber.**
One blue flag. **Linda Pastan.**
The one he loves. (The love sequence). **Sandra M. Gilbert.**
125th Street and Abomey. **Audre Lorde.**
One night. **Millicent Sutherland.**
One of too many. **Magdalena Gomez.**
One, The other, And. **Wendy Brooks Wieber.**

One-two-three. **Hannah Senesh.**
One way conversation. **Dorothy Livesay.**
One woman looking at another. (Two poems). **Diane Middlebrook.**
Only a second (1940). **Conca Michel.**
Only in this way. **Margaret Goss Burroughs.**
The only language she knows. **Genny Lim.**
Opaque. **Paula Yup.**
An opium fantasy. **Maria White Lowell.**
Orange chiffon. **Jayne Cortez.**
The orgy. **Susan Kennedy Calhoun.**
Orgy (that is, vegetable market, at Sarno). **Gina Labriola.**
Oriflamme. **Jessie Redmon Fauset.**
Orinda to Lucasia. **Katherine Philips.**
Orinda upon little Hector Philips. **Katherine Philips.**
Orisha. **Jayne Cortez.**
The other. **Ruth Fainlight.**
The other. (One, The other, And). **Wendy Brooks Wieber.**
The other side of a mirror. **Mary Elizabeth Coleridge.**
Oughta be a woman. **June Jordan.**
OUR CHILDREN ARE OUR CHILDREN. **Geraldine L. Wilson.**
Our lady, solitude. **Alexandra Grilikhes.**
Our mother America. **Teresita Fernández.**
Our tongue was Nahuatl. **Ana Castillo.**
Our voice. **Noémia da Sousa.**
Our worlds. **Lucha Corpi.**
Out of chaos out of order out. **Michèle Roberts.**
Out of the darkness. **Frankie Armstrong.**
Out of the darkness. **Gertrud Kolmar.**
Out on the water. **Molly Vaux.**
Outside the Kampsongs, at the market, waiting. **Virginia Gilbert.**
Over shining shingle. **Else Lasker-Schüler.**
Over the top. **Sybil Bristowe.**
Owl woman's death song. **Anonymous.**
Oysters. **Anne Sexton.**

Pain. **Edith Södergran.**
Pain. **Alfonsina Storni.**
Painted steps. **Tess Gallagher.**
A painting of a young woman in a coffee-shop. *See* Standstill.
The palace of pleasant regard. *See* The assembly of ladies.
Palestine. **Lola Ridge.**
Palm-reading. **Cheryl Clarke.**
The palm-reading. **Jane Katz.**
Papers for a man's retirement. (excerpt). **Lina de Feria.**
Paperweight. **Audre Lorde.**

Paphnutius. (excerpt). **Hroswitha von Gandersheim.**
Pappouli. **Eleni Fourtouni.**
Para Teresa. **Inés Hernandez Tovar.**
Para un revolucionario. **Lorna Dee Cervantes.**
Para un viejito desconocido que aun conozco. **Inés Hernandez Tovar.**
Parade. **Gloria Gayles.**
Paradigm. **Phyllis Gotlieb.**
A paradox. **Georgia Douglas Johnson.**
A parallel cut of air. **Elaine Dallman.**
Paraphernalia for a suicide: a revelation of life. **Lateifa-Ramona Lahleet Hyman.**
Parentage. **Alice Meynell.**
Parenthood. **Dorothy Livesay.**
paris musée de cluny. **Carol Bergé.**
The park in winter. **Alfonsina Storni.**
The parson's job. **Madeline Ida Bedford.**
Part I. (Early losses: a requiem). **Alice Walker.**
Part II. The child. (Early losses: a requiem). **Alice Walker.**
Parting. **Eleni Fourtouni.**
A parting hymn. **Charlotte L. Forten.**
Parting of a newly wedded couple. **Tu Fu.**
Parting with Lucasia: a song. **Katherine Philips.**
Parturition. **Mina Loy.**
Party. **Alejandra Pizarnik.**
Passengers in transit. **Elsie Alvarado de Ricord.**
Passion without a name. **Lucha Corpi.**
Patience. **Elaine Feinstein.**
Patience. (Notes from the first year). **Susan Saxe.**
Patriarchal poetry. **Gertrude Stein.**
Patron of flawless serpent beauty. **Friederike Mayröcker.**
Pattern. **Edith Lovejoy Pierce.**
Patterns. **Amy Lowell.**
Paying dues. **Bernette Golden.**
Peace. **Eleanor Farjeon.**
Peace. **Paula Yup.**
the peacock poem. (The house of desire). **Sherley Anne Williams.**
The pear tree. **Hilda Doolittle.**
Pears. **Mary Swander.**
The pennywhistle man. **Frances Gill.**
Penobscot bird. **Rochelle Owens.**
The people gather. **Mari Evans.**
people, on a bad day. **Michelene Wandor.**
Perhaps—. **Vera Brittain.**
persephone descends to the underworld. **Michèle Roberts.**
Persona. **Faye Kicknosway.**
personal letter no. 2. **Sonia Sanchez.**
Peterborough. **Marilyn Hacker.**
Petrograd. **Babette Deutsch.**
Phallic root. *See* The man root.
Phantasia for Elvira Shatayev. **Adrienne Rich.**
Phantoms. **Elizabeth Keeler.**
Phenomenal woman. **Maya Angelou.**
Philosophy in warm weather. **Jane Kenyon.**
The phone. **Rosalie Moore.**
The photogenic ones. **Belkis Cuza Malé.**
Photographs of an unmade bed. **Adrienne Rich.**

Phraseology. **Jayne Cortez.**
Physics. **Jeanne Murray Walker.**
The phythoness. **Kathleen Raine.**
Picking up your mail. **Kate Ellen Braverman.**
Picnic. **Rose Macaulay.**
Picnic. **Victoria Theodorou.**
Picnic. **Sybil Wood.**
Pictures. **Sylvia Read.**
A piece of business. **Judith Kazantzis.**
Pieces of echoes. **Rota Silverstrini.**
Pierrot goes to war. **Gabrielle Elliot.**
Pilot captured by the Japanese, 1942. **Sharon Olds.**
Piropos de la chinita. **Frances C. Chung.**
The pitcher. **Hsiung Hung.**
Pitiful role. **Marilyn Bobes.**
Place in the morning. **May Miller.**
Planetarium. **Adrienne Rich.**
The plantation. **Eugenie Eersel.**
The planting. **Judith Goren.**
A plaster and plexiglas creation. **Jessica Tarahata Hagedorn.**
A play. **Alice Karle.**
Players. **Josephine Miles.**
Playing all a summer's day by the lake, to the tune "Clear bright joy." **Chu Shu-chên.**
Playing water polo in Angola in the words of an ex-South Africa mercenary, 32 Battalion, reported Feb '81. **Judith Kazantzis.**
Please say something. **Tomioka Taeko.**
Pluck. **Eva Dobell.**
Plum blossoms. **Chu Shu-chên.**
Pneumonia. **Joan Swift.**
Poem. **Celia Dropkin.**
Poem. **Charlotte L. Forten.**
Poem. **Gloria T. Hull.**
Poem. **Teresa Torres.**
The poem. **Diane Wakoski.**
Poem about a night out: Michael: good-bye for awhile. **June Jordan.**
The poem as mask. **Muriel Rukeyser.**
Poem at thirty. **Sonia Sanchez.**
Poem for a stranger. **Jana Harris.**
A POEM FOR ALL THE MENS IN THE WORLD. **Mae Jackson.**
Poem for Aretha. **Nikki Giovanni.**
Poem for Charley. **Patricia Henley.**
poem for david murray. **Patricia Jones.**
Poem for her thirty-fifth birthday. **Susan North.**
Poem for inaugural rose. **June Jordan.**
Poem for Jacqueline Hill. **Anonymous.**
Poem for Maya. **Carolyn Forché.**
Poem for my father. **Heidi Gitterman.**
Poem for Nana. **June Jordan.**
Poem for Rene Crevel. **Jessica Tarahata Hagedorn.**
Poem for some Black women. **Carolyn M. Rodgers.**
A poem for Sterling Brown. **Sonia Sanchez.**
Poem for Suzanne. **Patricia Henley.**
Poem: for the beginning. **Honor Moore.**

Poem for the young White man who asked me how I, an intelligent, well-read person, could believe in the war between the races. **Lorna Dee Cervantes.**

A poem for women in rage. **Audre Lorde.**

Poem from Llanbyri. **Lynette Roberts.**

Poem in which my legs are accepted. **Kathleen Fraser.**

Poem nr. 2 for inaugural rose. **June Jordan.**

Poem of profound truth. **Mirta Aguirre.**

Poem of the end. (excerpts). **Marina Tsvetayeva.**

Poem on azure. **Anna de Noailles.**

poem on midsummer's day. **Michèle Roberts.**

Poem: on my happy/matrimonial condition. **June Jordan.**

poem on St. Valentine's Day. **Michèle Roberts.**

poem on the day of the autumn equinox. **Michèle Roberts.**

poem on the day of the spring equinox. **Michèle Roberts.**

Poem on the occasion of not receiving the Academy of American Poets' Walt Whitman Award for an outstanding first manuscript of poetry. **Jan Clausen.**

Poem to an imaginary Japanese lover. **Barbara Szerlip.**

Poem to her daughter. (excerpt). **Mwana Kupona Msham.**

Poem to the tune of ''Tsui hua yin.'' **Li Ch'ing-chao.**

Poem to the tune of ''Yi chian mei.'' **Li Ch'ing-chao.**

Poem towards a final solution. **June Jordan.**

A poem written on a floating red leaf. **Han Ts'ui-p'in.**

Poema cinético. (third version). **Amanda Berenguer.**

Poems. **Judith Barrington.**

Poems for her sick mother. (excerpts). **Yunna Moritz.**

The poet. (How I managed to square the circle of dreams in the shape of a window at the top of the stairs in a tenement house). **Jenny Mastoraki.**

The poet and the butcher. **Catherine Durning Whetham.**

The poet invites the moon for supper. **Nancy Willard.**

The poet learns to fly like an angel but gets nothing to eat. **Nellie Hill.**

Poetry. **Nikki Giovanni.**

Poetry. **Ruth Stone.**

Poets/poems. **Marnie Walsh.**

A point of view. **Barbara Howes.**

The Policeman. **Julia Fields.**

The Polish husband. **Helen Dunmore.**

Political activist living alone. **Pat Arrowsmith.**

The pond at dusk. **Jane Kenyon.**

The Pope at Dublin Airport. **Judith Kazantzis.**

Poppies in October. **Sylvia Plath.**

POR TI, BRO. **Sandra María Esteves.**

Portrait. **Jeanette Adams.**

Portrait. **Lili Bita.**

Portrait. **Dahlia Ravikovitch.**

Portrait. **Carolyn M. Rodgers.**

Portrait. **Judith Wright.**

Portrait in available light. **Sara Miles.**

Portrait of a woman artist. **Safiya Henderson.**

Portrait of girl with comic book. **Phyllis McGinley.**

The portraits. **Anna Marie Lenngren.**

Portraits of the heart. **Eunice Odio.**

Portugal. (Not that far). **May Miller.**

Possession. **Michael Field.**

Postage due. **Alison Zier.**

Postcard. **Pamela Stewart.**

Posthumous story. **Maria Eugenia Vaz Ferreira.**

Potions. **Shirley Geok-Lin Lim.**

Potter. **Alexandra Grilikhes.**

Power. **Audre Lorde.**

Powwow '79, Durango. **Paula Gunn Allen.**

The practical clown. **Sandra Hochman.**

Praematuri. **Margaret Postgate Cole.**

Praise of future. **Marilyn Bobes.**

Prayer. **Gabrielle de Coignard.**

Prayer. (Birds of paradise). **Nzadi Zimele-Keita (Michelle McMichael).**

Prayer before execution. **Mary, Queen of Scots.**

Prayer for the little daughter between death and burial. **Diana Scott.**

Prayer of an ovulating female. **Dilys Laing.**

Prayer to Isis. **Christina Walsh.**

Pregnant woman. **Ingrid Jonker.**

Premonition. **Lucha Corpi.**

Premonition. **Dulce María Loynaz.**

Present. **Sonia Sanchez.**

Present tense. **Armitage Hargreaves.**

The president and the laser bomb. (Searching/not searching). **Muriel Rukeyser.**

Pretending. **Brenda Connor-Bey.**

The price of love. **Muriel Box.**

Pride. **Dahlia Ravikovitch.**

Primer for Blacks. **Gwendolyn Brooks.**

Prince Harlem. **Lois Elaine Griffith.**

Private entry in the diary of a female parent. **Dilys Laing.**

Prize-fighter. **Margery Smith.**

Pro femina: parts one, two, and three. **Carolyn Kizer.**

Problems of etiquette. **Angela de Hoyos.**

Problems of translation: problems of language. **June Jordan.**

The process of dissolution. **Susan Efros.**

Profile of my city. **Lourdes Casal.**

Progenitor. **Judith Kazantzis.**

The prologue. **Anne Bradstreet.**

Prologue. (A curse for a nation). **Elizabeth Barrett Browning.**

The promise. **Johari M. Kunjufu.**

Proof. **Bessie Calhoun Bird.**

Prophecy. **Elinor Wylie.**

The prophets. **Charlotte Perkins Gilman.**

Prophets for a new day. **Margaret Walker.**

Proportion poetry. **Majken Johansson.**

The proposition. **Betsy Orient.**

prose/poem Written after overhearing a conversation on a Greyhound bus just outside of Oxnard, California. **Marie-Elise.**

Prospective immigrants please note. **Adrienne Rich.**

Psalm lix. **Mary Sidney Herbert, Countess of Pembroke.**

Psalm lvii. **Mary Sidney Herbert, Countess of Pembroke.**

Psalm lii. **Mary Sidney Herbert, Countess of Pembroke.**

Psalm lxxi. **Mary Sidney Herbert, Countess of Pembroke.**

Psalm lxxii. **Mary Sidney Herbert, Countess of Pembroke.**

Psalm lx. **Mary Sidney Herbert, Countess of Pembroke.**

Psalm lxvii. **Mary Sidney Herbert, Countess of Pembroke.**
The pump. **Mary Barnard.**
Puritan sonnet. **Elinor Wylie.**
The purple, white and green. **L. E. Morgan-Browne.**
Putting Mother by. **Dona Stein.**
The pyramid of the musicians. **Janet Hamill.**

Quasi-liberation in Upstate New York. **Beverly Tanenhaus.**
Queen charming. **Pamela White Hadas.**
The question. **Sylvia Lynd.**
The question. (Searching/not searching). **Muriel Rukeyser.**
Questionnaire. (Notes from the first year). **Susan Saxe.**
The quiet house. **Charlotte Mew.**
Quiet water. **Samiati Alisjahbana.**
Quilts. **Barbara Guest.**

R. Alcona to J. Brenzaida. *See* Remembrance.
R.I.P. **Muriel Box.**
RSVP. **Rachel Maines.**
Radio photo. **Digdora Alonso.**
Rag doll (a song). **Teresita Fernández.**
The raiders. **Marian Allen.**
Rain. (excerpts). **Bella Akhmadulina.**
Rain. **Lucha Corpi.**
The rain sounds like a dombra. **Bella Akhmadulina.**
Raining the water. **Georgette Cerrutti.**
Rainwater. **Phyllis Thompson.**
Random thoughts on the love of God. (excerpt). **Simone Weil.**
Ranmore. **Elizabeth Dixon.**
Rape. **Jayne Cortez.**
Rape. **Minnie Bruce Pratt.**
Rape at Progresso: a critical study. **Cheri Fein.**
A rape poem for men. **Donna Allegra.**
Rapunzil. **Faye Kicknosway.**
Readers. **Josephine Miles.**
Reading da leaves. **Colette Inez.**
(reading Plath's *Letters Home*; rereading *Ariel*). (dialectics). **Jan Clausen.**

Reading the Kieu. (Searching/not searching). **Muriel Rukeyser.**
Real estate. **Mary Barnard.**
The reason for poetry. **Nancy Morejón.**
Rebecca. **Shirley Kaufman.**
Rebirth. **Catriona Stamp.**
Rebirth according to the New Testament. (Chicana evolution). **Sylvia Alicia Gonzales.**
Receiving Buddha. **Ping Hsin (Hsieh Wan-ying).**
The receptionist is by definition. **Karen Brodine.**
A recognition. (To George Sand). **Elizabeth Barrett Browning.**
Recognition. **Myra Glazer.**
Recollected in tranquility. **Margriet Schaye.**
a record for my friends. **Sherley Anne Williams.**
A recruit from the slums. **Emily Orr.**
recuerdos de la chinita en Guatemala. **Frances C. Chung.**
Red. **Ellen Wittlinger.**
Red sandalwood mouth. **Chao Luan-luan.**
Reflections. **Georgina Herrera.**
Reflections, written on visiting the grave of a venerated friend. **Ann Plato.**
Re-forming the crystal. **Adrienne Rich.**
The refugee. **Marjorie Battcock.**
REFUGEE MOTHER. **Geraldine L. Wilson.**
Refugee ship. **Lorna Dee Cervantes.**
Regina. **Mary Elizabeth Coleridge.**
Regrets. **Alice Meynell.**
Remains- Stratigraphy: **Cynthia Macdonald.**
Remembering. **Ping Hsin (Hsieh Wan-ying).**
Remembering Fannie Lou Hamer. **Thadious M. Davis.**
Remembrance. **Emily Brontë.**
Remembrance day in the dales. **Dorothy Una Ratcliffe.**
Reminder. **Mirta Yañez.**
Remorse came slowly. **Nishi Junko.**
Renacimiento segun el Nuevo Testamento. *See* Rebirth according to the New Testament. (Chicana evolution).
The renaming. **Valerie Sinason.**
. . . Repeating chorus . . . **Carmen Tafolla.**
Reported missing. **Anna Gordon Keown.**
reports. **Mariah Britton Howard.**
Representing the universe. **Alice Walker.**
Requiem 1935–1940. (excerpts). **Anna Akhmatova.**
Rescue. **Phoebe Hesketh.**
The resemblance. **Ruthe D. Canter.**
Reservoir at night. **Chelly Lima.**
The respite. **Ingeborg Bachmann.**
Rest. **Christina Rossetti.**
Restaurant. **Maxine Hong Kingston.**
Résumé. **Dorothy Parker.**
Resurrection. **Marie Luise Kaschnitz.**
Resurrection. **Yoshihara Sachiko.**
Return. **Johari M. Kunjufu.**
Return to Frankfurt. (excerpt). **Marie Luise Kaschnitz.**
Return to the home we made. **Dolly Bird.**
A return to the tree of time. **Vesna Parun.**
Returning from Flower Law Mountain on a winter day, to the tune ''Washing silk in the stream.'' **Wu Tsao.**

Reunion. **Beverly Tanenhaus.**
rev pimps. (Memorial). **Sonia Sanchez.**
Revelation. **Carole C. Gregory.**
Revered quilts. (The mushroom quilt from water mill).
    Barbara Guest.
Revision. **Eileen Newton.**
Revolution. **Nishi Junko.**
Revolution. **Teru Kanazawa.**
Revolutionary blues. **Julie Blackwomon.**
Revolutionary dreams. **Nikki Giovanni.**
Revolutionary petunias. **Alice Walker.**
The rhetoric of Langston Hughes. **Margaret Danner.**
Rhodes. (Not that far). **May Miller.**
Rhyme of my inheritance. **Joan Larkin.**
Rhythms. **Diana Chang.**
Riches I hold in light esteem. **Emily Bronte.**
Ride. **Josephine Miles.**
Riding Hood, updated. **Adrien Stoutenburg.**
Riding the thunder. **Paula Gunn Allen.**
The rime of the ancient feminist. (excerpt). **Stephanie
    Markman.**
The ring. **Atsumi Ikuko.**
Riot. **Gwendolyn Brooks.**
rite de passage. **Michèle Roberts.**
Rites of passage. **Audre Lorde.**
Rites of spring. **Felice Newman.**
The ritual. **Virginia Gilbert.**
Ritual. **Okoyo Loving.**
ritual. **Michelene Wandor.**
The river. **Enid Vián.**
River boat. **Adrien Stoutenburg.**
The river god. **Stevie Smith.**
The river Honey Queen Bess. **Cynthia Macdonald.**
The river-merchant's wife: a letter. **Rihaku.**
(the road). (dialectics). **Jan Clausen.**
The road. **Helene Johnson.**
The road. **Cleve Solís.**
Robert G. Shaw. **Henrietta Cordelia Ray.**
Rock and roll. **Jessica Tarahata Hagedorn.**
Rock bottom nourishment. **Cheri Fein.**
The Rock of Levkas. **Mary Barnard.**
Rocking. **Gabriela Mistral.**
Roman fountain. **Louise Bogan.**
A romance. **Ellen Marie Bissert.**
The romance of the swan's nest. **Elizabeth Barrett
    Browning.**
The romancing poet. **Helen Hamilton.**
Rondel. **Muriel Rukeyser.**
Rookie dyke T. V. toddler. **Magdalena Gomez.**
Rooming houses are old women. **Audre Lorde.**
Rooms. **Charlotte Mew.**
Rosabel. **Angelina Weld Grimké.**
Rosalie. *See* Rosabel.
Rosas de la tarde. **Sara Miles.**
Rose in the afternoon. **Jenny Joseph.**
The roses of Saadi. **Marceline Desbordes-Valmore.**
Roseville, Minn., U.S.A. **Marcela Christine
    Lucero-Trujillo.**

Rouen. **May Wedderburn Cannan.**
Rouen. **Marguerite Wood.**
A royal princess. **Christina Rossetti.**
The runaway slave at Pilgrim's Point. **Elizabeth Barrett
    Browning.**
The runner wonders. **Grace Butcher.**
Running. **Leslie Ullman.**
Running scared. **Jana Harris.**
running to gone. **Esther Louise.**
Russian women. **Lola Ridge.**
Ruth. **Colleen J. McElroy.**

S

Sacrament. **Margaret Sackville.**
A sacred grove. **Fran Winant.**
Sacrificial victim. **Yoshiyuki Rie.**
A sadness which already knew me. **Lygia Guillén.**
Safed and I. **Molly Myerowitz Levine.**
SAGIMUSUME: The white heron maiden. **Jonny Kyoko
    Sullivan.**
Said the poet to the analyst. **Anne Sexton.**
Saint Catherine of Siena. **Alice Meynell.**
St. Marks, midnight. **Joan Murray Simpson.**
'Sal.' **Inez Quilter.**
Salome. **Leonora Speyer.**
Salvation. **Gayl Jones.**
San Antonio. **Carmen Tafolla.**
Santa Caterina. **Myra Glazer.**
Sappho's reply. **Rita Mae Brown.**
sassafrass. **Ntozake Shange.**
Satori. **Gayl Jones.**
Saturday: the small pox. **Mary Wortley Montagu, Lady.**
Say hello to John. **Sherley Anne Williams.**
Sayre (woman professor). **Lynn Strongin.**
Scarred. **Polly Joan.**
The scattering. **Muriel Grainger.**
Scenario. **Jan Clausen.**
scene. **Carol Bergé.**
Scene at evening. **Karen Gershon.**
The scholar. **Frances Cornford.**
Schrafft's Third Avenue and East 57th Street. **Rachel
    Maines.**
Scrawl. **Roberta Lefkowitz.**
The scream. **May Miller.**
Screens. **Winifred M. Letts.**
A script: beauty is the beginning of terror . . . **Jessica
    Tarahata Hagedorn.**
Sea flower. **Mary Dorcey.**
Sea shell. **Elizabeth Gross.**
The seacoast at Mera. **Takada Toshiko.**

Seamstress. **Susan MacDonald.**
The search for the perfect rye bread. **Bethami Auerbach.**
The searching. **Alice S. Cobb.**
Searching/not searching. **Muriel Rukeyser.**
Second home. (The segregated heart). **Minnie Bruce Pratt.**
second song. (Driving wheel). **Sherley Anne Williams.**
Second thoughts. **Michael Field.**
The second wife. **Mririda n'Ait Attik.**
The second wife. **Lizette Woodworth Reese.**
Secondhand coat. **Ruth Stone.**
Secret. **Gwendolyn B. Bennett.**
Secret. **Maria Teresa Horta.**
Secrets. **Gloria Frym.**
SEDUCTION. **Jo Ann Hall-Evans.**
Seedlings in the mail. **Marge Piercy.**
The Seed-Merchant's son. **Agnes Grozier Herbertson.**
Seeking a mooring. **Wang Wei.**
The segregated heart. **Minnie Bruce Pratt.**
Seizin. **Julia Fields.**
Selective service. **Carolyn Forché.**
Self. **Sharyn Jeanne Skeeter.**
Self and the otherself. *See* On monsieur's departure.
Self portrait 4. **Tove Ditlevsen.**
Self portrait 1. **Tove Ditlevsen.**
Self portrait 2. **Tove Ditlevsen.**
Self-criticism. **Monica Raymond.**
Self-portrait. (Käthe Kollwitz). **Muriel Rukeyser.**
Seminary. **Constance Carrier.**
Sending spring love to Tzu-an. **Yü Hsüan-chi.**
A sense of reality. **Jan Clausen.**
Sensitivity. **Angela Hamblin.**
Sent from the capital to her elder daughter. **Otomo no Sakanoe.**
Separation. (Of fruit whose black seed fire). **Olga Broumas.**
Sepia fashion show. **Maya Angelou.**
September. **Madge Hales.**
September 7. **Ellen Bass.**
A sequence for my mother. **Jan Heller Levi.**
Sequence from blue to blue. **Kristina McGrath.**
Serenade. **Anonymous.**
A serenade for two poplars. **Esther Raab.**
The sermon (Revelations). **Sister Bernadine.**
The serpent. **Phoebe Hesketh.**
The servant goddess. (Three women in the closet). **Gloria Anzaldúa.**
SESTINA, WINCHELL'S DONUT HOUSE. **Jan Clausen.**
Setting sail. **Molly Vaux.**
7 P.M. **Kate Ellen Braverman.**
The 7:25 trolley. **Mari Evans.**
72 hours: Yom Kippur. **Cynthia Kraman Genser.**
Sex. **Jean Valentine.**
Sex without love. **Sharon Olds.**
Sexual privacy of women on welfare. **Pinkie Gordon Lane.**
The shadow. **Rose Macaulay.**
Shadow Way. (Medicine song). **Paula Gunn Allen.**
Shadows of the burning. **Marge Piercy.**
Shall earth no more inspire thee? **Emily Brontë.**
The shallows. **Debora Greger.**

Shaman. **Maria Sabina.**
Shaman/Bear. **Anita Endrezze-Danielson.**
SHE. **Catherine Davis.**
She. **Zinaida Gippius.**
She is an older person now. **Clare Coss.**
She (Marina distant). (Marina). **Lucha Corpi.**
She scorns her husband the Caliph. **Lady Maisun.**
She walketh veiled and sleeping. **Charlotte Perkins Gilman.**
She warns him. **Frances Cornford.**
She went, she said, losing herself. **Yolanda Ulloa.**
She who understands. **Alfonsina Storni.**
She-bear. **Nia Francisco.**
Shellfish. **Ishigaki Rin.**
Shells. **Eugenie Eersel.**
A shepherd's coat. **Lilian Bowes Lyon.**
She's. **Osa Hidalgo-de la Riva.**
She's free! **Frances Ellen Watkins Harper.**
Shimmering threads like hair. **Suzanne Juhasz.**
Short biography of a washerwoman. **Yolanda Ulloa.**
Short history. **Lucha Corpi.**
The short order cook in the mountains. **Susan Schweik.**
shout. **Judith Kazantzis.**
The shrew who married God. **Belkis Cuza Malé.**
The Shulamite. **Else Lasker-Schüler.**
Shunpike. **Barbara Howes.**
Siblings. **Sharon Barba.**
The Sibyl's song. **Michèle Roberts.**
Sight. **Anne Welsh.**
Significant fevers. **Alison Fell.**
Silence. **Bella Akhmadulina.**
Silence. **Marianne Moore.**
Silence. She is six years old. **Lynn Emanuel.**
Silent is the House. **Emily Brontë.**
Silk-screen. **Maureen Owen.**
Simple-song. **Marge Piercy.**
'Since they have died.' **May Wedderburn Cannan.**
Sing a song of War-time. **Nina Macdonald.**
Sing with your body. **Janice Mirikitani.**
Singing aloud. **Carolyn Kizer.**
Sinking. **Lin Ling.**
Sir Patient Fancy. (excerpt). **Aphra Behn.**
Sister. **Gabriela Mistral.**
Sister. **Mririda n'Ait Attik.**
Sister. **Felice Newman.**
The sisters. **Alexis De Veaux.**
The sisters. **Nicki Jackowska.**
Sisters. **Adrienne Rich.**
6 a.m. **Jane Miller.**
Six years. **Alice Bloch.**
16/53. **Marge Piercy.**
Sixteenth day. (There is no evil only restlessness!). **Ruth Weiss.**
The skin trade. **Jeanne Lance.**
Slaughterhouse. **Takiguchi Masako.**
The slave mother. **Frances Ellen Watkins Harper.**
Sleep, darling. **Sappho.**
The sleeping. **Lynn Emanuel.**

Sleeping Beauty. **Olga Broumas.**
Sleeping on the left side. **Joan Larkin.**
Sleeping with Franz Kafka. **Anna Hartmann.**
Slender fingers. **Chao Luan-luan.**
Slow-motion elegy for Kathy King. **Madeline DeFrees.**
small comment. **Sonia Sanchez.**
A small contradiction. **Pat Parker.**
Small paths. **Henriette Roland-Holst.**
Small poem for Michael. **Susan North.**
The small square. **Sophia de Mello Breyner Andresen.**
a smart & final iris. **Carol Tinker.**
The smell, smell. **Marina Tsvetayeva.**
Smile, death. **Charlotte Mew.**
Smile lie rockets . . . **Iris Zavala.**
Smothered fires. **Georgia Douglas Johnson.**
Snow in April. **Judith McDaniel.**
Snow in Marin County! **Elizabeth Keeler.**
Snow in October. **Alice Ruth Moore Dunbar-Nelson.**
Snowless February. **Bella Akhmadulina.**
So abruptly. **Shlomit Cohen.**
So few sleep soundly. **Shirley Bridges.**
So many feathers. **Jayne Cortez.**
So to tell the truth. **Janet Dubé.**
Socks. **Jessie Pope.**
soeurs du mal. **Judith Kazantzis.**
"Sois sage o ma douleur." **Marie Ponsot.**
Solemn inventory. **Amanda Berenguer.**
The solitary. **Sara Teasdale.**
Solitude. **Ella Wheeler Wilcox.**
Solo. **Jayne Cortez.**
Solstice. **Audre Lorde.**
solution #9 "to touch you." **Mariah Britton Howard.**
Some of my best friends. **Elizabeth Cook-Lynn.**
Some pieces I lost. **Marsha Peterson.**
Some unsaid things. **Joan Larkin.**
Some verses upon the burning of our house July 10th, 1666.
     Anne Bradstreet.
Someone else. **Rosario Castellanos.**
Someone like no one else. **Forŭgh Farrokhzäd.**
Someone you love. **Ellen Wittlinger.**
Sometimes, as a child. **Olga Broumas.**
Sometimes as women only. **Gloria Gayles.**
Sometimes you look like lady day. **Jessica Tarahata**
     Hagedorn.
son. **Susan MacDonald.**
Song. **Aphra Behn.**
Song. **Gwendolyn B. Bennett.**
Song. (The convent of pleasure). **Margaret Cavendish,**
     Duchess of Newcastle.
Song. **Anne Collins.**
Song. **Ann du Cille.**
A song. **Anne Finch, Countess of Winchilsea.**
Song. **Joan Larkin.**
Song. **Cecilia Meireles.**
Song. **Pauli Murray.**
Song. **Christina Rossetti.**
Song. **Annie Louisa Walker.**
Song. **Marya Zaturenska.**

Song: a thousand martyrs I have made. **Aphra Behn.**
Song: Ah, this is not enough, I cry—. **Elizabeth Daryush.**
Song: As the inamour'd Thirsis lay. **Aphra Behn.**
Song for a girl on her first menstruation. **Anonymous.**
Song for a young girl's puberty ceremony. **Anonymous.**
Song for bringing a child into the world. **Anonymous.**
Song for my father. **Jessica Tarahata Hagedorn.**
Song for the new year. **Judith Kazantzis.**
Song for the newborn. **Anonymous.**
A song in the front yard. **Gwendolyn Brooks.**
Song: Love arm'd. **Aphra Behn.**
Song My. **Susan Griffin.**
Song of a girl journeying to the country of the dead.
     Anonymous.
Song of a woman in labor. **Anonymous.**
A song of Chin Men District. **Hsüeh Ch'iung.**
Song of circles. **Alice Karle.**
Song of Deborah. **Deborah.**
A song of grief. **Pan Chieh-yü.**
A song of Hsi-ling Lake. **Su Hsiao-hsiao.**
A song of magpies. **Lady Ho.**
Song of perfect propriety. **Dorothy Parker.**
Song of rootless people. **Chung Ling.**
A song of the dice. **Anonymous.**
Song of the diner waitress. **Roswell Spafford.**
Song of the old woman. **Anonymous.**
song of the ostrich. **Michelene Wandor.**
Song of the rejected woman. **Kibkarjuk.**
Song of the Sabbath. **Kadia Molodowsky.**
Song of the woman painted hot and cold. **Roswell Spafford.**
The song of the woman with her parts coming out. **Susan**
     Griffin.
A song of white hair. **Chuo Wên-chün.**
Song: the calling-up. (Käthe Kollwitz). **Muriel Rukeyser.**
Song: the willing mistress. **Aphra Behn.**
Song to earth mother. **Anonymous.**
Song to Ishtar. **Denise Levertov.**
Song to my Nisei mother. **Teru Kanazawa.**
A song to your blood. **Molly Myerowitz Levine.**
Songs in flight. (excerpts). **Ingeborg Bachmann.**
Songs of divorce. **Jane Green.**
Songs that cannot be silenced. **Hien Luong.**
Sonnet. **Alice Ruth Moore Dunbar-Nelson.**
Sonnet. **Louise Labé.**
Sonnet. **Edna St. Vincent Millay.**
A sonnet. (Patriarchal poetry). **Gertrude Stein.**
Sonnet. **Elinor Wylie.**
sonnet/for pedro pietri. **Patricia Jones.**
Sonnet to a sister in error. **Dilys Laing.**
Sonnet to Eurydice. **Sophia de Mello Breyner Andresen.**
Sonnets from a lock box. **Anna Hempstead Branch.**
Sonnets from the Portuguese. (excerpts). **Elizabeth Barrett**
     Browning.
Soon. **Kate Ellen Braverman.**
Sorceries. **Alejandra Pizarnik.**
The sorrow of departure, to the tune "Butterflies love flow-
     ers." **Li Ch'ing-chao.**
Sortin-out. **Amina Baraka.**

A soul. **Christina Rossetti.**
The soul's garment. **Margaret Cavendish, Duchess of Newcastle.**
The soul's home. **Anne Collins.**
The sound of one fork. **Minnie Bruce Pratt.**
Sound out your voices, morning prayers. **Zelda.**
South Bronx girl. **Esther Silverman.**
Sovereign queen. **Padeshah Khatun.**
Soweto song. **Amina Baraka.**
Space. **Shindó Chie.**
Spain. (Not that far). **May Miller.**
The sparrow's skull. **Ruth Pitter.**
Speak the truth to the people. **Mari Evans.**
Speaking of Gabriel. **Rosario Castellanos.**
Special delivery to Curtis: the future of the world. **Carol Muske.**
Special report for International Women's Day. **Minerva Salado.**
Speeding ship. **Erica Marx.**
Spelling out the cosmos. **Margarita Cota-Cárdenas.**
Sphinxes inclined to be. **Olga Orozco.**
Spires. **Lola Ridge.**
Spirit flowers. **Della Burt.**
Spitting backward,. **Faye Kicknosway.**
Split a passionflower. **Rochelle Owens.**
Spoil. **Malka Heifetz Tussman.**
Spring ends, to the tune ''Spring in Wu-ling.'' **Li Ch'ing-chao.**
Spring in the woods. **Marguerite Clerbout.**
Spring in war-time. **Edith Nesbit.**
Spring in war-time. **Sara Teasdale.**
Spring joy. **Chu Shu-chên.**
Spring night, to the tune ''Panning gold.'' **Chu Shu-chên.**
Spring song. **Mêng Chu.**
Spring Street bar. **Mei-mei Berssenbrugge.**
The spring waters. (excerpts). **Ping Hsin (Hsieh Wan-ying).**
Spring-joy praising God. Praise of the Sun. **Catharina Regina von Greiffenberg.**
Springtime in Vietnam. **Mirta Yañez.**
Sprout. **Tuo Ssu.**
Stalingrad. **Lina de Feria.**
Standing by on the third day. **Madeline DeFrees.**
Standstill. **Kiki Dimoula.**
Stanzas. **Emily Brontë.**
Starkweather House. **Chase Twichell.**
The stars. (excerpts). **Ping Hsin (Hsieh Wan-ying).**
Starting at dawn. **Sun Yün-fêng.**
Starvation camp near Jasło. **Wisława Szymborska.**
The starving vicuna. **Diane Wakoski.**
State mental hospital, 5 PM, summer. **Grace Butcher.**
Static. **Mary Barnard.**
Station. **Marina Rivera.**
The statue. (Largely because of coincidence and partly because of chance, I have taken up a new address at 47th Street and Avenue F). **Diane Wakoski.**
Statue of a woman with hands tied. *See* Mark of recognition.
Statues. **Kathleen Raine.**

Stepping westward. **Denise Levertov.**
The stepsisters. **Belkis Cuza Malé.**
Sticheron for Matins, Wednesday of Holy Week. **Kassia.**
Still falls the Rain. **Edith Sitwell.**
Still I rise. **Maya Angelou.**
Still life. **Diana Chang.**
Still life. **Anita Endrezze-Danielson.**
Stillbirth. **Barbara Noel Scott.**
The stone maiden. **Celia Gilbert.**
Stone soup. **Lisel Mueller.**
Stop. **Joan Larkin.**
Storm. **Kathleen Raine.**
Story for the remainder. **Johari M. Kunjufu.**
Story of a hotel room. **Rosemary Tonks.**
Strange plant. **Zelda.**
Strange victory. **Sara Teasdale.**
The stranger. **Kathleen Fraser.**
Stranger. **Gabriela Mistral.**
Strawberries. **Barbara Noda.**
Street demonstration. **Margaret Walker.**
Street of the women of the world. **Georgina Herrera.**
Striking out. **Kathleene West.**
Struggle of class. **Rashidah Ismaili.**
Struggling at the kill. **Shlomit Cohen.**
Student. **Cheng Min.**
Subalterns. **Elizabeth Daryush.**
Substitution. **Anne Spencer.**
SUBTERRANEOUS/Subterraneous. **Janet Hamill.**
The succubus. **Harriet Rose.**
The sudden appearance of cherry blossoms. **Empress Jitō.**
Sufi quatrain. **Rabi'a bint Isma'il of Syria.**
Sugarman. **Margaret Porter.**
Suicide. **Alice Karle.**
Summer acres. **Anne Wilkinson.**
Summer beach. **Frances Cornford.**
Summer freezes here. **Hsiung Hung.**
Summer in England, 1914. **Alice Meynell.**
Summer matures. **Helene Johnson.**
Summer murder. **Julia Vinograd.**
Summer 1970. **Lindiwe Mabuza.**
Summer oracle. **Audre Lorde.**
Summer street. **Sharyn Jeanne Skeeter.**
Summer words for a sister addict. **Sonia Sanchez.**
Sunday. **Pat Parker.**
Sunday morning. **Christina Jenkins.**
Sunday morning ritual. **Pat D'Alessandro.**
sunday parlor park freeway. **Carol Tinker.**
The Sunderland children. **Alice Meynell.**
Sundown sigh. **Melba Joyce Boyd.**
Sunflowers and Saturdays. **Melba Joyce Boyd.**
Sunni's unveiling. **Elouise Loftin.**
The sunset on the sea Saturday the 4th of March, 1972. **Amanda Berenguer.**
Superstition. **Minji Karibo.**
The suppliant. **Georgia Douglas Johnson.**
The supremes-cuz they dead. (Memorial). **Sonia Sanchez.**
The surfer. **Judith Wright.**
Susanna and the elders. **Adelaide Crapsey.**

susie. **Alta.**
Swallows. **Mary Webb.**
The swan bathing. **Ruth Pitter.**
Swannery. **Dorothy Wellesley.**
The swans. **Edith Sitwell.**
Sweet Ethel. **Linda Piper.**
Sweet Otis Suite. **Anasa Jordan.**
Sweet revenge. **Barbara Szerlip.**
Sweet rough man. **Gertrude "Ma" Rainey.**
Swift floods. **Kata Szidónia Petroczi.**
Swineherd. **Eilean ni Chuilleanain.**
A sword. **Karin Boye.**
Sympathy. **Viola Meynell.**

T

Table. **Ana Ilce.**
Take the skin off the mama. **Stephanie Mines.**
The takers. **Nikki Grimes.**
The takers. **Sharon Olds.**
The tale of the Genji. (excerpts). **Murasaki Shikibu.**
Talk to me, talk to me. **Chedva Harakavy.**
Talking about it. **Sara Miles.**
Talking to myself. **Kiki Dimoula.**
Tambourine song for soldiers going into battle. **Hind bint Utba.**
Tampax. **Frances Landsman.**
Tangled hair. (excerpts). **Yosano Akiko.**
Tanka. **Fatimah Afif.**
Tarantella. **Jeanne Sirotkin.**
A teacher taught me. **Anna Lee Walters.**
The tearing of the skin. **Yvonne.**
Tears. **Myrtle Bates.**
Tel Aviv beach, Winter, '74. **Raquel Chalfi.**
X. **Enid Vián.**
10:15 A.M.—April 27, 1969. **Sonia Sanchez.**
Ten leagues beyond the wide world's end. **Dilys Laing.**
Tenebris. **Angelina Weld Grimké.**
Tengo Puerto Rico en mi Corazón. **Maxine Shaw.**
Tenson. **Carenza** and **Iselda.**
The tenth Armistice Day. **S. Gertrude Ford.**
A terrible heart. **Yona Wallach.**
Territory. **Susan Wood-Thompson.**
tessa's song. **Carol Bergé.**
The testimony of Sister Maureen. **Toi Derricotte.**
Textile women: (Lowell, Lawrence, Fall River, Amoskeag, Gastonia, Marion, Columbia, Oneita). **Rachel Maines.**
thank you capitalism for the expanding universe. **Carol Tinker.**
Thanking my mother for piano lessons. **Diane Wakoski.**
That poem I didn't write. **Leah Goldberg.**

Thee to a dead mountain. **Emily Katherine Harris.**
Theft. **Barbara Smith.**
Theorem. (How I managed to square the circle of dreams in the shape of a window at the top of the stairs in a tenement house). **Jenny Mastoraki.**
There and here. **Barbara Anderson.**
There is a point. **Susan North.**
There is a woman in this town. **Pat Parker.**
There is no evil only restlessness! **Ruth Weiss.**
There is no title: only echoes. **Johari M. Kunjufu.**
There it is. **Jayne Cortez.**
There let thy bleeding branch atone. **Emily Brontë.**
There should be time. **Myrtle Bates.**
There was a dance, sweetheart. **Joy Harjo.**
'There will come soft rains.' **Sara Teasdale.**
Thermodynamics II. **Fanchon Lewis.**
These women at thirty-five. **Suzanne Juhasz.**
They clapped. **Nikki Giovanni.**
they did not build wings for them. **Irene Klepfisz.**
They go by, go by, love, the days and the hours. **Teresa de Jesús.**
They never thought. **Anna Akhmatova.**
They say that the plants do not speak. **Rosalía de Castro.**
they're always curious. **Irene Klepfisz.**
They're making a girl for the age. **Belkis Cuza Malé.**
They've come. **Alfonsina Storni.**
Thinking of someone. **Hsiung Hung.**
Third home. (The segregated heart). **Minnie Bruce Pratt.**
The third house. (excerpts). **Amy Károlyi.**
Thirty-eight. **Charlotte Smith.**
This child is the mother. **Gloria C. Oden.**
this city-light. (The house of desire). **Sherley Anne Williams.**
This is a poem about Vieques, Puerto Rico. **June Jordan.**
THIS IS MY CENTURY . . . Black synthesis of time. **Margaret Walker.**
This is the story of the day in the life of a woman trying. **Susan Griffin.**
This is the sword. **Elizabeth Daryush.**
This is to be told in the manner of . . . **Charlotte Carter.**
This page too. **Fina García Marruz.**
This place. **Barbara Szerlip.**
This road. **Mirta Aguirre.**
This room in which I lie sick. **Anna Akhmatova.**
This thing only. **Anna Rydstedt-Dannstedt.**
This woman is a lesbian be careful. (A woman is talking to death). **Judy Grahn.**
Thomas Iron-Eyes. Born circa 1840. Died 1919, Rosebud Agency, S. D. **Marnie Walsh.**
thoughts about Clara Schumann. **Mary Winfrey.**
Thoughts on the unicorn. **Elise Passavant.**
Three. **Miriam Dyak.**
The three lads. **Elizabeth Chandler Forman.**
Three nights on Hoffman Street. **Sandy Boucher.**
3 serendipitous poems. **Pat Crutchfield Exum.**
Three songs to mark the night. **Judith Ivaloo Volborth.**
3-31-70. (Journal). **Gayl Jones.**
Three women in the closet. **Gloria Anzaldúa.**

Through the weather. **Sara Miles.**
Tied down. **Kiki Dimoula.**
Tiger year. **Laura Tokunaga.**
Tiger-lily. **Raquel Chalfi.**
Tigers. **Fleur Adcock.**
The tightrope walker. **Diane Wakoski.**
Time caught in a net. **Dahlia Ravikovitch.**
Time of waiting in Amsterdam. **Ingrid Jonker.**
The tired poem: last letter from a typical unemployed Black
    professional woman. **Donna Kate Rushin.**
To _____. **Hsiung Hung.**
To a child born in time of small war. **Helen Sorrells.**
To a dark girl. **Gwendolyn B. Bennett.**
To a friend going blind. **Jorie Graham.**
To a gentleman and lady on the death of the lady's brother
    and sister, and a child of the name Avis, aged one year.
    Phillis Wheatley.
To a gone era (My college days - class of '73). **Irma
    McClaurin.**
To a hero dead at al-Safra. **Hind bint Uthatha.**
to a male intellectual. **Michèle Roberts.**
To a young man on his thirtieth birthday. **Jean Overton
    Fuller.**
To Alexis in answer to his poem against fruition. **Aphra
    Behn.**
To an autocrat. **Diane Wakoski.**
To an uneducated woman. **Sappho.**
To an unfaithful lover. **Adelaide Crapsey.**
To be of use. **Marge Piercy.**
To begin. **Fran Winant.**
To confirm a thing. **May Swenson.**
To conscripts. **Alice Meynell.**
"To count a million objects, even in 12 years, one cannot
    spend much time on each one." **Adrianne Marcus.**
To Dr. Swift on his birthday, 30th November 1721. **Esther
    Johnson.**
To every birth its pain. **Akua Lezli Hope.**
To, from, for and about Detroit. **Jeanne Sirotkin.**
To George Sand. **Elizabeth Barrett Browning.**
To grave, to cradle. **Patricia Henley.**
To her husband, at the wedding. **Fukuda Chiyo-Ni.**
To her portrait. **Juana Inés de la Cruz (Sister).**
To his father on praising the honest life of the peasant.
    Parvin E'tesami.
To Ibn Zaidun. **Wallada.**
To imagination. **Emily Brontë.**
To J. S. Collis. **Ruth Pitter.**
To Judith, taking leave. **Adrienne Rich.**
To Julia de Burgos. **Julia de Burgos.**
To keep the memory of Charlotte Forten Grimké. **Angelina
    Weld Grimké.**
To Lumi Videla. **Reina María Rodríguez.**
To Lysander, on some verses he writ, and asking more for
    his heart than 'twas worth. **Aphra Behn.**
To Mr. F. now Earl of W. **Anne Finch, Countess of
    Winchilsea.**
To my brother. **Vera Brittain.**
To my daughter the junkie on a train. **Audre Lorde.**

To my dear and loving husband. **Anne Bradstreet.**
To my excellent Lucasia, on our friendship. **Katherine
    Philips.**
To my father. **Blaga Dmitrova.**
To my father. **Henrietta Cordelia Ray.**
To my godson. **Carla Lanyon Lanyon.**
To my son, approaching 11. **Linda Pastan.**
To name you. **Alejandra Pizarnik.**
To other women who were ugly once. **Inés Hernandez
    Tovar.**
To our daughter. **Jennifer Armitage.**
To S. M. a young African painter, on seeing his work. **Phillis
    Wheatley.**
To say whose side you're on. **Kathleen Lignell.**
to Shannon and Kenneths. **Alice Karle.**
To sister for Mother. **Akua Lezli Hope.**
To sleep. **Bella Akhmadulina.**
(To someone I met on 125th Street, 1966). **Mae Jackson.**
To soulfolk. **Margaret Goss Burroughs.**
To the anxious mother. **Valente Malangatana.**
To the dark god. **Paula Ludwig.**
To the fair Clarinda, who made love to me, imagin'd more
    than woman. **Aphra Behn.**
To the first of August. **Ann Plato.**
To the ladies. **Mary Lee (Lady Chudleigh).**
To the memory of J. Horace Kimball. **Ada.**
To the newborn. **Judit Tóth.**
To the nightingale. **Anne Finch, Countess of Winchilsea.**
To the poet Wordsworth. **Felicia Hemans.**
To the portrait of Lermontov. **Margarita Aliger.**
To the Right Honorable William, Earl of Dartmouth. **Phillis
    Wheatley.**
To the short tune "The magnolias." **Li Ch'ing-chao.**
To the tune "A branch of bamboo." **Chu Chung-hsien.**
To the tune "A dream song." **Sun Tao-hsüan.**
To the tune "A dream song." **Wu Tsao.**
To the tune "A floating cloud crosses Enchanted Moun-
    tain." **Huang O.**
To the tune "A hilly garden." **Li Ch'ing-chao.**
To the tune "A watered silk dress." **Ho Shuang-ch'ing.**
To the tune "Eternal happiness." **Li Ch'ing-chao.**
To the tune "Flowers along the path through the field." **Wu
    Tsao.**
To the tune "I paint my lips red." **Anonymous.**
To the tune "Intoxicated with shadows of flowers." **Yü
    Ch'ing-tsêng.**
To the tune "Picking mulberries." **Anonymous.**
To the tune "Plucking a cinnamon branch." **Huang O.**
To the tune "Red embroidered shoes." **Anonymous.**
To the tune "Red embroidered shoes." **Huang O.**
To the tune "Soaring clouds." **Huang O.**
To the tune "The Bodhisattva's barbaric headdress." **Lady
    Wei.**
To the tune "The fall of a little wild goose." **Huang O.**
To the tune "The honor of a fisherman." **Li Ch'ing-chao.**
To the tune "The joy of peace and brightness." **Wu Tsao.**
To the tune "The Narcissus by the river." **Chi'iu Chin.**
To the tune "The pain of lovesickness." **Wu Tsao.**

To the tune "The Phoenix hairpin." **T'ang Wan.**
To the tune "The river is red." **Ch'iu Chin.**
To the tune "The river is red." **Wang Ch'ing-hui.**
To the tune "Washing silk in the stream." **Ho Shuang-ch'ing.**
To those of my sisters who kept their naturals. **Gwendolyn Brooks.**
To Tony (aged 3). **Marjorie Wilson.**
To turn from love. **Sarah Webster Fabio.**
To usward. **Gwendolyn B. Bennett.**
To W. L. G. on reading his 'Chosen Queen.' **Charlotte L. Forten.**
Today I am modest. **Esther Raab.**
Toe'osh: a Laguna coyote story. **Leslie Marmon Silko.**
tokens for "t." **Esther Louise.**
Tomorrow noon. **Nia Francisco.**
Tonight. **Laura Beausoleil.**
Tonight. **Ada Negri.**
too late. **Astra.**
The tooth quilt. (The mushroom quilt from water mill). **Barbara Guest.**
The total influence or outcome of the matter: THE SUN. **Marge Piercy.**
Touch. Poem 5. **Carolyn M. Rodgers.**
Touch. Poem 4. **Carolyn M. Rodgers.**
Touché. **Jessie Redmon Fauset.**
Touching a friend. **Marie-Elise.**
Tourist in Rumania. **Michelene Wandor.**
Toward a 44th birthday. **Nellie Wong.**
Tracks (after reading Blaise Cendrars). **Kate Ellen Braverman.**
The trail up Wu Gorge. **Sun Yün-fêng.**
Train. **Tuo Ssu.**
Transcendental etude. **Adrienne Rich.**
Transit. **Adrienne Rich.**
The transit of the gods. **Kathleen Raine.**
Transition. (Natural birth). **Toi Derricotte.**
Translations. **Adrienne Rich.**
the transplant. **Jan Clausen.**
Transport of wounded in Mesopotamia, 1917. **Margery Lawrence.**
Trapped. **Adelaide Crapsey.**
Travel notes. **Michelle Cliff.**
The traveller. **Dulce María Loynaz.**
The traveller. **Cleva Solís.**
Travelling in the mountains. **Sun Yün-fêng.**
The tree of begats. **Martha Shelley.**
Tree women quest for sun . . . **Malkia M'buzi.**
The trees are down. **Charlotte Mew.**
Trees at night. **Helene Johnson.**
Triad. **Adelaide Crapsey.**
Trip. **Josephine Miles.**
The trip back. (Not that far). **May Miller.**
Tripart. **Gayl Jones.**
Trojan. **Melanie Kaye.**
The Trojan women. (excerpt). **Ann Stanford.**
The trout. **Marion Marlowe.**
A true dream. **Elizabeth Barrett Browning.**

The truth of the matter in Coolidge, Arizona. **Susan North.**
Tulips. **Sylvia Plath.**
Tunisia. (Not that far). **May Miller.**
Turkey. (Not that far). **May Miller.**
Turning. **Lucille Clifton.**
Turning corners. **Lynn Suruma.**
The twelve dancing princesses. **Sandra M. Gilbert.**
Twenty-year marriage. **Ai.**
The twins. **Judith Wright.**
Two. **Margarita Aliger.**
2. **Jessica Tarahata Hagedorn.**
2-15-43/2-15-76. **Rachel Maines.**
Two gardens. **Yona Wallach.**
Two poems. **Anna Akhmatova.**
Two poems. **Diane Middlebrook.**
Two poems for my granddaughter. **Digdora Alonso.**
Two poems: in commemoration of a friend's happiness. **Virginia Gilbert.**
two poetry readings. **Michelene Wandor.**
Two poets on the way to the palace. **Sonya Dorman.**
Two, remembered. **Constance Carrier.**
Two songs. **Adrienne Rich.**
The two times table. **Amanda Berenguer.**
the tyer-in. **Rachel Maines.**

U name this one. **Carolyn M. Rodgers.**
Ugly things (a song). **Teresita Fernández.**
Ultimatum. **Dorothy Parker.**
Under the days. **Angelina Weld Grimké.**
Under the edge of february. **Jayne Cortez.**
Under the sword. **Cynthia Kraman Genser.**
Unemployment/monologue. **June Jordan.**
The unequal fetters. **Anne Finch, Countess of Winchilsea.**
Unfinished. **Rota Silverstrini.**
The unicorn. **Ruth Pitter.**
the union educator. **Rachel Maines.**
Unknown girl in the maternity ward. **Anne Sexton.**
Unknown warrior. **Elizabeth Daryush.**
Unlearning to not speak. **Marge Piercy.**
Unrecorded speech. **Anna Adams.**
Unspeakable. **Delmira Augustini.**
Untitled. **Lynda Efros.**
untitled. **Rosemari Mealy.**
Untitled. **Jeanne Sirotkin.**
Untitled. **Paula Yup.**
Up from D.C. **Marilyn Hacker.**
Up up on the disorders of the hairs. **Rochelle Owens.**
Upon her soothing breast. **Emily Brontë.**
Upon seeing an etching. **Helen Aoki Kaneko.**

Upon the double murther of King Charles I, in answer to a libellous copy of rimes by Vavasor Powell. **Katherine Philips.**

Upon the saying that my verses were made by another. **Anne Killigrew.**

Upstairs. **Marlene Leamon.**

Upstate. **Jan Clausen.**

(upstate poetry tour). (dialectics). **Jan Clausen.**

Urban life. **Xelina.**

Useless day. **Rosario Castellanos.**

Useless frontiers. **Alejandra Pizarnik.**

a using. **Mariah Britton Howard.**

Utanikki, August 1978. **Sandra McPherson.**

The V.A.D. scullery-maid's song. **M. Winifred Wedgwood.**

Vacant possession. **Janet Frame.**

The vacuous rime. **María Eugenia Vaz Ferreira.**

Vagabond in the tower. **Gladys Zaldivar.**

''Vagina'' sonnet. **Joan Larkin.**

Vague apprehension, to a gambler. **Lin Ling.**

Valediction. **Barbara Banks.**

van Gogh painting his way out of the asylum. **Dona Stein.**

The vanguard artist dreams her work. **Alexandra Grilikhes.**

Vanishing point: urban Indian. **Wendy Rose.**

Vashti. **Frances Ellen Watkins Harper.**

Venus—Aghia Sophia. **Catherine de Vinck.**

Venus of the Louvre. **Emma Lazarus.**

Venus petrified. **Dilys Laing.**

Venus transiens. **Amy Lowell.**

Vera, from my childhood. (The common woman). **Judy Grahn.**

A verse on the 50th day. **Rochelle Owens.**

Verses about Moscow. (excerpt). **Marina Tsvetayeva.**

Verses addressed to the imitator of the first satire of the second book of Horace. **Mary Wortley Montagu, Lady.**

Verses for Anna. **Carilda Oliver Labra.**

Verses to Blok. (excerpt). **Marina Tsvetayeva.**

The very rose. **Naomi Rachel.**

The veteran. **Margaret Postgate Cole.**

Veterans. **Dilys Laing.**

Vickie Loans-Arrow 1972. **Marnie Walsh.**

Villages cities. **Minerva Salado.**

Villanelle. **Dilys Laing.**

Violet twilights. **Edith Södergran.**

The virgin capture. **Kathleen Herbert.**

Vision. **Delmira Augustini.**

A vision. **Maria Konopnicka.**

Vision of the cuckoo. **Ruth Pitter.**

A visitation. **Margaret Stanley-Wrench.**

Visiting. **Chung Ling.**

Visiting. **Sandra Maria Esteves.**

Visiting a son in Java. **Elizabeth Keeler.**

Visiting M. at the Happy Valley Nursing Home. **Dona Stein.**

The visitor. **Albis Torres.**

The visits. (excerpts). **Mirta Yañez.**

Vitalie. **Janet Sternburg.**

Vocation. **Judith Herzberg.**

Voice. **Frances Mayes.**

The voice of return. **María Eugenia Vaz Ferreira.**

Voices from the diaspora home. **Wilmette Brown.**

The voices of Eden. **Else Lasker-Schuler.**

A volunteer. **Helen Parry Eden.**

Voodoo. **Gloria Frym.**

Voronezh. **Anna Akhmatova.**

W. rings on her fingers & bells on her toes she shall have music wherever she goes. **Diane Wakoski.**

Waiting. **Ellen Wittlinger.**

Waiting for her man too long. **Sandra Rogers.**

Waiting for mother. **Anonymous.**

Waiting for truth. **Susan Griffin.**

Waitresses. **Ranice Henderson Crosby.**

Waking at the bottom of the dark. **Jan Clausen.**

Wa-Ko-Da. (Birds of paradise). **Nzadi Zimele-Keita (Michelle McMichael).**

Walking-with-a-cane-pass. **Ishigaki Rin.**

The walls do not fall. (excerpts). **Hilda Doolittle.**

Waltz of the Angelus I. **Blanca Varela.**

Waltz of the Angelus II. **Blanca Varela.**

War dispatch. **Marilyn Bobes.**

A war film. **Teresa Hooley.**

War girls. **Jessie Pope.**

Warnings. **Vidaluz Meneses.**

Warpath song. **Anonymous.**

Wash. **Eilean ni Chuilleanain.**

Washing and pounding clothes. **Tu Fu.**

Watching crow, looking south towards the Manzano Mountains. **Joy Harjo.**

Watching the dance (for Martha Graham). **Alexandra Grilikhes.**

Water games. **Dulce María Loynaz.**

Water lily on Loch Bran. **Alice V. Stuart.**

Water without sound. **Malka Heifetz Tussman.**

Waterlilies. **Ma Hsiang-lan.**

The way we were. **Georgina Herrera.**

We are not forgetting the patience of the mad, their love of detail. **Lyn Hejinian.**

We shall come no more. **Vera Brittain.**
We shall not escape hell. **Marina Tsvetayeva.**
We visit the gorilla at his 47th Street address. (Largely because of coincidence and partly because of chance, I have taken up a new address at 47th Street and Avenue F). **Diane Wakoski.**
We women. **Edith Södergran.**
The weaver's lamentation. **Anonymous.**
Weaving. **Lucy Larcom.**
Wedding. **Maria Banus.**
The wedding coat. **Harriet Rose.**
Wedding poem. **Adrianne Marcus.**
Weekend man. **Kate Ellen Braverman.**
The welcome. **Y. W. Easton.**
The welcome. **Rochelle Nameroff.**
Welcome home from Vietnam. **Laura Beausoleil.**
The welder. **Cherríe Moraga.**
Well enough alone. **Debora Greger.**
We're OK. **Gloria Fuertes.**
The Western Wall. **Shirley Kaufman.**
wet green hallelujahs. **Carol Tinker.**
Wet your fingers. **Lina de Feria.**
Whale. **Laura Jensen.**
What a little girl had on her mind. **Ibaragi Noriko.**
What are years? **Marianne Moore.**
What can you do? **Ruth Stone.**
What does she dream of? **Charlotte Brontë.**
What is love if it is only known through words saying it would be hard for me to leave you? (The house of desire). **Sherley Anne Williams.**
What love is. (De arte honeste amandi). **Linda Gregerson.**
What Matisse is after. **Diana Chang.**
What reward? **Winifred M. Letts.**
What shall I give my children? **Gwendolyn Brooks.**
What the bones know. **Carolyn Kizer.**
What the sirens sang. **Rachel Loden.**
what we know. **Nzadi Zimele-Keita (Michelle McMichael).**
What you need. **Kathleen Fraser.**
When I married. **Vidaluz Meneses.**
when i rite. **Margaret Porter.**
When I think of him. **Anonymous.**
When I was a fat woman. **Rebecca Gordon.**
When I was fair and young. **Elizabeth I, Queen of England.**
When I was growing up. **Nellie Wong.**
When maidens are young. **Aphra Behn.**
When mother died, rows of cans. **Judith McDaniel.**
When people ask. **Donna Allegra.**
When poets dream. **Colleen J. McElroy.**
When she was no longer. **Miriam Oren.**
When the Emperor Tenji ordered Fujiwara Kamatari to judge between the beauty of cherry blossoms and the red autumn leaves on the hills, Princess Nukada gave judgment with this poem. **Princess Nukada.**
When the furnace goes on in a California tract house. **Ruth Stone.**
When the moon floats. **Anna Akhmatova.**
'When you become that cold sullen creature man.' **Rachel Loden.**

When you have forgotten Sunday: the love story. **Gwendolyn Brooks.**
When you laugh. **Ingrid Jonker.**
When you read this poem (for citizens opposed to [book] censorship, Baton Rouge). **Pinkie Gordon Lane.**
When your husband goes to prison. **Susan North.**
When your mouth said goodbye. **Elsie Alvarado de Ricord.**
Whenever the snakes come. **Chedva Harakavy.**
Where are the men seized in this wind of madness? **Alda do Espirito Santo.**
Where do these steps lead? **Gavriela Elisha.**
Where have you gone. **Mari Evans.**
Where iguanas still live. **Colleen J. McElroy.**
Where mountain lion lay down with deer. **Leslie Marmon Silko.**
Where, O, Where? **Elinor Wylie.**
Where will you be? **Pat Parker.**
Wherever. **Muriel Rukeyser.**
The white and the black. **Caroline N. M. Khaketla.**
White bears. **Veronica Porumbacu.**
The white bird. **Anna Akhmatova.**
The white color of nearness. (excerpt). **Lan Ling.**
The white horse. **Rita Spurr.**
White night. **Adrienne Rich.**
The white women. **Mary Elizabeth Coleridge.**
The white worm. **Alison Colbert.**
Who in one lifetime. **Muriel Rukeyser.**
Who is my brother? **Pinkie Gordon Lane.**
Who killed brown love? **Angela de Hoyos.**
Who stops the dance? **Hsiung Hung.**
Who will finally say. **Barbara Szerlip.**
Whodunit. **Sonya Dorman.**
Whores. **Margaret Walker.**
whose death at easter (on the train between London and Leeds). **Michèle Roberts.**
Why? **Melba Joyce Boyd.**
Why I like movies (for Charlotte). **Patricia Jones.**
Why should I be jealous. **Anonymous.**
Why so many of them die. **Susan Wallbank.**
Why we are late. **Josephine Miles.**
Wicked neighbor. **Zelda.**
Widow. **Dorothy Livesay.**
The widow's song. **Anonymous.**
Wife of Kohelet. **Shlomit Cohen.**
The wife's lament. (modern version of anonymous poem). **Ann Stanford.**
Wild nights. **Virginia de Araújo.**
Wild orchards. **Nurit Zarchi.**
The wild poppies. **Barbara Noel Scott.**
Wild women blues. **Ida Cox.**
Will you come out now? **Valerie Sinason.**
William Carlos Williams' buddy. **Naomi Rachel.**
Willow eyebrows. **Chao Luan-luan.**
Wimmin. **Carolyn M. Rodgers.**
Wind. **Helen Aoki Kaneko.**
The wind from Mt. Fuji. **Tagami Kikusha-Ni.**
The wind on the downs. **Marian Allen.**
Wind song. **Anonymous.**
A window. **Forūgh Farrokhzād.**

The window. **Sara Jackson.**
Winds of Africa. **Dorothy S. Obi.**
Winter. **Bella Akhmadulina.**
Winter day. **Bella Akhmadulina.**
Winter: my secret. **Christina Rossetti.**
Winter sacrament. **Michèle Roberts.**
Winter solstice—for Frank. **Asphodel.**
Winter solstice 1975. **Miriam Dyak.**
Winter solstice poem. **Diana Scott.**
A winter twilight. **Angelina Weld Grimké.**
Winterpoem. **Sandra M. Gilbert.**
The wiping moss from the ruins. **Anonymous.**
Wisdom has broken my arms. **Anne Hébert.**
A wish. **Fanny Kemble.**
the wishon line. **Sherley Anne Williams.**
The witch. **Mary Elizabeth Coleridge.**
The witch. **Adelaide Crapsey.**
Witch! **Leonora Speyer.**
Witch. **Jean Tepperman.**
A witch cracking up. **Raquel Chalfi.**
A witch without a cover. **Raquel Chalfi.**
Witch-woman. **Amy Lowell.**
With a ring. **Veronica Porumbacu.**
With child. **Genevieve Taggard.**
With my velvet gun. **Jan Zaleski.**
With no immediate cause. **Ntozake Shange.**
With words (for Tony). **Diane Wakoski.**
Witnesses. **Xelina.**
The woman. (Three women in the closet). **Gloria Anzaldúa.**
Woman. **Kōra Rumiko.**
Woman. **Elouise Loftin.**
A woman. **Siti Nuraini.**
Woman. **Magda Portal.**
Woman alone. **Denise Levertov.**
Woman as market. **Muriel Rukeyser.**
A woman at the window. **Nellie Wong.**
A woman dead in her forties. **Adrienne Rich.**
Woman free. (excerpts). **Elizabeth Wolstenholme-Elmy.**
Woman in a tobacco factory. **Nancy Morejón.**
The woman in Buffalo is given to waiting. **Becky Birtha.**
The woman in my notebook. **Lorna Dee Cerventes.**
The woman in the next room. **Adrianne Marcus.**
A woman is talking to death. (excerpts). **Judy Grahn.**
A woman making advances publicly. **Judith Kazantzis.**
Woman me. **Maya Angelou.**
A woman mourned by daughters. **Adrienne Rich.**
Woman poem. **Nikki Giovanni.**
A woman shaman's song. **Uvavnuk.**
The woman thing. **Audre Lorde.**
A woman to her lover. **Christina Walsh.**
Woman waiting in the park. **Magaly Sánchez.**
Woman wall. **Lin Ling.**
The woman who lives in the botanical gardens. **Alexis De Veaux.**
The woman who lives inside the world. **Michele Murray.**
The woman who swims in her tears. **Susan Griffin.**
the woman who wanted to be a hero. **Michèle Roberts.**
A woman who's arrived at a ripe old age. **Zelda.**

The woman's dream. **Frances Horovitz.**
The women's Marseillaise. **F. E. M. Macaulay.**
A woman's plea. **Sappho.**
A woman's song. **Colleen J. McElroy.**
Woman's song. **Judith Wright.**
A woman's song, about men. **Anonymous.**
A woman's song for her drowned brother. **Anonymous.**
A woman's tribal belt. **Willyce Kim.**
Womb. **Lili Bita.**
Women. **Adrienne Rich.**
Women. **May Swenson.**
Women. **Alice Walker.**
Women at munition making. **Mary Gabrielle Collins.**
The women gather. **Nikki Giovanni.**
Women of my land. **Frankie Armstrong.**
The women of Rubens. **Wisława Szymborska.**
Women of the baths. **Ellen Bass.**
Women songs I. **Kadia Molodowsky.**
Women Transport Corps. **Anonymous.**
Women's lib. **Margaret Danner.**
Wonder woman. **Genny Lim.**
Wonderland. **Michelene Wandor.**
Wood smoke. **Albis Torres.**
The wooden chamber. **Anne Hébert.**
Wool season. **Paula Gunn Allen.**
The word. **Bonnie Lateiner.**
the words of a woman who breathes fire: one. **Kitty Tsui.**
Words South. **Rafaela Chacón Nardi.**
The world. **Christina Rossetti.**
Would I might go far over sea. **Marie de France.**
Writing a poem. **Naomi Long Madgett.**
Written at a party where my lord gave away a thousand bolts of silk. **Ch'ien T'ao.**
Written in the sunset. **Hsiung Hung.**
The Wykhamist. **Nora Griffiths.**

Xantippe. **Amy Levy.**

Y.M.C.A. **C.A.L.T.**
Years. **Anna Margolin.**

The yellow linen dress: a sequence. **Ann Lauterbach.**
Yesterday. **Fran Winant.**
Yon pastures green. **Femi Sisay.**
You are always new. **Anna Akhmatova.**
You are stolen kisses in my unsuspecting sleep. **Marté Jones.**
You discover you're in love with the dead prince. (The love sequence). **Sandra M. Gilbert.**
You do not know the breaking through. **Ellen Bass.**
You fall. (The love sequence). **Sandra M. Gilbert.**
You know. **Jayne Cortez.**
You made it rain. **Fareedah Allah.**
You may go on the warpath. **Anonymous.**
You meet the real dream mother-in-law. (The love sequence). **Sandra M. Gilbert.**
You must break through old thought. **Elizabeth Daryush.**
you, phoebusapollo. **Barbara Moraff.**
You refuse to own. **Margaret Atwood.**
You, seated near a lamp. (Two poems). **Diane Middlebrook.**
You too. **Fina García Marruz.**
You upset the whole system of this place. **Cherríe Moraga.**
You, walking past me. **Marina Tsvetayeva.**
you were never miss brown to me. **Sherley Anne Williams.**
You were sleeping. **Bella Akhmadulina.**
You who occupy our land. **Manuela Margarido.**
A young deer/dust. **Hemda Roth.**
The young emerald, Evening Star. (excerpt). **Carol Tinker.**

Young girl. **Ricarda Huch.**
The young girl and the beach. **Sophia de Mello Breyner Andresen.**
The young rat and his dam, the cock and the cat. **Anne Finch, Countess of Winchilsea.**
Young woman's blues. **Bessie Smith.**
Your olive face. **Lorraine Sutton.**
Your small hands. **Adrienne Rich.**
Your story. **Susan Wood.**
Your window is on the eastern side. **Bella Akhmadulina.**
Youth gone. (Monna Innominata: a sonnet of sonnets). **Christina Rossetti.**
Yugoslavia. (Not that far). **May Miller.**

Zeppelins. **Nancy Cunard.**
Zhaleyka. **Bella Akhmadulina.**
zocalo. **Barbara Szerlip.**
Zoia. **Rafaela Chacón Nardi.**

Part 3
First Line Index

The ACLU Mountain States Regional Office came across
a **Pinkie Gordon Lane.** Sexual privacy of women on
welfare.

A.T. 30 lies in the siding. **Carola Oman.** Ambulance train
30.

abode pueblos/woven of white sun tierra **Xelina.** Witnesses.

Abortions will not let you forget. **Gwendolyn Brooks.** The
mother.

Above the waves/the lady stands in the pink shell, **Catherine
de Vinck.** Venus—Aghia Sophia.

According to the calendar/I am 36 years old. **Helen Wong
Huie.** The odyssey.

Across one of the hills **Leah Goldberg.** Illuminations 2.

Across the aisle from/me on the subway **Sapphire.** New
York City tonight.

Across the blinded lowlands the beating rain blows chill,
Muriel Elsie Graham. The battle of the swamps.

Across the flesh and feeling of soledad **Jayne Cortez.**
Orisha.

Across the street—the freeway, **Lorna Dee Cervantes.** Beneath the shadow of the freeway.

Adam, come here, I'm gathering heavens. **Reina María
Rodríguez.** Adam.

Adrastes Ears with that dear Voice are blest, **Aphra Behn.**
To Lysander, on some verses he writ, and asking more
for his heart than 'twas worth.

Affirming./What affirmation makes it turn, **Eunice Odio.**
Portraits of the heart.

Afraid of the sunlight,/You cover your face with your silk
sleeves. **Yü Hsüan-chi.** Advice to a neighbor girl.

After a night of whippoorwills **Miriam Dyak.** Dying.

After having been acquitted by a hung jury **Frankie Hucklenbroich.** Due process.

After kicking on the swing, **Anonymous.** To the tune "I
paint my lips red."

After my girl's first gerbils die, **Sharon Olds.** The house of
fecundity.

After the birth of each of my grandmother's five children the
cord was **Michelle Cliff.** Obsolete geography.

After the fretful hours were done— **Babette Deutsch.**
Moving.

After the laboring birth, the clean stripped hull **May Sarton.**
My father's death.

"After the terrible rain, the Annunciation"— **Edith
Sitwell.** Anne Boleyn's song.

after these years/as iron comes by fire **Michele Murray.**
Coming to self.

After this crisis,/nothing being conquered, **Muriel
Rukeyser.** The question. (Searching/not searching).

After years of relative clumsiness/she found her fingers, ten
shuttles **Judith Kazantzis.** Arachne.

Again this morning trembles on the swift stream the image
of **Kathleen Raine.** Images.

again you slept with mr no man **Yona Wallach.** again you
slept with mr no man.

Against any city   that has denied homage **Enheduanna.**
Inna exalted.

Against this wall/where they stood me up barefoot to take my
measurements—**Victoria Theodorou.** Picnic.

age/envelops your strong/soft frame **Bernette Golden.**
Paying dues.

Agnes keeps to herself./That's the trouble. **Kathleen Fraser.** Agnes.

Ah, Dona Mariquita! **Lucha Corpi.** Dona Mariquita.

AH hapless sex! who bears no charms, **Aphra Behn.** To Alexis in answer to his poem against fruition.

Ah, I never, never can forget **Anonymous.** Warpath song.

Ah, little road all whirry in the breeze, **Helene Johnson.** The road.

Ah no! not these!/These, who were childless, are not they who gave **Alice Meynell.** Parentage.

Ah, this is not enough, I cry— **Elizabeth Daryush.** Song: Ah, this is not enough, I cry—.

Ah, to clean and pretend it was nothing **Ingrid Wendt.** Dust.

Ah! why, because the dazzling sun/Restored my earth to joy **Emily Brontë.** Ah! why, because the dazzling sun.

Aim straight at my heart **Rita Boumi-Pappas.** Krinio.

Ain't been on Market Street for nothing **Margaret Walker.** Ballad of the Hoppy-Toad.

ain't got time for a bite to eat **Mari Evans.** The 7:25 trolley.

the air hums at night **Toi Derricotte.** The testimony of Sister Maureen.

The air is cold here. **Teru Kanazawa.** The look of success.

the air is swimming **Janet Hamill.** In my taboo.

Airplane shadows moved across the mountains; leaving me to clear rivers, **Michelle Cliff.** Obsolete geography.

Ajaija-ja,/my playmate **Anonymous.** Love-making.

Aj-ja-japa-pe./Bring out your hair-ornaments! **Anonymous.** untitled.

Alarm clock/sure sound/loud **Mari Evans.** The alarm clock.

Alas, alas, O Goddess, what misfortune has brought me here? **Anonymous.** untitled.

Alas! for all the pretty women who marry dull men, **Anna Wickham.** Meditation at Kew.

Alas, I draw breath heavily, **Akjartoq.** An old woman's song.

Alas, that I should die, **Anonymous.** untitled.

All alone with my shadow, **Ch'iu Chin.** A letter to Lady T'ao Ch'iu, to the tune "Walking through the sedges."

All arguments break down before the news. **Minerva Salado.** The news.

All around the jailhouse/Waiting for a trial; **Ella May Wiggins.** All around the jailhouse.

All a-tremble she awoke **Amrita Pritam.** The annunciation.

All day in exquisite air/The song clomb an invisible stair, **Katharine Tynan.** Larks.

All day long having/buried himself/in the peonies, **Okamoto Kanoko.** untitled.

All day on the phone. All day **Janet Frame.** Vacant possession.

All day she stands before her loom; **Lucy Larcom.** Weaving.

All day the guns had worked their hellish will, **Muriel Elsie Graham.** The lark above the trenches.

All Greece hates/the still eyes in the white face, **Hilda Doolittle.** Helen.

All Igbo come and see that my **Anonymous.** untitled.

All may come by the roads/we least suspect. **Mirta Aguirre.** All may come.

ALL MEN FROM ALL LANDS/KNEEL BEFORE YOU GO **Frances Cornford.** Inscription for a wayside spring.

All month a smell of burning, of dry peat **Anna Akhmatova.** July 1914.

All morning I've had this Rain around me. **Bella Akhmadulina.** Rain.

All night had shout of men and cry. **Alice Meynell.** Easter night.

All night we sang, the invisible sea **Pamela Melnikoff.** The lighthouse at Acre.

All of a sudden a morning is a night. **Nancy Morejón.** In praise of dialectics.

All old women sometimes come to this: **Miriam Waddington.** Old women of Toronto.

"All summer, Sheep's Green and Coe Fen were pick with boys, as naked **Judith Moffett.** "Cambridge University Swimming Club/no public access to river."

All the way back I watch the mountains. **Wu Tsao.** Returning from Flower Law Mountain on a winter day, to the tune "Washing silk in the stream."

All the windows are shining. A great waltz flows **Dilys Laing.** Venus petrified.

All the years waiting, the whole, barren, young **Jean Valentine.** Sex.

all these heads these ears these eyes **Anonymous.** Song of the old woman.

All these voices; whose house am I? Every **Faye Kicknosway.** Persona.

All things within this fading world hath end, **Anne Bradstreet.** Before the birth of one of her children.

All this so tasteless and threatening **Yona Wallach.** All this so tasteless and threatening.

All this takes place as David is **Sharon Barba.** Siblings.

all those straight lovers waiting **Jacqueline Lapidus.** Caution.

All too. We ran away from the burrow of family **Cynthia Macdonald.** My familiar lover.

All veiled from view/she moves toward the altar. **Daniela Gioseffi.** Birth dance, belly dancer.

All white/the boards, the shutters **Yvonne.** The tearing of the skin.

All you violated ones with gentle hearts; **Margaret Walker.** For Malcolm X.

almost newyork with sagging arms. **Rachel Maines.** almost newyork.

Almost sheer fatigue/and yet a steadfastness **Penelope Shuttle.** Early pregnancy.

Alone the sea/and the sky alone; **Alfonsina Storni.** Dog and sea.

Along the way/We met a man **May Miller.** The Holy Land. (Not that far).

Already the buoys/are sounding **Molly Vaux.** Setting sail.

Already yesterday's lips have broken **Lan Ling.** The white color of nearness.

Although he said it **Anonymous.** When I think of him.

Although I come to you constantly **Ono no Komachi.** untitled.

although it is late, it's night,/and you can't. **Alejandra Pizarnik.** I ask silence.

Always/keep in mind/that posterity is for **Mirta Yañez.** Reminder.

Ambushed myself discovered/The counterfeit blossoms **Marie Luise Kaschnitz.** Humility.

America was a new dream and a new world for dreaming. **Pauli Murray.** Dark testament.

American life, you said, is not possible **Carolyn Forché.** Expatriate.

Among the hours facing the sea it rains **Magaly Sánchez.** Among the hours.

Among the Persian rugs & cushions, **Patricia Henley.** Poem for Suzanne.

Amyntas let me to a Grove, **Aphra Behn.** Song: The willing mistress.

Ancient legends/of the coffee fields **Albis Torres.** Coffee field dorm.

ancient stone fences separating nothing **Barbara Szerlip.** The crossing.

and/every thing/that is any/thing **Sonia Sanchez.** 10:15 A.M.—April 27, 1969.

And after we damned each other, **Anna Akhmatova.** And after we damned each other.

And afterwards, when honour has made good, **Iris Tree.** untitled.

And again I was like one of those little girls, **Dahlia Ravikovitch.** Time caught in a net.

And Elizabeth fell in love/with the tree of Springtime **Alice Karle.** An epic (with renaissance flute).

And every Hour still more unjust you grow, **Aphra Behn.** To Lysander, on some verses he writ, and asking more for his heart than 'twas worth.

and finally/she said this is enough **Irena Klepfisz.** The monkey house and other cages.

And from that hour our spirits grew **Elizabeth Barrett Browning.** The runaway slave at Pilgrim's Point.

And he cast it down, down, on the green grass, **Fredegond Shove.** The new ghost.

And he moaned and trembled from foot to head, **Elizabeth Barrett Browning.** The runaway slave at Pilgrim's Point.

And how does one begin again **Susan Sherman.** Lilith of the Wildwood, of the Fair Places.

And I had loved that house, always, for **Bella Akhmadulina.** Rain.

And I, I was a good child on the whole, **Elizabeth Barrett Browning.** Aurora Leigh.

And I made myself a surrogate wedding-day **Nicki Jackowska.** The sisters.

And I put this skull on an old **Susan Griffin.** Deer skull.

And I took myself for a walk in the woods that day **Nicki Jackowska.** Family outing—a celebration.

And I, woman, cloaked in blues **Irma McClaurin.** I, woman.

And if any man should ask me/If I would sell my vote, **Frances Harper.** Deliverance.

and if they close my garrulous throat (Epilogue) **Anna Akhmatova.** Requiem 1935–1940.

And in that instant remembered you/had been in that body of **Susan Griffin.** Deer skull.

And in the end I'll say—/goodbye, don't commit yourself to love. **Bella Akhmadulina.** Goodbye.

And in the land, there were four. **Chaya Shenhav.** Four.

And it's hard to see the mountains **Dolly Bird.** Can I say.

And last night a man came in/to tell her of stars and clouds moving fast **Mei-Mei Berssenbrugge.** Spring Street bar.

. . . and nights i just lay awake in bed **Mae Jackson.** Night.

And nothing's wrong with the other two. **Kathleen Fraser.** Agnes.

And now a ''goodbye forever'' . . . a ''thank you'' . . . **Claudia Lars.** Letters written when night grows.

And now without Respect or Fear, **Aphra Behn.** The disappointment.

and of course/you promise to do/the same for me. **Carolyn M. Rodgers.** Masquerade.

And she is beautiful, our daughter. **Jennifer Armitage.** To our daughter.

And should I thank you, my dear skin, **Annette Lynch.** Gratitude.

And so Rimbaud and I set out to sea **Belkis Cuza Malé.** Oh, my Rimbaud.

And so the stork,/that long-legged bird of the grand venture, **Georgina Herrera.** Birth.

And so through the Jaffa Gate, the street **Shirley Kaufman.** The Western Wall.

and so who/was the city's mother? did it **Michèle Roberts.** city limited.

And still God's sunshine and his frost, **Elizabeth Barrett Browning.** The runaway slave at Pilgrim's Point.

And the ladies dressed in red for my pain and with **Alejandra Pizarnik.** Sorceries.

And the new space she find was an antique **Lois Elaine Griffith.** For all the homseick sunshine girls in spring.

and the old women gathered/and sang His praises **Marie Evans.** . . . And the old women gathered (The Gospel Singers).

And there is nothing at all—neither fear, **Natalya Gorbanevskaya.** untitled.

And there was stormy silence in that city, **Babette Deutsch.** Petrograd.

And this is death's gift-dream to me: **Jan Heller Levi.** After her death. (A sequence for my mother).

And thus I thought that I would come **Elizabeth Barrett Browning.** The runaway slave at Pilgrim's Point.

And thus we two were reconciled, **Elizabeth Barrett Browning.** The runaway slave at Pilgrim's Point.

and tom, the existentialiste, drives, off, in his **Barbara Moraff.** untitled.

And up again because/going is not enough **Shirley Kaufman.** Jerusalem notebook.

and what shall i be today, what **Fay Kicknosway.** untitled.

and what will we do/together/in this place **Jan Clausen.** the kitchen window.

And when I cleaned the skull **Susan Griffin.** Deer skull.

and when I say to my sisters **Julie Blackwomon.** Revolutionary blues.

And when our sense is dispossest, **Katherine Philips.** Parting with Lucasia: a song.

and when the center opened/I saw myself **Sandra Maria Esteves.** Ahora.

And when they asked her what she wanted to be **Judith Herzberg.** Vocation.

And wilt thou have me fashion into speech **Elizabeth Barrett Browning.** Sonnets from the Portuguese. (XIII).

And yet bring flowers and heap them, all this day, **S. Gertrude Ford.** The tenth Armistice Day.

And yet He has made dark things **Elizabeth Barrett Browning.** The runaway slave at Pilgrim's Point.

And you as well must die, beloved dust, **Edna St. Vincent Millay.** Sonnet. (XIX).

Androgynous child whose hair curls into flowers, **Marge Piercy.** The total influence or outcome of the matter: THE SUN.

Angel of declaring, you opened before us walls, **Muriel Rukeyser.** For Dolci. (Searching/not searching).

Angela Davis/Tall, fair and wiry-haired, **Alice S. Cobb.** Angela Davis.

anger/is killing/my face. **Susan Efros.** An expression.

Anna, fierce/in her will/to control the kittens: **Jan Clausen.** the kitchen window.

Annual celebration of mating/sends buglegs to collect pollen **Pamela Victorine.** Menses: a seasonal.

Another cruel letter today. **Izumi Shikibu.** untitled.

Another full moon. I knew without checking **Ruth Fainlight.** Another full moon.

Another loneheart evening **Akua Lezli Hope.** Gowanus Canal (because you said look again).

Another story still: a porch with trees **Marilyn Hacker.** Peterborough.

Another time, another life, another place, **Marnie Walsh.** Thomas Iron-Eyes. Born circa 1840. Died 1919, Rosebud Agency, S.D.

Another youthful advocate of truth and right has gone; **Ada.** To the memory of J. Horace Kimball.

Apples in gales drop like footsteps **Madge Hales.** September.

appreciation of the ordinary/sets in **Rota Silverstrini.** The fish tank.

April 30, 1975/Moving backwards suddenly **Miriam Dyak.** Dying.

the arch of her foot/dark, like a grey breath **Michèle Roberts.** masochism one.

are you among the animals whose secret names **Barbara Szerlip.** Breech.

Are you there still? . . . nights, late, **Virginia de Araújo.** Letter to Connie in the Maine woods.

Aren't you afraid of me? **Judith Kazantzis.** And in Richmond.

Arise! Thou pain or loss betide, **F. E. M. Macaulay.** The woman's Marseillaise.

Arise ye daughters of a land/That vaunts its liberty! **F. E. M. Macaulay.** The woman's Marseillaise.

Arms full of bland death **Albis Torres.** The dead one.

Arrogant tourists, attracting/only their own **Ingrid Wendt.** Dust.

As a child I pressed my fingers against my closed eyes—watched the stars, **Michelle Cliff.** Travel notes.

as a child i recall/waiting for my father **Mae Jackson.** Just one in a series.

As a child I saved maps. Haunted airports. Begged for travel brochures **Michelle Cliff.** Travel notes.

as a child i was/constantly reminded **Elouise Loftin.** Woman.

As a hungry fledgling, who sees and hears **Vittoria Colonna.** untitled.

As a man who soon must be without **Gaspara Stampa.** Hunger.

As a young woman, who had known her? Tripping **Alice Walker.** Burial.

As evening comes/A sudden rain and wind **Anonymous.** To the tune "Picking mulberries."

As I am unhappy/and feel myself becoming a coward, **Yosano Akiko.** untitled.

As I came home through Drury's woods, **Elizabeth Madox Roberts.** Cold fear.

As I descend from ideal to actual touch **Ann Stanford.** The descent.

As I lie roofed in, screened in, **Harriet Monroe.** On the porch.

As I stood/Ling'ring upon the threshold, half-concealed **Amy Levy.** Xantippe.

As I was a child/hearing timber fall **Teru Kanazawa.** Aborting.

As I was passing there, in that green field, **Rivka Miriam.** In that green field.

As if suddenly/a star had exploded in our hands, **Elsie Alvarado de Ricord.** A letter.

As in those medieval maps/the three known continents **Shirley Kaufman.** Jerusalem Notebook.

As it came to the dawning I awoke: **Anonymous.** The mother.

as light goes/it pierces the river **Carol Tinker.** The young emerald, Evening Star.

As long as it took fasten it back to a place where **Gertrude Stein.** Patriarchal poetry.

As loving Hind that (Hartless) wants her Deer, **Anne Bradstreet.** A letter to her husband, absent on public employment.

As one who does not mind/the transitory touch, **Elizabeth Cook-Lynn.** Contradiction.

As soon as the day is shoved **Ellen Warmond.** Change of scene.

As the first spring mists appear **Lady Ise.** untitled.

As the inamour'd Thirsis lay **Aphra Behn.** Song: As the inamour'd Thirsis lay.

As the plane flies flat to the trees **June Jordan.** Problems of translation: problems of language.

As the plant on the smooth of the hill **Evelyn Underhill.** Mountain flora.

As the season changes,/I change my clothes **Shunzei's daughter.** untitled.

As the Word came to prophets of old, **Margaret Walker.** Prophets for a new day.

As we pass through the field of purple herbs **Princess Nukada.** untitled.

As we slip along the stair way/mounting the garden **Sybil Wood.** Picnic.

as when the person's bones and thoughts **Carol Bergé.** of roots and sources.

As, when the seaward ebbing tide doth pour **Alice Meynell.** Regrets.

As you sit like a captured king **Zelda.** The light is my delight.

Ashes of me,/Whirl in the fires I may not name. **Leonora Speyer.** Witch!

Ask me not/If now I write poems— **Yosano Akiko.** Tangled hair.

At dusk heavy clouds grieve the long day; **Li Ch'ing-chao.** Poem to the tune of "Tsui hua yin."

At end-of-month/you keep on turning to the fear **Molly Vaux.** February.

At first, I hunted deer. **Nellie Hill.** My inheritance.

At first I was given centuries **Margaret Atwood.** Untitled.

At four in the morning I hear/her scream again. **Minnie Bruce Pratt.** Rape.

at her arrival   she was/stunned and bruised. she **Irena Klepfisz.** The monkey house and other cages.

At Ichiyiama/Boating on Lake Nio **Matsumoto Koyū-Ni.** untitled.

At last, my old inveterate foe, **Anne Finch, Countess of Winchilsea.** Ardelia to melancholy.

at least once:/every one/should know/lightning **Pat Crutchfield Exum.** 3 serendipitous poems.

At mass/at meat **Alberta Turner.** Bliss. (A dictionary of common terms).

At Meron I look down/into nothing. The sky is huge **Shirley Kaufman.** Meron.

At midnight, a candle glowed/in the heart **Zelda.** Strange plant.

At my father's wake,/The old people/Knew me, **Janet Campbell.** Desmet, Idaho, March 1969.

at night,/in the day, in the/day's dream **Rochelle Nameroff.** Invocation.

At night, she sees voices. **Chedva Harakavy.** At night, she sees voices.

At night the wallpaper shakes/itself loose from the walls, **Margherita Guidacci.** At night.

At Nigitazu we wait for the moon **Princess Nukada.** untitled.

At noon you call/Feed the birds **Judith McDaniel.** Snow in April.

At sixty, it might be well to start **Desirée Flynn.** The collector.

At the ceremony of Emobo/I feel your embrace, **Kattie M. Cumbo.** Ceremony.

At the corner/One glimpses/Occasional dreams **Jessica Tarahata Hagedorn.** Fillmore Street poems: August, 1967.

At the end of the day I stack the galleys, **Irena Klepfisz.** Contexts.

At the fire's conjuring/the old wound re-opens. **Lucha Corpi.** Short history.

At the first of the month/Money to buy flowers is given **Hua Jui, Lady.** Life in the Palace.

At this bed and quiet hour/what else are we but children **Chelly Lima.** Ballad by one who doesn't want to make love blindly.

At this time I find the bed very arid **Nancy Morejón.** The reason for poetry.

at times all week/i have felt my life **Jan Clausen.** A sense of reality.

At 20, I began to know/I wanted to grow/Up to be a woman. **Becky Birtha.** untitled.

at two/my upper lip split open **Cherríe Moraga.** For the color of my mother.

An atomic sprite/perched on a polished **Mina Loy.** Crab-angel.

August 'twas, the twenty-fifth, **Lucy Terry.** Bars fight, August 28, 1746.

awaken a flower/petal/torn from the bulb **Fayola Kamaria Ama.** for "Mamie."

The awning of funeral homes/along Harlem's broad avenues, yawn **Adrienne Ingrum.** Friday the 13th Candlelight march.

Ay me, to whom shall I my case complaine, **Mary Sidney Herbert, Countess of Pembroke.** The dolefull lay of Clorinda.

Ayii, Ayii, Ayii,/I am good looking. **Anonymous.** untitled.

Azouou! Evening Breeze! What a perfect name! **Mririda n'Ait Attik.** Azouou.

Azure, 'tis I, come from Elysian shores **Janet Lewis.** Helen, the sad queen.

B

Babe, by your helplessness/Conjure pity in my breast: **Rosamund Greenwood.** The bairn.

Baby,/You shall be free: **Jessie Sampter.** Kadia the young mother speaks.

Backed up against time **Venus Khoury.** untitled.

Background/Four brothers went by train **Kate Ellen Braverman.** Job interview.

bailando por pesetas/sylvia earns to quench **Xelina.** Nightmare.

The banished thrush, the homeless rook **S. Gertrude Ford.** Nature in war-time.

The bare branches tremble **Tzu Yeh.** untitled.

Barely twelve years old/Conscripted into a marriage bed **Evelyn Arcad Zerbe.** In memory of my Arab grandmother.

the battle before us. Walk through **Alexandra Grilikhes.** Watching the dance.

Bavaria/Market Einerstein **Alice Karle.** Liebfraumilch.

Be careful! Be careful! **Ōme Shūshiki.** untitled.

Be just, my lovely *Swain,* and do not take **Aphra Behn.** To Lysander, on some verses he writ, and asking more for his heart than 'twas worth.

Be White man's Slave. **Sonja Åkesson.** The marital problem I.

A beast is among us. **Margaret Walker.** Prophets for a new day.

A beautiful person awakes/singing in the forest. **Yoshiyuki Rie.** Sacrificial victim.

Beauty is dead and rotten. **Babette Deutsch.** Epistle to Prometheus. (VIII).

The beauty of the Friend it was that taught me **Makhfi (Zibu'n-Nisa).** untitled.

because beer tingles/like tear drippings **Melba Joyce Boyd.** Beer drops.

Because I know deep in my own heart **Pauli Murray.** Song.

Because the sea is also **Roberta Spear.** Fishes at Saint-Jean: Chagall, 1949.

Because we were friends and sometime lovers; **Rosario Castellanos.** Chess.

Because ye have broken your own chain **Elizabeth Barrett Browning.** The curse. (A curse for a nation).

Become that which arises behind dawn, **Eunice Odio.** Portraits of the heart.

The bed on which we used to sit. **Anonymous.** Untitled.

Bees hummed and rooks called hoarsely outside the quiet room **Margaret Adelaide Wilson.** Gervais.

Before I came to Holloway, **M. C. R.** untitled.

Before me/when I look into the mirror **Anonymous.** untitled.

Before one drop of angry blood was shed **Cicely Hamilton.** Non-combatant.

Before rain I notice seagulls. **Lorna Dee Cervantes.** Beneath the shadow of the freeway.

before she was a woman/she was an angel   hence **Michele Stepto.** her song.

Before the Altar of the world in flower, **Margaret Sackville.** Sacrament.

Before the light grows/a woman curls over the seedbed **Molly Vaux.** March.

Before the sun rises my brothers call the spotted dogs in **Sarah Kirsch.** Before the sun rises.

Before your waking I only knew **Anna Gréki.** Before your waking.

behind glass, my room is neat **Michèle Roberts.** Out of chaos out of order out.

Behind the temple/Where the white bell-flowers bloom, **Yosano Akiko.** Tangled hair.

Behind the warmth and light are dark and damp/behind the wet sugar, **Michelle Cliff.** Obsolete geography.

Being full grown means letting go of small comforts **Donna Allegra.** A rape poem for men.

being property once myself/I have a feeling for it, **Lucille Clifton.** being property once myself.

being un-rigid conduit for/whatever is of purpose or design **Desirée Flynn.** From the rain forest.

Believe the light, believe the eye, **Kathleene West.** Striking out.

The bell in the hollow chapel/and the bell in the throat of the donkey **Yunna Moritz.** The bell.

Beneath awkward branches clipped of birds, **Frances Gill.** The Pennywhistle man.

Beneath the deep blue nightshade of the sky **Jean Overton Fuller.** Mask and essence.

Better to live as a rogue and a bum, **Mahsati.** untitled.

Between/night and dark/nearness and far **Alexandra Grilikhes.** Potter.

Between Awajishima and Suma **Anonymous.** untitled.

Between your life and mine, there's a fresh air **Zaida del Río.** untitled.

Beyond the bars I see her move, **Laura Grey.** untitled.

Beyond those who live beyond the mountain **Albis Torres.** Cocosi.

Beyond windowfog/last year's garden tools **Suellen Mayfield.** Baking bread.

Big mother you have on your worn smile and **Frances Mayes.** Nesting dolls.

Billy de Lye was a reckless gambler **Deidre McCalla.** Billy de Lye.

binding by sincerity/hating that kindness **Anna Lee Walters.** A teacher taught me.

A bird comes/delicately as a little girl **Yosano Akiko.** untitled.

The bird that saw sings/Tseutse's child is dead **Anonymous.** untitled.

A bird twittered like crazy **Dahlia Ravikovitch.** The noise of the waters.

A birdless sky, seadawn, one lone star, **Ann Lauterbach.** The yellow linen dress: a sequence.

Bits of city/fragments out of context, the links lost. **Lourdes Casal.** Profile of my city.

Bitter rain in my courtyard **Wu Tsao.** To the tune "The joy of peace and brightness."

Bitter tea,/Hot or cold,/Equally good **Shirley Geok-Lin Lim.** Potions.

"The bitter wormword shivers in the endless plains" **Carol Tinker.** untitled.

Black and glossy as a bee and curled was my hair; **Ambapali.** untitled.

Black is; slavery was; I am. **Gloria C. Oden.** This child is the mother.

Black men were safe when tom-toms slumbered **Pauli Murray.** Dark testament.

Black pride, black pride, we remember well **Margaret Goss Burroughs.** Black pride.

Black skin against bright green, **Kattie M. Cumbo.** Black sister.

black sugar-cane Lady/papa Doc wa'nt your daddy **Amina Baraka.** Haiti.

Blackman/let that white girl go. **June Jordan.** Getting down to get over.

Blackness/is a title,/is a preoccupation, **Gwendolyn Brooks.** Primer for Blacks.

Blessed above women/shall Jael the wife of Heber the Kenite be **Deborah.** Song of Deborah.

Blind, as a child./As a child unsteady. **Mirta Aguirre.** This road.

The blind man balances easily in the rocking **Irena Klepfisz.** Contexts.

Blizzards of paper/in slow motion/sift through her. **Marge Piercy.** Unlearning to not speak.

Blood falling in drops to the earth **Alda do Espirito Santo.** Where are the men seized in this wind of madness?

Blood gushes out of the throat **Takiguchi Masako.** Slaughterhouse.

Blood is/poetry. **Phyllis Koestenbaum.** Blood journey.

Blood red, blood purple, jet and jade **Debora Greger.** Well enough alone.

Blood rising under the Andes and above **June Jordan.** Problems of translation: problems of language.

Blood sister,/our fingers join beneath the veins **Toi Derricotte.** For a godchild, Regina, on the occasion of her first love.

Blood. Tears. The vital/salt of our body. Each **Olga Broumas.** Sleeping Beauty.

a blossom/not far from night **Alejandra Pizarnik.** Lovers.

Blossoming plum and cherry/Flowering apple and quince **Adelaide Crapsey.** Blossoming plum and cherry.

The blow/muffled through years of/forgetting, of not knowing: **Marina Tsvetayeva.** Epitaph.

Blow on the embers, an' sigh at the sparkles! **Moira O'Neill.** A bud in the frost.

Blue evening. The winds limply die. **Anna Akhmatova.** Deception.

Blue is this night of stars **Pauli Murray.** Inquietude.

Blues Lady/with the beaded face/painted lips **Jayne Cortez.** Grinding vibrato.

The body is the Victory of dreams **Katerina Anghelaki-Rooke.** The body is the Victory and the Defeat of dreams.

The body of a young guerrilla **Alison Colbert.** The white worm.

A bolt of silk for each clear toned song. **Ch'ien T'ao.** Written at a party where my lord gave away a thousand bolts of silk.

A bony foot/Attached to three red sticks of/Dynamite by **Heidi Gitterman.** The experiment.

Books, books, books!/I had found the secret of a garret-room **Elizabeth Barrett Browning.** Aurora Leigh.

Boots are being polished/Trumpeters clean their horns **Pat Parker.** Where will you be?

Boston, Massachusetts, three years ago. **Dorothy Allison.** Boston, Massachusetts.

Boy, bring me candles on a silver salver, **Hélène Swarth.** Candles.

Boys and girls come out to play **Anne Wilkinson.** Boys and girls.

Bradford Lindstrom was once Wall Street **Colleen J. McElroy.** Catacombs: dream poem number one.

Braown-Bom-bo/with your chocolate skin **Rota Silverstrini.** Unfinished.

Brasov/losing count after ten **Michelene Wandor.** Tourist in Rumania.

Brassica (oleracea) is a cabbage **Rosemary Norman.** Cabbage.

Break open the loaf of yourself **Michele Murray.** The woman who lives inside the world.

Breaking the morning ice on the well's bucket was no great hardship **Asphodel.** On the pilgrim's way in Kent, as it leads to the Coldrum Stones.

Breaks/Day/Unspecial dockside arising life **Cynthia Kraman Genser.** 72 hours: Yom Kippur.

Brecht saying: Galileo talking astronomy **Muriel Rukeyser.** Brecht's Galileo. (Searching/not searching).

Bright moon—/All grief, sorrow, loneliness completed— **Ping Hsin (Hsieh Wan-ying).** Multitudinous stars and spring waters.

The bright sunbeams/Shoot down upon/Tauwara, whose **Anonymous.** untitled.

brighteyed black kid/sweet/so sweet in your **Eugenie Eersel.** First communion picture.

bring out the glasses of crystal **Mae Jackson.** For the count.

Britannia's isles proclaim/That freedom is their theme; **Ann Plato.** To the first of August.

A broken rainspout. **Maria Southwick.** Doors opening here, and there.

The broken soldier sings and whistles day to dark; **Katharine Tynan.** The broken soldier.

The bronze head came from the sea, **Vera Rich.** The bronze of Poseidon.

The bronzed man came from the sea, **Vera Rich.** The bronze of Poseideon.

The brother of the woman/with the cut breast **Alison Colbert.** The white worm.

Brothers, today we drink/the fresh milk of dawn **Angela de Hoyos.** Brindis: for the barrio.

Brought to book at last,/what did you say on your day **Marie Ponsot.** "Sois sage o ma douleur."

Brown woman face plump/over 116th Street watching **Sharyn Jeanne Skeeter.** Summer street.

A brush of evening clouds. **Yü Ch'ing-tsêng.** To the tune "Intoxicated with shadows of flowers."

the builder of continents/Is not the surging billow **Ping Hsin (Hsieh Wan-ying).** The stars.

The building across the street/has an ordinary facade, a view of the park **Irena Klepfisz.** Contexts.

Buildings above the leafless trees **Sara Teasdale.** Central Park at dusk.

The buildings of the/Projects were arrayed/like barracks in **Sherley Anne Williams.** The iconography of childhood.

But beyond the/anxiety/the querulous and reckless intersecting **June Jordan.** No poem because time is not a name.

But he as much unus'd to Fear, **Aphra Behn.** The disappointment.

But I am the shining   High Priestess of Nanna **Enheduanna.** Inanna exalted.

But I am Thomas. I am here, **Marnie Walsh.** Thomas Iron-Eyes. Born circa 1840. Died 1919, Rosebud Agency, S.D.

''but I don'/really/give a fuck/Who/my daughter/ marries—'' **Alice Walker.** Once.

But I had an invitation to a house, where **Bella Akhmadulina.** Rain.

But in the crowding darkness not a word did they say. **Gwendolyn Brooks.** the old-marrieds.

But it must make sense. The mad cascade **Ann Stanford.** Composing the garden.

But it was right that she/looked back. Not to be **Shirley Kaufman.** His wife.

But it was when I touched the place **Susan Griffin.** Deer skull.

But look/but look/man breaks out **Nelly Sachs.** But look.

But love is a large bag **Katerina Anghelaki-Rooke.** My mama and satan.

But *my* fruit . . . ha, ha!—there, had been **Elizabeth Barrett Browning.** The runaway slave at Pilgrim's Point.

But set a springe for him, 'mio ben,' **Elizabeth Barrett Browning.** Bianca among the nightingales.

but she envied them all **mary hope lee.** on not bein.

But the Navajos say he won a contest once. **Leslie Marmon Silko.** Toe'osh: a Laguna coyote story.

but then: he might kill me in his madness. **Carol Bergé.** all wars.

But there was/once/a time/when the bones, great/skeletons **Eleni Vakalo.** untitled.

But too much stands between us and this **Robin Morgan.** Documentary.

—But we that are no Polliticians, **Aphra Behn.** The Cabel at Nickey Nackeys.

But *we* who are dark, we are dark! **Elizabeth Barrett Browning.** The runaway slave at Pilgrim's Point.

but with you, i would want it. **Jan Clausen.** likeness.

The butcher's wife—after she has cleaned the tripe—comes to wax the **Michelle Cliff.** Obsolete geography.

Buy us a little grain of reality! **Christine Lavant.** Buy us a little grain.

By day I watch the sensual/wisteria cluster burst into **Barbara Bravelle.** The new Joan come out of the fire.

By day she woos me, soft, exceeding fair: **Christina Rossetti.** The world.

By Heaven 'tis false, I am not vain; **Aphra Behn.** The defiance.

By July/she's become a matter/of breathing **Kristina McGrath.** By July. (Sequence from blue to blue).

By near resemblance see that bird betrayed **Anne Finch, Countess of Winchilsea.** The bird and the arras.

by that summer snapshot taken/on someone else's porch, skewed to one **Bella Akhmadulina.** I swear.

By the day I perish in the barrel **Katerina Anghelaki-Rooke.** Diogenes.

By this we shall be truly great, **Katherine Philips.** Parting with Lucasia: a song.

call me dine asdzaani/i am child of winter nights **Nia Francisco.** Iridescent child.

Call me names/listening to you **Marie-Elise.** Gemini.

the call of chinita/the sound of Cantonese **Frances C. Chung.** recuerdos de la chinita en Guatemala.

Calling you from my kitchen to the one where/you cook. **June Jordan.** Poem nr. 2 for inaugural rose.

Cameleopard is the classic term **Judith McCombs.** Games mammals play.

Can I easily say,/I know you of course now, **Adrienne Rich.** Sisters.

Can these movements which move themselves **Diane Wakoski.** Belly dancer.

Can this farm girl/in farm-girl finery burn your heart? **Sappho.** Andromeda, what now?

can you imagine the ocean still in my mouth **Cindy Bellinger.** Children and other reasons.

can you imagine where my love goes **Cindy Bellinger.** Children and other reasons.

Can't we find some way/to meet again **Wallada.** To Ibn Zaidun.

Carson, turn your coat collar up, throw the cigarette from **Kay Boyle.** The invitation in it.

Cased in your bone and plaster/you stare where the land stretches **Harriet Rose.** The succubus.

casket/of leaf green **Carol Tinker.** wet green hallelujahs.

The castle is sprinkled with sleeping powder. **Rachel Loden.** Mother.

Casuist, quibbler, jelly-heart, equivocater, hedger, shuffler, beater about **Kathleen Fraser.** Casuist.

Catch your breath in the wind, where the mountains **Desirée Flynn.** From the rain forest.

Cats making love in the temple **Kawai Chigetsu-Ni.** untitled.

Cause nobody deals with aretha—a mother with four children— **Nikki Giovanni.** Poem for Aretha.

The Certainty we two shall meet by God **Gwendolyn Brooks.** Appendix to the Anniad: leaves from a loose-leaf war diary.

The chains that bind my thinking **Alice S. Cobb.** The searching.

changes pain **Sapphire.** New York City tonight.

Charcoals/and blues poured from you. **Anasa Jordan.** Sweet Otis Suite.

Charlie Coyote wanted to be governor **Leslie Marmon Silko.** Toe'osh: a Laguna coyote story.

the child/with her wounded knee **Jeanne Sirotkin.** To, from, for and about Detroit.

the child is dead./they bring him in a white boat/to my bed **Toi Derricotte.** The testimony of Sister Maureen.

Child of water, desert mind **Paula Gunn Allen.** The dead spider. (Medicine song).

The child sleeps in the daytime, **E. J. Scovell.** Child waking.

Child, the current of your breath is six days long. **Anne Sexton.** Unknown girl in the maternity ward.

Child who within me gives me dreams and sleep, **Muriel Rukeyser.** Nine poems for the unborn child.

Child, you conceived in my upstairs room, **Helen Sorrells.** To a child born in time of small war.

childhood remembrances are always a drag/if you're Black **Nikki Giovanni.** Nikki-Rosa.

The childless years alone without a home **Muriel Rukeyser.** Nine poems for the unborn child.

The children in my care/with wisp-thin wings **Toi Derricotte.** The testimony of Sister Maureen.

Children of wealth in your warm nursery, **Elizabeth Daryush.** Children of wealth in your warm nursery.

The children shout in Hide-and-Seek: **Florence Randal Livesay.** Gold ladies.

Children we have not borne/bedevil us by becoming/themselves **Audre Lorde.** To my daughter the junkie on a train.

Children, who do you fear, why turn away? **Marjorie Oludhe Macgoye.** For Miriam.

China fights a border war with/Vietnam: all the pundits **Judith Kazantzis.** Progenitor.

China is fighting with ordinary rockets. **Judith Kazantzis.** Progenitor.

The Chinaman has truth/Locked up **Jessica Tarahata Hagedorn.** Fillmore Street poems: August, 1967.

The Chinaman knows it all **Jessica Tarahata Hagedorn.** Fillmore Street poems: August, 1967.

Christmas is coming and I think of home: **Shirley Geok-Lin Lim.** Christmas in exile.

Christmas, season of streamers, coloured lights; **Pat Arrowsmith.** Christmas story (1980).

The circus entered their lives **Mirta Yañez.** The visits.

The cities of dream wander under the bark of a **Vesna Krmpotic.** A December forest.

the city./the dance. **Barbara Szerlip.** Beehive. (Four short poems).

city blues pay tribute to:/massage parlors **Xelina.** Urban life.

city bred/I watch the moon/through glass **Frances Horovitz.** Moon.

City by the sea/mamma can't stand the damp **Katerina Anghelaki-Rooke.** My mama and satan.

The city had not organized itself. **Teresinha Pereira.** Austin: foreign city.

The city of Esteli/woke up taken by the kids. **Magdalena de Rodríguez.** June 10.

the city persists name the joy **Sara Miles.** Rosas de la tarde.

City-center, mid-/traffic, I/wake to your public kiss. Your name **Olga Broumas.** Sleeping Beauty.

Clanged the keys on the table; **Anonymous.** untitled.

Class dismissed! Half the activists pitched **Jane Shore.** Basic training.

Classic heritage/the window open on all the rooftops **Zaida del Río.** untitled.

The clear water of the imperial pond **Ise Tayū.** untitled.

Climb the spruce tree and dance on the tip **Paula Gunn Allen.** Riding the thunder.

Climbing the air, prophet beyond prophet **Muriel Rukeyser.** The floor of ocean. (Searching/not searching).

Climbing the stairs/wearing blue sunglasses and a new smile, **Kate Ellen Braverman.** Picking up your mail.

Clinging to my neck, the children cried out, **Ts'ai Yen.** The lamentation.

The clock sucks me back. I calculate the loss, **Irena Klepfisz.** Contexts.

Cloris returning from the Trance **Aphra Behn.** The disappointment.

Cloud capped peaks fill the eyes **Yü Hsüan-chi.** On a visit to Ch'ung Chen Taoist temple I see in the South Hall the list of successful candidates in the Imperial examinations.

clouds fill the sky/the breeze is cool **Kattie M. Cumbo.** The morning after . . . love.

Clouds surround us,/cupolas surround us, **Marina Tsvetayeva.** Verses about Moscow.

Cobra is the night image of a chinese water-print **Joyce Mansour.** North express.

Coffee-stained, knife-cut tablecloth **Amy Károlyi.** The third house.

Cold and shiny/long and hard **Rashidah Ismaili.** Murderous intent with a deadly weapon.

Cold and starry twins— **Judith Kazantzis.** Progenitor.

Cold, cold this night is my bed, **Anonymous.** The lullaby of the snow.

The cold felt cold until our blood **Adrienne Rich.** Phantasia for Elvira Shatayev.

Cold in the earth, and the deep snow piled above thee! **Emily Brontë.** Remembrance.

a cold place/detention house **Sandra Maria Esteves.** Visiting.

The colors of the flowers fade **Ono no Komachi.** untitled.

come & see   you/have shown me/passion **Carol Tinker.** buddha's birthday.

Come back to me, who wait and watch for you:— **Christina Rossetti.** Monna Innominata: a sonnet of sonnets.

Come, dark-eyed Sleep, thou child of Night, **Michael Field.** And on my eyes dark sleep by night.

Come here/Come over here **Ann Dunn.** untitled.

Come into animal presence. **Denise Levertov.** Come into animal presence.

''Come quickly, quickly!'' The words **Margaret Stanley-Wrench.** A visitation.

Come right in this house, Will Johnson! **Clara Ann Thompson.** Mrs. Johnson objects.

Come, the wind may never again/Blow as now it blows for us; **Emily Brontë.** D.G.C. to J.A.

Come to me from Crete to this holy temple, **Sappho.** untitled.

Come to me in the night—let us sleep entwined. **Else Lasker-Schüler.** A love song.

Come to me in the silence of the night; **Christina Rossetti.** Echo.

come to thy beloved one **Anonymous.** untitled.

"Coming at an end the lovers"/could be a beginning for each other's **Kathleen Fraser.** Improvisation on lines by Spicer, No. 2.

Coming late to your bed in sleet-ridden **Madeline DeFrees.** Standing by on the third day.

Coming on since Christmas. **Kathleen Fraser.** Agnes.

The comino morning sits down on the dawn **Carmen Tafolla.** Bailar . . .

Completely worn out,/We sleep soundly **Tuo Ssu.** Train.

Con la mañana oscura, **Angela de Hoyos.** Blues in the barrio.

Concentric reminiscences in the movement of the bird **Gladys Zaldivar.** Vagabond in the tower.

The concubine next door/chants sutras. **Tomioka Taeko.** Girlfriend.

Conditioned by two split things—/Atoms and seconds— **Margery Smith.** Prize-fighter.

Connecticut/Lucite clothespins color this September sky. **Elizabeth Keeler.** Looking for light and finding the sea.

connecticut has trees/and white has two faces: **Gayl Jones.** Tripart.

The conquerors are sad whose victory so often **Elisabeth Cluer.** The last enemy.

Consider a poem. Cup/your hand, put the fingers of the other hand in **Phyllis Koestenbaum.** Blood journey.

Consider the mysterious salt: **May Sarton.** In time like air.

Consider the queen/hand on her hip **June Jordan.** Getting down to get over.

Consider this/a photograph. **Willyce Kim.** A fistful of flowers for Vivian's kid.

Content that now the bleeding bone be swept **Babette Deutsch.** Lioness asleep.

contracting/to time/contracting/in time **Desirée Flynn.** From the rain forest.

contradictions, ice cream/at the demo, a beautiful **Jan Clausen.** (Assata on trial in New Jersey). (dialectics).

A core of the conversations we never had/lies in the distance **Audre Lorde.** Morning is a time for miracles.

Cou'd our first father, at his toilsome plough, **Anne Finch, Countess of Winchilsea.** Adam pos'd.

Cou'd we stop the time that's flying **Anne Finch, Countess of Winchilsea.** The unequal fetters.

the country girl in Paris/rises early **Mary Winfrey.** Charlotte Corday/Marat (July 13, 1793).

country woman/cards/slit/gypsy eyes **Jan Clausen.** Upstate.

The courage that my mother had **Edna St. Vincent Millay.** The courage that my mother had.

Covered the flowered linen/where I graze **Marilyn Hacker.** Home, and I've.

The covert man is sitting on a/screened veranda **Alison Colbert.** The white worm.

The cranes in the harbor/are lugging up the night **Katerina Anghelaki-Rooke.** Magdalen the great mammal.

. . . Creatures speak in sounds. The word of God is silence.

Simone Weil. Random thoughts on the love of God.

credence crawled over like/a rat **Michelene Wandor.** untitled.

The cricket sings on Twelfth-night, **Natayla Gorbanevskaya.** untitled.

Crippled for life at seventeen, **Eva Dobell.** Pluck.

A crocodile-cloud swallowed/a cloud-cloud **Raquel Chalfi.** Tel Aviv beach, Winter, '74.

crossed desires, the sun/glinting on edge-days, **Michelene Wandor.** untitled.

crow floats in winter sun/a black sliver **Joy Harjo.** Watching crow, looking south towards the Manzano Mountains.

Cruelty is rarely conscious **Adrienne Rich.** Photographs of an unmade bed.

Crying's not so easy/when you cuss the aches **Pat Nottingham.** Entries: 13.

"Cuckoo!"/"Cuckoo!" **Fukuda Chiyo-Ni.** untitled.

Cunts have faces/Did you know? **Elsa Gidlow.** Cunts have faces: dialogue among rumpled sheets.

Cupbearer, O victorious Falcon, come! **Qorratu'l-Ayn (Umm-i Salam).** He the beloved.

The Curandera arrived too late/One Santa Fe Day in 1848. **Marcela Christine Lucero-Trujillo.** The advent of my death.

(*A curse for the Ripper: we turn your hatred back at you*) **Anonymous.** Poem for Jacqueline Hill.

Cut off from each other— **Anne Blackford.** Family script.

The cypress stood up like a church **Elizabeth Barrett Browning.** Bianca among the nightingales.

D

D. says the mirror is a snake. **Beverly Dahlen.** D.

Dad is disappointed in Agnes. **Kathleen Fraser.** Agnes.

Daddy/is a shadow on/the silver screen his **Sherely Anne Williams.** Generation: (Daddy is a shadow on).

Daddy and Mummy/also the midwife **Tomioka Taeko.** Life story.

daddy sits/in his brown/leather chair **Melba Joyce Boyd.** Sunflowers and Saturdays.

Damit blackman/what are you going to **Katie M. Cumbo.** Domestics.

dancin is the movement of oceans/ **Ntozake Shange.** cypress.

Dandelions meet me wherever I am they overrun Ger- **Sarah Kirsch.** Dandelions for chains.

Dappling shadows on the summer grass, **Viviane Verne.** Kensington gardens.

dark and who/can see properly and a waste **Michelene Wandor.** untitled.

Dark as the spring river, the earth **Ellen Bryant Voigt.** Farm wife.

The dark covers watched petals **Alejandra Pizarnik.** Dusk.

Dark on a bright day, fear of you is two-poled, **Marie Ponsot.** Late.

Dark sea-shelter/of our land, come **Alda do Espírito Santo.** Far from the beach.

Dark was the day for Childe Rolandine the artist **Stevie Smith.** Childe Rolandine.

Dark young pine, at the center of the earth **Anonymous.** untitled.

The darkened bedroom, the double bed, **Sherley Anne Williams.** first story. (Driving wheel).

The dark-plumed rider striking the iron door **Sylvia Read.** The dark rider.

Dateline Saigon: Marines wait in the rain **Carolyn Kizer.** The first of June again.

Daughter, take this amulet **Mwana Kupona Msham.** Poem to her daughter.

Dawn has flashed up the startled skies, **Muriel Stuart.** Forgotten dead, I salute you.

Day after day I've longed for my husband, **Yosami, Wife of Hitomaro.** untitled.

The day before he died/Martin Luther King **Fina García Marruz.** At the death of Martin Luther King.

A day before Maggie's journey. The impossible is no hindrance, **Shlomit Cohen.** The impossible is no hindrance.

The day will come when I will/Share once more the quilts. **Huang O.** A farewell to a southern melody.

The days and nights of the river **Alice Karle.** untitled.

The days fall upon me;/One by one, they fall, **Angelina Weld Grimké.** Under the days.

The day's gone/and you're left with a telephone coin, **Jenny Mastoraki.** untitled.

Days I was in school/Mother cleaning everything we didn't **Ingrid Wendt.** Dust.

Daytime—/as it happened **Judith Kazantzis.** Progenitor.

The dead's right grain/is woven in our flesh **Andrée Chedid.** The future and the ancestor.

Dear Colette,/I only want to thank you: **Erica Jong.** Dear Colette.

Dear Colette,/I want to write to you **Erica Jong.** Dear Colette.

Dear friend/and stalwart gazelle **Jessica Tarahata Hagedorn.** Letter to Rafael: 1966.

Dear Godmother, Another year and the annual **Pamela White Hadas.** Queen charming.

Dear Husband,/Your letters are here; **Jana Harris.** Running scared.

Dear Samson,/I put your hair/in a jar **Carole C. Gregory.** Love letter.

Dear San: Everybody doesn't write poetry. **Marilyn Hacker.** Feeling and form.

dear sirs;/i am a Good Cause applying for funds. i am a **Susan MacDonald.** the application.

Dear, when we sit in that high, placid room, **Jessie Redmon Fauset.** Touché.

Dearest. I know that they body is but transitory; that **Anonymous.** untitled.

Death halves us:/every loss/divides **Dorothy Livesay.** After grief.

death is a five o'clock door forever changing time. **Sonia Sanchez.** Kwa mama zeto waliotuzaa.

Death, that struck when I was most confiding **Emily Brontë.** Death, that struck when I was most confiding.

Death's treat!   Today I have known laughter **Muriel Rukeyser.** Nine poems for the unborn child.

Debra and I are different. Fundamentally different. **Michelle T. Clinton.** Debra.

December thirty first **Olga Elena Mattei.** untitled.

deep along the reaches of me **Johari M. Kunjufu.** There is no title: only echoes.

Deep, in the earth,/it was broken **Virginia Gilbert.** Leaving, the sepulcre city.

Deep in this grave her bones remain, **Ann Plato.** Reflections, written on visiting the grave of a venerated friend.

Deeper than sleep but not so deep as death **Muriel Rukeyser.** Night feeding.

Deeply repentant of my sinful ways **Gaspara Stampa.** untitled.

Defiled is my name full sore **Anne Boleyn.** Defiled is my name full sore.

degeneration was the way backwards **Katharine Morton.** untitled.

The demonstrators who filled the streets of/Seoul **Fukunaka Tomoko.** It's not the same.

Desire makes you/beautiful. **Ann Smith.** untitled.

a desire to embrace you/becomes a kiss of spring **Nia Francisco.** Friday noon feelings.

Destroyer of lands on storm-lent wings **Enheduanna.** Inanna exalted.

the diagnosis complete, I tried to become **Michèle Roberts.** poem on St. Valentine's Day.

The diamond studded/slave bracelet he/gave me **Elizabeth Gross.** Do women have souls?

diamonds glitter in black hair **Frances C. Chung.** Cantonese opera at Sun Sing Theater.

Diapering this poem,/I listen to my hands/folding fatigue, **Marie-Elise.** Diapering this poem.

Did I, my lines intend for publick view, **Anne Finch, Countess of Winchilsea.** The introduction.

Did my longing create/the black rose you gave me/in a dream, **Zelda.** A black rose.

Did you ever fall in love with a man that was no good **Bessie Smith.** Dirty no gooder blues.

did you ever wonder at the woolen flannels **Rachel Maines.** Textile women: (Lowell, Lawrence, Fall River, Amoskeag, Gastonia, Marion, Columbia, Oneita).

did you hear me start/my herding song that **Sonia Sanchez.** Old words.

Did you see in the shadowy woods **Shinkawa Kazue.** An event which makes no news.

didn't you receive my note? **Carol Bergé.** moss, like cauls.

The difference between loving and being loved, **Diane Wakoski.** Largely because of coincidence and partly

because of chance, I have taken up a new address at 47th Street and Avenue F.

The difference between poetry and rhetoric **Audre Lorde.** Power.

difficult Monday. Rosemary fired. could have been any of us. **Karen Brodine.** Making the difference.

Digging with my finger, parrot **Anonymous.** untitled.

Dipping each nail in grease, **Mary Swander.** Pears.

Dipping our bread in oil tins **Carolyn Forché.** Poem for Maya.

Disarm'd with so genteel an air, **Anne Finch, Countess of Winchilsea.** The answer.

The disasters numb within us **Denise Levertov.** Life at war.

Disguised in my mouth as a swampland **Jayne Cortez.** In the morning.

Distance does not occur. You carry **Adrianne Marcus.** Wedding poem.

The distance from Satan to God/has grown shorter, **Eeva-Liisa Manner.** Apathy. (Cambrian).

disturbed by consciousness/god created creation **Gayl Jones.** Satori.

Divide your bread in two, **Leah Goldberg.** Heavenly Jerusalem, Jerusalem of the earth.

divisions aren't limits/on my mind anymore **Sharyn Jeanne Skeeter.** Self.

Do I have the right to end **Ana Blandiana.** I have the right.

do it carefully/when you choose **Susan North.** Farmers' almanac, or a guide to loving.

Do not ask what rips the night **Christine Lavant.** Do not ask.

Do not lose sight/of the skipping children: **Manuela Margarido.** You who occupy our land.

do not speak to me of martyrdom **Sonia Sanchez.** Malcolm.

Do ye hear the children weeping, O my brothers, **Elizabeth Barrett Browning.** The cry of the children.

do you/have a turnkey **Barbara Moraff.** you, phoebusapollo.

Do you blame me that I loved him? **Frances Ellen Watkins Harper.** A double standard.

Do you come to me to bend me to your will **Christina Walsh.** A woman to her lover.

Do you remember,/your face in the soup, **Olga Elena Mattei.** untitled.

Do you remember how we used to panic **Inés Hernandez Tovar.** To other women who were ugly once.

Do you remember now the night that we, **Jean Mollison.** untitled.

do you struate?/a little girl/asked my youngest son **Frances Landsman.** Frustruation.

the doctor has explained/and your sister has been **Susan North.** It isn't that you don't understand.

The doctors, white as candles, say/*You will lose your child.* **Nancy Willard.** Bone poem.

A dodder clinging to a flax-plant finds **Tu Fu.** Parting of a newly wedded couple.

Does that bird/think of bygone times **Princess Nukada.** untitled.

Doesn't he realize/that I am not **Ono no Komachi.** untitled.

The dog body and cat mind/Lay in the room with the fire dying. **Jenny Joseph.** Dog body and cat mind.

Don't/go./We've shored/up, foreigners **Olga Broumas.** Lament. (Of fruit whose black seed fire).

Don't ask a geologist about rocks. **Diane Wakoski.** No more soft talk.

Don't be in a hurry, Miranda . . . **Judith Kazantzis.** For my daughter.

Don't do ill to anyone/good, when it's within your reach **Vidaluz Meneses.** Warnings.

Don't give me food/But give me delight **Anonymous.** untitled.

Don't lock me in wedlock, I want/marriage, an **Denise Levertov.** About marriage.

Don't scold me, grannie **Anonymous.** untitled.

Don't sleep, look!/Behind the curtains the day is beginning to dance **Ingrid Jonker.** Don't sleep.

Don't tell them about my/dress **Maria Teresa Horta.** Secret.

Don't touch me/Don't touch me **Lorna Mitchell.** The hermaphrodite's song.

The doors of the long semi-trailer truck **Jeanne Murray Walker.** Physics.

Dorothy Bradford waited for her husband. **Robin Becker.** The landing.

The doubt of future foes exiles my present joy, **Elizabeth I, Queen of England.** The doubt of future foes.

Douglass, DuBois, Garvey, King, and Malcolm X. **Margaret Walker.** FIVE BLACK MEN . . . and ten will save the city . . .

Down in the dell,/A rose-gleam fell **Henrietta Cordelia Ray.** Idyl: sunrise.

Down streams of centuries grown old, **Frankie Armstrong.** Women of my land.

Down the long hall she glistens like a star, **Emma Lazarus.** Venus of the Louvre.

Down the porphyry stair/Headlong into the air **Anne Ridler.** A matter of life and death.

Down the road rides a German lad, **Elizabeth Chandler Forman.** The three lads.

Down to the Puritan marrow of my bones **Elinor Wylie.** Puritan sonnet.

down to the wharf/there waz always **Ntozake Shange.** sassafrass.

Drafty winds and fine rain/Make a chilly Spring. **Chu Shu-chên.** Spring joy.

Dragon seas breathed white death. **May Miller.** Tunisia. (Not that far).

The drawers of my mother's bedroom/have been searched. What man **Toi Derricotte.** The damned.

Dreadful memories, how they linger, **Sarah Ogan Gunning.** Dreadful memories.

Dried up old cactus/yellowing in several limbs **Elaine Feinstein.** June.

The drivers are dead now **Pauli Murray.** Dark testament.

driving/a wooded stretch/bedside the quick Columbia **Melanie Kay.** Trojan.

The drunken sun/totters among the clouds **Gina Labriola.** Orgy (that is, vegetable market, at Sarno).

The dry brown coughing beneath their feet, **Gwendolyn Brooks.** Beverly Hills, Chicago.

A dull grey man arrives, hands you his **Adrianne Marcus.** "To count a million objects, even in 12 years, one cannot spend much time on each one."

Dull swish of runners/over the buried/lake: **Antonia Pozzi.** Landing.

Dull-headed, with dull fingers/I patch once more **Adrienne Rich.** To Judith, taking leave.

during one period I remember/you made poems all day **Ramona C. Wilson.** Eveningsong 2.

dusk, the sea is between colors **Pamela Stewart.** Postcard.

A dusky owl in velvet moth-like flight, **Marie Carmichael Stopes.** Night on the shore.

the dust has not settled on my heart **Patricia Jones.** sonnet/ for pedro pietri.

Dust wouldn't be/dust forever **Ingrid Wendt.** Dust.

Each/is personal as a thumbprint. **Judith Moffett.** "Cambridge University Swimming Club/no public access to river."

Each age brings its questions of reality: **Diane Wakoski.** Medieval tapestry and questions.

each day is a full/spool, and death winds me in **Michèle Roberts.** after my grandmother's death.

Each day's morning tastes of thinking of you, **Teresita Fernández.** Every day that I love you.

Each even I watch my mother fight/the meaning of words without pictures. **Laureen Mar.** Chinatown 4.

Each poem has its own pattern of tones. **Hsüeh T'ao.** An old poem to Yüan Chên.

Each subtlety hard for the pedant to solve **Mehri (Mihru'n-Nisa of Herat).** Coming across.

Each Sunday/the people of this town **Pat Parker.** Sunday.

Early and very early, by a moon dawn-dimmed, **Lilian Bowes Lyon.** Northumbrian farm.

early April he began to sniff it: **Judy Dothard Simmons.** Linseed oil and dreams.

the early burghers of Florence persuading the churchmen **Mary Winfrey.** historical footnote.

early in the mornin/j w brown/whippin' his woman **Mari Evans.** early in the mornin.

Early morning now and I remember **June Jordan.** Problems of translation: problems of language.

Early morning over Rouen, hopeful, high, courageous morning, **May Wedderburn Cannan.** Rouen.

Earning high wages?Yus,/Five quid a week. **Madeline Ida Bedford.** Munition wages.

The ears of doves are tender **Silvia Barros.** untitled.

Earth/Depth from all its body. **Francisca Ossandón.** Games of earth and light.

The earth turns/like a rainbow **Pinkie Gordon Lane.** When you read this poem (for citizens opposed to [book] censorship, Baton Rouge).

East, west, north, south/Tell me in which river **Anonymous.** The abortion.

Eating sleep, eating sunlight, eating meat, **Muriel Rukeyser.** Nine poems for the unborn child.

ebb/with the flow/of this soft movement **Mari Evans.** Daufuski (Four movements).

Echoes. Angels./Hosannas. Consecrations of mercy. **Carolyn M. Rodgers.** Mannessahs.

The eggplants have pins and needles. **Novella Matveyeva.** The eggplants have pins and needles.

Egotistical minutiae of *stitch* **Barbara Guest.** Medieval. (Quilts).

The eighth part (at least) of everything/is death. Its weight is not great. **Leah Goldberg.** The eighth part (at least) of everything.

Either you will/go through this door **Adrienne Rich.** Prospective immigrants please note.

Ejaja-eja./A bit of song comes back. **Anonymous.** untitled.

El Salvador erupts/Zimbabwe quiets **Adrienne Ingrum.** Loomit.

Elaina/I almost got killed, **Jana Harris.** Elaina Elaina I almost got killed.

Elegant replaced by delicate and tender, delicate and **Gertrude Stein.** Patriarchal poetry.

"Elizabeth the Beloved"—/So much says the stone **Sylvia Townsend Warner.** Elizabeth.

The embankment. I hold on to/water as dense and deep **Marina Tsvetayeva.** Poem of the end.

The embankment. The last./That's it. Separate, our hands apart **Marina Tsvetayeva.** Poem of the end.

Emilia/strung her lines of white laundry **Yolanda Ulloa.** Short biography of a washerwoman.

Emma Lee's husband beat her up **Joy Harjo.** Conversations between here and home.

Emptied with weeping/my eyes are **Safiya bint Musafir.** At the Badr Trench.

The empty woman took toys! **Gwendolyn Brooks.** The empty woman.

empty-eyed building reflect nothing/of abandoned life **Regina Williams.** I AM NOT MY SISTER'S KEEPER: I AM MY SISTER.

Encircled by the traffic's roar **Eleanour Norton.** In a restaurant, 1917.

The end of a line/is movement the **Sherley Anne Williams.** the wishon line.

endings are fond of/sneaking round shoulders **Pat Nottingham.** Entries: 21.

Endlessly sinking—/My wings into the waves of your eyes. **Lin Ling.** Sinking.

Enter the Old Count/and the Jilted Lady, **Joan Murray Simpson.** St. Marks, midnight.

Enveloping the air is Ougluup **Alice Karle.** An epic (with renaissance flute).

'Er looked at me bunnet (I knows 'e ain't noo!) **Lillian Gard.** Her 'allowance'!

Eros, blind father, I want to guide you. **Delmira Augustini.** Another race.

Europe 1953: **Adrienne Rich.** For Ethel Rosenberg.

Even after Confession,/Sister Mary Leonette told me **Janet Campbell.** On a Catholic childhood.

—Even blue mold is/A map of dream, **Kanai Mieko.** In the town with cat-shaped maze.

Even flaming fire/can be snatched up, smothered **Empress Jitō.** On the death of the Emperor Temmu.

Even if she settles doesn't mean she/can't select. The simple stitch well **Akua Lezli Hope.** To sister for Mother.

Even in dreams/I do not want him to know **Lady Ise.** untitled.

Even rocks crack, I tell you, **Dahlia Ravikovitch.** Pride.

Even the sun-clouds this morning cannot manage such skirts. **Sylvia Plath.** Poppies in October.

even though it is not now/now is never **Alejandra Pizarnik.** The great words.

Evening comes and sorrow crowds my mind, **Kasa no Iratsume.** untitled.

Events like the weeping of the girl in the classroom **Josephine Miles.** Denial.

ever since I found out I was hired to teach a class, **Karen Brodine.** Making the difference.

Ever since the great planes were murdered at the end of **Charlotte Mew.** Domus caedet arborem.

Every day I hang a different picture. They are **Madeline DeFrees.** Hanging the pictures.

every day in autumn/our cat presents a corpse as the mice **Judith McDaniel.** November passage.

Every five years the Thracians chose by lot a messenger to **Frances Horovitz.** The messenger.

Every morning at half-past four **Anonymous.** Hard times in the mill.

Every morning I get up/Beautiful as the Goddess **Huang O.** To the tune ''A floating cloud crosses Enchanted Mountain.''

Every morning I run **Leslie Ullman.** Running.

every 3 minutes a woman is beaten **Ntozake Shange.** With no immediate cause.

Every time I think of it/there's a peculiar tickle. **Eleni Fourtouni.** Child's memory.

Everyone buys his own/unhappiness **Antonia Pozzi.** Canzonetta.

Everyone is asleep **Enomoto Seifu-Jo.** untitled.

Everyone knows how much I admire/beautiful women, **Margaret Danner.** Women's lib.

Everything is hers: she went through it. **Ann Lauterbach.** the yellow linen dress: a sequence.

Everything is plundered, betrayed, sold, **Anna Akhmatova.** Everything is plundered.

Everything that was a rose, electric and heroic **Juana de Ibarourou.** Chronicle.

Evil hands took your life. **Gabriela Mistral.** Death sonnets.

Evolution fall foul of/Sexual equality **Mina Loy.** Love songs (IV).

Exert thy Voice, sweet Harbinger of Spring! **Anne Finch, Countess of Winchilsea.** To the nightingale.

Expensive, her throat/the white of a fattened column. **Judith Kazantzis.** Ave Gardner in the film *Earthquake*.

The eye of this storm is not quite. **Irma McClaurin.** To a gone era (My college days - class of '73).

The eyes of the little girls are lit with projects **Dilys Laing.** The little girls.

Eyes, what are they? Coloured glass, **Mary Elizabeth Coleridge.** Eyes.

The faces of women long dead, of our family, **Kadia Molodowsky.** Women songs I.

Faces surround me that have no smell or color no time **Audre Lorde.** Chain.

Facing it:/''What did you do today?'' **Ingrid Wendt.** Dust.

Fair lovely Maid, or if that Title be **Aphra Behn.** To the fair Clarinda, who made love to me, imagin'd more than woman.

The fairy people flouted me, **Mary Webb.** Fairy-led.

The fairy tales were right and they were wrong, **Helen Forsyth.** Dichotomy.

A fallen needle on the pavement, **Teresita Fernández.** A fallen needle . . .

The fallow deer are filtering along the tangled track, **Diana Witherby.** The leafy day.

The familiar rhythms/when the house goes quiet **Nancy Bacelo.** In a very, very quiet voice.

Farewell, incomparable element,/Whence man arose, where he shall not return; **Elinor Wylie.** Hymn to earth.

Farewell, old friend, thy work is done; **Eliza Cook.** My old straw hat.

Farewell, old friend,—we part at last; **Eliza Cook.** My old straw hat.

The farmer's clothes are soaked through and never dried, **Ise Tayū.** untitled.

Fashionable women in luxurious homes, **Charlotte Perkins Gilman.** The anti-suffragists.

The father and mother of the son/in the grave and the daughter with **Alison Colbert.** The white worm.

The father goes out on dates **Jan Heller Levi.** After her death. (A sequence for my mother).

The father remarries **Jan Heller Levi.** After her death. (A sequence for my mother).

Father, your strawberry-stained/skin a field brown **Barbara Noda.** Strawberries.

The fear of death disturbs me constantly; **Gabrielle de Coignard.** Prayer.

the fear stays, im/all alone near this huge **Faye Kicknosway.** Spitting backward.

Fear took off my/dancing shoes **Magdalena Gomez.** He got
me the first time.

Feel the coming rains and/speak in Thunder Tongue. If
Melanie Ellis. Feel the coming rains.

Female giants, fauna of women **Wisława Szymborska.** The
women of Rubens.

The field has not been ploughed **Anonymous.** The abortion.

a field of rationalizations over/a network of black poppies
that **Honor Johnson.** Maxims.

Fifteen boys, or perhaps even more, **Bella Akhmadulina.**
Fifteen boys, or perhaps even more.

50 insulin comas./Apparently well. **Kathleen Fraser.** Agnes.

'Fight the year out!' the War-lords said: **S. Gertrude Ford.**
'A fight to a finish.'

Fighting cocks, in the dark, **Diane Wakoski.** Cock fight
under the magnolias.

The Filipino is rotting in a ditch **Alison Colbert.** The white
worm.

The final wind will tear this page out too, **Fina García
Marruz.** This page too.

Finally I see your skin so scarred **Eleanor Lerman.** Finally
I see your skin.

Fine clothes have come for you **Anonymous.** untitled.

The fire advances/cold, resplendent with the calm **Amanda
Berenguer.** The sunset on the sea Saturday the 4th of
March, 1972.

The fireflies' light./How easily it goes on **Chine-Jo.**
untitled.

The fireplace in the backyard,/cocky, disheveled masonry,
Lorna Dee Cervantes. Beneath the shadow of the
freeway.

first,/take me to dinner/let me eat **Nikki Grimes.** The
takers.

the first day i shot dope **Sonia Sanchez.** Summer words for a
sister addict.

The first Day's Night had come— **Emily Dickinson.** 410.

First having read the book of myths, **Adrienne Rich.** Diving
into the wreck.

First, he paints the concrete/floor brown. Then with grey
Dona Stein. van Gogh painting his way out of the
asylum.

first I lowered my head **Anonymous.** A woman's song,
about men.

The first ivory gulls to reach Seymore Island **Elizabeth
Keeler.** Phantoms.

the first person I loved/was a woman my passion **Jacqueline
Lapidus.** Coming out.

First rule of the road/attend quiet victims first. **Audre
Lorde.** The evening news.

The First Separation/must have been a relief—of our **Elise
Young.** untitled.

the first task was to persuade them/a woman could go
Michèle Roberts. the woman who wanted to be a hero.

The first time we climbed the stairs **Mirta Yañez.** The visits.

First you wait for yourself **Ellen Wittlinger.** Waiting.

fish tank/representative cages/ **Rota Silverstrini.** The fish
tank.

A fisherman's net forgotten in the sun— **Victoria
Theodorou.** Picnic.

5 shirts/2 blouses/3 pairs of jeans and the iron's on hot **June
Jordan.** ON THE REAL WORLD: Meditation #1.

The flame of kerosene flickers. **Margarita Aliger.** Great
expectations.

A flavor of vanilla drifts/on the Sunday air. **Lucha Corpi.**
Dark romance.

A flight of birds has arrived in/their many-coloured coats.
Yunna Moritz. Poems for her sick mother.

floats on water/beasts enter the windows cleanly **Karen
Bunting.** her immaculate house.

The floors are slippery with blood: **Edith Sitwell.** The
dancers.

The florist was told, cyclamen or azalea; **Carolyn Kizer.**
Lines to accompany flowers for Eve (who took heroin,
then sleeping pills and who lies in a New York hospital).

The floss of the reed flowers/Is like flying snow. **Ma
Hsiang-lan.** Waterlilies.

A flow of people looking. **Judith Kazantzis.** At the National
Gallery.

the flow of sound breaks even from the minds of/artists
Katharine Morton. untitled.

Foam fluttered on the sea like birds' wings. **Dahlia
Ravikovitch.** Hills of salt.

Fold your impetuous hands and kneel **Jill Furse.** Gloria in
excelsis.

Foolish men, who do accuse/Women without reason, **Juana
Inés de la Cruz (Sister).** Foolish men.

For all the lovers among us, bloated with dreams **Frankie
Hucklenbroich.** For all the lovers among us.

For days the pond is the only pond. **Georgette Cerrutti.**
Raining the water.

for fifty years/his breathing at my back **Jan Clausen.**
grandma.

For grief/he wore those colorful bells, **Saniya Sālih.** Exile.

For hark! I will tell you low, low, **Elizabeth Barrett Browning.** The runaway slave at Pilgrim's Point.

For how long known this boundless wash of light, **Frances
Cornford.** Summer beach.

For how many years along this street of mine have I **Bella
Akhmadulina.** For how many years.

For long, in jealousy for corporal power, **Elizabeth
Wolstenholme-Elmy.** Woman free.

For love he offered me his perfect world. **Anna Wickham.**
Gift to a jade.

For me/it is not guilt/that haunts **Akua Lezli Hope.** D & C.

For my people everywhere singing their slave songs repeat-
Margaret Walker. For my people.

For nine days it rained/and this morning. **Elizabeth Keeler.**
Autumnal claque.

For pride of life/I plant this tree. **Karen Gershon.** On planting a tree.

for some reason/sometimes/you remind me/of a seascape **Michelene Wandor.** geography.

For the sake of a night of a little sleep **Minamoto no Toshitaka, The daughter of.** untitled.

For the woman/African in ancestry, **Carole C. Gregory.** A freedom song for the Black woman.

For 35 years I have fought you **Susan Sherman.** Amerika.

For twelve years I worshipped Siva, and what is my reward? **Anonymous.** untitled.

For two nights it snowed/on our green local mountain. **Elizabeth Keeler.** Snow in Marin County!

for us who sometimes fly in dreams, **Esther Louise.** for us.

For Violeta was the name/of a flower, **Yolanda Ulloa.** She went, she said, losing herself.

For weeks my heart has been camping out. **Jan Heller Levi.** After her death. (A sequence for my mother).

For years I thought I knew, at the bottom of the dream, **Louise Bogan.** The meeting.

For you I have stored up an ocean of thought, **Hsiung Hung.** Thinking of someone.

for your Easter vacation, I would like **Rachel Maines.** RSVP.

Forbear, bold youth, all's Heaven here, **Katherine Philips.** An answer to another persuading a lady to marriage.

the forehead cherished the dead son **Lina de Feria.** Kinfolk.

The forest cover gives way; pitch pines **Robin Becker.** Dorothy Bradford's dream. (The landing).

forgive, forgive/that the cosmic waters do not turn from me **Diane di Prima.** Brass furnace going out: song, after an abortion.

forgot to turn down the shades/you always do **Fay Chiang.** choreopoem VI.

the form small form/that to me it doesn't matter **Christina Meneghetti.** untitled.

Forward, sons of the tribe! **Hind bint Utba.** Tambourine song for soldiers going into battle.

Fountain of tears, river of grief **Christine de Pisan.** untitled.

Four brothers went by train **Kate Ellen Braverman.** Job interview.

'Four years,' some say consolingly. 'Oh well, **Vera Brittain.** The lament of the demobilised.

Fragile blades of grass,/Be proud! **Ping Hsin (Hsieh Wanying).** The stars.

The fragrance of the red lotus fades, **Li Ch'ing-chao.** Poem to the tune of "Yi chian mei."

Fragrant with powder, moist with perspiration, **Chao Luanluan.** Creamy breasts.

Frame it. Everyone lies, you say. The light's bad. **Sara Miles.** Portrait in available light.

Fred Kessler, of the East and West of Castro Street **Linda Gregerson.** What love is. (De arte honeste amandi).

Free earth hungered for free men but **Pauli Murray.** Dark testament.

Free I have my own self-reliance **Ingrid Jonker.** I drift in the wind.

Freed from the island-camp **Victoria Theodorou.** Galatia Kazanzaki.

Freedom is a dream/Haunting as amber wine **Pauli Murray.** Dark testament.

Friction. That shock/two stones in the dark click, igneous, **Sara Miles.** Contrary ways to make fire.

A friend calls us/an old married couple **Alice Bloch.** Six years.

From a flower carrying pole **Li Ch'ing-chao.** To the short tune "The magnolias."

from cavities of bones/spun/from caverns of air **Pat Parker.** From the cavities of bones.

From dark abodes to fair etherial light **Phillis Wheatley.** On the death of a young lady of five years of age.

From days spent bending over the pattern, **Sandra M. Gilbert.** Daguerreotype: lace maker.

From fair Jamaica's fertile plains, **Ada.** Lines.

From far away/my friend sent me a book of paintings. **Nellie Hill.** My inheritance.

From me she Ravishes those silent hours, **Aphra Behn.** To Lysander, on some verses he writ, and asking more for his heart than 'twas worth.

From Mt. Arima,/over the bamboo plains of Ina, **Daini no Sanmi.** untitled.

from my slackjaw eyes **Carol Bergé.** tessa's song.

From out the dragging vastness of the sea, **Amy Lowell.** Convalescence.

From Sappho to myself, consider the fate of women. **Carolyn Kizer.** Pro femina: parts one, two, and three.

from the bone there comes a drumbeat **Ann du Cille.** from the bone, the blood, the rib.

From the dream where we made love **Anonymous.** untitled.

From the heart of Earth, by means of yellow pollen **Anonymous.** untitled.

From the Isle of Awaji/each night there comes **Anonymous.** untitled.

from the laps of women/who have known hard toil **Gloria Gayles.** Parade.

From the North send a message **Murasaki Shikibu.** untitled.

From the photograph the child/(Dutch-boy bob, cross-stitched yoke, **Diana Chang.** Allegory.

From the ravine pours silent angry darkness **Fadwa Tuqān.** Behind bars.

From the sea of albino secrets **Lucha Corpi.** Absence.

From the shoaling/waters, pebbles. **Robin Becker.** The landing.

From the tender/The water went too fast **May Miller.** Yugoslavia. (Not that far).

from the train, the metal jaws/of yellow diggers slashing **Michèle Roberts.** Leeds weekend.

From the white man's house, and the **Elizabeth Barrett Browning.** The runaway slave at Pilgrim's Point.

From you from me painted dwellers **Nancy Bacelo.** untitled.

The frost: lucid as a child's face **Bella Akhmadulina.** Winter day.

Frozen cans of orange juice. **June Jordan.** From sea to shining sea.

The full days come striding with measured **Henriette Roland-Holst.** Concerning the awakening of my soul.

A full moon lamps it in a cloudless sky, **Alice Alment.** On a picture by Smith Haldy.

Full moon round/and the earth like a glass. **Enid Vian.** X.

Funny how he always comes/right when no one else is here **Roswell Spafford.** Song of the diner waitress.

The future is for tomorrow **Anna Gréki.** untitled.

Gain without gladness/Is in the bargain I have struck; **Liadain.** untitled.

The garden at last/begins to yield **Miriam Dyak.** Dying.

Garden of Shushan!/After Eden, all terrace, **Anne Spencer.** Before the Feast of Shushan.

The garden's shading. Let there be **Judith Moffett.** Key West (Triple ballade with enjambed refrain, plus envoy).

gave me life/what a hell on wheels she was **Catherine Davis.** SHE.

Gay colors flow/down streets that swirl **Gotō Miyoko.** untitled.

Gay little Girl-of-the-Diving-Tank, **Anne Spencer.** At the carnival.

Geared to the sterility/of machine-made symbols, **Angela de Hoyos.** The missing ingredient.

Gemini/a poem for two voices **Marie-Elise.** Gemini.

Gemmed with white daisies was the great green world **Marjorie Wilson.** To Tony (aged 3).

The genitals of woods/in full bloom; **Yagi Mikajo.** untitled.

Gentlemen: how are you? Here things go well. **Marie Ponsot.** Half-life: copies to all concerned.

Gentlemen of the Jury: I have had the time and opportunity to appear **Susan Saxe.** I argue my case. (Notes from the first year).

Gently traced,/this hand of bark-dry grooves **Lois Bissell Jircitano.** Love, Grandma.

Gertrude died not from love nor self. **Marilyn Bobes.** Notes on Gertrudis Gómez de Avellaneda.

The girl being chosen stood in her naked room **Muriel Rukeyser.** Mortal girl.

Girl in the moon, are you sorry **Chung Ling.** The fall of moon lady before the landing of Apollo X.

A girl of six, drenched, throws the covers off. **Susan Wood-Thompson.** Fever.

Girl of the lovely glance, looking out through the **Praxilla.** untitled.

The girl thinks/if I can only manage **Marie Luise Kaschnitz.** Return to Frankfurt.

Giulio, my Giulio!—sing they so, **Elizabeth Barrett Browning.** Bianca among the nightingales.

Give a seat to your visitor **Anonymous.** untitled.

Give me my little hoe **Anonymous.** untitled.

give me something/some slacks **Carol Bergé.** tessa's song.

Give them my regards when you go to the school reunion; **Muriel Rukeyser.** More of a corpse than a woman.

A glass of water in a time of scorching thirst: **Marina Tsvetayeva.** Earthly name.

Gleam ochre/and a light breaks **Ingrid Jonker.** Ladybird (a memory of my mother).

The gleaming of gold deceives— **Leah Goldberg.** Last brightness.

Go ahead, break something. You need to **Cynthia Kraman Genser.** Hootchie Kootchie man.

Go slowly/Like oxen dragging carts **May Miller.** Madeira. (Not that far).

God certainly wasn't/sun stubbornly continued rising **Yoshihara Sachiko.** Blasphemy.

God if he exists/Or if he doesn't **Shiraishi Kazuko.** The man root.

God if he isn't is/and laughs a lot *See* God if he exists/ Or if he doesn't.

God in me is the fury on the bare heath **Kathleen Raine.** Storm.

God, on us thy mercy show, **Mary Sidney Herbert, Countess of Pembroke.** Psalm lxvii.

Goddamn the empty sky **Violeta Parra.** Goddamn the empty sky.

The Gods of heaven are irrational. **Kasa no Iratsume.** untitled.

Going/Gone/Don't be going/Be gone **Yoshihara Sachiko.** Candle.

Going and/coming I/remain/exactly where I am **Alexandra Grilikhes.** Isabel Rawsthorne standing in a street in Soho (the portrait by Frances Bacon).

Going into the show one heard nothing but closing sounds, **Josephine Miles.** Nine o'clock show.

Going to Menlo Park/early, with time to spare, **Phyllis Koestenbaum.** Minor poem.

Going to the Desert/is the old term **Rae Armantrout.** Extremities.

the gold band/plays its roll/across europe **Michelene Wandor.** My mother's funeral in Waltham Abbey.

gold will not buy this voyage **Colleen J. McElroy.** Looking for a country under its original name.

GOLDSTEIN'S—GOLDFARB'S—WE BUY AND SELL **Jessica Tarahata Hagedorn.** Fillmore Street poems: August, 1967.

Gone are the games we played all night, **Mahsati.** untitled.

Gone is the sleepgiver, **Penelope Shuttle.** Gone is the sleepgiver.

A gone-forever spring,/lifted on the aroma **Audrey Lee.** Nostalgia.

Good Friday. Half-past three./Aunt Ida's hairdressing parlor **Yvonne.** The tearing of the skin.

Good Heav'n, I thank thee, since it was design'd **Anne Finch, Countess of Winchilsea.** On myselfe.

Good like locoweed **Rochelle Owens.** O supreme Domine.

Good repute is water carried in a sieve. **Lalleswari (Lalla).** untitled.

Good writing, the book tells you,/begins at home. **Rosellen Brown.** The Famous Writers School opens its arms in the next best thing to welcome.

The good-looking boy/Is waiting for me in the lane. **Anonymous.** The good-looking boy.

Good-looking, I'll never stoop for you **Mahsati.** untitled.

Grain-mother, thou art still our mother: now **Dorothy Wellesley.** Demeter in Sicily.

Granada/Seville and Cordoba/But we saw Malaga **May Miller.** Spain. (Not that far).

"Grandchild, I am an old woman/but I have nothing to tell about **Elizabeth Cook-Lynn.** History of Unchi.

Grandfather of the four mysteries **Nzadi Zimele-Keita.** Wa-Ko-Da. (Birds of paradise).

Grandmother holds my hand **Wendy Rose.** Native American studies, University of California at Berkeley, 1975.

grandmother's little feet/carried seven children **Bobbie Bishop.** untitled.

Grandpa:/Any day now you'll go off with your **Zaida del Río.** untitled.

Grandpa, I saw you die in the Indian hospital at Pawnee, **Anna Lee Walters.** Hartico.

A grandson is/not/the wing-sprouting cherub **Margaret Danner.** A grandson is a hoticeberg.

Granted that you write verse, **Helen Hamilton.** The romancing poet.

Grasshoppers/Chirping in the sleeves **Kawai Chigetsu-Ni.** untitled.

Grave mother of ours/rankled and sleeping. **Teresita Fernández.** Our mother America.

The great mammoth dreams quixotes **Iris Zavala.** The great mammoth . . .

Great Nature clothes the soul, which is but thin, **Margaret Cavendish, Duchess of Newcastle.** The soul's garment.

Great rocks frighten/Little people **May Miller.** Gibraltar. (Not that far).

The great sea stirs me. **Uvavnuk.** A woman shaman's song.

The great tiger/loved me—/and I loved him. **Esther Raab.** Folk tune.

Great-winged, as thirstily as an athlete you **Babette Deutsch.** Niké at the Metropolitan.

Green enravishment of human life, **Juana de Asbaje.** untitled.

Green lawn/a picket fence/flowers— **Alice Walker.** Once.

green moss between stonegrey shows **Carol Bergé.** paris musée de cluny.

Green stream full of life **Ingrid Jonker.** Dark stream.

green tinsel/chicken/green eyes **Michelene Wandor.** 'chick.'

Grey and dingy house in Meudon, **Margarita Aliger.** House in Meudon.

Grief/o grief/grief for ever **Urszula Kozioł.** Alarum.

The grim age turned me like a river, **Anna Akhmatova.** Northern elegy.

Grim, wandering Jew, helpless orphan. **Concha Michel.** Genesis.

growing/growing/i'm gagging on jelly **Carol Tinker.** Ishtar or the explosion in a shingle factory.

Gunfire spit/In the distance **Jessica Tarahata Hagedorn.** Fillmore Street poems: August, 1967.

Gunshot, or a pin oak falling; I still **Martha Boethel.** Falling South.

Ha, ha, the trick of the angels white! **Elizabeth Barrett Browning.** The runaway slave at Pilgrim's Point.

Ha!—in her stead, their hunter sons! **Elizabeth Barrett Browning.** The runaway slave at Pilgrim's Point.

Had I only known/My longing would be so great, **Otomo no Sakanoe.** Envoy.

Had nothing to do on Wednesday/but watch the house grow hot and silent **Paula Gunn Allen.** Moonshot: 1969.

had you not chosen the dangerous business of freedom, **Cheryl Clarke.** Freedom flesh.

Hail, happy day, when, smiling like the morn, **Phillis Wheatley.** To the Right Honorable William, Earl of Dartmouth.

The hair ornament of the sun/has sunk **Mitsuhashi Takajo.** untitled.

Half of me died at Bapaume, **Olive E. Lindsay.** Despair.

Half of our borders, rivers and mountains were gone, **Wu Tsao.** In the home of the scholar Wu Su-chiang from Hsin-An, I saw two psalteries of the late Sung General Hsieh Fang-tê.

Halloween has passed/for you, dear friends, **Teru Kanazawa.** Dumb patronage.

A hand extends toward me/Holding a steel hammer, **Hsiung Hung.** To—.

the hands examine./the tongue tests **Susan Macdonald.** son.

Handsome friend, charming and kind, **Beatritz de Dia.** untitled.

Hang the children by/their buttons to the gate. **Barbara Szerlip.** untitled.

Hanging on the wall, an iron face watches me. **Irma McClaurin.** The mask.

Happiness doesn't have any songs, happiness doesn't **Edith Södergran.** Pain.

Hard way of learning **Lisel Mueller.** Fracture.

A harder time is coming. **Ingeborg Bachmann.** The respite.

The hardest thing in the world/Is to reveal a hidden love. **Ho Shuang-ch'ing.** To the tune "A watered silk dress."

The hare is vanished from the darkening hill, **Jill Furse.** The hare is vanished.

Harriet there was always somebody calling us crazy. **Audre Lorde.** Harriet.

the hat-check girl in white tie and tails. **Rachel Loden.** Mother.

Hate is the cure. Dislike. Contempt. Rage. Hate. **Sandra M. Gilbert.** The cure. (The love sequence).

Hate me or love, I care not, as I pass **Ruth Pitter. The** unicorn.

Hath any loved you well, down there, **Marie de France.** Chartivel.

Have been thinking and dreaming a lot about death **Eugenie Eersel.** 4 A.M.

Have you ever held hands with a woman? **Judy Grahn.** A mock interrogation. (A woman is talking to death).

haven't been to one in almost three years **Paula Gunn Allen.** Powwow '79.

Having died he becomes more vivid. **Elizabeth Keeler.** The face in the camera.

having hooded my face with hair **Michèle Roberts.** The Sibyl's song.

Having tried to use the/witch card **Carolyn M. Rodgers.** It is deep.

The hawk's nose/Crows/Offbeat hearts **Alice Karle.** Earthquake.

He always had   a special kind of feeling/for the country-side **Angela Hamblin.** Sensitivity.

he and i do not resemble conventional lovers, **Carol Bergé.** letter from point lobos.

He bathes his soul in women's wrath; **Ruth Pitter.** The Irish patriarch.

He calls you in his wedding coat **Harriet Rose.** The wedding coat.

he came/with silver plated word **Nikki Grimes.** The takers.

He came and he sat **Sherry Hollingsworth.** untitled.

He came early, the song of his liquid voice **Albis Torres.** The visitor.

He does not come./Tonight in the dark of the moon **Ono no Komachi.** untitled.

He dreamed that he bestrode the sun. **Juanita Peirse.** Lament for a dictator.

He flooded everything, like a peaceful climate . . . **Elsie Alvarado de Ricord.** Interior dawn.

He forgets me/the air far from my shadow tastes better **Magaly Sánchez.** He forgets me.

He fumbles at your Soul/As Players at the Keys **Emily Dickinson.** 315.

he had/A Dream/e x p loded/down/his/throat. **Mari Evans.** A good assassination should be quiet.

He had no heart for war, its ways and means, **Helen Parry Eden.** A volunteer.

He has felt your heavy hair slide through his hands **Diane Middlebrook.** One woman looking at another. (Two poems).

He heard them in the silence of the night **Agnes Grozier Herbertson.** Airman, R.F.C.

He is leaving/the front end/of the calendar, **Marina Rivera.** Station.

He is my own fault. Let me see it straight. **Dilys Laing.** Private entry in the diary of a female parent.

He marched away with a blithe young score of him **Ruth Comfort Mitchell.** He went for a soldier.

He moaned and beat with his head and feet, **Elizabeth Barrett Browning.** The runaway slave at Pilgrim's Point.

He opened the car door. There was a low rumble **Nicki Jackowska.** The meeting.

He prayed for patience; Care and Sorrow came, **Clara Ann Thompson.** His answer.

he said no other/could be wiser/and offered me the job **Frances Landsman.** Advice.

He saw how at her Length she lay; **Aphra Behn.** The disappointment.

He say/I'm beautiful and/for real chant about **Sherley Anne Williams.** the peacock poem. (The house of desire).

he says he would like each of our rooms to contain **Carol Bergé.** letter from point lobos.

He says to her what moves her most. **Elizabeth Barrett Browning.** Bianca among the nightingales.

He sniffs the autumn air,/fur bristling, rippling, like a red robe **Anita Endrezze-Danielson.** Shaman/Bear.

He speaks in a big voice through all the air **Muriel Rukeyser.** The president and the laser bomb. (Searching/not searching).

He thrust his joy against the weight of the sea, **Judith Wright.** The surfer.

He waits for her to arrive/in the family carriage. **Ann Lauterbach.** The yellow linen dress: a sequence.

He wanted her to be with him **Brenda Conner-Bey.** The dancer.

he was growing old/without a wife **Frances C. Chung.** untitled.

He was just a boy, as I could see, **Mary H. J. Henderson.** An incident.

He was once a tiny, helpless thing, **Janet Campbell.** Aaron Nicholas, almost ten.

He was still Uncle/Jack to me the first **Sherley Anne Williams.** The Empress brand trim: Ruby reminisces.

He was wounded and he fell in the midst of hoarse shouting. **Alice Corbin.** Fallen.

He who stole my virginity/is the same man/I am married to **Śilabhattarika.** untitled.

He who was wont to give me beautiful things, the son of Noworb, **Anonymous.** untitled.

He will meet me in a matched set **Sharon Barba.** Siblings.

He won't come./The date was for the sun's hour **Magaly Sánchez.** Woman waiting in the park.

He would   in the case of a divorce **Tove Ditlevsen.** Divorce 1.

Head bent, walking through snow **Audre Lorde.** 125th Street and Abomey.

A head that's hard to define. **Eliana Rivera.** Identification card.

Head wrapped in the sleeve/of a neighbor's old dress **Magdalena Gomez.** One of too many.

Hear now a curious dream I dreamed last night, **Christina Rossetti.** My dream.

Hear one voice/for another/the bird **Marguerite Clerbout.** Spring in the woods.

Heard you that shriek? It rose/So wildly in the air, **Frances Ellen Watkins Harper.** The slave mother.

The heart of a woman goes forth with the dawn, **Georgia Douglas Johnson.** The heart of a woman.

A heart requires a Heart Unfeign'd and True, **Aphra Behn.** To Lysander, on some verses he writ, and asking more for his heart then 'twas worth.

The heart thinks constantly. this can't be changed **Janet Hamill.** SUBTERRANEOUS/Subterraneus.

heaven declares/the heron of oblivion **Carol Tinker.** Heron of oblivion.

The heavens join with the clouds. **Li Ch'ing-chao.** To the tune "The honor of a fisherman."

Heavy breathing fills all my chamber **Donna Whitewing.** August 24, 1963—1:00 a.m.: Omaha.

The heavy sobs which rise up and choke me **Anonymous.** untitled.

Held among wars, watching/all of them/all these people **Muriel Rukeyser.** Käthe Kollwitz.

Held between wars/my lifetime/among wars, the big hands of the world of death **Muriel Rukeyser.** Käthe Kollwitz.

Hence, Cupid! with your cheating toys, **Katherine Philips.** Against love.

Her Balmy Lips incountring his, **Aphra Behn.** The disappointment.

Her birdcage bones/ridge through the flesh **Sandy Boucher.** Copy clerk—North American Aviation.

Her Bright Eyes sweet, and yet severe, **Aphra Behn.** The disappointment.

Her creamy child kissed by the black maid! square on the mouth! **Gwendolyn Brooks.** Bronzeville woman in a red hat.

Her dark head fallen forward in her grief, **Alfonsina Storni.** She who understands.

Her daughter wore a linen dress and **Ann Lauterbach.** The yellow linen dress: a sequence.

Her delicate way/came from a blue planet **Rafaela Chacón Nardi.** Amelia's color.

Her eyes glowed pale as radium. **Sandra M. Gilbert.** The dream kitchen.

Her father and mother will pay/for the silver knife that cuts **Alison Colbert.** The white worm.

her grandmother called her from the playground **Nikki Giovanni.** Legacies.

Her hand passing slowly under her hair. over her neck under the weight of **Cynthia Kraman Genser.** Under the sword.

Her—"last Poems"—/Poets—ended— **Emily Dickinson.** 312.

Her mother testifies against her **Adrienne Rich.** For Ethel Rosenberg.

her name is nada/born of ainu and t'boli **Jessica Tarahata Hagedorn.** Canto de Nada/para ti, M'wandishi.

Her name was Mercedes. And she was good. **Carilda Oliver Labra.** Elegy for Mercedes.

Her neighbors are telling the truth:/she is filthy, **Susan North.** The truth of the matter in Coolidge, Arizona.

her personal life has very little to do with **Karen Brodine.** The receptionist is by definition.

Her thin puny little body, **Jo Barnes.** Clinic day.

Here am I—tall as the pine-tree. **Marguerite Johansen.** High-heeled boots.

Here an establishment, its sunny rooms, **Josephine Miles.** Demeanor.

Here are the Schubert *lieder.* Now begin. **Frances Cornford.** For M. S. singing *Fruhlingsglaube* in 1945.

Here comes my secular skirt again **Milagros González.** First dialogue.

Here I lived with the other women prisoners **Victoria Theodorou.** Picnic.

here I sit/like a bird/in the wilderness, **Safiya Henderson.** Portrait of a woman artist.

here is my room I sit at a drawing table **Diane de Prima.** Brass furnace going out: song, after an abortion.

Here is the wooden/dirt bridge. And here **Virginia Gilbert.** Impressions at dawn.

Here lies a woman. Pause as you go along **Muriel Box.** R.I.P.

Here suddenly on your tightrope. **Minerva Salado.** The city.

Here the scanted daisy glows **Elizabeth Daryush.** Flanders Fields.

Here they are, what you hid,/what shamed you, the **Marie Ponsot.** "Sois sage o ma douleur."

Here too the Spirit shafts/Such heavenly floods of light **Mechthild von Magdeburg.** untitled.

Here's the gate from the sea. The top of it curves. **Diana Ó Hehir.** Alicia's dream: entering Knossos.

Here's where our gypsy/brotherhood led! **Marina Tsvetayeva.** Poem of the end.

Heritage/I look for you all day in the streets of Oaxaca. **Lorna Dee Cervantes.** Heritage.

Hey Chicano bossman/don't tell me that/machismo is part of our culture **Marcela Christine Lucero-Trujillo.** "Machismo is part of our culture."

hey music and/me/only white, **Lucille Clifton.** my dream about being white.

Hey my man/you know we can't/stay in these city trappings **Dolly Bird.** Return to the home we made.

Hey there brother man/Black prince come to save me from the white night **Donna Allegra.** A rape poem for men.

Hey you death/ho and ho poor death **Judy Grahn.** A woman is talking to death.

heye neye yana/Now she is dressing up her child, **Anonymous.** untitled.

hieroglyphs found under cypress bark at point lobos **Carol Bergé.** letter from point lobos.

High above shores and times, **Muriel Rukeyser.** Miriam: the Red Sea. (Searching/not searching).

High bare white walls/and the facts of separation. **Elaine Dallman.** Later.

High waving heather, 'neath stormy blasts bending, **Emily Brontë.** High waving heather.

His artificial feet calumped in holy rhythm **Naomi Long Madgett.** Deacon Morgan.

His eyelids are dark as coffee, the Southerner, **Yunna Moritz.** Midday in Gantiadi.

His instrument is reddish like Mars **Kathleen Teague.** The harmony of sirens.

His life is umber./From earth colours olives grow, **Sheila Wingfield.** Envy.

His pains so racked my heart **Viola Meynell.** Sympathy.

His quick probings, much like a pike **Elena Wilkinson.** Face: border.

His right hand holds his slingshot, **Ping Hsin (Hsieh Wan-ying).** For the record (given to my little brother).

his roots/went back to the reservation old **Chrystos.** He saw.

His sad brown bulk rears patient as the hills **Babette Deutsch.** A bull.

His teeth are white as curds **Anonymous.** untitled.

His woman knows/he is a war older. **Laura Beausoleil.** Welcome home from Vietnam.

Hitler entered Paris the way my **Sharon Olds.** The takers.

ho and ho poor death **Judy Grahn.** Hey you death. (A woman is talking to death).

Ho Chi Minh,/winter won't come to your veranda anymore. **Mirta Yañez.** Springtime in Vietnam.

Hold, hold it tight, **Anonymous.** Song for a girl on her first menstruation.

Hold it up, show it, bring the torch! **Ann Stanford.** Cassandra's wedding song. (The Trojan women).

Homesickness! That weariness/I've felt so long! **Marina Tsvetayeva.** Homesickness.

honey people murder mercy U.S.A./the milkland turn to monsters teach **June Jordan.** In memoriam: Rev. Martin Luther King, Jr. (Part one).

Honeyed by time/the shining walls **Anne Hébert.** The wooden chamber.

Hop hop, thump thump,/Oh I am holy, o I am plump, **Stevie Smith.** The dedicated dancing bull and the water maid.

The hope I dreamed of was a dream, **Christina Rossetti.** The hope I dreamed of.

Hope is a crushed stalk/Between clenched fingers. **Pauli Murray.** Dark testament.

"Hope" is the thing with feathers— **Emily Dickinson.** 254.

Horror's happy guest,/invited by hunger, **Carilda Oliver Labra.** Last conversation with Rolando Escardó.

The horses of instruction/tell slowly forward **Judith Kazantzis.** The horses of instruction, the tigers of wrath.

The hostess poured me out another cognac. **Bella Akhmadulina.** Rain.

Hot wind sweeps over the vegetable patches **Cheng Min.** The drought.

An hour I waited for you. And her. Gold. Black. *First* **Honor Moore.** In Mrs. N's palace.

The house feels unfinished like **Sherley Anne Williams.** The house of desire. (The house of desire).

The house is a body/from which we come; **Jane Augustine.** I help my mother move out of her old house in the country.

How beautiful the Buddhist statutes **Imaizumi Sogetsu-Ni.** untitled.

How beautiful the young woman! How beautiful and how **Excilia Saldaña.** Obba (a patakin).

How can I blame the cherry blossoms **Shunzei's daughter.** untitled.

How can I complain/that you have shaved your hair? **Yokobue.** untitled.

How can I entertain you,/Traveler, **Yosano Akiko.** (Tangled hair).

How can I look/at this sun? **Shirely Kaufman.** Jerusalem notebook.

How can you stare out at the Neva, **Anna Akhmatova.** How can you stare out at the Neva.

how could I ever make a friend/of death? though he behaves **Michèle Roberts.** persephone descends to the underworld.

How did we get to this place, anyway? **Jenny Mastoraki.** How did it happen?

How do I differ from a woman with a flower, **Bella Akhmadulina.** How do I differ from a woman with a flower.

How do I enter the silence of stones **Mona Sa'udi.** untitled.

How do I love thee? Let me count the ways. **Elizabeth Barrett Browning.** Sonnets from the Portuguese. (XLIII)

How do they do it, the ones who make love **Sharon Olds.** Sex without love.

How does it help me if, with flawless art, **Louise Labe.** Elegy XXIII.

How fast this water flows away! **Han Ts'ui-p'in.** A poem written on a floating red leaf.

How frail/Above the bulk/Of crashing water hangs, **Adelaide Crapsey.** Niagara.

How heavy the trees are with rain, **Chase Twichell.** Starkweather House.

How I long for the man who climbed Mt. Yoshino **Shizuka.** untitled.

how is it possible/space/around a life **Jan Clausen.** the kitchen window.

How is living with another woman—/simpler? An oar stroke! **Marina Tsvetayeva.** An attempt at jealousy.

How it comes/in answer/to a question **Susan Sherman.** Amerika.

How long, how long must I regret? **Ruth Pitter.** The lost tribe.

How long will it last? **Lady Horikawa.** untitled.

How many hours/is it? In the darkened hole **Virginia Gilbert.** Leaving, the sepulcre city.

How many wise men and heroes/Have survived the dust and dirt of the world? **Ch'iu Chin.** To the tune "The river is red."

How old was Mary out of whom you cast **Charlotte Mew.** Madeleine in church.

how patiently/how lonely/you weave your tapestries/Penelope **Margarita Cota-Cárdenas.** Gullible.

How rudely you speak to me! **Fina García Marruz.** How rudely you speak to me.

How say that by law we may torture and chase **Frances Ellen Watkins Harper.** She's free!

how the light shines through your skin! **Toi Derricotte.** For a godchild, Regina, on the occasion of her first love.

How they came into the world,/the women-loving-women **Judy Grahn.** A history of lesbianism.

How to lay down her death,/Bring her back living **May Sarton.** After four years.

How to weave your web of medicinal flesh into words **Jayne Cortez.** Big fine woman from Ruleville.

How will you call me, brother **Mari Evans.** How will you call me, brother.

How would you cry out to me? **Bella Akhmadulina.** At night.

Howard, some day will you buy me a horse? **Betsy Orient.** The proposition.

Howling and roaring/Toe'osh scattered white people **Leslie Marmon Silko.** Toe'osh: a Laguna coyote story.

The huddled bean-sheaves under the moon, **Mary Webb.** Autumn, 1914.

The human heart has hidden treasures, **Charlotte Brontë.** Evening solace.

The human race is going to the cemetery **Etel Adnan.** The Beirut—Hell Express.

An Humble *slave* the Buyer must become. **Aphra Behn.** To Lysander, on some verses he writ, and asking more for his heart then t'was worth.

hungry, you with/the wish come **Carol Tinker.** Naramasu.

The hunters are back from beating the winter's face **Audre Lorde.** The woman thing.

HUSH! YO' MOUTH/IT IS TIME TO BE QUIET **Fareedah Allah.** HUSH, HONEY.

hymns to the tunes/that/wove their way **Wendy Stevens.** The hymns my mother sang.

Hypocrite women, how seldom we speak **Denise Levertov.** Hypocrite women.

I/is the total black, being spoken **Audre Lorde.** Coal.

i)/My garnet necklace goes **Anna Hartmann.** Sleeping with Frank Kafka.

I/never liked/white folks **Alice Walker.** Once.

I, a princess, king-descended, decked with jewels, gilded, **Christina Rossetti.** A royal princess.

"I accept the universe."—Margaret Fuller **Michele Murray.** The woman who lives inside the world.

"I always compare you to a drifting log with iron nails in it. **Miriam Dyak.** Dying.

I always like summer/best **Nikki Giovanni.** Knoxville, Tennessee.

I am/in the mean/hot/cold/warm/red **Abbey Lincoln (Aminata Moseka).** In the middle.

I am a Black woman/and I hold my head up high, **Margaret Walker.** MY TRUTH AND MY FLAME.

I am a black woman/the music of my song **Mari Evans.** I am a black woman.

I am a blood-priestess **Lili Bita.** The blood criminal.

I am a bourgeois wife/with a swollen belly **Olga Elena Mattei.** untitled.

I am a lamp, a lamp that is out; **Frances Cornford.** She warns him.

i am a lesbian, forfeit/the universal. i cannot **Jan Clausen.** dialectics.

I am a lioness/and will never allow my body **'Aisha bint Ahmad al-Qurtubiyya.** untitled.

I am a thief/your guardian angel/who watches you **Jessica Tarahata Hagedorn.** Listen.

I am a tractor/useful and physically strong, **Natasha Morgan.** He said: Mostly I feel like a tractor.

I am a union woman,/As brave as I can be; **Molly (Aunt) Jackson.** I am a union woman.

I am a victim of/migraines/insomnia/the taxman **Judith Barrington.** Poems.

I am a welder./Not an alchemist. **Cherríe Moraga.** The welder.

I am a white rabbit in a hutch **Naomi Wolf.** Alice James.

I am a woman controlled./Remember this: I never scream. **May Miller.** The scream.

i am a woman in ice/melting **Martha Courtot.** untitled.

I am a woman made of fragments **Rivka Miriam.** Flute.

"I am a woman running into my own country . . ." *See* she is in a white dress

I am about to sing this song of yours, **Anonymous.** untitled.

I am always aware of my mother, **Nagase Kiyoko.** Mother.

I am an ostrich/this is my credo **Michelene Wandor.** song of the ostrich.

i am anxious for answers/this night after **Akua Lezli Hope.** August.

I am as awful as my brother War, **Eleanor Farjeon.** Peace.

I am being followed. **Mary Crow.** Not volcanoes, not minerals.

I am black, I am black! **Elizabeth Barrett Browning.** The runaway slave at Pilgrim's Point.

I am bleeding/the blood seeps in red **Susan Griffin.** The song of the woman with her parts coming out.

I am Chicana/And I turn to you, **Sylvia Alicia Gonzales.** In search of the messiahs of nativism. (Chicana evolution).

I am Chicana/something inside revolts. **Sylvia Alicia Gonzales.** Genesis and the original sin. (Chicana evolution).

i am declaring war/on my refrigerator **Margaret Porter.** inflation.

I am fixed in waiting/by these silks that bind me **Jonny Kyoko Sullivan.** SAGIMUSUME: The white heron maiden.

I am forgotten now. **Lady Ukon.** untitled.

i am glad you mention/while mononucleosis is my favorite disease the doctor smiles **Mary Winfrey.** at the diagnostician's office.

I am growing into your husk **Michele Murray.** The woman who lives inside the world.

I am helping proofread the history **Irena Klepfisz.** Contexts.

I am here/seated in this place **Olga Elena Mattei.** untitled.

I am here with my beautiful bountiful womanful child **Isabella Gardner.** At a summer hotel.

I am in Hong Kong. **Dahlia Ravikovitch.** How Hong Kong was destroyed.

I am in my lady skin coming/Down my ordinary stair, **Dona Stein.** Lady and the wolf.

I am in the euphoria of your white wings **Maya Islas.** untitled.

i am indeed the lady in the supermarket slapping her kid **Jan Zaleski.** In answer to what he said.

I am like a field waiting. **Raquel Chalfi.** Like a field waiting.

I am like the traveller **Dulce María Loynaz.** The traveller.

i am lonely./all the people i know/i know too well **Carolyn M. Rodgers.** Poem for some Black women.

I am not a Black Goddess **Donna Kate Rushin.** The Black goddess.

I am not human, **Kathleen Raine.** Maternal grief.

I am not lazy./I am on the amphetamine of the soul. **Anne Sexton.** Frenzy.

I am not mad: I am black. **Elizabeth Barrett Browning.** The runaway slave at Pilgrim's Point.

I am now so weary with waiting, **Gaspara Stampa.** untitled.

I am on my way running, **Anonymous.** Song for a young girl's puberty ceremony.

I am pretending/To listen to the/Battered radio **Jessica Tarahata Hagedorn.** Poem for Rene Crevel.

I am putting you in a painting. **Hsiung Hung.** Summer freezes here.

I am sick today,/sick in my body, **Yosano Akiko.** Labor pains.

i am sick with knives, knives **Olga Broumas.** the knife & the bread.

I am silver and exact. I have no preconceptions. **Sylvia Plath.** Mirror.

I am still making my body in the dark **Michele Murray.** The woman who lives inside the world.

i am stronger here: **Carol Bergé.** letter from point lobos.

I am that serpent-haunted cave **Kathleen Raine.** The phythoness.

I am that woman whose works are good **Padeshah Khatun.** Sovereign queen.

I am the Black woman/& i have been all over **Pat Parker.** untitled: Movement in Black.

I am the Black woman/I am Bessie Smith **Pat Parker.** untitled: Movement in Black.

I am the Black woman/I am the child of the sun **Pat Parker.** untitled: Movement in Black.

I am the blossom pressed in a book **Jane Kenyon.** Briefly it enters, and briefly speaks.

I am the centre/Of a circle of pain **Mina Loy.** Parturition.

I am the chariot/rolling through alleys **Marnie Walsh.** Poets/poems.

I am the downtrodden/I am the poor and deprived **Judy Dothard Simmons.** Minority.

I am the 4th fish/the others lie in their **Rota Silverstrini.** The fish tank.

"*I am the Great Drum of Justice*" **Fina García Marruz.** At the death of Martin Luther King.

I am the Kiwi bird **Nina Cassian.** The Kiwi bird.

I am the North Pole **Tzu Yeh.** untitled.

I am the one who is inside you **Michele Murray.** The woman who lives inside the world.

I am the scholar of the dark armchair—the crimson **Sandra M. Gilbert.** The twelve dancing princesses.

I am the wall at the lip of the water **Judy Grahn.** untitled.

I am the weaver. **Abbey Lincoln (Aminata Moseka).** I am the weaver.

I am the woman moving into your life **Susan MacDonald.** untitled.

I am the woman of the principal fountain **Maria Sabina.** Shaman.

I am too near, too clear a thing for you, **Lizette Woodworth Reese.** A flower of mullein.

I am trying to imagine/how it feels to you **Adrienne Rich.** Re-forming the crystal.

i am warm/great/i am undulating life **Johari M. Kunjufu.** The promise.

I am wary of need/that tastes like destruction. **Audre Lorde.** NEED: a chorale of Black women's voices.

I am weaving a song of waters, **Gwendolyn B. Bennett.** Song.

I am your mother. **Cherríe Moraga.** Like I am to no one.

i arrive/in the unbearable heat **Jessica Tarahata Hagedorn.** Song for my father.

I ask her what she will do **Susan Griffin.** Deer skull.

i ask no more than/you're willing to give **Esther Louise.** enough.

i ask what lake this is./they tell me Erie. **Jan Clausen.** (upstate poetry tour). (dialectics).

I ask you, sir, to/Stand face to face **Sappho.** untitled.

I awake in a church in Quebec. **Virginia Gilbert.** Awakening, in a church.

I bargain:/my blood or my poetry. **Phyllis Koestenbaum.** Blood journey.

I bathe thy palms/In showers of wine, **Anonymous.** untitled.

i became a woman/during the old prayers **Lucille Clifton.** apology (to the panthers).

I begin with an itching in the middle/of the palm **Katerina Anghelaki-Rooke.** Magdalen the great mammal.

I, being born a woman and distressed **Edna St. Vincent Millay.** Sonnet. (XLI).

I believe I will die young/The boy said to me **Jessica Tarahata Hagedorn.** The Blue Swan Cafe.

I bend over the woman./This is the third time between abortions. **Ai.** The country midwife: a day.

I, Boudica **Judy Grahn.** I, Boudica.

I break the surface/grasp for air **Susan Sherman.** Amerika.

I bring no throat-slit kid/no heart-scooped victim **Dilys Laing.** Prayer of an ovulating female.

i bring roses to the arms of the sea— **Evelyn Posamentier.** I bring roses.

I bring you a goat/snatched half dead from the jaws of wolves— **Hroswitha von Gandersheim.** Paphnutius.

I brush the spider webs from the dismantled sky **Amanda Berenguer.** Housework.

I burn/arch/zero/frontier **Amanda Berenguer**. The fire advances (second version).

I burn/arch/zero/frontier **Amanda Berenguer**. Poema cinetico (third version).

I call you Miss in tribute/to the women of that time, **Sherley Anne Williams**. you were never miss brown to me.

i called you/because i became frightened **Ellen Marie Bissert**. Groves II.

I came out a winner **Forūgh Farrokhzād**. O realm bejewelled.

I can charm the man **Anonymous**. Love charm song.

I can give myself to her/In her dreams **Ysano Akiko**. untitled.

I can no longer tell dream from reality. **Akazome Emon**. untitled.

I can not:/cook/wear a hat **Tove Ditlevsen**. Self portrait 1.

I can only say I have waited for you **Ingrid Jonker**. Time of waiting in Amsterdam.

I can only strip/my spoil of wisteria/and sing **Barbara Gravelle**. The new Joan come out of the fire.

I can remember the time, it's not so long ago, when I wanted nothing/more than to be small. **Charlotte Carter**. Days and nights before winter.

I can see the street/from barricaded windows **Rota Silverstrini**. Pieces of echoes.

I can still smell the spray off the sea they made me cross. **Nancy Morejón**. Black woman.

I cannot let you die. **May Miller**. Death is not master.

I cannot raise my hand/To knock at your door **Cheng Min**. Evening rendezvous.

I cannot recall you gentle **Audre Lorde**. Black mother woman.

I cannot sleep/For the blaze of the full moon **Tzu Yeh**. untitled.

i can't get anything done on time **Ellen Marie Bissert**. ode to my true nature.

I can't hold you and I can't leave you, **Juana Inés de la Cruz (Sister)**. I can't hold you and I can't leave you.

I can't see you now, rushing down the aisle dizzy **Sara Miles**. Calling on the live wire.

I care not how the busy Market goes, **Aphra Behn**. To Lysander, on some verses he writ, and asking more for his heart then 'twas worth.

i carry the whole weight of this paper today. **Reina María Rodríguez**. To Lumi Videla.

I catch the movement of his lips. **Marina Tsvetayeva**. Poem of the end.

i change,/illumined by them, **Carol Bergé**. the friends, a celebration.

I climb the black rock mountain **Leslie Marmon Silko**. Where mountain lion lay down with deer.

I come from far away. I have forgotten my country. **Rosario Castellanos**. Foreign woman.

i come from the womb of Africa **Amina Baraka**. Soweto song.

I come to White Painted Woman, **Anonymous**. untitled.

I come to you already dreaming **Cate Abbe**. Khmer woman.

I could have lived close to you **Claudia Lars**. Letters written when night grows.

i could help you./i could become the vital **Carolyn M. Rodgers**. Masquerade.

i could never explain/why you move me so **Akua Lezli Hope**. Lovesigns.

i crawl to his door/peek through dilating iris **Nikki Grimes**. Fragments: mousetrap.

i cried tonite/oba-san/remembering you **Chris Kobayashi**. Oba-san.

I danced for Herod, yes. My mother's eyes, **Leonora Speyer**. Salome.

I declare/That this is/A baby machine **Jessica Tarahata Hagedorn**. Rock and roll.

i dedicate this poem/to my unborn daughters **Astra**. Daughters.

I did/-dijo el hombre blanco-/with my little knife **Angela de Hoyos**. Who killed brown love?

I did not live until this time **Katherine Philips**. To my excellent Lucasia, on our friendship.

I didn't bolt the door/or light the candle. **Anna Akhmatova**. On a white night.

I did't hear the door/slam when it closed. **Mariana Sanson**. untitled.

i didn't know bobby/hutton in fact it is **Sonia Sanchez**. bobby hutton. (Memorial).

I didn't want this,/not this. (Silence: listen!) **Marina Tsvetayeva**. Poem of the end.

I disapprove even of eloquent **Corinna**. untitled.

I discover you in bits and pieces **Odette Aslan**. untitled.

I do not consider myself worth counting, **Kujō Takeko**. untitled.

I do not know how to write silken verses, **Iris Zavala**. Escritura desatada. XXI.

I do not love thee! No! I do not love thee! **Caroline Norton**. I do not love thee.

i do not understand very much. **Evelyn Posamentier**. Immigration.

I do not want to be your weeping woman **Alison Boodson**. I do not want to be your weeping woman.

I do not want to meet you in the winter. **Margarita Aliger**. For a man on his way.

i done got so thirsty that my mouth waters/at the thought of rain **Patricia Jones**. I done got so thirsty that my mouth waters at the thought of rain.

I don't have a home,/and I live there **Julia Vinograd**. Downhill.

I don't have your way of staring in a mist **Carilda Oliver Labra**. Verses for Anna.

I don't know about that/one. **Michelene Wandor**. ritual.

i don't know anything/about the pain **Jan Clausen**. the kitchen window.

I don't know if the one who is writing here **Olga Casanova-Sanchez**. The girl who is always with me.

I don't know politics but I know the names **Kamala Das**. An introduction.

I don't know what I would've done **Jenny Mastoraki**. Marble busts. (How I managed to square the circle of dreams

in the shape of a window at the top of the stairs in a tenement house).

I don't know where I found the nerve. **Susan North.** Aunt Lenore at forty-five.

I don't know where to find a vase **Rachel Loden.** Mother.

I don't know why, but my hand knew **Ishigaki Rin.** untitled.

I don't think/integration/entered/into it/officer **Alice Walker.** Once.

I don't want any more of your gentle abuse. **Helen Wong Huie.** untitled.

I don't want feelings, his wife said more **Linda Gregerson.** Between what persons love may exist. (De arte honeste amandi).

I drag my shirt across the floor **Kendra Kopelke.** Eager Street.

I drank a cup of sunlight to have you. **Elsie Alvarado de Ricord.** On the birth of a child.

I dream of Serenity,/Peace,/Calmness. **Kattie M. Cumbo.** I'm a dreamer.

I dream of you, to wake: would that I might **Christina Rossetti.** Monna Innominata: a sonnet of sonnets.

I dream only of gulls. **Molly Vaux.** Out on the water.

I dreamed (God pity babes at play) **Lesbia Thanet.** In time of war.

I dreamed I held/A sword against my flesh. **Kasa no Iratsume.** untitled.

I dreamed that someone's coming **Forūgh Farrokhzād.** Someone like no one else.

I dreamt (no 'dream' awake—a dream indeed) **Alice Meynell.** In sleep.

I dreamt of walking on icy waves. **Chung Ling.** On the melting lake.

I dug in with all the spirit of spring **Mary Coghill.** Knowing.

I dwell alone—I dwell alone, alone, **Christina Rossetti.** Autumn.

I dwell in Possibility— **Emily Dickinson.** 657.

I emerged one spring/to ride with the earth **Frances Mayes.** Epitaph.

I emptied, I emptied like a pool **Yona Wallach.** I emptied.

I entered the marble hall **Sybil Wood.** The civil servant is eaten too.

I envy the solitude you/learned from me **Barbara Szerlip.** This place.

I envy you/your steady silence/inside your calm world **Marie-Elise.** Definition.

I escape from the anguish of beating **Teresita Fernández.** I escape.

I exit, trying to find some meaning in this. **Jeanne Murray Walker.** Making the painting.

I expected my skin and my blood/to ripen **Wendy Rose.** I expected my skin and my blood to ripen.

I fall, I swoon! I look at the sky. **Elizabeth Barrett Browning.** The runaway slave at Pilgrim's Point.

I feared your wrath Eurynome **Eleni Fourtouni.** Eurynome.

I fed upon flowers, the pungent essence of grasses **Kathleen Herbert.** The virgin capture.

I feed off you./I breathe from you. **Fanchon Lewis.** Love poem to the earth.

I feel empty/unfinished like/this poem **Sapphire.** New York City tonight.

I feel in her pockets; she wore nice cotton gloves, **Ruth Stone.** Secondhand coat.

I feel of others' affairs **Murasaki Shikibu.** untitled.

I feel so good I ain't written a fuckin' thing in a year. **Chocolate Waters.** I feel so good I ain't written a fuckin' thing in a year.

I feel the child cry/from in my womb. **Anonymous.** I dream.

I feel the Spring far off, far off, **Sara Teasdale.** Spring in war-time.

I feel the stubborn humming **Kata Szidónia Petröczi.** Swift floods.

I fell asleep thinking of him, **Ono no Komachi.** untitled.

I fell in love with the Lord Buddha **Hayashi Fumiko.** The Lord Buddha.

I felt rough from the needs that took me away, **Carole C. Gregory.** Revelation.

I finally saw it was poliomyelitis behind the pepsicola **Minerva Salado.** Nela.

i find/women can slip/from the pages of a book **Mary Winfrey.** meeting.

I find no edge to this mourning. **Rachel Loden.** Mother.

I fire at the face/Of the country where I was born, **Shiraishi Kazuko.** I fire at the face of the country where I was born.

I followed a path. **Pat Parker.** I followed a path.

I followed the ink-blue water of the glove. **Gerda S. Norvig.** Hand fantasy.

I forgot that my lips/were rouged, **Fukuda Chiyo-Ni.** untitled.

I found her, rich loser of all, **May Sarton.** Joy in Provence.

I gave my small son/a plastic rose/and then forgot. **Nancy Willard.** Night rising.

I gave the jewel away to its owner. **Otomo no Sakanoe.** untitled.

i get her up/then she say/there aint nothing in it **Marnie Walsh.** Vickie Loans-Arrow 1972.

I get my degree/The Spring of '52 **Fareedah Allah.** Lawd, dese colored chillum.

I go one step forward,/Then stumble one step back. **Cheng Min.** Student.

I go out of darkness/Onto a road of darkness **Izumi Shikibu.** untitled.

I go to visit her where she stays— **Becky Birtha.** Maria de Las Rosas.

I got up and opened the shoji **Anonymous.** untitled.

I grieve and dare not show my discontent, **Elizabeth I, Queen of England.** On monsieur's departure.

I guess you love me now./I guess you admire me now. **Jane Green.** Songs of divorce.

I guided you by rote— **Anne Wilkinson.** Letter to my children.

I had a baby/two babies/three **Polly Joan.** Scarred.

I had a dream three walls stood up wherein a raven bird **Stevie Smith.** Anger's freeing power.

I had a sudden vision in the night, **Leonora Speyer.** The ladder.

I had become callous like most **Della Burt.** On the death of Lisa Lyman.

I had been hungry, all the Years— **Emily Dickinson.** 579.

I had no thought of violets of late, **Alice Ruth Moore Dunbar-Nelson.** Sonnet.

I had not an evil end in view, **Elizabeth Barrett Browning.** A true dream.

I had not fastened my sash over my gown, **Tzu Yeh.** untitled.

I had wanted a daughter. **Lesley Saunders.** Mothers of sons.

I hadn't thought of calling the poem Autumn Rains. **Soleida Ríos.** Autumn rains.

I hate it when you/fill my glass up **Joan Larkin.** Stop.

I hate the company bosses, **Sara Ogan Gunning.** I hate the company bosses.

I have a question for all the sisters/who love their sons **Donna Allegra.** Before I dress and soar again.

i have all/my mother's habits **Nikki Giovanni.** Mother's habits.

I have been/stuck on your spike **Michele Roberts.** masochism two/man of iron.

I have been a guest/in enough kitchenettes **Adrienne Ingrum.** Loomit.

I have been expecting it so much. **Lin Ling.** Woman wall.

I have been measuring miles all day **Adrien Stoutenburg.** Icarus on wheels.

I have closed the double doors. **Wu Tsao.** To the tune "Flowers along the path through the field."

I have come to/hear Monk/forever funky **Sherley Anne Williams.** a record for my friends.

(I have come to His press conference, or **Jan Heller Levi.** After her death. (A sequence for my mother).

I have done it again./One year in every ten **Sylvia Plath.** Lady Lazarus.

I have gone out, a possessed witch, **Anne Sexton.** Her kind.

I have had tomorrow/stripped from/My soul, **Barbara Wolf Booth.** In the shallows.

i have heard of tortures/yet remain/strangely safe. **Irena Klepfisz.** The monkey house and other cages.

I have imagined all this: **Lynn Emanuel.** The sleeping.

I have leaned my flat belly/against six different stoves. **Marsha Peterson.** Some pieces I lost.

I have lived in rented houses, where I learned **Minnie Bruce Pratt.** Second home. (The segregated heart).

I have lived with that forbidding rigidness of limbs, **Rachel Loden.** 'When you become that cold sullen creature man.'

I have lived without/music except what **Sherley Anne Williams.** a record for my friends.

I have moved to this home of Immortals. **Yü Hsüan-chi.** Living in the summer mountains.

I have much/good to give **Sapphire.** New York City tonight.

I have never seen the place wher I was born **Tahereh Saffarzadeh.** Birthplace.

I have no desire to live, but I am afraid of death. **Ts'ai Yen.** Eighteen verses sung to a Tatar reed whistle.

I have no veins, **Naomi Wolf.** Alice James.

I have no wit, no words, no tears; **Christina Rossetti.** A bitter resurrection.

I have only one reason for living/and that's you **Judy Grahn.** Confrontations with the devil in the form of love.

I have painted my eyes **Anonymous.** untitled.

I have prepared the hibachi **Anonymous.** untitled.

I have reached the right age. Speeding **Phyllis Janowitz.** Mrs. Lucky.

I have robbed the garrulous streets, **Elsa Gidlow.** For the goddess too well known.

I have the delusion/that you are with me **Yosano Akiko.** untitled.

I have walked a great while over the snow, **Mary Elizabeth Coleridge.** The witch.

I hear a footstep on the walk outside. **Laura Tokunaga.** Behind locked doors.

i hear a mandolin **Barbara Moraff.** untitled.

I hear a rumbling underground. **Margaret Walker.** I HEAR A RUMBLING . . .

I hear the heart of the child, **Concha Michel.** Genesis.

I heard a Fly buzz—when I died— **Emily Dickinson.** 465.

I heard an angel speak last night, **Elizabeth Barrett Browning.** Prologue. (A curse for a nation).

I heard the wind sing that/the recipe for Ougluup **Alice Karle.** An epic (with renaissance flute).

I heard this morning/dawn's trumpet stampede **Lindiwe Mabuza.** Summer 1970.

I hold my head and think/—what conspiracies- **Marina Tsvetayeva.** Akhmatova.

I hold you tight in my jade white arms. **Anonymous.** To the tune "Red embroidered shoes."

'I, if I perish, perish'—Esther spake: **Christina Rosetti.** Monna Innominata: a sonnet of sonnets.

I imagine Gertrude making love to Alice **M. F. Hershman.** Making love to Alice.

I imagine her all in white **Belkis Cuza Malé.** The shrew who married God.

I inherited this anger from my lunches **Zaida del Río.** untitled.

I keep my parents in a garden **Margaret Atwood.** Eden is a zoo.

I keep placing my hands over/my face, the finger tips just **Susan Griffin.** Deer skull.

I knew like a song your vows weren't strong, **Mahsati.** untitled.

I know/that when a grumbling old woman **Minji Karibo.** Superstition.

I know, friend,/It is all within me as in **Mirta Aguirre.** Certainty.

I know not if the voice of man can reach to the sky; **Anonymous.** The Hako.

I know not whether thou has been absent: **Anonymous.** untitled.

I know now that once I longed to be white. **Nellie Wong.** When I was growing up.

I know that you will not come back from war. **Tu Fu.** Washing and pounding clothes.

I know the reputation/of the idle ways **Lady Kii.** untitled.

I know the script **Anne Blackford.** Family script.

I know what there is, she says **Kristina McGrath.** August. (Sequence from blue to blue).

I know. You don't want to hear about it, **Sharon Olds.** Homage.

I know you love me better cold **Georgia Douglas Johnson.** A paradox.

I leave all the scarlet flowers **Yamakawa Tomiko.** untitled.

I left in the early morning/despite the warning. **Bella Akhmadulina.** Zhaleyka.

I lie awake listening to Ken's breathing **Jan Heller Levi.** After her death. (A sequence for my mother).

I lie like a stone on the hill,/indifferent and silent **Leah Goldberg.** In the Jerusalem Hills.

I lie under the crust of the night singing, **Ingrid Jonker.** Pregnant woman.

I lift my heavy heart up solemnly, **Elizabeth Barrett Browning.** Sonnets from the Portuguese.

I lift my songs/I, Macuilxochitl **Macuilxochitl.** Battle song.

I like a look of Agony, **Emily Dickinson.** 241.

I like it here just fine/And I don't want no bail **Margaret Walker.** Girl held without bail.

I like movies because **Patricia Jones.** Why I like movies (for Charlotte).

I like the backs of houses. Fronts are smug, **Margaret Stanley-Wrench.** Hinterland.

I, like the fog,/was born with a veil **Audrey Lee.** The maudlin mist of morning.

I like to think of Harriet Tubman. **Susan Griffin.** I like to think of Harriet Tubman.

I like to think of you as brown and tall, **Marian Allen.** The wind on the downs.

I line up five stones on the ground. **Linda Gregg.** Lilith.

I listen to the pulse of a life **Gōto Miyoko.** untitled.

I listened to your lost words **Anna Akhmatova.** In a shattered mirror.

I live, I die. I drown, I am aflame. **Louise Labé.** The eighth sonnet.

I live in Cuba. **Lourdes Casal.** I live in Cuba.

I live on a hill/in the city that **Sherley Anne Williams.** Generations: II.

I live on an island/and there I tend/a little heap of stones. **Mary Crow.** My barrow stones.

I lived under the house for quite a few years. **Cheri Fein.** The earliest days.

I look at my hands and remember **Pat D'Alessandro.** Sunday morning ritual.

I look on the sea and the sky. **Elizabeth Barrett Browning.** The runaway slave at Pilgrim's Point.

I look on the sky and the sea. **Elizabeth Barrett Browning.** The runaway slave at Pilgrim's Point.

I looked for a sounding-board and I found none. **Henriette Roland-Holst.** I looked for a sounding-board.

I looked so wretched—passers by were alarmed. **Bella Akhmadulina.** Rain.

I lost my mind to a late night movie **Magdalena Gomez.** Rookie dyke T.V. toddler.

I love it, I love it; and who shall dare **Eliza Cook.** The old arm-chair.

I love you for your brownness, **Gwendolyn B. Bennett.** To a dark girl.

I love you . . . Why do you hate me? **Rosalía de Castro.** I love you . . . Why do you hate me?

I loved you first: but afterwards your love, **Christina Rossetti.** Monna Innominata: a sonnet of sonnets.

I make fast my white barge **Chung Ling.** Visiting.

I make this song about me full sadly **Ann Stanford.** The wife's lament. (Modern version of anonymous poem).

I married a man of the Croydon class **Anna Wickham.** Nervous prostration.

I marvel how the birds can sing, **Elizabeth Barrett Browning.** Bianca among the nightingales.

I may be smelly and I may be old, **Stevie Smith.** The river god.

I mean/the fiddleheads have forced their babies, **Maxine Kumin.** May 10th.

I mean, I'm a no shoes hillbilly an' home **Fay Kicknosway.** Gracie.

I meet two women in Texas — **Michelle Cliff.** Travel notes.

I met my Solitude. We two stood glaring. **Naomi Replansky.** I met my Solitude.

I met you once,/wingtip, the most delicate **Georgette Cerrutti.** Raining the water.

I might have had a sister **Shirley Kaufman.** Claims.

I must be calm. What if he did? What if he does? **Virginia Moore.** "In dejection near Naples."

I must be ill, of course. I've been shivering **Bella Akhmadulina.** Fever.

I must be mad, or very tired, **Amy Lowell.** Meeting-house Hill.

I must remember the details. **Kate Ellen Braverman.** Details.

I must take a grip on myself/sitting in cinders, I to myself. **Judith Kazantzis.** Cinderella.

I need not die to go/So far you cannot know **Elinor Wylie.** Where, O, Where?

I need the/wisdom of the/ancients **Sapphire.** New York City tonight.

I need you/here and now **Christina Meneghetti.** untitled.

I never believed that in my broken life **Ts'ai Yen.** Eighteen verses sung to a Tatar reed whistle. (XIII).

I never hear the word "escape" **Emily Dickinson.** 77.

I never learned the names of/flowers or herbs **Myra Glazer.** Santa Caterina.

I never saw that stone tablet. **Margit Szécsi.** The death of Moses.

I never talk of hunger. No. **Lizette Woodworth Reese.** I never talk of hunger.

I, no sense of being alive,/live next door to death. **Nakamura Chio.** A diary without dates.

I often wonder/just to get your attention **Maureen Owen.** How to get by.

I, Olga Orozco, tell everyone from your heart that I die. **Olga Orozco.** "Olga Orozco."

I outgrew childhood once,/served the full sentence **Linda Pastan.** To my son, approaching 11.

I parted/like a note divided/in search of itself. **Lucha Corpi.** Mexico.

I pass my life/through the eye of the same rusty/old needle **Katerina Anghelaki-Rooke.** Magdalen the great mammal.

I passed by the house of the young man who loves me; **Anonymous.** Love song.

I pitied him/Standing by the door **Yosano Akiko.** Tangled hair.

I placed my dream in a boat/and the boat into the sea; **Cecilia Meireles.** Song.

I play man games/play war games **Barbara Gravelle.** The new Joan come out of the fire.

I praise the disk of the rising sun, **Vidya (Vijjika).** untitled.

I pray for long life and health. **Sappho.** A woman's plea.

I pray that the great world's flowering stay as it is, **Mona Van Duyn.** The gardener to his god.

I pray to the light in the window. **Anna Akhmatova.** I pray to the light in the window.

"I primaled it," she said **Joan Larkin.** Sleeping on the left side.

I pulled the kerchief very close: **Elizabeth Barrett Browning.** The runaway slave at Pilgrim's Point.

I pursue him, the loved one all unsolved, **Dilys Laing.** Ten leagues byond the wide world's end.

I quarreled with kings till the Sabbath, **Kadia Molodowsky.** Song of the Sabbath.

I really don't want to say anymore **Miriam Dyak.** On having to go round the circle and state our philosophies.

I recognize the diamond on my hand **Marie Ponsot.** Late.

I recreate you out of light and shadow, **Phoebe Hesketh.** Epitaph.

I remember/seeing/a little girl, **Alice Walker.** Once.

I remember in Hsi T'ing,/All the many times **Li Ch'ing-chao.** Happy and tipsy, to the tune "A dream song."

I remember rooms that have had their part **Charlotte Mew.** Rooms.

i remember sunshine/and summers by rivers **Safiya Henderson.** letter to my father . . . a solidarity long overdue.

I remember the days/When the lily **Yosano Akiko.** untitled.

i remember the grasp of her claws **Irena Klepfisz.** The monkey house and other cages.

I remember the time/he dared me to understand **Della Burt.** A little girl's dream world.

I ride in a red painted carriage. **Su Hsiao-hsiao.** A song of Hsi-ling Lake.

I rode with my darling in the dark wood at night **Stevie Smith.** I rode with my darling . . .

i rode you piggyback/through groundless sky, **Toi Derricotte.** Hester's song.

I roll the pebble of this word on my tongue, feel **Madeline DeFrees.** Slow-motion elegy for Kathy King.

I said to my mother,/"What have you done with God?" **Celia Watson Strome.** Nr. 19.

I said to Poetry, "I'm Finished/With You; **Alice Walker.** I said to poetry.

I sailed in my dreams to the Land of Night **Gwendolyn B. Bennett.** Fantasy.

I sang his name instead of a song, **Elizabeth Barrett Browning.** The runaway slave at Pilgrim's Point.

I sat before my glass one day, **Mary Elizabeth Coleridge.** The other side of a mirror.

I sat staring at an anthill for almost forever **Alice Karle.** Elizabeth.

I saw,/With a catch of the breath and the heart's uplifting, **Teresa Hooley.** A war film.

I saw a pale tree, the leafless boughs—but two— **Hélène Swarth.** Ecstasy.

I saw a picture of your embryo **Kathleen Teague.** untitled.

I saw a screamer this morning/crossin' Broad Street as I **Y. W. Easton.** The welcome.

I saw her in a Broadway car, **Sara Teasdale.** The old maid.

I saw the best women of my generation destroyed by anonymity, **Roberta Lefkowitz.** Scrawl.

I saw the people climbing up the street **Nancy Cunard.** Zeppelins.

I saw thee, child, one summer's day **Emily Brontë.** I saw thee, child, one summer's day.

I saw you once, Medusa; we were alone. **May Sarton.** The muse as Medusa.

I saw you there in that dark hole **Mae Jackson.** (To someone I met on 125th Street, 1966).

I saw your coffin today/a friend made it **Miriam Dyak.** Dying.

I say I wanted what I found at your side. **Marie Ponsot.** Late.

I say that words are men and when we spell **Anna Hempstead Branch.** Sonnets from a lock box. (XXXI).

I say things to myself/in a bitch of a syllable **Jayne Cortez.** Phraseology.

I scan shapes in a sea/where all the islands **Molly Vaux.** Landing.

I searched,/I looked, but did not find. **Anonymous.** untitled.

i see/her sit/every noon/except winter's **Mariah Britton Howard.** a using.

I see smiles/gestures plaintive, eyes **Teru Kanazawa.** untitled.

I see the four mountains in Chile higher **June Jordan.** Problems of translation: problems of language.

I seek mercy/for the women stoned **Desanka Maksimovic.** For all Mary Magdalenes.

I seem to float, we seem to float **Elizabeth Barrett Browning.** Bianca among the nightingales.

I sent my love a little bird, **Rosamund Greenwood.** The gift.

I set forth hopeful—cotton-blossom Lal. **Lalleswari (Lalla).** untitled.

I shall die, but that is all that I shall do for Death. **Edna St. Vincent Millay.** Conscientious objector.

I shall hate you/Like a dart of singing steel **Gwendolyn B. Bennett.** Hatred.

I shall hide myself **Chino Masako.** untitled.

I shall lie hidden in a hut **Elinor Wylie.** Prophecy.

I shall make a song like your hair . . . **Gwendolyn B. Bennett.** Secret.

I should like to creep/Through the long brown grasses **Angelina Weld Grimké.** A Mona Lisa.

I sing my song in/a cycle a round/spiral up spiral **Sherley Anne Williams.** The collateral adjective.

I sing of myself because by force of love/I stand, **Soleida Ríos.** I also sing of myself.

I sing the cycle of my country's year, **Victoria Sackville-West.** The land.

I sit and sew—a useful task it seems, **Alice Ruth Moore Dunbar-Nelson.** I sit and sew.

I sit on the bed./The ashes have been dumped at sea. **Ann Lauterbach.** The yelllow linen dress: a sequence.

I sit with my cup **Ruth Stone.** Poetry.

i skim like a thriller/these last communiques. **Jan Clausen.** (reading Plath's *Letters Home*; rereading *Ariel*). (dialectics).

I sleep, I sleep/too long, sheer hours **Olga Broumas.** Sleeping Beauty.

I slept in the past,/that will never come back, **Princess Shikishi.** untitled.

i slice the bread/in the kitchen, i hold the knife **Olga Broumas.** the knife & the bread.

I sneak looks at young girls in class, **Phyllis Koestenbaum.** Blood journey.

I sought them./Down in the wadi, no deer. **Hemda Roth.** Four ways of writing one poem.

I speak but only in an illusion/For I see and I don't **Judy Lucero.** I speak in an illusion.

i speak skimpily to/you about apartments i **Sonia Sanchez.** personal letter no. 2.

I speak to you a friend speaks/or a true lover **Audre Lorde.** Conversation in crisis.

I sprouted in a hothouse **Jenny Mastoraki.** Birth. (How I managed to square the circle of dreams in the shape of a window at the top of the stairs in a tenement house).

I spy on myself. **Eunice Odio.** Portraits of the heart.

I stand here. I have arisen—into the dazzling, the different **Sarah Appleton.** Book of my hunger, book of the earth.

I stand high in the belfry tower, **Annette von Droste-Hülshoff.** On the tower.

I stand on the mark beside the shore **Elizabeth Barrett Browning.** The runaway slave at Pilgrim's Point.

I stand still under an orange tree, **Ibaragi Noriko.** Dialogue.

I started Early—Took my Dog— **Emily Dickinson.** 520.

I stop him in the hall. Gun/blazing, he throws **Toi Derricotte.** The damned.

I stroked her cheek with my finger **Jeanne Murray Walker.** For my daughter's twenty-first birthday.

I surprise myself in places/where I would never be **Nancy Bacelo.** untitled.

I swear I ain't done what Richard **Sherley Anne Williams.** Say hello to John.

I swore not to love you, **Otomo no Sakanoe.** untitled.

I take as my theme, ''The Independent Woman,'' **Carolyn Kizer.** Pro femina: parts one, two, and three.

I takes up for my colored men **Fareedah Allah.** The generation gap.

i talk filth and energy **Carol Bergé.** tessa's song.

I talked clearly/too much. Too much/to be clear **Jill Gernand.** Lenore.

I taste a liquor never brewed— **Emily Dickinson.** 214.

I tear off the calendar, **Ping Hsin (Hsieh Wan-ying).** Remembering.

I tell my secret? No indeed, not I: **Christina Rossetti.** Winter: my secret.

I think I hear him, how he cried **Elizabeth Barrett Browning.** Bianca among the nightingales.

I think I see her sitting bowed and black, **Jessie Redmon Fauset.** Oriflamme.

I think I was enchanted/When first a sombre Girl— **Emily Dickinson.** 593.

I think not on the State, nor am concern'd **Katherine Philips.** Upon the double murther of King Charles I, in answer to a libellous copy of rimes by Vavasor Powell.

I think of her so often, **Janet Lewis.** The Anasazi woman.

I think they give us uniforms/so we remember who we are **Ranice Henderson Crosby.** Waitresses.

I thought, as I wiped my eyes on the corner of my apron: **Edna St. Vincent Millay.** An ancient gesture.

I thought of leaving her for a day **Michael Field.** Second thoughts.

I thought once how Theocritus had sung **Elizabeth Barrett Browning.** Sonnets from the Portuguese. (I).

I thought the chrysanthemum bloomed in autumn **Ise Tayū.** On receiving the gift of a robe with a pattern of mingled plum blossoms and chrysanthemums.

I thought: you're my enemy, **Bella Akhmadulina.** I thought: you're my enemy.

I too am now among the others **Fina García Marruz.** I too am now among the others.

i too was little boy little girl **Reina María Rodríguez.** Neighborhood in the breast.

I took a piece of the fine cloth of Ch'i, **Pan Chieh-yü.** A song of grief.

I tried to build Perfection with my hands **Anna Wickham.** Inspiration.

I tried to tell her:/This way the twig is bent. **Naomi Long Madgett.** Offspring.

I trim my lamp, and weeping write this letter, **Shao Fei-fei.** A letter.

I try not to write about tigers, **Fleur Adcock.** Tigers.

I turn to my Rand McNally Atlas. **June Jordan.** Problems of translation: problems of language.

I unfolded my fear/and watched **Lucha Corpi.** Passion without a name.

I unsealed my veins: unstoppable,/irreparable, life gushes out- **Marina Tsvetayeva.** I unsealed my veins: unstoppable.

i used to dream militant/dreams of taking **Nikki Giovanni.** Revolutionary dreams.

I used to think/I can't be a poet **Chirlane McCray.** I used to think.

I used to wait under that tree **Jana Harris.** I canned them pears and I canned them pears.

I, Uva A. Clavijo,/who left Cuba still a child, **Uva A. Clavijo.** Declaration.

I visited my distant relative/by Lake Suwa in Shinshū. **Ishigaki Rin.** Walking-with-a-cane-pass.

I waited in a map of dreams/and I found the town **Kanai Mieko.** In the town with cat-shaped maze.

I wake at midnight. **Ishigaki Rin.** Shellfish.

I wake earlier, now that the birds have come **Mary Oliver.** No voyage.

I wake to the sound of horses' hooves clacking **Maxine Kumin.** Leaving my daughter's house.

I wake up, cold and dark. In Moscow **Yunna Moritz.** Autumn morning frost.

I walk down the garden paths, **Amy Lowell.** Patterns.

I walk in your house and see your loneliness **Eleni Fourtouni.** Homecoming.

I walk with you in the woods/as I walked in my dream **Rochelle Nameroff.** Eucalyptus grave.

I walked into a moon of gold last night, **Millicent Sutherland.** One night.

I want a language/Structured like my body. **Stephanie Mines.** My own impression.

i want flowers/bring me fresh bouquet **Nikki Grimes.** The takers.

I want for my name/gray and cutting grave diggers. **Ángela María Dávila.** I want for my name . . .

i want the chains/i want the blood **Amina Baraka.** I wanna make freedom.

I want to be bad, but I'm not. There's a warm breath **Jane Miller.** 6 a.m.

I want to be your love/I want to be your strength **Margarita Aliger.** For a man on his way.

I want to catch it while it's still fresh **Cherríe Moraga.** For amber.

I want to die while you love me, **Georgia Douglas Johnson.** I want to die while you love me.

I want to lament the princess who was killed, **Judith Kazantzis.** In memory, 1978.

I want to see the slim palm-trees, **Gwendolyn B. Bennett.** Heritage.

I want to visit my mother's school where she broke her ankle playing **Michelle Cliff.** Obsolete geography.

I want to write/I want to write the songs of my people. **Margaret Walker.** I want to write.

I want you in a bottle to send to your father **Diane di Prima.** Brass furnace going out: song, after an abortion.

I wanted to be a nature poet **Thadious M. Davis.** "Honeysuckle was the saddest odor of all, I think.''

I wanted to be the lone figure on the landscape. **Michelle Cliff.** Travel notes.

I wanted to grow up somewhere else. **Shirley Kaufman.** Claims.

I wanted to hear/Sappho's laughter **Mary Barnard.** Static.

I wanted to see the lines of it **Susan Griffin.** Deer skull.

I wanted to *talk* to my father and he said, **Chocolate Waters.** Father poem II.

i wanted to write/a poem/that rhymes **Nikki Giovanni.** For Saundra.

I was a giraffe,/Small of head, **Judith McCombs.** Games mammals play.

i was a saint/went up in a/basket **Carol Tinker.** golden triangle.

I was always fascinated/with lights then, **Alma Villanueva.** untitled.

I was as you say/born under the moon **Pamela Victorine.** Menses: a seasonal.

I was born in a time of peace, **Ts'ai Yen.** Eighteen verses sung to a Tatar reed whistle. (I).

I was born in the old home of the sun, **Lin Ling.** Cloud dissects itself.

I was born in war **Judith Kazantzis.** Progenitor.

I was born the year of the loon **Mei-Mei Berssenbrugge.** Chronicle.

I was busy, with the normal course of events, **May Ivimy.** On a death in an old people's home.

I was cast in steel and darkness **Eleni Fourtouni.** Monovacia.

I was comiing down the wide, painted steps. **Tess Gallagher.** Painted steps.

I was never there./But I know the cave **Hemda Roth.** A young deer/dust.

I was not going to say/how you lay with me **Joan Larkin.** Some unsaid things.

I was seventy-seven, come August, **Dorothy Parker.** The little old lady in lavender silk.

i was sick/and my motha called me **Carolyn M. Rodgers.** Jesus was crucified or: it must be deep (an epic pome).

I was strange/as a neighbor of distant lights **Alejandra Pizarnik.** Green paradise.

I was sure I would never get lost **Kenrei Mon-in Ukyō no Daibu.** untitled.

I was tired of being a woman, **Anne Sexton.** Consorting with angels.

I wash my hands several times a day **Majken Johansson.** Proportion poetry.

I wasn't afraid of death **Rita Boumi-Pappas.** Erasmina.

I watch cypress/trees through the smoke **Carol Tinker.** untitled.

I watch her in the corner there, **Rose Terry Cooke.** Arachne.

I watch the light/that pumps your heart **Toi Derricotte.** For a godchild, Regina, on the occasion of her first love.

I watch the red buds turn to green leaves. **Wu Tsê-t'ien.** A love song of the Empress Wu.

I watched her go/from her invention/to her destruction. **Helen Wong Huie.** untitled.

I wear barricaded woven/pigtails **Rota Silverstrini.** Pieces of echoes.

I well remember the swan's nest **Dorothy Wellesley.** Swannery.

I went into my garden to gather some herbs; **Bertha Jacobs (Suster Bertken).** A ditty.

I went to thank Her—/But She Slept— **Emily Dickinson.** 363.

I, who cut off my sorrows/like a woodcutter, **Akazome Emon.** untitled.

I will answer he will say mother died my brother his voice will **Phyllis Koestenbaum.** Friday.

I will be one of them. **Phyllis Koestenbaum.** Blood journey.

I WILL BE PATIENT WHILE MY LORD **Fareedah Allah.** CINDERELLA.

I will be still soon. **Kate Ellen Braverman.** Soon.

i will be your mouth now, to do your singing **Judy Grahn.** A funeral plainsong from a younger woman to an older woman.

I will carry my belly to Timbuctoo! **Chana Bloch.** Magnificat.

I will look with detachment/on the signing of contracts, **Pinkie Gordon Lane.** On being head of the English department.

I will speak about women of letters, for I'm in the racket, **Carolyn Kizer.** Pro femina: parts one, two, and three.

I will stay with you, most likely, **Barbara Banks.** Valediction.

i will take you with me **Irena Klepfisz.** Conditions.

I will work with my hands/I will not work with my hands **Michele Stepto.** I will work with my hands I will not work with my hands.

i wish for her fantastic hands, **Lucille Clifton.** for her.

I wish I could remember that first day, **Christina Rossetti.** Monna Innominata: a sonnet of sonnets.

I wish it were over the terrible pain, **Christina Rossetti.** Introspection.

. . . I wish to accomplish something in life, something of value **Gloria Truvido.** My people are the poor.

I woke before the day, when the night bird **Marnie Walsh.** Thomas Iron-Eyes. Born circa 1840. Died 1919, Rosebud Agency, S.D.

I woke from death and dreaming. **Lilian Bowes Lyon.** A shepherd's coat.

I woke up this morning **Gertrude "Ma" Rainey.** Sweet rough man.

I wonder in what fields today **Fukuda Chiyo-Ni.** On her child's death.

. . . I would have tied my breasts in a black slip **Barbara Szerlip.** untitled.

I would like to be happy as a servant: **Shirley Geok-Lin Lim.** I would like.

I would never calm/those wild hairs **Marie-Elise.** Touching a friend.

I would not for her white and pink, **Elizabeth Barrett Browning.** Bianca among the nightingales.

I wrapped my eyeballs/in soft cloth and tucked them away **Eleni Fourtouni.** Parting.

I write poems, gentleman, I write poems, **Gloria Fuertes.** I write poems.

I wrote a poem about a metaphor **Judith McCombs.** Horse and rider.

I wrote down words/that for a long time I couldn't say. **Anna Akhmatova.** Deception.

Idlers and cowards are here at home now, **Anonymous.** Wind song.

If ever two were one, then surely we. **Anne Bradstreet.** To my dear and loving husband.

If everything I cannot learn to bear **Margarita Aliger.** If everything.

If everything were different/I would not have a long journey **Claudia Lars.** Letters written when night grows.

If he bores her, always falling **Sonya Dorman.** Whodunit.

If I come/I'll be more than a hole **Susan Wallbank.** If I come.

If I consider/My body like the fields **Lady Ise.** untitled.

If I could trust mine own self with your fate, **Christina Rossetti.** Monna Innominata: a sonnet of sonnets.

If I die, don't take me to the cemetery. **Juana de Ibarbourou.** Life-hook.

If I had a child/by everyone I love **Jacqueline Lapidus.** untitled.

if I hear you/say my body is softer than yours **Miriam Dyak.** January 23, 1976 the axe.

If I leave all for thee, wilt thou exchange **Elizabeth Barrett Browning.** Sonnets from the Portuguese. (XXXV).

If I were only sure/I could live as long as I wanted to, **Shirome.** untitled.

If I would have a daughter/I would want her alone **Jane Creighton.** Ceres in an open field.

If it is art you are looking for/go away. **Roswell Spafford.** Song of the woman painted hot and cold.

If it were real/Perhaps I'd understand it; **Ono no Komachi.** untitled.

If I've lost it,/I've lost it twice, **Lourdes Casal.** Profile of my city.

If, Lord, thy love for me is strong **Teresa of Ávila.** If, Lord, thy love for me is strong.

If my soul lies down on her side **Zelda.** The fine sand, the terrible sand.

If no revolution come/star clusters/will brush heavy on the sky **Helen Dunmore.** If no revolution come.

If only we knew each other! **Ellen Wittlinger.** In cahoots.

If orange chiffon sadness/flowed from my chin of three bumps **Jayne Cortez.** Orange chiffon.

if raisins grew in you from the sole of your foot up to your head **Yona Wallach.** Two gardens.

If she chose sin, some gentler guise **Elizabeth Barrett Browning.** Bianca among the nightingales.

If the arms and the legs of the lover **Anonymous.** untitled.

If the blower is on **Ruth Stone.** When the furnace goes on in a California tract house.

If there be any one can take my place **Christina Rossetti.** Monna Innominata: a sonnet of sonnets.

If thou must love me, let it be for naught **Elizabeth Barrett Browning.** Sonnets from the Portuguese. (XIV).

If we could speak to death, what would we say? **Jan Heller Levi.** After her death. (A sequence for my mother).

If we have to begin I want to tell you everything **Excilia Saladaña.** Autobiography.

if we were stars we'd be nova **Patricia Jones.** poem for david murray.

If you are dealing in the flesh/trade, you'd better know what **Jeanne Lance.** The skin trade.

If you come my way that is. . . . **Lynette Roberts.** Poem from Llanbyri.

If you don't know, why pretend? **Huang O.** To the tune "Red embroidered shoes."

If you have been there,/you know the bed rises **Dona Stein.** Carol's house.

If you look down and there's no link **Virginia de Araújo.** Letter to Connie in the Maine woods.

If you own/your soul/the mornings come/heavy **Melba Joyce Boyd.** Sundown sigh.

If you press a stone with your finger, **Babette Deutsch.** Natural law.

If you saw a Negro lady/sitting on a Tuesday **June Jordan.** If you saw a Negro lady.

If you think with fire/Then life is a road that leads **Hsiung Hung.** If you think with fire.

If you understood how much I need this **Eleanor Lerman.** The community of women causes an operation.

I'll sing, although I'm loath to make this plea, **Beatritz de Dia.** I'll sing, although I'm loath to make this plea.

I'll start far away: from there, not here; **Bella Akhmadulina.** Chapters from a poem.

I'll take the skin off the mama,/My daughter said, **Stephanie Mines.** Take the skin off the mama.

I'll take you from the icy niche where they placed you, **Gabriela Mistral.** Death sonnets.

''I'll tell you something,'' he said/his voice creased and wrinkled **Marie-Elise.** prose/poem Written after overhearing a conversation on a Greyhous bus just outside of Oxnard, California.

I'm a rag doll, a doll made of rags, **Teresita Fernández.** Rag doll (a song).

I'm a rapper/a stoned out trapper. **Lois Elaine Griffith.** Prince Harlem.

I'm ceded—I've stopped being Theirs— **Emily Dickinson.** 508.

I'm folding up my little dreams **Georgia Douglas Johnson.** My little dreams.

I'm lying on a cot in the jungle **Janet Hamill.** The pyramid of the musicians.

I'm middle-aged,/a child; **Pat Arrowsmith.** Political activist living alone.

I'm no longer the bitter girl **Gloria Fuertes.** Love which frees.

I'm none of yer London gentry, **Inez Quilter.** 'Sal.'

I'm not interested in facts **Nancy Bacelo.** untitled.

I'm only a little womn,/who's happy to slave, **Kibkarjuk.** I'm a little woman who's happy to slave.

i'm playing word games with myself **Brenda Connor-Bey.** Pretending.

I'm really very fond of you/he said. **Alice Walker.** I'm really very fond.

I'm talkin' about/a sickness/inside **Sapphire.** New York City tonight.

I'm telling you,/stubborn Móir, **Nuala ní Dhomhnaill.** Móir hatching.

I'm the little black child, **Marie-Thérèse Rouil.** Childhood.

I'm thinking tonight of an old southern town **Sarah Ogan Gunning.** Old southern town.

i'm tired/i know what you want from my life **Nikki Grimes.** The takers.

I'm two times twenty/I learned to multiply by two **Amanda Berenguer.** The two times table.

I'm wearied of wearying love, my friend, **Dorothy Parker.** Ultimatum.

I'm ''wife''—I've finished that— **Emily Dickinson.** 199.

Imagine a moon/walking in pallor **Raquel Chalfi.** Lunatics.

Imagine lamenting our longing, no, **Yona Wallach.** Cradle song.

Immobile, transparent,/with neither blood nor pulsing vein **Rafaela Chacón Nardi.** Zoia.

In a chariot driven by droves, Aphrodite **Shlomit Cohen.** Aphrodite.

In a chinese Hanyak/herb hospital, the sick **Virginia Gilbert.** Two poems: in commemoration of a friend's happiness.

In a flash I understand/how poems are unlike photographs **Adrienne Rich.** Photographs of an unmade bed.

In a green woodland,/Beneath a slender tree, **Dorothy Howard.** Eurydice.

in a hospital room from a halfclosed eye from a half **Barbara Moraff.** untitled.

In a lone Thicket made for Love, **Aphra Behn.** The disappointment.

In a press conference this afternoon the Secretary **June Jordan.** Poem towards a final solution.

in a redwalled cave, tied down **Judith Johnson Sherwin.** Miranda's birthspell.

in a spathe of silence/he moves **Frances Horovitz.** The messenger.

in an age of napalmed children **Nikki Giovanni.** Atrocities.

In an old worn out basin/I planted violets for you **Teresita Fernández.** Ugly things (a song).

In Aprils like this, I search/for rest in the Carmel market. **Shulamit Apfel.** A big woman screams out her guts.

In back of our exit was Ezmeralda **Alice Karle.** An epic (with renaissance flute).

In bed you think of her **Stephanie Strickland.** How we love now.

In Belgrade, the windows of the tourist **Carolyn Forché.** Endurance.

in Bohack/a woman my age, **Jan Clausen.** the kitchen window.

in childbirth/you focus on technique **Jan Clausen.** dialectics.

In Cubero/days too hot, arroyo dry **Paula Gunn Allen.** Wool season.

In December I needed light. **Elizabeth Keeler.** Light.

In dreams without sleep/I lie inside myself **Ann du Cille.** Lady in waiting.

in early autumn darkness/I drive past the corpse a deer hung **Judith McDaniel.** November passage.

In early youth's unclouded scene, **Charlotte Smith.** Thirty-eight.

In February/sometime/you gave me/an iris stalk **Jessica Tarahata Hagedorn.** For Bruce who's on smack: may 31, 1967.

In harness/in bed with your shoes on **Alberta Turner.** Die. (A dictionary of common terms).

In Hässelby,/on the Earth,/some pilot's wife **Sonja Åkesson.** Evening walk.

In human need/of the familiar/I see God/woman-shaped **Dilys Laing.** Let them ask their husbands.

In Indiana/the corn comes up sharp **Mary Mackey.** In Indiana.

In intimacy there's a secret place **Anna Akhmatova.** In intimacy there's a secret place.

in jr hi/a boy no color/transparent skin **Anna Lee Walters.** A teacher taught me.

In lamplight she saw the smoke of another's dream: **Roberta Hill.** Leap in the dark.

In late May the grasses/are so tall their plumy **Mary Barnard.** Real estate.

In legend told/by smoky fires **Paula Gunn Allen.** Riding the thunder.

In life, you came/now and then **Eleni Fourtouni.** I have no poem for you father.

In love longing/I listen to the monk's bell. **Izumi Shikibu.** At the Sutra chanting of her dead daughter.

In May it drops down fresh from the mountains, **Cynthia Macdonald.** The river Honey Queen Bess.

In misery buds music-words, **Ann Dunn.** untitled.

In my bath—/Submerged like some graceful lily **Yosano Akiko.** Tangled hair.

In my dream, the man with black hair **Nellie Hill.** My inheritance.

In my dreams/I want to teach **Ana Kowalkowska.** Azteca IV.

In my garden there are roses: **Dulce María Loynaz.** Eternity.

in my grandmother's day they would have called us **Maxine Shaw.** For Mrs. W., who would not be Black, White or other.

In my heart's depth/I keep our secret smothered **Akazome Emon.** untitled.

In my land there are no distinctions. **Lorna Dee Cervantes.** Poem for the young white man who asked me how I, an intelligent, well-read person, could believe in the war between the races.

. . . In my melodious city cupolas burn, **Marina Tsvetayeva.** Akhmatova.

In my mother's bedroom, he/pulls down his pants. Underneath, **Toi Derricotte.** The damned.

In Naples/It was beads/The sailors were buying **May Miller.** Italy. (Not that far).

In Nara, the ancient capital, **Ise Tayū.** untitled.

In New York/the breast of her daughter/is cut open **Alison Colbert.** The white worm.

In New York we took one day to gawk **Olga Broumas.** Deja vu. (Of fruit whose black seed fire).

In one of London's most exclusive haunts, **Helen Dircks.** After Bourlon Wood.

In our content, before the autumn came **Elinor Wylie.** Sonnet. (XII).

In our town people live in rows. **Anna Wickham.** The fired pot.

In Roseville, one notices/a speck on a white wall **Marcela Christine Lucero-Trujillo.** Roseville, Minn., U.S.A.

In secret place where once I stood **Anne Bradstreet.** The flesh and the spirit.

In shadowy formation up they rise, **Marian Allen.** The raiders.

In shaping the snow into blossoms— **Ping Hsin (Hsieh Wan-ying).** The spring waters.

In silent night when rest I took **Anne Bradstreet.** Some verses upon the burning of our house July 10th, 1666.

In silk gown and jade belt/I am graceful as a phoenix, **Hua Jui, Lady.** Life in the Palace.

In such a *Night,* when every louder Wind **Anne Finch, Countess of Winchilsea.** A nocturnal reverie.

In sunlight she was a falling leaf of gold **Leah Goldberg.** A look at a bee.

In that country sacred to the wolf, **Carol Muske.** Fairy tale.

In the anteroom of silence you waited to meet **Sandra M. Gilbert.** You meet the real dream mother-in-law. (The love sequence).

In the autumn when words sound **Baba Akiko.** untitled.

In the back bedroom, laughing when you pull **Honor Moore.** First time: 1950.

in the beginning, I was/carried away by him; helpless; he **Michèle Roberts.** persephone descends to the underworld.

In the bird scream and whistle, **Natalya Gorbanevskaya.** untitled.

In the blue distance **Nelly Sachs.** In the blue distance.

In the cemetery on North Hill **Kuan P'an-p'an.** Mourning.

In the chapel/the floor was linoleum **Susan Wood-Thompson.** Territory.

In the clearing stands/A three story white brick structure. **Linda Piper.** Missionaries in the jungle.

In the closed box of the darkroom— **Marge Piercy.** Images emerging.

In the cold I will rise, I will bathe **Adelaide Crapsey.** The lonely death.

In the country they call it Black. **Bella Akhmadulina.** Black brook.

In the daytime/I can cope with them, **Ono no Komachi.** untitled.

In the dining room painting of my childhood **Joan Swift.** Father.

In the dry riverbed/barefoot desire **Zelda.** In the dry riverbed.

In the dusk the path/You used to come to me **Izumi Shikibu.** untitled.

In the early morning/Of the Spring day **Hua Jui, Lady.** Life in the Palace.

In the earnest path of duty, **Charlotte L. Forten.** Poem.

In the gazebo-life café, you gave/me food from your plate, alert **Olga Broumas.** Amazon twins.

In the great night my heart will go out, **Anonymous.** Owl woman's death song.

In the great wild orchards of the Carmel **Nurit Zarchi.** Wild orchards.

In the green harbour muck, the gulls, **Betty Parvin.** Gulls aground.

In the green light of water, like the day **Edith Sitwell.** The swans.

In the Hanging Gardens at Graz stands Grosswunch, **Cynthia Macdonald.** The mosiac hunchback.

In the high stars are all the souls **Anna Akhmatova.** In the high stars are all the souls.

In the Hotel of Infinite Space **Janet Hamill.** The big sleep.

In the house with the tortoise chair **Anonymous.** untitled.

In the huge, rectangular room, the ceiling **Laureen Mar.** My Mother who came from China, where she never saw snow.

In the last letter that I had from France **Eleanor Farjeon.** Easter Monday.

in the last question/i ask, the answer **Esther Louise.** it's all in the name.

In the military hospital where I worked **Judy Grahn.** This woman is a lesbian be careful. (A woman is talking to death).

In the Moon/when the ponies had shed **Willyce Kim.** A woman's tribal belt.

in the morning/the room is sharp with mirrors **Olga Broumas.** the knife & the bread.

in the morning light i look upon your face **Patricia Jones.** a no blues love poem.

in the night I would hear it/glass bottles shattering on the street **Lorna Dee Cervantes.** Beneath the shadow of the freeway.

In the nuptial room there was a black, cosmic cold. **Maria Banus.** Wedding.

In the painted quiet/of snow ridges **Mary Barnard.** The pump.

In the parque Beiria/the armless and legless **Mary Crow.** The heat in Medellin.

In the picture the Siamese twins who worked *See* The First Separation/must have been a relief—of our

In the place of sustenance   what am I, even I? **Enheduanna.** Inanna exalted.

In the season when the world leafs and flowers, joy grows for all **Compiuta Donzella.** untitled.

In the sheltered garden, pale beneath the moon, **Gabrielle Elliot.** Pierrot goes to war.

In the south the cloud flower blossoms, **Anonymous.** Lullaby.

In the spastic hand of a corpse, **Alejandra Pizarnik.** Abodes.

In the square of a lighted window— **Leah Goldberg.** A look at a bee.

In the stillness,/uterine,/hidden from me, **Penelope Shuttle.** Expectant mother.

In the sun she was a falling leaf, **Leah Goldberg.** A look at a bee.

In the sunny ground between the canes, **Elizabeth Barrett Browning.** The runaway slave at Pilgrim's Point.

In the sunny Spring of March and April, **Mêng Chu.** Spring song.

In the third country of white/She is the ghost of color. **Adrianne Marcus.** Alone, we dream as gods.

In the unploughed rice field, elder brother **Anonymous.** The abortion.

In the wake of the yellow sunset one pale star **Nora Griffiths.** The Wykhamist.

in the way that the indians ground acorns **Carol Bergé.** farewell.

In the wintertime/at night/we tell coyote stories **Leslie Marmon Silko.** Toe'osh: a Laguna coyote story.

In the Year of the Tiger, we have our last fight **Dona Stein.** In the Year of the Tiger.

In these, my father and mother are divorced. **Jan Heller Levi.** After her death. (A sequence for my mother).

in this city/there are/no fountains/at night **Naomi Rachel.** The very rose.

in this one/your're the woman/i'm the man **Jan Clausen.** Scenario.

In this room, holding hands, **Sarah Webster Fabio.** All day we've longed for night.

In this room where voices spin the light **Paula Gunn Allen.** Shadow Way. (Medicine song).

In this so Amorous Cruel Strife, **Aphra Behn.** The disappointment.

In those two silent moments, when we stand **Eileen Newton.** Revision.

In times like these we have **Bella Akhmadulina.** Rain.

In twilight, in smells of whitewash, **Yunna Moritz.** In twilight.

In two large columns on thy motley page, **Mary Wortley Montagu, Lady.** Verses addressed to the imitator of the first satire of the second book of Horace.

In Vieques/"The Ocean is Closed on Mondays" **June Jordan.** This is a poem about Vieques, Puerto Rico.

In water nothing is mean. The fugitive **Elaine Feinstein.** Patience.

In western skies/Rare radiance lies **Henrietta Cordelia Ray.** Idyl: sunset.

In wood, in vault, in Baltimore. **Jan Heller Levi.** Formal feeling (A sequence for my mother).

In your country how do you say copper **June Jordan.** Problems of translation: problems of language.

Incensed nights/Jazz floats **Akua Lezli Hope.** Ode.

An incident here and there, **Hilda Doolittle.** The walls do not fall. (I).

Including the Galapago turtle out of time **Amanda Berenguer.** Solemn inventory.

Indeed we live beneath the sky, **Elizabeth Barrett Browning.** The runaway slave at Pilgrim's Point.

Infinite gentleness, infinite irony **Sara Teasdale.** Effigy of a nun.

Initially glimpsing/an ivory Pharoah figure **Barbara Guest.** Clouet of silks. (Quilts).

Inland,/far inland go my thoughts, **Kibkarjuk.** Song of the rejected woman.

Instructed in love/by ten thousand books, **Ingeborg Bachmann.** Songs in flight.

the intensity of the motion of the pebble is **Barbara Szerlip.** The crossing.

Internal angel . . ./Hiding behind God. **Eunice Odio.** Portraits of the heart.

Intimate after weeks of close quarters, **Robin Becker.** The landing.

Into her mother's bedroom to wash the ballooning body. **Gwendolyn Brooks.** Jessie Mitchell's mother.

Into my green and greedy lap you poured **Phoebe Hesketh.** Rescue.

Into the chamber   you beckoned me enter **Enheduanna.** Inanna exalted.

Into the deepest mornings/Strange harmonious cries are sung **Jessica Tarahata Hagedorn.** Fillmore Street poems: August, 1967.

Into the spacious bay the sun of afternoon/Shone, **Josephine Miles.** Players.

Into the void behold my shuddering flight, **Anna Hempstead Branch.** Sonnets from a lock box. (XXV).

Into this city room your pungent scent **Eiluned Lewis.** Flowering current.

Into your arms I came/when you bore me, very anxious **Valente Malagatana.** To the anxious mother.

Inventing means to see you, I stay awake, **Diane Wakoski.** We visit the gorilla at his 47th Street address. (Largely because of coincidence and partly because of chance, I have taken up a new address at 47th Street and Avenue F).

Irresistible, the earth carries/the weight of another planet. **Virginia Gilbert.** Two poems: in commemoration of a friend's happiness.

is a man. who. sleeping on a hill and a bench among the Chinese **Alexis De Veaux.** The woman who lives in the botanical gardens.

is an enchanted thing/like the glaze on a **Marianne Moore.** The mind is an enchanting thing.

is dancing under the Mtskheta moon, **Bella Akhmadulina.** To sleep.

Is it because you always hope, my heart, **Yosano Akiko.** untitled.

Is it to me, this sad lamenting strain? **Mary Wortley Montagu, Lady.** An answer to a love-letter.

Is it your command/that we must pass through this life, **Lady Ise.** untitled.

Is Life itself but many ways of thought, **Anne Spencer.** Substitution.

Is our love over? **Mother of Michitsuna.** untitled.

Is the air political today? **Susan Griffin.** untitled.

Is the clock wound up, is it wound? **Nicki Jackowska.** The insect kitchen.

Is this the end? Is there no end but this? **Christina Rossetti.** Is this the end?

is this the turbulence of which you spoke then pilot **Carol Bergé.** tessa's song.

Is "vagina" suitable for use/in a sonnet? I don't suppose so. **Joan Larkin.** "Vagina" sonnet.

Is't not enough, I gave you Heart for Heart, **Aphra Behn.** To Lysander, on some verses he writ, and asking more for his heart then 'twas worth.

It appears on the fleeting face unaccompanied. **Eunice Odio.** Portraits of the heart.

It began in her pram/when she named the blue-plate sky **Valerie Sinason.** The renaming.

It doesn't live in mornings, **Eunice Odio.** Portraits of the heart.

it doesn't matter /what I hear inside **Laura Tokunaga.** Geography.

It encircles the reeds and flows **Lan Ling.** A melody.

It happens sometimes; a pair of eyes a profile **Magaly Sánchez.** Almost love.

It has not rained/And shall not rain. **Heidi Gitterman.** Poem for my father.

it has taken me until now/to be able to say/even this **Barbara Szerlip.** Mute's definition Blind man's definition Deaf man's definition.

It has turned crystal clear lately **Hsüeh T'ao.** The autumn brook.

It hasn't been said of the Sierra/that it's the smile's altar **Soleida Ríos.** Of the Sierra.

It involves a simplicity,/the difference between men and women, **Grace Wade.** The difference.

It is a being somewhat like a well. **Kōra Rumiko.** Woman.

It is a bright house; **Fukao Sumako.** Bright house.

It is a gesture I do/that grew/out of my mother/in me. **Beverly Dahlen.** Gesture.

it is a pearl, a universe of mouths **Barbara Szerlip.** Mute's definition Blind man's definition Deaf man's definition.

it is a shell in thick beds **Barbara Szerlip.** Mute's definition Blind man's definition Deaf man's definition.

It is a year of good harvest. **Li Chü.** Harvesting wheat for the public share.

it is all so thoroughly/predictable say no **Rochelle Nameroff.** Machine.

It is already so late at night **Ise Tayū.** untitled.

it is always the quiet ones/whom the whirlwind picks: **Michèle Roberts.** rite de passage.

it is beautiful where i go **Carol Bergé.** tessa's song.

It is because you were my friend, **Mary Elizabeth Coleridge.** Mortal combat.

It is dangerous for a woman to defy the gods; **Anne Spencer.** Letter to my sister.

It is hard, loving this way. **Anonymous.** To the tune "Red embroidered shoes."

it is horrible to be./gigantic fornicators advance **Sonia Sanchez.** Old words.

It is I in the cities, in the bars, in the **Wendy Rose.** Vanishing point: urban Indian.

it is midnight/no magical bewitching/hour for me **Sonia Sanchez.** Poem at thirty.

It is night again **Tzu Yeh.** untitled.

It is not easy/to be alone **Tove Ditlevsen.** Divorce 3.

It is not known if those/who warred and hunted on the plains **Paula Gunn Allen.** Beloved women.

It is not likely now. **Frances Bellerby.** It is not likely now.

It is not my life/under these lichened oaks, **Jane Augustine.** I help my mother move out of her old house in the country.

It is not until I see my first grade teacher **Alice Walker.** Burial.

it is not words but the lack/of them. **Barbara Szerlip.** Nothing of innocence.

it is now the day after mother's day. on mother's day, all four **Fay Chiang.** impressions.

It is politically incorrect/to demand monogamous **Pat Parker.** A small contradiction.

It is sad that the mist and fog are gathering **Chu Shu-chên.** Playing all a summer's day by the lake, to the tune "Clear bright joy."

It is that, in fact, that first among others, He **Anonymous.** untitled.

It is that, when she has given birth to a child, as soon **Anonymous.** untitled.

It is the first day of spring & you have taken everything **Rachel Nahem.** End.

It is the pool that first accepts the season's **Jean Kenward.** Moorhens.

It is the room around the bowl/of fruit, the man around the body **Anita Endrezze-Danielson.** Still life.

It is the time of rain and snow. **Izumi Shikibu.** untitled.

It is this way the work builds **Sarah Appleton.** Book of my hunger, book of the earth.

It is time that my mother comes home! **Anonymous.** untitled.

It is too cold to work. **Ann Stanford.** Composing the garden.

It is true—/I've always loved/the daring **Alice Walker.** Once.

It is unreasonable to ask my tears **Shunzei's daughter.** untitled.

"It is yourself you fall in love with" when the mysterious stranger appears **Kathleen Fraser.** The stranger.

it isn't as easy as you think **Kathleen Spivack.** Humanitarian.

It isn't that the threat of the bomb is great **Ishigaki Rin.** Cocoon.

It must be true I love you well **Anna Wickham.** The economist.

It must have been some day for me to die unaware! **Olga Casanova-Sanchez.** Neither from before nor ever.

It seems unlikely that we'll talk again **Jean Mollison.** untitled.

It surprised the night and me/like a suburb of lights **Adrien Stoutenburg.** River boat.

It ticks out of the walls/like lives **Ingrid Wendt.** Dust.

it took 27 years to write this poem **Colleen J. McElroy.** Ruth.

It was/the morning/before/it rained **Virginia Gilbert.** The drought.

It was a dance./Her back against the wall **Joy Harjo.** There was a dance, sweetheart.

It was a heartfelt game, when it began— **Judith Wright.** Portrait.

It was a mirror above the mountains, **Enid Vián.** In the mirror.

it was a mistake to pretend that we were on intimate terms with wildlife **Monica Raymond.** Self-criticism.

It was a season/when even music/was expensive; dimes **Sherley Anne Williams.** a record for my friends.

it was as if there were not enough chances or places **Fay Chiang.** it was as if.

It was crunched out/of my life it/was my life **Alexandra Grilikhes.** Being drivin.

It was gentle,/Far away, the moon crumbled into the sea **Chedva Harakavy.** It was gentle.

It was hot. A size too large, **Jane Shore.** High holy days.

It was in Helios' heart to break, in Athene's not to be broken. **Hilda Doolittle.** Helios and Athene.

It was in the month of January the hills **Frankie Armstrong.** Month of January.

It was the presence of the soul, **Eunice Odio.** Portraits of the heart.

It was when my songs became quite. **Wendy Rose.** How I came to be a graduate student.

It was your idea to come/that's for sure **Susan Kennedy Calhoun.** The orgy.

It will be possible for me to arrange/for your benefit a sort of **Elena Wilkinson.** The logical mind of the martyr.

it works so slow it/takes days and **Carol Tinker.** untitled.

It would have been better that I slept **Akazome Emon.** untitled.

It's a fine kind thought! And yet—I know **Dorothy Una Ratcliffe.** Remembrance day in the dales.

It's a hell/creeping back into/the garden, **Sarah Webster Fabio.** Back into the garden.

It's all been taken away: strength, love. **Anna Akhmatova.** It's all been taken away.

It's all familiar,/the fall air, clear and sober, **Bella Akhmadulina.** A dream.

It's all over—I told you **Kiki Dimoula.** Talking to myself.

its almost a dream   she says/or a chapter from a story book **Mary Winfrey.** hera of the locker room.

It's been years since she arrived/from the USA **Kiki Dimoula.** Standstill.

It's logical. It's serious. **Nellie Hill.** My inheritance.

It's my/what you call my/melancholy temperament/temperamental melancholy **Judith Kazantzis.** Marginal.

It's no joke being born a pig **Jeanne Lance.** New Jersey.

It's not my world, I grant, but I made it. **Josephine Miles.** Ride.

It's not the rest of the world we track in **Ingrid Wendt.** Dust.

IT'S RAINING/in Teotecacinte Cusmapa **Yolanda Blanco.** IT'S RAINING.

It's snowing today in the last great **Sara Miles.** Native dancer.

It's the day of never/I am bloodied/beat **Abbey Lincoln (Aminata Moseka).** A name change.

It's the duplicity that sticks— **Shirley Kaufman.** Rebecca.

It's the quality of light/that excites me. **Kate Ellen Braverman.** 7 P.M.

Its the things we feel most/we never say for fear perhaps **Susan Sherman.** Lilith of the Wildwood, of the Fair Places.

It's to possess more than the skin **Ruth Whitman.** Cutting the Jewish bride's hair.

it's too late, mother,/for you to know/i think of you **Astra.** too late.

It's true. My belly will soon be as round **Roberta Spear.** Fishes at Saint-Jean: Chagall, 1949.

Its waters alert/running between pebbles and whirlpools, **Enid Vián.** The river.

I've been inside all day. **Cherríe Moraga.** You upset the whole system of this place.

I've been tired lately./It's not any one thing. **Julia Vino-grad.** Analysis.

I've come back many times today **May Miller.** Gift from Kenya.

I've come this far to freedom and I' won't turn back. **Naomi Long Madgett.** Midway.

I've forgotten whose apartment **Leslie Ullman.** Running.

I've got a different system/And a way of my own, **Ida Cox.** Wild women blues.

. . . I've got this very bad problem. **Stephanie Smolensky.** I told you when we started this relationship what to expect.

I've had enough/I'm sick of seeing and touching **Donna Kate Rushin.** The bridge poem.

I've never got anything in my gray purse, **Gloria Fuertes.** I've never got anything.

I've passed you before,/And nodded, thinking **Kathryn Hellerstein.** For water, for air.

I've stayed in the front yard all my life. **Gwendolyn Brooks.** A song in the front yard.

I've unrolled my orphan's legacy **Alejandra Pizarnik.** Party.

I've worked in a cotton mill all of my life **Anonymous.** Hard times cotton mill girls.

Joseph the Stepfather,/Joseph forbearing, slow **Griselda Scott.** Joseph and the magi.

Joy shakes me like the wind that lifts a sail, **Clarissa Scott Delany.** Joy.

A jug of water in the hand, and on **Rachel.** Dawn.

jumbo jets/never spit flame/like your fists **Michelene Wandor.** He-man.

The jungle says to the bank of america crack **Frances Mayes.** Voice.

Just/Look/At me/A typical black woman **Mae Jackson.** A POEM FOR ALL THE MENS IN THE WORLD.

Just look, 'tis a quarter past six, love— **Mary Weston Fordham.** The coming woman.

just once. Just long enough/to snap up the words, fish-hooked **Wendy Rose.** For the white poets who would be Indian.

K

Kangiak, while you take me for a fool, **Anonymous.** untitled.

The 'Kat' can play ball, Man **Fareedah Allah.** Funky football.

Katerina, Rotho, and Theano wear their heavy dresses. **Melpo Axiote.** The homestead.

katherine/is warm,/chocolate marsh-/mallow/floating on/the turquoise/carpet, **Melba Joyce Boyd.** Why?

Keep that discourse, hummingbird brief, **Enid Vián.** IV.

A killing summer heat wraps up the city **Audre Lorde.** A poem for women in rage.

Kindness glides about my house. **Sylvia Plath.** Kindness.

The kingdoms fall in sequence, like the waves on the shore. **Ruth Pitter.** The sparrow's skull.

Kingfisher green lines the deserted shore, **Yü Hsüan-chi.** Composed on the theme "Willows by the Riverside."

Kiss me again, re-kiss and kiss me whole; **Louise Labé.** Sonnet XVIII.

Knock, listen/The harsh fly shines/the beetle rubs **Sarah Appleton.** Book of my hunger, book of the earth.

Knowing it was a prisoner of chance **Eunice Odio.** Portraits of the heart.

Known by the ear; sweet voice, sour reputation; **Ruth Pitter.** Vision of the cuckoo.

Kool I/Bruce/Head 155/Steam One/Chino **Joan Larkin.** Notations—the F Train.

Kore is back, my daughter returns **Mary Winfrey.** Demeter's song.

Kotaro shall we go to a country **Barbara Szerlip.** Poem to an imaginary Japanese lover.

J

Jade turns dull, flowers wilt **Nieh Shêng-ch'iung.** Farewell to Li, to the tune "A partridge sky."

Jake the best damn cap'n in the world **Mari Evans.** Jake.

A January night. Moonlight/strikes the window. Six sweaters **Alison Fell.** Significant fevers.

Japanese women of the baths, rinsing and sudsing and rinsing your hair, **Ellen Bass.** Women of the baths.

Jealousy fans the night   a moth   its rapid wings **Diane Middlebrook.** You, seated near a lamp. (Two poems).

Jest bronze—you wouldn't ever know, **May Herschel-Clarke.** 'For valour.'

Jesukin/Lives my little cell within; **Saint Ita.** Jesukin.

Jewel towers relay to jewel towers **Amy Károlyi.** The third house.

Jill thinks/This is an angry text. **Josephine Miles.** Readers.

Jingo-woman/(How I dislike you!) **Helen Hamilton.** The Jingo-woman.

John Cabot, out of Wilma, once a Wycliffe, **Gwendolyn Brooks.** Riot.

John Delaney of the Rifles has been shot. **Winifred M. Letts.** Casuality.

José, big brother/how broad the plough has made your back **Zaida del Río.** untitled.

Labour was normal, a birth, like any other. **Barbara Noel Scott.** Stillbirth.

Lace, velvet, my grandmother's dresses hang **Adelaide Blomfield.** Attics.

'The ladies should be thinking that there is, in the career of **Felica Hemans.** Corinne at the capitol.

Lady . . ./Janis . . ./i never rode no horse like you **Maxine Shaw.** For Billie Holiday and Janis Joplin.

lady in brown/dark phrases of womanhood **Ntozake Shange.** Dark phrases.

lady in orange/ever since i realized there waz someone callt/a colored girl **Ntozake Shange.** No more love poems #1.

Lady, Lady, I saw your face, **Anne Spencer.** Lady, Lady.

Lady, Sister, it is cold/Out here, there is snow falling, monstrous, **Adrianne Marcus.** Lady, Sister: for Janis Joplin.

The Lady Supreme   pride of the throne **Enheduanna.** Inanna exalted.

Lady T'ao Ch'ui-tse gave a farewell party in T'ao Jan **Ch'iu Chin.** To the tune "The Narcissus by the river."

Lady, the fresh lake trout you ask for **Susan Schweik.** The short order cook in the mountains.

The lake is ravenous. **Beverly Tanenhaus.** First you tell him all your problems.

lambs to the slaughter/sheep to the altar **Michelene Wandor.** untitled.

The land is cold and its men gather earth for no reason. Their **Colleen J. McElroy.** A woman's song.

The land is flat/And my head throbs. **Colleen J. McElroy.** Flight.

The landscape comes apart/in birds **Diana Chang.** Rhythms.

Languid swirl of light/on his cap. And on his drooping lids, **Soleida Ríos.** The clown.

a large tree shakes and the/skies move **Marguerite Clerbout.** Matinal.

Last/bridge   I won't **Marina Tsvetayeva.** Poem of the end.

Last autumn/The three of us tossed acorns **Yosano Akiko.** untitled.

The last bridge./(I don't take back my hand. I don't take it out of his!) **Marina Tsvetayeva.** Poem of the end.

the last chapter of a maturity **Christina Meneghetti.** untitled.

The last day I live in a strange house, **Bella Akhmadulina.** The last day I live in a strange house.

Last night I dreamed/we put you in the toybox **Miriam Dyak.** Dying.

Last night I dreamt in Chinese. **Shirley Geok-Lin Lim.** Modern secrets.

last night I met my mother again **Michèle Roberts.** winter sacrament.

last night when you fell asleep/in my arms **Judith Barrington.** Poems.

last nite/i shoulda told you/you're not my friend/anymore **Geraldine Kudaka.** i shoulda told you.

The last shred of light falls on your wrist **Jeanne Murray Walker.** The last migration: Amherst, Mass., Winter 1981.

last spring I got two dozen chicks **Judith McDaniel.** November passage.

last time I got married was/yesterday (in **June Jordan.** Poem: on my happy/matrimonial condition.

the last time i was home/to see my mother we kissed **Nikki Giovanni.** Mothers.

The last time we played together **Eugenie Eersel.** Ada.

Last time you left/The moon shone on heavy frosts. **Li Yeh.** A greeting to Lu Hung-Chien.

Last year the fields were all glad and gay **Edith Nesbit.** The fields of Flanders.

Late at night/that sort of thing **Kristina McGrath.** The nights in June. (Sequence from blue to blue).

Late-born and woman-souled I dare not hope, **Emma Lazarus.** Echoes.

Lately my neighbor wheezes **Leslie Ullman.** Running.

later i'll say/i spent my life/loving a great man **Lucille Clifton.** later i'll say.

Laugh, and the world laughs with you; **Ella Wheeler Wilcox.** Solitude.

Laughed every goblin/When they spied her peeping: **Christina Rossetti.** Goblin market.

Laughing, exulting and rebellious **Bella Akhmadulina.** Laughing, exulting and rebellious.

Laughing eyes followed/the gold everywhere in our circle **Thadious M. Davis.** Asante sana, Te Te.

Laughter rough as a carthorse/tangles our sheets like wrinkles in velvet. **Julia Vinograd.** Morning.

A leaf floats in endless space. **Wang Wei.** Seeking a mooring.

A leaf from Freedom's golden chaplet fair, **Henrietta Cordelia Ray.** To my father.

Leaning against the wind, he stands. **Lan Ling.** A melody.

The least be be oaklike colorless. Or. Or the **Rochelle Owens.** Up up on the disorders of the hairs.

Leave him: he's quiet enough: and what matter **Charlotte Mew.** Here lies a prisoner.

Leave them while they're still clapping. Go to bed before you re-coup **Gloria Frym.** Secrets.

Leaves don't fall. They descend. **Malka Heifetz Tussman.** Leaves.

The leaves of the bush clover rustle in the wind. **Kenrei Mon-in Ukyō no Daibu.** untitled.

Leaves that whisper whisper ever **Angelina Weld Grimké.** Rosabel.

The leftovers beasts of prey leave **Shlomit Cohen.** Struggling at the kill.

Legs!/How we have suffered each other, **Kathleen Fraser.** Poem in which my legs are accepted.

the legs of the piano/stool are clawing glass **Carol Tinker.** sunday parlor park freeway.

The leopard was snow in the winter grief **Odette Tchernine.** The leopard.

'Lest we forget!' Let us remember, then, **S. Gertrude Ford.** The tenth Armistice Day.

Let go of the present and death. **Liz Sohappy.** Once again.

Let her be seen, a voice on a platform, heard **Muriel Rukeyser.** Ann Burlak.

Let her be to be to be to be let her be to be to be let **Gertrude Stein.** Patriarchal poetry.

Let joy go solace-winged **Mina Loy.** Love songs (VI).

let me introduce myself: **Evelyn Posamentier.** Immigration.

Let me not die for ever, when I'm gone **Fanny Kemble.** A wish.

Let me weep. He has left. **Mririda n'Ait Attik.** The abandoned.

Let no man call me good. I am not blest. **Eleanor Farjeon.** Peace.

Let nothing disturb thee, **Teresa of Ávila.** Bookmark.

let rivers tremble again between the breasts **Nzadi Zimele-Keita (Michelle McMichael).** Prayer. (Birds of paradise).

Let the pure sky ahead, this sky of long **Simone Weil.** Illumination.

let uh revolution come. uh/state of peace is not known to me **Carolyn M. Rodgers.** U name this one.

Let us ask fear to be silent **Mireya Robles.** untitled.

Let us be still/As ginger jars are still **Gwendolyn B. Bennett.** To usward.

Let us forget tomorrow! For tonight **Eileen Newton.** Last leave.

Let us go back to the point of departure, **Concha Michel.** Genesis.

Let us remember Spring will come again **Charlotte Mew.** May, 1915.

Let us suppose the mind/to be a reversible tea-kettle **Barbara Morall.** untitled.

Let us then love upon the honest Square, **Aphra Behn.** To Lysander, on some verses he writ, and asking more for his heart then 'twas worth.

Let's not have tea. White wine/eases the mind along **Olga Broumas.** Artemis.

letters of the alphabet/we are/sisters **Margarita Cota-Cárdenas.** Spelling out the cosmos.

libation./hey sisters, we the color of our men **Johari M. Kunjufu.** Ceremony.

Life, like a thread piercing through jewels, **Princess Shikishi.** untitled.

Life moves slowly through me **Margriet Schaye.** untitled.

Life with her weary eyes, **Marya Zaturenska.** Song.

lift the lonely from their corners **Jeanette Adams.** on the first day of summer in the twenty fifth year of our lives.

The light/drains me of what I might be, **Lisel Mueller.** A nude by Edward Hopper.

Light./Stage of dawn./Opening on new worlds **Paula Gunn Allen.** Creation story.

Light at a window. Someone up **Adrienne Rich.** White night.

Light burn all day./sun through the kitchen window, **Phyllis Koestenbaum.** Blood journey.

light falls cleanly on the back/step, a square gold puddle **Michele Roberts.** New England, 1980.

Light floats through the edges **Alice Karle.** untitled.

The light goes pale in the lenses of the eyes, **Diana Ó Hehir.** Final anatomy.

Light has the dull luster of pewter **Mary Barnard.** The gorge.

The light is on my body also. **Linda Gregg.** Lilith.

''Light! more light! the shadows deepen **Frances Ellen Watkins Harper.** Let the light enter.

Light up thy halls! 'Tis closing day; **Emily Brontë.** Light up thy halls! 'Tis closing day.

The light young man who was to die, **Alice Meynell.** Saint Catherine of Siena.

Like/treasure hidden in the ground **Mahadeviyakka.** untitled.

Like a ballooning pavilion with lances pinned down, **Joan Murray Simpson.** St. Marks, midnight.

Like a bone/Was the first child born **Anonymous.** The abortion.

Like a cloud hunted by the moon **Amy Károlyi.** The third house.

Like a crew of workers, loud, **Marina Tsvetayeva.** Poem of the end.

Like a path for sheep,/the descent. The din of the city. **Marina Tsvetayeva.** Poem of the end.

Like a pregnant nun/ruffling her habits at the back of some vestry **Excilia Saldaña.** Fish - bird.

Like a quince-apple/ripening on a top **Sappho.** Lament for a maidenhead.

Like a round loaf, that's how small you were. **Judit Tóth.** To the newborn.

Like a thick mane:/the rain in our eyes. Hills. **Marina Tsvetayeva.** Poem of the end.

Like a white stone in the depths of a well **Anna Akhmatova.** Like a white stone in the depths of a well.

Like all guests my son disturbed me **Rosario Castellanos.** Speaking of Gabriel.

Like an acrobat in a green suit, **Roberta Spear.** Fishes at Saint-Jean: Chagall, 1949.

Like jumping rope, **Elizabeth Spires.** Days.

Like Lightning through the Grove she hies, **Aphra Behn.** The disappointment.

Like mail order brides/they are lacking in glamor. **Marge Piercy.** Seedlings in the mail.

Like the criminal who waits across the street **Jeanne Murray Walker.** Making the painting.

Like the honeycomb dropping honey **Hildegard von Bingen.** untitled.

like the light reaching us/from stars **Barbara Szerlip.** No hay Olvido. (Four short poems).

like the ruby & silver stars for perfect attendance, **Evelyn Posamentier.** The gun is back.

Like the seed that waits/for gentle rain **Lucha Corpi.** untitled.

Like the very gods in my sight is he who **Sappho.** untitled.

like wet cornstarch/I slide past mi abuelita's eyes **Lorna Dee Cervantes.** Refugee ship.

like wild tea blossoms/One white skirt **Hsiung Hung.** Who stops the dance?

Linda, spun in liquid lace **Carol Simone.** Linda, come down.

A line in ebony starkness curved on the white page, **Helen Aoki Kaneko.** Upon seeing an etching.

The lines in your hand **Alice Karle.** untitled.

The linnet in the rocky dells, **Emily Brontë.** The linnet in the rocky dells.

The linnet is here, and the lark, and the yellowhammer **Jan Struther.** Glamour.

Listen:/everything is calm and smooth and sleeping. **Sophia de Mello Breyner Andresen.** Listen.

Listen./Sometimes, when you have innocently & mistakenly **Michelle T. Clinton.** For strong women.

Listen—help me!/I'm desperate./Listen! **Sonja Åkesson.** Ears.

Listen I am just like/the cuckoo down the hillside **Anonymous.** untitled.

listen listen/the vast centuries raise a mound **Mary Winfrey.** Kleis.

listen, my ancestors/rooted up stumps **Jan Clausen.** dialectics.

Listen to that silence, **Eunice Odio.** Dawn's territory.

Listen to the trumpets of your kingdom. Noah drowns **Blanca Varela.** Waltz of the Angelus II.

Listening for the sound/of my own/voice **Pinkie Gordon Lane.** Nocturne.

Lit major learned in "isms." **Marcela Christine Lucero-Trujillo.** untitled.

A little boy once found a brass coin with two faces on it. **Diane Wakoski.** The brass coin. (Largely because of coincidence and partly because of chance, I have taken up a new address at 47th Street and Avenue F).

Little dwarf/in a checkered cupcake dress **Carol Dine.** Babysitter.

Little Ellie sits alone, **Elizabeth Barrett Browning.** The romance of the swan's nest.

The little girls' frocks are frilly. **Phyllis McGinley.** Ballroom dancing class.

Little my lacking fortunes show **Adelaide Crapsey.** Expenses.

Little red hearts/come in rows from the sun **Yona Wallach.** A terrible heart.

Live or die, but don't poison everything . . . **Anne Sexton.** Live.

Live unlamenting through obscure remaining: **Ruth Pitter.** T. J. S. Collis.

Living my staid life here/among the conventional cows **Judith Kazantzis.** Song for the new year.

La Llorona/they took away her children **Victoria Moreno.** La Llorona, Crying Lady of the Creekbeds, 483 years old, and aging.

Lo! Freedom comes. Th' prescient Muse foretold, **Phillis Wheatley.** Liberty and peace, a poem.

The lochan in the mild September sun **Alice V. Stuart.** Water lily on Loch Bran.

Lola, do you still get what you want? **Yona Wallach.** Lola.

Long (as song so stricken goes) **Paula Gunn Allen.** Lament. (Medicine song).

Long have I beat with timid hands upon life's leaden door, **Georgia Douglas Johnson.** The suppliant.

Long have I yearned and sought for beauty **Mae V. Cowdery.** I sit and wait for beauty.

Long John Nelson and Sweetie Pie/Lived together on Center Street. **Margaret Walker.** Long John Nelson and Sweetie Pie.

The long wooden steps/are ripe with pine needles **Albis Torres.** Caguayo.

Longing for you,/loving you,/waiting for you, **Princess Nukada.** untitled.

Look at him, over there **Maureen Burge.** Disillusion.

Look at me, circles of silver/rising, dropping like stars! Around my waist **Anita Endrezze-Danielson.** The belly dancer's song.

"Look at that/nigger with those/white folks!" **Alice Walker.** Once.

Look at the map. If you forget **Shirley Kaufman.** Claims.

"look, honey/said/the/blond/ample/boobed/babe/in the/green/g/string **Alice Walker.** Once.

the look of him/the beauty of the man **Lucille Clifton.** the kind of man he is.

Look what you've made of me, the poorest saint in the **Blanca Varela.** Waltz of the Angelus I.

Looking hollow-eyed and haggard **Diane Wakoski.** The starving vicuna.

Looks like to me/folks ought to mind/they own business, Lula says. **Carolyn M. Rodgers.** Folk.

A loon/I thought it was **Anonymous.** My love has departed.

Lord, on thee my trust is grounded: **Mary Sidney Herbert, Countess of Pembroke.** Psalm lxxi.

Lorenzo swallowed his hot water and lemon **Yvonne.** The tearing of the skin.

Loss is also clearance./Emptiness is also receptivity. **Marge Piercy.** All clear.

Lost Eurydice who in the odours **Sophia de Mello Breyner Andresen.** Sonnet to Eurydice.

Love flows from God to man without effort **Mechthild von Magdeburn.** Love flows from God.

Love has come to me, the kind I am far more ashamed **Sulpicia.** untitled.

Love in Fantastique Triumph satt **Aphra Behn.** Song: love arm'd.

Love, in my wood, the small child sings— **Joan Forman.** For Sally.

Love is not the only face/a poem wears **Nikki Grimes.** Definition.

Love, love! What nonsense it is, **Natalya Gorbanevskaya.** untitled.

Love, making love all night,/I think, this can't be Buffalo. **Adrianne Marcus.** It's Buffalo, Boise, or Boston this time.

'Love me, for I love you'—and answer me, **Christina Rossetti.** Monna Innominata: a sonnet of sonnets.

Love me in thy gorgeous airs, **Elizabeth Barrett Browning.** A man's requirements.

Love me pure, as musers do, **Elizabeth Barrett Browning.** A man's requirements.

Love me, Sweet, with all thou art, **Elizabeth Barrett Browning.** A man's requirements.

Love me with their lids, that fall **Elizabeth Barrett Browning.** A man's requirements.

Love me with thine azure eyes, **Elizabeth Barrett Browning.** A man's requirements.

Love me with thine hand stretched out **Elizabeth Barrett Browning.** A man's requirements.

Love me with thine open youth. **Elizabeth Barrett Browning.** A man's requirements.

Love me with thy thinking soul, **Elizabeth Barrett Browning.** A man's requirements.

Love me with thy voice, that turns **Elizabeth Barrett Browning.** A man's requirements.

Love of my loves, man, stranger, **Concha Michel.** Genesis.

Love set you going like a fat gold watch. **Sylvia Plath.** Morning song.

Love that I bear/within my heart, O speak; **Hilda Doolittle.** Love that I bear.

Loveliest of what I leave behind is the sunlight, **Praxilla.** Of the sensual world.

lovely to grow a child up till her braids are long **Carol Bergé.** tessa's song.

The loves of a little while ago/and the smoke of tobacco **Anonymous.** untitled.

A loyal subject, thou, to that bright Queen, **Charlotte L. Forten.** To W. L. G. on reading his 'Chosen Queen.'

Lucila, you of the bread laden tables, tables heavy **Milagros González.** Mother light, mother wind.

Lucite clothespins color this September sky. **Elizabeth Keeler.** Looking for light and finding the sea.

The luck beyond birds that was our quest **Marie Ponsot.** Late.

Lucy goes down the celestial escalator in light **Diana Scott.** Lucy taking birth.

lying on the beach last Tuesday **Cindy Bellinger.** Children and other reasons.

M

Mad Rosalinda/in the early morning hours/did herself in. **Shulamit Apfel.** Mad Rosalinde.

Madeleine's dreads are fertile like the lips/of good friends **Alexis De Veaux.** Madeleine's dreads.

Madrid—/Blood drops, drip, drop, from the child in your arms. **Pai Wei.** Madrid.

A madwoman sits on the roof **Sandy Boucher.** Three nights on Hoffman Street.

A madwoman steals my grandfather's horse and tries to ride away. I know **Michelle Cliff.** Obsolete geography.

'Mae, not to change the subject but you look good.' **Bobbie Louise Hawkins.** Mae, not to change . . .

Maggots dance inside the sheep's head **Michele Murray.** The woman who lives inside the world. (9).

the magician of labor, you arrive **Rachel Maines.** the union educator.

mahjong and dice on the tables upstairs **Fay Chiang.** chinatown.

Maid of France! whose armèd hand **Annie Louisa Walker.** Song.

The mail-order houses/do a healthy business **Angela de Hoyos.** problems of etiquette.

The main cook lies sick on a banquette, and his assistant **Maxine Hong Kingston.** Restaurant.

Maintenant que tout c'est fini, **Dorothy Ann Brown.** Later, to Jean-Pierre.

make me a magic **Carol Bergé.** tessa's song.

Making love with fingertips and eyelashes **Victoria Moreno.** en público.

Male crane/you turn me on **Katerina Anghelaki-Rooke.** My mama and satan.

Mama, I never stop seeing you there **Sharon Olds.** The meal.

mama spent pennies/in uh gallon milk jug **Carolyn M. Rodgers.** Portrait.

mamita linda/muneca **Frances C. Chung.** Piropos de la chinita.

Mamma/is a silent movie/I hear her voice in **Sherley Anne Williams.** Generations: (Mama is a silent movie).

Mamma's heirs are/the things/I rub my nose/on them **Katerina Anghelaki-Rooke.** My mamma and satan.

A man and woman/alone in a vast sea, **Frances Horovitz.** The woman's dream.

a man comes in the bar,/this is a dream, it seems **Toi Derricotte.** The testimony of Sister Maureen.

(Man, drop that stone you dared to lift!—) **Elizabeth Barrett Browning.** The runaway slave at Pilgrim's Point.

A man goes up to a woman/with whom he had lived for twenty years. **Judith Kazantzis.** A piece of business.

The man in the Trilby hat has furtively shifted it; **Ursula Roberts.** The Cenotaph.

Man pays that debt with new munificence **Alice Meynell.** In time of war.

(the man she married/cuz he was the first one to ask/her **mary hope lee.** on not bein.

A man walks along the board. **Judith Kazantzis.** The diving board.

The mansions of the concubines/Surround the Imperial Palace. **Hua Jui, Lady.** Life in the Palace.

Many die here./I follow the footprints of strangers **Gayl Jones.** Many die here.

Many in aftertimes will say of you **Christina Rossetti.** Monna Innominata: a sonnet of sonnets.

MANY SUMMER MOUNTAIN NIGHTS AGO/LOS VIEJITOS WITH SQUEAKY VIOLINS, **Marcela Christine Lucero-Trujillo.** THE MUSICOS FROM CAPULÍN.

A marathon runner's legs/fan in and out. **Yagi Mikajo.** untitled.

Marble cools/The story **May Miller.** Greece (Not that far).

Marina, how I love to know that/like everyone else, like me— **Bella Akhmadulina.** Music lessons.

The Mariner that on smooth waves doth glide, **Anne Bradstreet.** Contemplations.

Marriage is a lovely thing **Christine de Pisan.** untitled.

Marriage is a sweet state, *See* Marriage is a lovely thing

Marriage, which might have been a mateship sweet, **Elizabeth Wolstenholme-Elmy.** Woman free. (XI).

Marry the man your parents want for a son. **Anita Endrezze-Danielson.** Making adjustments.

Martha kept no box/under the board/no jar in the flour **Yvonne.** Aunt Martha: severance pay.

A marvel of design/woven with precious **Lili Bita.** Womb.

mary's daughter/silver tipped sweet thing **Jeanette Adams.** for my mamma and hers.

Mask-face of old grief, death-mask, massive **Genevieve Taggard.** Image.

Massive, heavy, with a small Kepi **Margarita Aliger.** For Neruda.

The mauve light of evening fills the room **Sara Jackson.** The window.

. . . May your road be fulfilled. **Anonymous.** Grandmother's prayer while presenting an infant to the sun.

Maybe all I saw was the mirror/of my desires, an illusory **Delmira Augustini.** Vision.

Maybe all that my verses have expressed **Alfonsina Storni.** It may be.

Maybe—yes/it doesn't matter. **Anonymous.** Men's impotence.

Me, dear Ephelia, me, in vain you court **Anne Finch, Countess of Winchilsea.** Ardelia's answer to Ephelia.

Me eyes start to screw up tight **Lois Elaine Griffith.** Myth sight.

Me fui a la obra y te vi, Julia **Sandra Maria Esteves.** A Julia y a mi.

Meadowlarks nesting March to August yield **Madeline DeFrees.** Keeping up with the signs.

Meanwhile the children struck up in chorus nearby **Bella Akhmadulina.** Rain.

Meanwhile to amuse the guests, some **Bella Akhmadulina.** Rain.

Meat remembers. And I have pushed my pain **Rachel Loden.** Mother.

the meat rolls up and moans on the damp table. **Toi Derricotte.** Transition. (Natural birth).

The meeting place is a dark victory. **Fina García Marruz.** Oedipus.

melting out my emerald spring/I stretch a lazy butterfly-bloom **Carmen Tafolla.** . . . Repeating chorus . . .

Members in their seventies fail to recall/a filthier July. Mildew rots the roses **Judith Moffett.** "Cambridge University Swimming Club/no public access to river."

The memories of long love/gather like drifting snow, **Murasaki Shikibu.** The tale of the Genji.

Memory is a miser, spendthrift, thief, **Adrien Stoutenburg.** Memory album.

a memory of ivory chopsticks **Frances C. Chung.** untitled.

Memory of the sun faints in my heart. **Anna Akhmatova.** Memory of the sun faints in my heart.

Men, divide into two groups oo **Anonymous.** untitled.

Men go to women mutely for their peace; **Genevieve Taggard.** Everyday alchemy.

The men in her department envied her. **Lynn Strongin.** Sayre (woman professor).

Men who make war/rape women and children **Barbara Gravelle.** The new Joan come out of the fire.

Mending his broken *tabi* **Sugita Hisajo.** untitled.

Mercy kept me out of the river. **Jane Miller.** The long fingers of 1956.

The Meuse and Marne have little waves; **Katharine Tynan.** A girl's song.

Micah was a young man of the people **Margaret Walker.** Micah.

Midnight cold of oxygen/bronze vitriol of stars: **Yunna Moritz.** Midnight cold.

Midnight. The flowing water of Hu T'o River **Jen Jui.** Midnight.

Midway between Mecca and Medina **Hind bint Uthatha.** To a hero dead at al-Safra.

Mild and slow and young,/She moves about the room, **Janet Lewis.** Girl help.

Miles off in the dark,/my dark, **Chana Bloch.** Magnificat.

Milton, thou shouldest be living at this hour, **Catherine Durning Whetham.** The poet and the butcher.

Mine eyes have seen the glory of the coming of the Lord; **Julia Ward Howe.** The battle hymn of the Republic.

Minerva's helmet! what of that? **Eliza Cook.** My old straw hat.

The miraculous is no more than what/comes naturally after **Ann Lauterbach.** The yellow linen dress: a sequence.

Mis' Lou/Sunny as a poui **Jacquelyn Furgus Hunter.** Mis' Lou.

Misfortune is as huge/and heavy as this cold **Yunna Moritz.** Poems for her sick mother.

Mist-filled Moon/rising,/rising. **Judith Ivaloo Volborth.** Three songs to mark the night.

Mrs. Dubosky pulls a handful **Ruth Stone.** What can you do?

Mrs. Snatcher Thatcher/runs the land. **Gillian E. Hanscombe.** Jesus people. (Jezebel: her progress).

miz fitzhugh/it's gotta be done by **Ntozake Shange.** cypress.

A modern mysterious boy approaches/the stall with sparkling water **Bella Akhmadulina.** Automat with sparkling water.

Mole who knows,/Who burrows up for air **Jenny Joseph.** Back to base.

Momma, a unselfish woman, **Carole C. Gregory.** Revelation.

Momma had cut through, **Carole C. Gregory.** Revelation.

MOMMA MOMMA/MOMMA/momma momma/*mammy* **June Jordan.** Getting down to get over.

MOMMA MOMMA/momma momma/family face **June Jordan.** Getting down to get over.

momma took her outta/almost all black lincoln high **mary hope lee.** on not bein.

Moon, as you pass through the night **Sylvia Alicia Gonzales.** Rebirth according to the New Testament. (Chicana evolution).

The moon is a sow/and grunts in my throat **Denise Levertov.** Song to Ishtar.

The moon is eaten and renewed **Eeva-Liisa Manner.** The lunar games.

The moon is teaching Bible. **Zelda.** The moon is teaching Bible.

Moonlight and death were on the Narrow Seas, **Lilian M. Anderson.** Leave in 1917.

Moose in Mexico and little local deer. **Julia Vose.** untitled.

More and more frequently the edges/of me dissolve and I become **Margaret Atwood.** More and more.

More than the gems/Locked away and treasured **Otomo no Sakanoe.** Send from the capital to her elder daughter.

More wild, more rash, Eve, admit it **Else Lasker-Schüler.** The voices of Eden.

Morning:/a silent singing, a vibration **Mary Barnard.** Journey.

The morning dawns./Luanda's clocks: what time do they tell? **Marilyn Bobes.** Chronicle of a morning in 1976.

Morning is drunk with spring sun. **Anna Akhmatova.** Deception.

Morning is lost in a maze. **Gloria Fuertes.** We're OK.

The morning of your departure, off-handed and passionate, **Jane Miller.** Lightning storm.

Morning opens/her mouth. **Bobbie Bishop.** Love poem.

Morning sparrow/freckled with sun **Alice Karle.** to Shannon and Kenneths.

Mornings/I'm pressed to elevators **Sybil Wood.** untitled.

Mornings and the eggshells crack, the eggshells scatter **Nellie Wong.** Toward a 44th birthday.

Most beautiful of things I leave is sunlight; **Praxilla.** Of the sensual world.

Most of our love from the age of nine **Adrienne Rich.** A woman dead in her forties.

Mother,/If I am *where* I am/because I am *what* I am **Anne Stevenson.** From an asylum: Kathy Chattle to her mother, Ruth Arbeiter.

Mother/in a restaurant/you hug me **Beverly Tanenhaus.** Reunion.

Mother,/You did not leave me an inheritance of **Fawziyya Abu Khalid.** Mother's inheritance.

Mother picked up the fantastic cup, **Laura Jensen.** Mouse.

Mother said if I wore this hat **Stevie Smith.** My hat.

The mother sat on/the curve of her bed **Lateifa-Ramona Lahleet Hyman.** Paraphernalia for a suicide: a revelation of life.

The mother, the highest-ranking woman/in the C.I.A., is typing the footnotes for her **Alison Colbert.** The white worm.

mothers/cranking the machine, **Carole C. Gregory.** The Greater Friendship Baptist Church.

Mother's description of my brother's apartment: **Maria Southwick.** Doors opening here, and there.

A mother's hardest to forgive. **Phyllis McGinley.** The Adversary.

The mountain path is steep **Yü Hsüan-chi.** Sending spring love to Tzu-an.

The mountain range, a gust of heights **Rosario Castellanos.** Elegy.

mourning suns filter thru her/opaque eyes **Regina Williams.** ASYLUM.

Mouth looking directly at you **Muriel Rukeyser.** Self-portrait. (Käthe Kollwitz).

Movement in Black/movement in Black/can't keep em back **Pat Parker.** untitled.

Moving backwards suddenly/we come to the edge of our lives **Miriam Dyak.** Dying.

much like/the heat of a leaf **Rochelle Nameroff.** The welcome.

Much too happy always/in the strength of your love **Margarita Aliger.** Much too happy.

Mud dark above the stream the factory's finger **Marjorie Battcock.** The refugee.

Music! Lilting, soft and languorous, **Alice Ruth Moore Dunbar-Nelson.** Music.

the music of the drawing-in/she knows the loops and eyes **Rachel Maines.** the tyer-in.

Music screams in the mind **Akua Lezli Hope.** Music screams in the mind.

musical forest/in my eyes the birds used to sketch **Alejandra Pizarnik.** Before.

must be used with caution for the altitude **Cynthia Macdonald.** Remains—Stratigraphy:

A mutual shiver./Our creamery! **Marina Tsvetayeva.** Poem of the end.

My answer would have to be music **Elaine Feinstein.** The medium.

My body and her pleasure **Vassar Miller.** First intimation.

My body haunts me/thieves in on me at night **Dorothy Livesay.** Aging.

My body is braille./Come touch me. **M. F. Hershman.** Eyes.

my body is the grapevine that grows and lengthens **Mary Winfrey.** at menopause.

My breadwinner/I have eaten your salt **Amrita Pritam.** The breadwinner.

My brother, a Central State graduate in elementary education, **Carole C. Gregory.** Revelation.

My business is words. Words are like labels, **Anne Sexton.** Said the poet to the analyst.

My cabinets are oyster-shells, **Margaret Cavendish, Duchess of Newcastle.** Song. (The convent of pleasure).

My child is like a stone **Dorothy Livesay.** Parenthood.

my chocolate egg/of a boy/silver and blue laughing **Michelene Wandor.** chocolate egg.

My city's profile yellows/and wears thin, always moving **Lourdes Casal.** Profile of my city.

my contraceptive history/pregnant with pain **Akua Lezli Hope.** Lament.

My dad was a practical man. **Sandra Hochman.** The practical clown.

My daddy come home this morning **Gertrude "Ma" Rainey.** Don't fish in my sea.

My daughter, at eleven/(almost twelve), is like a garden. **Anne Sexton.** Little girl, my string bean, my lovely woman.

My daughter marks the day that spring begins. **Audre Lorde.** Equinox.

My daughter pleads with me/for the life of our goldfish **Susan Griffin.** Chile.

My dear friend/your husband, **Anonymous.** He stared at me.

My dear girl, I know there is very little I can say to you **Summer Brenner.** Letter to an unborn daughter.

My dearest dust, could not thy hasty day **Katherine Dyer.** Epitaph on the monument of Sir William Dyer at Colmworth, 1641.

My disordered perfumed clouds are still damp, **Chao Luan-luan.** Cloud hairdress.

My dressing mirror is a humpbacked cat. **Jung Tzu.** My dressing mirror is a humpbacked cat.

my egg for breakfast/I eat me **Michelene Wandor.** Wonderland.

My eye on the storm, still T.V., **Virginia de Araújo.** Letter to Connie in the Maine woods.

My eyes catch and stick/As I wade in bellysoft heat. **Marge Piercy.** The consumer.

My face is black. See the moon? My eyes. **Faye Kicknosway.** Crystal.

My father has big skin like a soldier's cape **Venus Khoury.** untitled.

my father thought/himself/a buddy/of william carlos williams **Naomi Rachel.** William Carlos Williams' buddy.

My father used to say, **Marianne Moore.** Silence.

My father was Ouranos/and my mother Queen Zenobia **Etel Adnan.** The Beirut—Hell Express.

My fathers,/Our Sun Father./Our Mother, Dawn, **Anonymous.** untitled.

My first flash/on the newsprint/face **Janice Mirikitani.** Attack the water.

my first language was wet/and merging. **Joan Larkin.** Native tongue.

My friend/they don't care/if you're an individualist **Jayne Cortez.** There it is.

My friend in the east says it's raining **Adrianne Marcus.** The child of earthquake country.

My friend who haunts antique stores says **Ellen Wittlinger.** Red.

My friend, you face/is showing **Pinkie Gordon Lane.** Who is my brother?

My garnet necklace goes **Anna Hartmann.** Sleeping with Franz Kafka.

My girl found it on the way to the garden, **Sharon Olds.** The mole.

My girlfriend/(when we were still girls) **Nurit Zarchi.** Furtively.

my grampaw was a smooth black, way back then **Delores S. Williams.** Little girl talk.

My grandfather used to pray:/"Lead us not into temptation, nor into disgrace." **Zelda.** Wicked neighbor.

My Grandmama/don't believe they walked in space: **Thadious M. Davis.** It's all the same.

my grandmother grips my hands as if they were truth and **Karen Brodine.** Making the difference.

My grandmother had braids/at the thickest, pencil wide **Ramona C. Wilson.** Keeping hair.

My grandmother's verandah before they renovated the house sloped down- **Michelle Cliff.** Obsolete geography.

My grandmothers were strong. **Margaret Walker.** Lineage.

My hair is springy like the forest grasses **Naomi Long Madgett.** Black woman.

My heart has grown rich with the passing of years, **Sarah Teasdale.** The solitary.

My heart is like a singing bird **Christina Rossetti.** A birthday.

My heart is like the sun, **Yosano Akiko.** untitled.

My heart, like my clothing/is saturated with your fragrance. **Kenrei Mon-in Ukyō no Daibu.** untitled.

My heart, thinking/"How beautiful he is" **Otomo no Sakanoe.** untitled.

My home is the mountain. **Akhtar Amiri.** I am a woman.

My hope, I know you're dead. **María Eugenia Vaz Ferreira.** The floating casket.

My host's invitation was something of **Bella Akhmadulina.** Rain.

My hunter of dragonflies, **Fukuda Chiyo-Ni.** untitled.

my husband held me/responsible for his failures. **Susan Efros.** The process of dissolution.

My husband in a closed room listening to Pachelbel. **Maria Southwick.** Doors opening here, and there.

My husband who is not my husband/sleeps face up, **Kate Ellen Braverman.** My husband who is not my husband.

My infant godson, I would teach you other things, **Carla Lanyon Lanyon.** To my godson.

My jade body, like my gold hairpins, **Chu Shu-chên.** Spring night, to the tune "Panning gold."

My life had stood—a Loaded Gun— **Emily Dickinson.** 754.

My life had taken the shape of the small square **Sophia de Mello Breyner Andresen.**

My lips are salt, and my eyelashes. **Margarita Aliger.** My lips are salt.

My little body, kerchiefed fast, **Elizabeth Barrett Browning.** The runaway slave at Pilgrim's Point.

My little son/Where have they hidden you? **Anonymous.** untitled.

My Lord/if I worship Thee from fear of Hell **Rabi'a al-Adawiyya.** Two prayers.

My lord contemplates a pool **Chang Wên-chi.** The bamboo shaded pool.

My Lord, fallen, sin-stained/She falls before You **Kassia.** Sticheron for Matins, Wednesday of Holy Week.

My Lord raised a flag of surrender **Hua Jui, Lady.** The Emperor asks why my husband surrendered.

My lord, you only want to/Torture me. Into whose courtyard **Huang O.** To the tune "Plucking a cinnamon branch."

My love hurts me because you cannot know it— **Otomo no Sakanoe.** untitled.

My love, like my hair, is pure, **Chuo Wên-chün.** A song of white hair.

My lover capable of terrible lies/at night lay close to me **Kaccipettu Nannakaiyar.** untitled.

My Mama moved among the days/like a dreamwalker in a field; **Lucille Clifton.** My Mama moved among the days.

My mamma is a/silent movie my/daddy a quiet **Sherley Anne Williams.** Generations: I.

My man is a bone ringed with weed. **Brenda Chamberlain.** Lament.

my man is a fine fine man **Sherley Anne Williams.** second song. (Driving wheel).

My mirror is always a little taller than I am. **Tada Chimako.** Mirror.

my mother/even in her encroaching senility **Clare Coss.** She is an older person now.

My mother/had eyes/in the back/of her head **Maxine Kumin.** The marriage.

My mother always said/make the most of what you've got. **Minnie Bruce Pratt.** Oconeechee Mountain.

My mother always said/that in her youth she was **Sappho.** Headdress.

My mother and I/bear resemblance. **Ruthe D. Canter.** The resemblance.

My mother bids me bind my hair **Mrs. John Hunter.** My mother bids me bind my hair.

My mother gave me a bitter tongue. **Joan Larkin.** Rhyme of my inheritance.

my mother her sad eyes worn as bark **Lucille Clifton.** morning mirror.

my mother is an indictment **Akua Lezli Hope.** 1.

My mother is my grandmother's daughter. My acquaintance with my **Michelle Cliff.** Obsolete geography.

My mother is very beautiful/And not yet old. **Jessica Tarahata Hagedorn.** The death of Anna May Wong.

My mother knew I lost/my good leather glove **Janet Sternburg.** At my house.

My mother loves women. **Minnie Bruce Pratt.** untitled.

My mother remembered how she sat **Shirley Kaufman.** Claims.

My mother used to serve/the thick black earth on round and warm **Margriet Schaye.** My fat Mama.

My mother's mother died/in the spring of her days. And her daughter **Leah Goldberg.** From my mother's home.

My mother's phantom hovers here **Fadwa Tuqān.** Behind bars.

My name is "I am living." **Anna Lee Walters.** I have bowed before the sun.

My name's Polly Parker I come o'er/from Worseley, **Frankie Armstrong.** The Collier lass.

My native Florence! dear, foregone! **Elizabeth Barrett Browning.** Bianca among the nightingales.

My night sweats grease his breakfast plate. **Sylvia Plath.** The jailor.

My Old Straw Hat, my conscience tells **Eliza Cook.** My Old Straw Hat.

My other life of notebooks, lessons, homework continues. I try not to pay **Michelle Cliff.** Obsolete geography.

My own, own child! I could not bear **Elizabeth Barrett Browning.** The runaway slave at Pilgrim's Point.

. . . My parched and frayed dreams, **Marté Jones.** A flame within.

My pillow is hot on both sides. **Anna Akhmatova.** Two poems.

My poet, thou canst touch on all the notes **Elizabeth Barrett Browning.** Sonnets from the Portuguese. (XVII).

My poor raging sisters/floating on turbulent waves **Esther Raab.** My poor raging sisters.

My Queen her sceptre did I lay down, **Mary Elizabeth Coleridge.** Regina.

My silverware it seemed/was yoked to people's faces **Rebecca Gordon.** When I was a fat woman.

My sister will bring the baby, **Sharon Barba.** Siblings.

My skin grows black./I burn. **Toi Derricotte.** The testimony of Sister Maureen.

My snow was azure,/yours,/pale green. **Leah Goldberg.** Hill excursion.

my son is becoming a spider **Michelene Wandor.** crafty.

My son wears a nappy/And waterproof pants **Rosemary Norman.** My son and I.

My song is curdled in my throat **Juana de Ibarbourou.** Chronicle.

My soul is awakened, my spirit is soaring **Anne Brontë.** Lines composed in a wood on a windy day.

My soul of heaven's light blue **Edith Södergran.** Love.

My spirit leans in joyousness tow'rd thine, **Ada.** Lines, Suggested on reading 'An appeal to Christian women of the South,' by A. E. Grimké.

My straying thoughts, reduced stay, **Anne Collins.** Song (II).

My sunlight came pre-packaged **Naomi Long Madgett.** Nomen.

My thin mother began it at the bottle, **Honor Moore.** Abundance and scarcity.

My thought shall never be that you are dead: **Anna Gordon Keown.** Reported missing.

My three sisters are sitting/on rocks of black obsidian. **Adrienne Rich.** Women.

My time is carved in my poems **Leah Goldberg.** On myself I.

My traveling provisions are short, and won't see me through— **Rabi'a bint Isma'il of Syria.** Sufi quatrain.

My tree my tree/where do you go **Alice Karle.** Song of circles.

my trouble/is that I have the spirit of Gertrude Stein **Diane Wakoski.** My trouble.

My true love makes me happy **Beatritz de Dia.** untitled.

My twenty-six year old ensign, **Margarita Aliger.** To the portrait of Lermontov.

My uterus is a clay pot **Phyllis Koestenbaum.** Blood journey.

My voice rings down through thousands of years **Rita Mae Brown.** Sappho's reply.

My whole house is sprinkled with my poems. **Gioconda Belli.** The mundane.

My wish for you/that God should make your love **Rabi'a of Balkh.** untitled.

The mysteries remain,/I keep the same **Hilda Doolittle.** The mysteries remain.

N

Naked/hair flowing/sandals left by the road/I danced. **Lucha Corpi.** Movement.

The naked Greek, the youth in athletic contest, **Hilda Doolittle.** Helios and Athene.

Naked trees/run a race/around the square's rectangle. **Alfonsina Storni.** The park in winter.

The name, the haunch, just like by Byron a assy **Rochelle Owens.** The name, the haunch.

named for a circus performer/who dropped from the high wire **Maxine Shaw.** Damaris.

natural brown sweetener of life **Jeanette Adams.** Portrait.

Natural order is being restored **June Jordan.** From sea to shining sea.

the nature of the beast is the/man or to be more specific **Sonia Sanchez.** small comment.

Nature's support, (without whose Aid) **Aphra Behn.** The disappointment.

Nay, then to meet we may conclude, **Katherine Philips.** Parting with Lucasia: a song.

Nay, we have felt the tedious smart **Katherine Philips.** Parting with Lucasia: a song.

Nearby sea the same that brought Columbus **Minerva Salado.** Villages cities.

Necessary to the calculation/of the living process—the energy **Fanchon Lewis.** Thermodynamics II.

Neither of us wanted/this flame to run the street. **Judith Kazantzis.** Fire.

never seen such a slow day **Michelene Wandor.** hell.

new moon,/you lie/in shadow— **Laura Tokunaga.** Tiger year.

Newborn, on the naked sand **Anonymous.** Song for the newborn.

Newington Butts were lively, **Alice Ker.** untitled.

Next Heaven, my vows to thee, O sacred Muse! **Anne Killigrew.** Upon the saying that my verses were made by another.

Nieves/You are snow/with flaming red hair **Jessica Tarahata Hagedorn.** Dream war.

night:/bright starlight dark/velvet quiet: **Pat Crutchfield Exum.** 3 serendipitous poems.

Night/The silence of night **Anne Hébert.** Night.

The night dreams come as ivory gulls **Elizabeth Keeler.** Phantoms.

'Night. Fog. Tall through the murky gloom **Aelfrida Tillyard.** A letter from Ealing Broadway Station.

nightly/I dream that I am clay **Lynda Koolish.** my flesh is flesh.

1979: Forty-nine inches in New York this year: **Cynthia Macdonald.** Remains—Stratigraphy:

No,/I cannot/turn from love, **Sarah Webster Fabio.** To turn from love.

No backporch in my mind/but there was beauty: sun **Akua Lezli Hope.** To every birth its pain.

No cautions of a matron, old and sage, **Anne Finch, Countess of Winchilsea.** The young rat and his dam, the cock and the cat.

No coward soul is mine **Emily Brontë.** No coward soul is mine.

No, it is not I, it is someone else who suffers **Anna Akhmatova.** Requiem 1935–1940.

No, it's not a solution/to throw oneself under a train like Tolstoy's Anna **Rosario Castellanos.** Meditation on the brink.

no legs./toe; a sock beginning. **Faye Kicknosway.** untitled.

No longer/violent storms,/they fall as **Myrtle Bates.** Tears.

No longer any man needs me **Dorothy Livesay.** Widow.

No moon, no chance to meet; **Ono no Komachi.** untitled.

no more wondering   when the grass was taller than **Katharine Morton.** untitled.

No, not under an alien sky **Anna Akhmatova.** Requiem 1935–1940.

No one cares about the flowers **Forūgh Farrokhzād.** I feel sorry for the garden.

No one near me getting late **Lygia Guillén.** A sadness which already knew me.

no one uses words such as/marvelous here. The scent **Frances C. Chung.** untitled.

No one worth possessing/Can be quite possessed; **Sara Teasdale.** Advice to a girl.

No Phoenix pen, nor Spenser's poetry, **Anne Bradstreet.** In honour of that high and mighty Princess Queen Elizabeth of happy memory.

No punts in view, no paddlers? Good. **Judith Moffett.** "Cambridge University Swimming Club/no public access to river."

No Rack can torture me— **Emily Dickinson.** 384.

No romance/To sound of pouring coffee **Emily Katherine Harris.** I do not like it here.

No se puede traducir/el aullido de viento: **Angela de Hoyos.** Below zero.

No second spring can melt this winter-sadness **Margaret Willy.** Lament of Heloise.

No, she's not lying down there now for love **Margaret Stanley-Wrench.** In the radiotherapy unit.

No sooner, FLAVIO, was you gone, **Anne Finch, Countess of Winchilsea.** To Mr. F. now Earl of W.

no   warning   she is/tormenting the myths that torment/you you **Alexandra Grilikhes.** The film by the woman.

no words, you say/we slip/through the nets **Jan Clausen.** the kitchen window.

nobody banged/a fist on the table **Michèle Roberts.** and so it all goes on.

nobody's blind/they said they said/over your **Yvonne.** The tearing of the skin.

Nocturnal water, primaeval silences, **Rosario Castellanos.** Useless day.

None of them came for me. **Shirley Kaufman.** Meron.

a non-negotiable issue for both of us/my child exists **Maxine Shaw.** Issue.

Noon students slid onto the unfolded chairs **Josephine Miles.** Noon.

Noon, the sky gray, the snow not falling in earnest, so **Honor Moore.** Poem: for the beginning.

Not because of their beauty- though they are slender **Judith Wright.** The twins.

Not by wayout hairdos, bulbous Afro blowouts and certainly **Margaret Goss Burroughs.** Only in this way.

Not even in dreams/Can I meet him anymore- **Lady Ise.** untitled.

Not for Nanna, but Inanna   these praises I sing **Enheduanna.** Inanna exalted.

Not for the dead, but for memories. None of/them sad. **Alice Walker.** Burial.

Not just the message but the sound. **June Jordan.** Problems of translation: problems of language.

Not like the brazen giant of Greek fame, **Emma Lazarus.** The new colossus.

Not like the memories/first homes we lived in **Shirley Kaufman.** Jerusalem notebook.

Not rose of death:/drawing in to your centre each wave of colour **Jenny Joseph.** Rose in the afternoon.

Not that broad path chose he, which whoso wills **Elizabeth Daryush.** Unknown warrior.

Not that I wish to take the liberty **Pernette de Guillet.** Not that I wish to take the liberty.

Not the poem of your absence, **Alejandra Pizarnik.** To name you.

Not what the light will do but how he shapes it **Elizabeth Jennings.** The diamond cutter.

Not while, but long after he had told me, **Tess Gallagher.** Each bird walking.

Not wholly this or that, **Georgia Douglas Johnson.** Cosmopolite.

Not with my thoughts shall you be weighted **Phyllis Mégroz.** The crystal tree.

Not working, not breathing, **Bella Akhmadulina.** Autumn.

Not yet will those measureless fields be green again **Charlotte Mew.** The Cenotaph.

Nothing remains from the shipwrecked survivor; nothing: **María Eugenia Vaz Ferriera.** The voice of return.

Nothing soft in this skull/hung up, somewhere— **Joan Larkin.** Cow's skull with calico roses.

Noticed the apparent closeness of a couple **María Southwick.** Doors opening here, and there.

November days, and the vague shape of a wing, **Madeline DeFrees.** Extended outlook.

november 28/so today finally I was no longer waiting **Miriam Dyak.** Dying.

Now/the polar nights/startle the **Veronica Porumbacu.** White bears.

Now a whole year has waxed and waned and whitened **Isabel C. Clarke.** Anniversary of the Great Retreat.

Now, age came on, and all the dismal traine **Anne Finch, Countess of Winchilsea.** Clarinda's indifference at parting with her beauty.

Now all the doors and windows **Jane Kenyon.** Philosophy in warm weather.

Now, glass in hand, another woman guest, who **Bella Akhmadulina.** Rain.

Now I am slow and placid, fond of sun, **Genevieve Taggard.** With child.

Now I know/that distance is three-dimensional. **Lourdes Casal.** Now I know.

Now I see myself making the stars. Within me I hold a vast **Sarah Appleton.** Book of my hunger, book of the earth.

now I wear skirts/that know what my hips will hold **Cindy Bellinger.** Children and other reasons.

Now I'm going to tell you **Gloria Fuertes.** Now.

Now is the time/Oh Bird! **Fukui Hisako.** Now is the time.

now is the year's fullness; like/a pregnant bride **Michèle Roberts.** poem on midsummer's day.

Now let me tell you about minutes of lead, **Jan Heller Levi.** Formal feeling (A sequence for my mother).

Now let no charitable hope/Confuse my mind with images **Elinor Wylie.** Let no charitable hope.

Now my heart turns to and fro **Hatshepsut.** The Obelisk inscriptions.

Now, not a tear begun,/we sit here in your kitchen, **Adrienne Rich.** A woman mourned by daughters.

Now on three sides the darkness grows deeper **Bella Akhmadulina.** Night.

Now rock the boat to a fare-thee-well. **Audre Lorde.** Rites of passage.

Now, stealing fearful or chaperoned through the shadowed **Anonymous.** Poem for Jacqueline Hill.

Now that I am fifty-six **Muriel Rukeyser.** Rondel.

Now that my loves are dead **Irene Claremont de Castillejo.** The last years.

Now that you too must shortly go the way **Eleanor Farjeon.** 'Now that you too.'

Now the fingers and toes are formed, **Chana Bloch.** Magnificat.

Now the ideas all change to animals **Muriel Rukeyser.** Nine poems for the unborn child.

Now the lotuses in the imperial lake **Wang Ch'ing-hui.** To the tune "The river is red."

Now the sprinkled blackthorn snow **Edith Nesbit.** Spring in war-time.

Now the wings of madness/hover in my soul **Anna Akhmatova.** Requiem 1935–1940.

Now then, I've shown you/how I managed to square **Jenny Mastoraki.** Theorem. (How I managed to square the circle of dreams in the shape of a window at the top of the stairs in a tenement house).

Now to be clean he must abandon himself **Ruth Pitter.** The swan bathing.

Now we'll go homeward/in search of a bed **Yunna Moritz.** Now we'll go.

Now, while we dance/Come here to us **Sappho.** untitled.

Now you are standing face to face with the clear light **Diana Scott.** Prayer for the little daughter between death and burial.

Nowadays I call no one place home. **Minnie Bruce Pratt.** First home. (The segregated heart).

Nowhere, not among the warriors at their festival, **Atimantiyar.** untitled.

Ntabuu/Ntabuu Selina and/Ntabuu of the red dirt road in
     New Orleans. Red dirt morning. **Alexis De Veaux.** The
     sisters.
nun meets me at the station. **Toi Derricotte.** November.
     (Natural birth).
Nurse Malloy taps me **Rota Silverstrini.** Pieces of echoes.
Nyanu was appointed/as my Lord. The husband
     chosen **Alice Walker.** Part I. (Early losses: a requiem).
The nymph, in vain, bestows her pains, **Anne Finch,
     Countess of Winchilsea.** A song.
The *Nymph's* Resentments none but I **Aphra Behn.** The
     Disappointment.

Oh,/I am thinking **Anonymous.** untitled.
O/Potent head pouncing, **Rochelle Owens.** Split a passion-
     flower.
O/to be a man! **Anonymous.** Serenade.
Oh Beverly, do you remember/how we sat together in that
     brook, touching **Ellen Bass.** September 7.
O bird's singing!/The dead walk **Mitsuhashi Takajo.**
     untitled.
O black warrior,/Hurl a dark spear of song **Pauli Murray.**
     Dark testament.
O Bride brimful of/rosy little loves! **Sappho.** Bridesmaids'
     carol I.
O brightness/of peony's buds **Hoshino Tatsuko.** untitled.
O brother, why do you talk/to this woman,
     Mahadeviyakka. untitled.
O cold white moonlight of the north, **Elizabeth Barrett
     Browning.** Bianca among the nightingales.
Oh come and live with me, my love, **Aelfrida Tillyard.**
     Invitation au Festin.
O crimson blood/Which fell from that high place **Hildegard
     von Bingen.** untitled.
O do not grieve, Dear Heart, nor shed a tear, **Margaret
     Cavendish, Duchess of Newcastle.** untitled.
O Earth, lie heavily upon her eyes; **Christina Rossetti.** Rest.
O Faithless thorn/He has my heart no longer **Anonymous.**
     untitled.
O flower garment!/When I take it off, **Sugita Hisajo.**
     untitled.
O Flowery Mountain slopes,/Now that my lover is
     dead **Anonymous.** On the slope of Hua mountain.
O, from your sweet mouth I have come **Else Lasker-
     Schüler.** The Shulamite.
O God of Mercy/For the time being/Choose another people.
     Kadia Molodowsky. God of Mercy.
(Oh God, she said.)/It began a beautiful day by the sun
     up **Susan Griffin.** Song My.

Oh, golden flower opened up **Anonymous.** untitled.
Oh, half of my being, my very self! **Concha Michel.** Only a
     second (1940).
Oh I am a cat that likes to/Gallop about doing good **Stevie
     Smith.** The galloping cat.
Oh, I see myself as I was/then skinny little **Sherley Anne
     Williams.** this city-light. (The house of desire).
Oh, I should like to ride the seas, **Dorothy Parker.** Song of
     perfect propriety.
O Isis, Mother of God, to thee I pray! **Christina Walsh.**
     Prayer to Isis.
O King, I know you gave me poison. **Mira Bai.** untitled.
O lady of all truths   bright light going forth **Enheduanna.**
     Inanna exalted.
Oh little island,/How can you be so secure, **Ping Hsin
     (Hsieh Wan-Ying).** Multitudinous stars and spring
     waters.
O, Lord—/If in life eternal **Ping Hsin (Hsieh Wan-ying).**
     The spring waters.
Oh! Love, that stronger art than wine, **Aphra Behn.** The
     lucky chance. Song.
O lovely raw red wild/autumn turning **Dorothy Livesay.**
     Grandmother.
Oh lover/when you laugh with me **Ann du Cille.** Song.
O man, behold your destiny./Look on this life **Margaret
     Walker.** THIS IS MY CENTURY . . . Black synthesis
     of time.
O merciful Father, my hope is in Thee! **Mary, Queen of
     Scots.** Prayer before execution.
Oh Monday night's the night for me! **C.A.L.T.** Y.M.C.A.
O Mother, do not again give me a woman's birth **Anony-
     mous.** untitled.
O move in me, my darling, **Judith Wright.** Woman's song.
"Oh muther" sings the Chinese dishwasher, *2am,* "I'm
     tired **Sara Miles.** Talking about it.
Oh, my beloved, shall you and I **Margaret Postgate Cole.**
     Afterwards.
O my dear little man, O my dear little man, **Gabriela Mis-
     tral.** Dear little man.
O my heart's heart, and you who are to me **Christina Ros-
     setti.** Monna Innominata: a sonnet of sonnets.
O my love/My mind has broken **Anonymous.** The abortion.
Oh, my lovely mountain **Anonymous.** Corn grinding song.
Oh not again this coupled/hump, lump, bundle of love **Olga
     Broumas.** Breaking camp. (Of fruit whose black seed
     fire).
Oh, oh, you will be sorry for that word! **Edna St. Vincent
     Millay.** Sonnet. (XXXI).
O pilgrim-souls, I speak to you! **Elizabeth Barrett Brown-
     ing.** The runaway slave at Pilgrim's Point.
O, poet gifted with the sight divine! **Henrietta Cordelia
     Ray.** Milton.
O pregnant womanhood that scarce can drag **Sylvia Pank-
     hurst.** The mothers.
O smooth adder/who with fanged kisses changedst my natural
     blood **Augusta Webster.** Medea in Athens.
O stop, Jade Rabbit! **Chung Ling.** The fall of moon lady
     before the landing of Apollo X.

Oh the relief of the children! **Judith Kazantzis.** The Pope at Dublin Airport.

oh this man/what a meal he made of me **Michèle Roberts.** Magnificat.

O thy bright eyes must answer now, **Emily Brontë.** O thy bright eyes must answer now.

O Time the fatal wrack of mortal things, **Anne Bradstreet.** Contemplations.

O to go home at last— **Else Lasker-Schüler.** Over shining shingle.

O tucumcari lady took good care of you **Carol Tinker.** thank you capitalism for the expanding universe.

O Ukko, god on high,   come look here, **Anonymous.** untitled.

Oh, when this earthly tenement **Ada.** untitled.

O wicked tyrant, send me back my heart, **Gaspara Stampa.** untitled.

Oh, Woman dear, and did ye hear the news that's going round, **L. E. Morgan-Browne.** The purple, white and green.

O woman with child, it was good you gave birth. **Anonymous.** untitled.

Oh yes, even more than this **Forūgh Farrokhzād.** Mechanical doll.

O you who are my heavenly pain of Hell, **Edith Sitwell.** Mary Stuart to James Bothwell.

Oak burns steady and hot and long **Marge Piercy.** Shadows of the burning.

The oars are silenced. **Laura Jensen.** Whale.

Obediently we walked/over a crystal bridge **Lucha Corpi.** The crystal bridge.

Observe the weary birds ere night be done, **Katherine Philips.** Orinda to Lucasia.

Obviously, it was necessary/a long time ago **Miriam Oren.** At least.

The occult note/the influenze **Pamela Victorine.** Menses: a seasonal.

The ocean has befriended me; **Diane Wakoski.** On Barbara's shore.

October and no rain falls . . . **Lucha Corpi.** For an attempted suicide of the 20th century.

October. Now I dream **Jan Heller Levi.** Formal feeling (A sequence for my mother).

O'de wurl' ain't flat/An' de wurl' ain't roun', **Lucy Ariel Williams.** Northboun'.

Of all the days of my life, I would choose that which is **Marilyn Bobes.** Praise of future.

Of all who died in silence far away **Iris Tree.** untitled.

Of children nine and twenty that I bore, **Anonymous.** A joyful mother of children.

Of course/the sun is angry **Nadia Tuéni.** untitled.

Of course I love them, they are my children. **Anne Stevenson.** The mother.

Of her own accord, before the altar **Lucha Corpi.** Marina virgin. (Marina).

Of that last climb in the hills of Arad **Leah Goldberg.** Hill excursion.

Of the [seven] and seven mother-wombs, seven **Anonymous.** untitled.

Of the two kinds of wing-shaped rings on his/desk **Atsumi Ikuko.** The ring.

Of us who darkly stand/Bared to the spittle of every curse, **Pauli Murray.** Dark testament.

off First Avenue the filipinos sell freshly cut pineapple **Patricia Jones.** 14th St/new york. (VII).

Often rebuked, yet always back returning **Emily Brontë.** Stanzas.

Old age has come, my head is shaking **Anonymous.** untitled.

The old church building had no altar any more, **Betsy Orient.** The divorce.

Old enemies/ten year adversaries **Molly Myerowitz Levine.** Safed and I.

The old gods are no longer bountiful **Marina Tsvetayeva.** In praise of Aphrodite.

Old houses have the most **Ingrid Wendt.** Dust.

An old man crosses/the road/thin ends of his beard **Shirley Kaufman.** Jerusalem notebook.

Old man walking into Mi Tierra, **Inés Hernandez Tovar.** Para un viejito desconocido que aun conozco.

Old Molly Means was a hag and a witch; **Margaret Walker.** Molly Means.

Old plant of Asia—/Mutilated vine **Lola Ridge.** Palestine.

An old woman, her butt spread on the stoop, **Faye Kicknosway.** Rapunzil.

An old woman in me walks patiently to the hospital, **Carole C. Gregory.** Revelation.

An old woman who sometimes works for us has built a house by the road— **Michelle Cliff.** Obsolete geography.

The old women move quietly up/and touch Sis Rachel's face. **Alice Walker.** Burial.

On a hillside I search for mangoes. As I shake the tree the fruit drops: its **Michelle Cliff.** Obsolete geography.

On a lit-up window square, **Leah Goldberg.** A look at a bee.

On an empty stomach,/with the pang of mendicant yesterdays, **Angela de Hoyos.** The final laugh.

On Death's domain intent I fix my eyes, **Phillis Wheatley.** To a gentleman and lady on the death of the lady's brother and sister, and a child of the name Avis, aged one year.

On Good Friday/Virgin Mary becomes again the belle of the ball **Katerina Anghelaki-Rooke.** My mama and satan.

On London fell a clearer light; **Alice Meynell.** Summer in England, 1914.

On my balcony, not a lover **Elizabeth Keeler.** Visiting a son in Java.

On my birthday I never woke up. I was singing **Molly Vaux.** On my birthday.

On one hillside next to the house is the coffee piece: the bushes are low, **Michelle Cliff.** Obsolete geography.

on second avenue even in november the corner stays hot **Patricia Jones.** 14th St/new york. (IV).

On the altar/faint stars of fire burning **Ping Hsin (Hsieh Wan-ying).** Receiving Buddha.

On the beach where we had been idly/telling the shell coins **Marge Piercy.** Gracious goodness.

on the bus the medical personnel: two women and a man **Patricia Jones.** 14th St/new york. (VI).

on the corner where s. klein's used to be **Patricia Jones.** 14th St/new york. (I).

On the edge of his tongue, it was the one word **Abbey Lincoln (Aminata Moseka).** On being high.

On the first day of school the teacher asked me: **Nellie Wong.** How a girl got her Chinese name.

On the green leaf/they are sleeping,/the beetles, **Judith Ivaloo Volborth.** Three songs to mark the night.

On the Ile de Gorée, M. Diop elegant/in steel-gray cardigan **Thadious M. Davis.** Double take at Relais de l'Espadon.

On the last year's trip I enjoyed this place. **Sun Yün-fêng.** On the road through Chang-Te.

On the Moon's rim/abalone horses/circling, **Judith Ivaloo Volborth.** Three songs to mark the night.

On the 19th and Jefferson block,/the trees are evenly spaced. **Laureen Mar.** Chinatown 2.

On the other side of that line, up the hill, **Georgina Herrera.** Street of the women of the world.

On the porch outside my door/girls are lying **Audre Lorde.** Chain.

On the road at night there stands the man **Dahlia Ravikovitch.** On the road at night there stands the man.

On the road through the clouds/Is there a short cut **Den Sute-Jo.** untitled.

''on the roof of the beer garden, **Shiraishi Kazuko.** untitled.

On the subway/home/people look at u/like u crazy **Sapphire.** New York City tonight.

On the terrace, violins played **Anna Akhmatova.** In the evening.

On the webbed finger of a water dream swims **Paula Gunn Allen.** The duck-billed god. (Medicine song).

on these branches I left/my youth **Victoria Theodorou.** Picnic.

On winter nights when the wind was cold, **Sylvia Lynd.** The question.

On your breast,/In your arms— **Lin Ling.** Vague apprehension, to a gambler.

On your slender body/Your jade and coral girdle ornaments chime **Wu Tsao.** For the courtesan Ch'ing Lin.

Once above the sea/And glittering sands **May Miller.** Portugal. (Not that far).

Once again a yellow twilight **Wu Tsao.** To the tune "The pain of lovesickness."

Once again they've quarrelled on a tram, **Margarita Aliger.** Two.

Once and for all, I go my chosen way, **Virginia Moore.** Avowal.

once, the canyons say,/there was but one cloud **Nzadi Zimele-Keita (Michelle McMichael).** once. (Birds of paradise).

Once there were stones in our pockets to hold **Adelaide Blomfield.** Attics.

Once upon a time I was/Beautiful and seductive, **Huang O.** To the tune ''The fall of a little wild goose.''

Once when I walked into a room **Audre Lorde.** Between ourselves.

One autumn evening in a train **Adrienne Rich.** A woman dead in her forties.

One blue flag is the only color left **Linda Pastan.** One blue flag.

One child died—a son, at eighteen. His grave is in the flower garden, shaded **Michelle Cliff.** Obsolete geography.

One Christmas eve my lovers and I **Judy Grahn.** Death and disfiguration. (A woman is talking to death).

one could be so close/after all the dark spells **Ruth Weiss.** Sixteenth day. (There is no evil only restlessness!).

One darkness/I was a tiger-lily. **Raquel Chalfi.** Tiger-lily.

One day in/Georgia/Working around/the Negro section **Alice Walker.** Once.

One day, not here, you will find a hand **Charlotte Mew.** Again.

One day she awoke and saw that her life **Raquel Chalfi.** A witch without a cover.

One day the Amorous *Lysander,* **Aphra Behn.** The disappointment.

One day this summer,/I swam on the seacoast at Mera, **Takada Toshiko.** The seacoast at Mera.

one day, you stepped/into my horoscope **Colleen J. McElroy.** Dancing with the fifth horseman.

One face looks out from all his canvases, **Christina Rossetti.** In an artist's studio.

One hand, two hands. Nothing more. **Olga Orozco.** Sphinxes inclined to be.

one has to throw it all away/notes—numbers **Ruth Weiss.** Desert journal   Second day.

One is an ex-professor of biology **Sharon Barba.** Dykes in the garden.

one knitted dress inventories/a satin future **Michelene Wandor.** people, on a bad day.

One minute we was laughin', me an' Ted, **May Herschel-Clarke.** 'Nothing to report.'

one night/i place my ear/against the wall **Toi Derricotte.** The testimony of Sister Maureen.

One night they woke me, **Molly Vaux.** Northern lights.

One reason the parlor floor is waxed on Saturday is that my grandmother **Michelle Cliff.** Obsolete geography.

One said to me, 'Seek Love, for he is Joy **May Wedderburn Cannan.** Love, 1916.

One should always practice/going mad first: **Grace Butcher.** My name in lights.

One swallow did not follow/The departed Spring **Wu Tsao.** To the tune "A dream song."

1. The sea./2. The disappearance of the sun. **Jessica Tarahata Hagedorn.** A script: beauty is the beginning of terror . . .

One time in the cool of dawn/Angels came and worked with me. **Anna Hempstead Branch.** The monk in the kitchen.

One. Two. How do you do. **Beverly Dahlen.** For Darlene Tower.

One—two—three . . . /eight feet long, **Hannah Senesh.** One-two-three.

One wept whose only child was dead, **Alice Meynell.** Maternity.

The one who cleans, knows: **Ingrid Wendt.** Dust.

The one who'd seen it all turned her face away. She was **Blanca Varela.** Madonna.

One window for seeing **Forūgh Farrokhzād.** A window.

One woman say a good man make her want/to shout. **Carolyn M. Rodgers.** Wimmin.

One year/the politicians got fancy/at Laguna. **Leslie Marmon Silko.** Toe'osh: A Laguna coyote story.

Only consider, said my author, contemporary painters **Barbara Guest.** From water mill. (Quilts).

Only for the sake of art/Millicent, do you rise **Gabrielle Daniels.** Millicent Fredericks.

Only the bathroom/is private. I lock myself in **Melanie Kaye.** Brooklyn 1956: The walls are full of noise.

Only the fastidiously unheroic dare **Robin Morgan.** Lunch hour.

Only the stubble is left where the barley, **Celia Randall.** Harvest.

Only the virgin knows the life story, **Kathleen Raine.** The clue.

Only the waning morning moon **Ise Tayū.** untitled.

Only when the face is blotted out **Dahlia Ravikovitch.** Memory.

Ooooooo la-la cheri/catches on the lips the phrase, **Lois Elaine Griffith.** Juxtaposer.

An open world/within its mountain rim: **Denise Levertov.** Lonely man.

Orange in the middle of a table: **Margaret Atwood.** Against still life.

The orange tree/we planted in my garden **Otomo no Sakanoe.** untitled.

oranges & jade at the shrine **Diane di Prima.** Brass furnace going out: song, after an abortion.

Order is a lovely thing; **Anna Hempstead Branch.** The monk in the kitchen.

The orphan boat of my heart **Ping Hsin (Hsieh Wan-ying).** Multitudinous stars and spring waters.

Osiris, Isis, black and beauteous gods, **Margaret Walker.** THIS IS MY CENTURY . . . Black synthesis of time.

Other loves I have known. **Bessie Calhoun Bird.** Proof.

The others/who buy one quart of lowfat milk **Phyllis Koestenbaum.** Blood journey.

Our argument echoed down the steps of our hotel, soaked into the carpet. **Diana Ó Hehir.** Casualty in Mexico City.

Our collective wastebin/where the air sticks **Mitsuye Yamada.** In the outhouse. (Camp notes).

Our family was so poor. **Georgina Herrera.** The way we were.

Our father works in us, **Alice Meynell.** A father of women: ad sororem E.B.

Our flat bottomed boat/glides through the reeds of the bay. **Mei-Mei Berssenbrugge.** Old man let's go fishing in the yellow reeds of the bay.

Our husbands they may scold or snore, **Annie Louisa Walker.** Song.

Our loves are not many. **Leah Goldberg.** Hill excursion.

Our mound of earth dug up for a new sidewalk **Olga Broumas.** Epithalmion.

our neighbor brings us venison **Judith McDaniel.** November passage.

Our secret does not lie/in the groin **Akua Lezli Hope.** Avatar.

Our skin loosely lies across grass borders; **Wendy Rose.** Long division: a tribal history.

Our sons, our sons! **Lesley Saunders.** Mothers of sons.

Our victories at this time/seem so minute **Rosemari Mealy.** A love poem to an African freedom fighter.

Our voice lifts/over the white selfishness of men **Noémia da Sousa.** Our voice.

Our walls were thick. **Venus Khoury.** untitled.

Our white sisters/radical friends/love to own pictures of us **Jo Carrillo.** And when you leave, take your pictures with you.

Our wounds are different. Your white men **Elizabeth Barrett Browning.** The runaway slave at Pilgrim's Point.

Out; Dangerous **Rochelle Owens.** A verse on the 50th day.

Out from his bed the breaking seas **Anne Ridler.** A dream observed.

Out here the dogs of war run loose, **Maud Anna Bell.** From a trench.

Out of her own body she pushed/silver thread, light, air **Paula Gunn Allen.** Grandmother.

Out of the darkness/on a dark path, **Izumi Shikibu.** untitled.

Out of the darkness comes the fear of/what's to come **Frankie Armstrong.** Out of the darkness.

Out of the darkness I come, a woman. **Gertrud Kolmar.** Out of the darkness.

Outside are the silent streets, the sleeping lights. **Marilyn Bobes.** Elvira.

Outside the study door the candles wait, **Barbara Vere Hodge.** The night-light.

Over my house/one late swallow. **Leah Goldberg.** Heavenly Jerusalem, Jerusalem of the earth.

Over North Mountain/dark clouds rise. **Empress Jitō.** On the death of the Emperor Temmu.

overflow their yards/brilliant skirts smother the earth **Karen Bunting.** the neighbor women.

Overnight, very/Whitely, discreetly,/Very quietly **Sylvia Plath.** Mushrooms.

Overwhelming, the torpor/of your twisted lives how you lay **Alexandra Grilikhes.** Listening to the story of your life.

The owl sings/a plaintive overture. **Lucha Corpi.** Premonition.

Owlish, warty/prickly of speech **Yvonne.** The tearing of the skin.

Oye Mr. Chico . . .spic/bro **Sandra Maria Esteves.** POR TI, BRO.

Oysters we ate,/sweet blue babies, **Anne Sexton.** Oysters.

The pain and laughter of the day are done, **Eva Dobell.** Night duty.

Paintings done when I was 18, 22 **Jane Augustine.** I help my mother move out of her old house in the country.

Pairs/of soda crackers/part **Olga Elena Mattei.** untitled.

pale curry-yellow and grapefruit-pink **Eugenie Eersel.** Shells.

Pan, grant that I may never prove **Aphra Behn.** Song.

Paper is neither kind nor cruel/only white in its neutral-ity **Audre Lorde.** Paperweight.

partially/off course the moment rises **Carol Tinker.** lank pier.

Partly grasped,/my meaning,/simply given **Irene Friis.** Mother, child.

past mosquito bites and brown/soft black hair and moles **Elouise Loftin.** Sunni's unveiling.

Path-let . . . leaving home, leading out, **Stella Ngatho.** Footpath.

Patriarchal poetry does not make it never made it **Gertrude Stein.** Patriarchal poetry.

Patriarchal poetry makes no mistakes makes no **Gertrude Stein.** Patriarchal poetry.

Patriarchal she said what is it I know what it is it is I **Gertrude Stein.** Patriarchal poetry.

Patron of flawless serpent beauty **Friederike Mayröcker.** Patron of flawless serpent beauty.

Pearl of the sea! Star of the West! **Gertrudis Gómez de Avellaneda.** On leaving Cuba, her native land.

A peculiar woman he used to think **Brenda Connor-Bey.** The dancer.

penetrated death's dogma/with her hero's hands **Lina de Feria.** Stalingrad.

People are walking in the counterfeit city **Leah Goldberg.** Heavenly Jerusalem, Jerusalem of the earth.

The people I love the best/jump into work head first **Marge Piercy.** To be of use.

The perfect rye bread/is a light-colored rye, **Bethami Auerbach.** The search for the perfect rye bread.

Perhaps he went into the sun's trail **Anonymous.** A wom-an's song for her drowned brother.

perhaps i snapped/shut my mouth too late. **Esther Louise.** running to gone.

Perhaps in the spring **Blanca Varela.** untitled.

Perhaps some day the sun will shine again, **Vera Brittain.** Perhaps—.

Perhaps you will never answer my letters. **Claudia Lars.** Letters written when night grows.

The persimmon, lo!/No one can tell till he tastes it! **Fukuda Chiyo-Ni.** To her husband, at the wedding.

person who stole/landlady's wash left her **Carol Tinker.** untitled.

Peter always/thought/the only way to/"enlighten" **Alice Walker.** Once.

les petits mals/outside the swollen and scrolled black acanthus **Judith Kazantzis.** soeurs du mal.

The photo in the livingroom/and the *sun sun dambaé* **Nancy Morejón.** Bricklayer's fable.

the pianist was a different kind of person **Lina de Feria.** Kinfolk.

The picnic tables,/empty./The bright benches,/empty. **Grace Butcher.** State mental hospital, 5 PM, summer.

A piece of fossil ivory **Anonymous.** A song of the dice.

A piece of thread ripped-out from a fierce design, **Adrienne Rich.** Ghazals: Homage to Ghalib.

The pig is big, and hangs suspended by her hind legs from a tree in the **Michelle Cliff.** Obsolete geography.

The pillow that knows all **Izumi Shikibu.** untitled.

Pillowed on your arm/only for the dream of a spring night, **Lady Suwō.** untitled.

The pine branch of Heaven— **Ping Hsin (Hsien Wan-ying).** Multitudinous stars and spring waters.

The pistol, yes./Sheets of paper horizontally folded. **Jessica Tarahata Hagedorn.** Autobiography part one: Manila to San Francisco.

Pity the poor who hate— **Pauli Murray.** Dark testament.

a place/I do not say a space **Alejandra Pizarnik.** Useless frontiers.

Place changes, dawn breaks **Anonymous.** Song of a girl journeying to the country of the dead.

a place of women and toast/husbands divorced and divorc-ing **Rachel Maines.** Schrafft's Third Avenue and East 57th Street.

The place was empty./We entered the room **Virginia Gil-bert.** Leaving, the sepulcre city.

the plants/reach out new hands/toward the light **Jan Clau-sen.** the transplant.

plants don't talk, people say **Rosalía de Castro.** They say that the plants do not speak.

A poem I keep forgetting to write/Is about the stars. **Josephine Miles.** Figure.

The poem is not written until the mind is so cut **Diane Wakoski.** The poem.

Poems come from incomplete knowledge. **Diane Wakoski.** With words (for Tony).

poems in hand, I follow/Helen's camera **Colleen J. McElroy.** Morning in Argentina.

The poet is a hunter of invisible beasts that die **Barbara Szerlip.** Four short poems.

Poetesses, they said./They shall be lukewarm **Marilyn Bobes.** Pitiful role.

poetry is motion graceful/as a fawn **Nikki Giovanni.** Poetry.

The poet's work/has simply got to be difficult. **Jenny Mastoraki.** The poet. (How I managed to square the circle of dreams in the shape of a window at the top of the stairs in a tenement house).

The Policeman/leaves his beat/follows me, **Julia Fields.** The Policeman.

Poor restless dove, I pity thee; **Anne Brontë.** The captive dove.

The portrait is in black and white, **Cheri Fein.** Rape at Progresso: a critical study.

Potato-colored the couple stepped a weary way **Emily Katherine Harris.** Thee to a dead mountain.

potent male rain/clouds so fertile **Nia Francisco.** Tomorrow noon.

Pots in piles of blue and white, **Alberta Vickridge.** In a V.A.D. pantry.

pounce the cat/chatterbox jerry **Paula Yup.** Untitled.

Pouting cause I left you at the party you know nothing **Sara Miles.** for Cynthia.

Poverty? wealth? seek neither— **Kassia.** untitled.

The powerfully confused,/the Leaders. **Rosalie Moore.** Near Cologne: 1212.

The power-saw, whirling, **Diane Wakoski.** Mill.

A pox of the Statesman that's witty, **Aphra Behn.** The Cabal at Nickey Nackeys.

Precious night-blooming cereus **Thadious M. Davis.** Remembering Fannie Lou Hamer.

Pretty Lady Carenza/Advise me as a sister **Carenza** and **Iselda.** Tenson.

Pretty women wonder where my secret lies. **Maya Angelou.** Phenomenal woman.

primrose. and lizard **Rochelle Owens.** Loon lord and master O jack pollock.

A Prison gets to be a friend— **Emily Dickinson.** 652.

the procession for San Martin de Porres the only **Patricia Jones.** 14th St/new york. (II).

the professor is a magician **Maxine Shaw.** Going back to school.

Proud inclination of the flesh, **Dilys Laing.** Villanelle.

Provincetown/The night **Lynda Efros.** Untitled.

Publication—is the Auction/Of the Mind of Man— **Emily Dickinson.** 709.

Puckering in a speckled porcelain **Yvonne.** 1936. (Aunt Martha: severance pay).

Punished in the moment of love. **Baba Akiko.** untitled.

Purple butterflies/fly at night through my dreams. **Yosano Akiko.** untitled.

que le pegaron tres tiros/what am I to say **Esther Silverman.** South Bronx girl.

Queen, mistress, crucified at the gates of the furthest city **Anne Hébert.** Eve.

The query:/woman among women/how far? **Jacqueline Lapidus.** I Ching.

question authority./question:/why should trees or rivers or even **Alexis De Veaux.** . . . And then she said.

The quick pale fingers of Sister Tutor **Monica Ditmas.** Annunciation.

The quiet/The quiet/The quiet kisses like the one hand claps **Alice Karle.** A play.

The quiet dead, they lie at ease **F. Tennyson Jesse.** De mortuis.

Quiet now, feel the kindly pressure of darkness: **Diana Scott.** Winter solstice poem.

Quiet, only tiny ripples. **Samiati Alisjahbana.** Quiet water.

Radiant/glorified/effervescent **Yvonne.** The tearing of the skin.

The radio says flooding in Mississippi and parts of Alabama. **Minnie Bruce Pratt.** Third home. (The segregated heart).

rafael laughed when i said i was puerto rican **Maxine Shaw.** Tengo Puerto Rico en mi Corazón.

The rain had them caught in the park **Lois Elaine Griffith.** Lena Lime thinking she up close but being far away.

Rain in torrents has washed out the road **Patricia Cumming.** Midsummer.

the rain is falling/through the gauze air **Laura Beausoleil.** Tonight.

The rain is slipping, dripping down the street; **Pauline Barrington.** 'Education.'

Rain on the lawn falls softly, **Ann Lauterbach.** The yellow linen dress: a sequence.

rain on the roof/i stroke the shape of your head **Jan Clausen.** the kitchen window.

The rain sounds like a dombra, **Bella Akhmadulina.** The rain sounds like a dombra.

Rainbow/Fountain **Alberta Turner.** Arch. (A dictionary of common terms).

Rainbow/space between earth and sky **Paula Gunn Allen.** Diné.

Rainbow-robed, immortal Aphrodite **Sappho.** Ode to Aphrodite.

Raja, my heart is mad for you **Anonymous.** untitled.

The rays of the low sun,/Reflected on the stream, **Lady Wei.** To the tune "The Bodhisattva's barbaric headdress."

Razors pain you;/Rivers are damp; **Dorothy Parker.** Résumé.

"Ready or not, you must be caught," **Florence Randal Livesay.** Gold ladies.

Ready to taste a thousand Joys, **Aphra Behn.** The disappointment.

the real american does not know what flan is **Patricia Jones.** mi chinita poem.

A red light is stuck/At the corner of Le Conte and Euclid. **Josephine Miles.** Why we are late.

Reform the past and not the future this is what the **Gertrude Stein.** Patriarchal poetry.

The relief of putting your fingers on the keyboard, **Diane Wakoski.** Thanking my mother for piano lessons.

Remember/the fiery blue of planets **May Miller.** Turkey. (Not that far).

Remember still the first, impetuous form **Lilian Bowes Lyon.** Leda.

Remembering the past/And gloating at it now, **Carolyn Kizer.** What the bones know.

Remembering those gentle deer/that watched me as I wept, **Susan Griffin**. Deer skull.

Renoula, Popi, Titika, Melpo/their names—singing birds **Victoria Theodorou**. Picnic.

Renouncing you,/forever/renouncing you. **Elsie Alvarado de Ricord**. Passengers in transit.

Resting on the alien garden of your forehead, **Lan Ling**. The arrival.

Restless/restless with the rolling rocks **Katerina Anghelaki-Rooke**. My mama and satan.

Restless night,/My tangled hair **Yosano Akiko**. Tangled hair.

The return is bleak. Where morning had **Virginia de Araújo**. Wild nights.

Ri rina rina wo ri ri nawo rina **Anonymous**. untitled.

Riches I hold in light esteem/and Love I laugh to scorn **Emily Brontë**. Riches I hold in light esteem.

Rider of dream, the body as an image **Muriel Rukeyser**. Nine poems for the unborn child.

Right away they call you a statue. **Kiki Dimoula**. Mark of recognition.

ripping the skin off a dead rabbit **Michelene Wandor**. untitled.

Risen from who knows what shadows **Antonia Pozzi**. Awakening.

Ritual brought us together under that wide **Madeline De-Frees**. Lecture under the moose.

The river—as I know it—runs from a dam at my cousins' sugar mill down to **Michelle Cliff**. Obsolete geography.

The river "comes down": the dam breaks; rocks shift; animals are carried **Michelle Cliff**. Obsolete geography.

the river for the poem **Barbara Moraff**. untitled.

the road is strewn with fallen wings **Wilmette Brown**. Bushpaths.

The road-makers made it well **May Sinclair**. Field ambulance in retreat.

The rock grows brittle/From which I spring, **Else Lasker-Schüler**. My people.

Rock of the dome/she said/not dome of the rock **Shirley Kaufman**. Jerusalem notebook.

Roll call, shout em out/Phyliss Wheatley/Sojourner Truth **Pat Parker**. untitled.

Rolling pants' legs, bundling skirts, **Debora Greger**. The shallows.

romeo couldn't come **Ellen Marie Bissert**. A romance.

the rooks and maidens in a/green row **Michelene Wandor**. fields.

The room deciduous/as autumn **Pamela Victorine**. Menses: a seasonal.

The room is one brown color **Alice Karle**. untitled.

Rooming houses are old women/rocking dark windows into their whens **Audre Lorde** Rooming houses are old women.

Root hanging in the air,/I want to hold you **Chung Ling**. Song of rootless people.

The rose of Heaven—/Its red appears **Ping Hsin (Hsien Wan-ying)**. Multitudinous stars and spring waters.

Rose whose soul unfolds white petaled **Angelina Weld Grimké**. Rosabel.

Rounding the edges/until precision feeds into form **Bonnie Lateiner**. The word.

Rrrrrrrraaarghr/We have paid you back **Hind bint Utba**. Fury against the Moslems at Uhud.

Rumor, stir of ripeness/rising within this girl **Muriel Rukeyser**. Song: the calling-up. (Käthe Kollwitz).

Running down/Atlanta/streets/With my sign **Alice Walker**. Once.

Running through the house, out the gate **Marina Rivera**. Chon.

Running to me—/My wiping moss— **Anonymous**. The wiping moss from the ruins.

Rustier than tin,/the finger of the post. **Marina Tsvetayeva**. Poem of the end.

Sad eyes, my owl, my groom **Celia Gilbert**. At the ball.

sadists use coal-tar soap **Michèle Roberts**. he is merely socially inept.

Safe in their Alabaster Chambers— **Emily Dickinson**. 216.

Said the Lion to the Lioness—'When you are amber dust,— **Edith Sitwell**. Heart and mind.

st. louis/such a colored town/a whiskey **Ntozake Shange**. Nappy edges (A cross country sojourn).

St. Patrick's Dean, your country's pride, **Esther Johnson**. To Dr. Swift on his birthday, 30th November 1721.

the salts. rhetorical sky against the sea. **Lina de Feria**. Kinfolk.

The same voice, the same glance, **Anna Akhmatova**. Two poems.

Sammy Lou of Rue/sent to his reward **Alice Walker**. Revolutionary petunias.

San Antonio,/They called you lazy. **Carmen Tafolla**. San Antonio.

Sand evy'where over/Janis sweepin **Mari Evans**. Janis.

Sand swirls a halo/round the dark mother   Africa **Geraldine L. Wilson**. REFUGEE MOTHER.

Sat in the pub/Drink flowing free **Maureen Burge**. The diet.

Satisfied, unsatisfied,/satiated or numb with hunger, **Hilda Doolittle**. The flowering of the rod. (V).

saturdays always come on/time— **Pat Nottingham**. Entries: 14.

Save me from such as me assaile, **Mary Sidney Herbert, Countess of Pembroke**. Psalm lix.

The saw gleams in her hand like a cat's teeth. **Joan Swift**. 1933.

saw spring smiles emerge **Jeanette Adams**. missed you.

Say farewell o tooth like the Isle/of Lump no longer will you be connected **Barbara Guest.** The tooth quilt. (The mushroom quilt from water mill.)

Say what you will in two/Words and get through. **Marie-Françoise-Catherine de Beauveau, La Marquise de Boufflers.** Air: Sentir avec ardeur.

Scared, not too bad, not past claiming **Virginia de Araújo.** Letter to Connie in the Maine woods.

a scarf blows off your head in the wind **Maureen Owen.** Cubism.

scarlike, the continent/puckers, drawn together **Jan Clausen.** dialectics.

scatter yourself/i told her moving **Irena Klepfisz.** the monkey house and other cages.

Scattered petals gather on the road, **Hatsui Shizue.** untitled.

Scattered, we fall/as in a game of jacks **Teru Kanazawa.** Song to my Nisei mother.

The scene is nature/in painted colors. **Paula Yup.** Opaque.

The scene shifts to morning and sunlight and splendour of flags, **Joan Murray Simpson.** St. Marks, midnight.

The scholar came in from the street, **Vera Rich.** The bronze of Poseidon.

Scholar-type from Winchester or (sometimes) Eton **Maida Stanier.** Freshmen.

The scream of a frog/comes to me from night ponds . . . **María Eugenia Vaz Ferreira.** The vacuous rime.

The sea/tore a rib from its side **Malka Heifetz Tussman.** Water without sound.

The sea its thousands of waves **Gabriela Mistral.** Rocking.

The sea of Scaramaga—tied down **Kiki Dimoula.** Tied down.

The sea was and is forever. **Cecilia Meireles.** Absolete sea.

Sealed in rainlight one/November sleepwalking afternoon streets **Elaine Feinstein.** The magic apple tree.

The season of changing clothes **Nakamura Teijo.** untitled.

a second woman arrives open/flipped thru doors her body **Susan Efros.** Kaiser Hospital trilogy: three women at the mercy of unknown gods.

Second-hand platitudes like antique watches **Paula Gunn Allen.** Catching one clear thought alive.

Secretly, I have always known and counted reasons for bad luck. **Diane Wakoski.** Dried flower under my pillow. (Largely because of coincidence and partly because of chance, I have taken up a new address at 47th Street and Avenue F).

Secretly I use you to masturbate several times a day. You don't know why **Gloria Frym.** Voodoo.

See, Girl, those metals in the moon **Wendy Rose.** Moon metals: inventing a new daughter.

See, Phoebus breaking from willing skies, **Anne Finch, Countess of Winchilsea.** The consolation.

See that apple tree, mellow and strong, **Nancy Morejón.** Apple tree in Oakland.

See! The gleam/on my fishing line **Fukuda Chiyo-Ni.** untitled.

see what you like **Barbara Szerlip.** Lines upon waking. (Four short poems).

The Seed-Merchant has lost his son, **Agnes Grozier Herbertson.** The Seed-Merchant's son.

Seeing tiny winter frost against cedar bough **Nia Francisco.** She-bear.

Seen on a Night in November **Adelaide Crapsey.** Niagara.

sees herself in a white silk linen blazer, **Nellie Wong.** A woman at the window.

Self expands to take in hawk take in hawk's gulf of air **Desirée Flynn.** From the rain forest.

send me your address a picture, I want to **Diane di Prima.** Brass furnace going out: song after an abortion.

The sensual children sucking drowsy thumbs **Joan Murray Simpson.** Le bonheur.

SENSUOUS/SLOE EYES/SOFT LIPPED **Jo Ann Hall-Evans.** SEDUCTION.

Sentence/And the word falls like a stone **Anna Akhmatova.** Requiem 1935–1940.

September born, reared in the sunset hour, **Anne Wilkinson.** Summer acres.

September. The rabbi didn't know her. **Jan Heller Levi.** Formal feeling (A sequence for my mother).

The serpent does not crouch at Athene's feet. **Hilda Doolittle.** Helios and Athene.

The setting sun is molten gold. **Li Ch'ing-chao.** To the tune "Eternal happiness."

seven years ago/at forty-five/i knew it was time **Astra.** Now or never.

seven years ago/or more/we heated it in the intensity of our dreams **Gloria Gayles.** Cracked.

The seventeenth stanza. My heart aches, my tears fall. **Ts'ai Yen.** Eighteen verses sung to a Tatar reed whistle. (XVII).

Sex. as they harshly call it, **Adrienne Rich.** Two songs.

The shades are pulled, but still I hear the rain. Under the streetlight **Phyllis Thompson.** Rainwater.

shadows deepen the road like water **Susan North.** Small poem for Michael.

Shadows dressed in silence/weaken the summer **Francisca Ossandón.** untitled.

The shadows of the torn gree/Plantain leaves toss in disorder. **Sun Tao-hsüan.** To the tune "A dream song."

Shake hands with time; make ready to depart **Phyllis Hartnoll.** A death abroad.

Shall earth no more inspire thee, **Emily Brontë.** Shall earth no more inspire thee?

Shall I charge like a bull/against this sleepy town, **Auvaiyar.** untitled.

Shall I come there, or you here? **Hafsa bint al-Hajj.** untitled.

Shall I come to see/plum blossoms in every stream **Lady Ise.** untitled.

shall we go to jonestown or the disco **Ntozake Shange.** jonestown or the disco.

Shall we not lay our holly wreath **Diana Gurney.** The fallen.

"Shame--ee, shamee-ee," they cried. "You have garments on your back. **Naomi Clark.** Magdalene.

Shape, the strong and awful Spirit, **Anna Hempstead Branch.** The monk in the kitchen.

Sharp, double-edged and gleaming like a sword **Muriel Box.** The price of love.

She/wolf/carries a prairie story **Lois Elaine Griffith.** Fire wind's song to Sundae (Loba).

She. A flower perhaps, a pool of fresh water . . . **Lucha Corpi.** She (Marina distant).

She acquired an eye/for cracks and chips **Janet Sternburg.** My mother's breakfront.

She boards the bus at Chinatown,/holding the brown paper shopping bag **Laureen Mar.** Chinatown 1.

She brought us a month noisy with rain **Asphodel.** Full moon in Malta.

she called to say she thought/she'd died **Regina Williams.** For our life is a matter of faith.

She calls you a rock./He calls you a rock. **Jo Carrillo.** Beyond the Cliffs of Abiquiu.

She can't wait for you to knock/so she can ignore you. **Sandra Rogers.** Waiting for her man too long.

She coaxes her fat in front of her **Naomi Long Madgett.** New day.

She comes to beg. Without a tambourine, without **Beverly Tanenhaus.** untitled.

She could paint with one hand **Joan Aleshire.** Exhibition of women artists (1790–1900).

She cried, 'Laura' up the garden, **Christina Rossetti.** Goblin market.

She curls her darkened lashes; manicures **May O'Rourke.** The minority: 1917.

She died away from home/Moved to floral rooms **Diana Chang.** On seeing my great-aunt in a funeral parlor.

she explains/i used to do surface dives **Mary Winfrey.** the conditioning.

she gives herself to a burning man, **Nzadi Zimele-Keita (Michelle McMichael).** long road rhythms.

She had not reached him at my heart **Elizabeth Barrett Browning.** Bianca among the nightingales.

She had thought the studio would keep itself; **Adrienne Rich.** Living in sin.

She has come, the stranger. **Mririda n'Ait Attik.** The second wife.

She has taken a woman lover **Judy Grahn.** Carol, in the park, chewing on straws. (The common woman).

She has thee all; whilst *I* with silent Greif, **Aphra Behn.** To Lysander, on some verses he writ, and asking more for his heart then 'twas worth.

She has tight,/protruding eyes. She is behind **Virginia Gilbert.** Leaving, the sepulcre city.

She hated the rain. Never could figure out what people be **Sapphire.** untitled.

she hated the women/who worshipped her falsely **Michelene Wandor.** Olive Schreiner.

She is a black crow being driven out of sight. **Tan Ying.** Drinking the wind.

She is a Sybil/of ignorant possibilities **Elizabeth Gross.** blackbirds over water.

She is cut away: a rising **Angela Langfield.** The chariot.

She is dead, thank God. **Elizabeth Keeler.** Daughter's funeral dirge at a Saturday burial (Union gravediggers quit at noon).

She is graceful/My young darling **Anonymous.** untitled.

she is in a white dress/kneeling **Susan Griffin.** Breviary.

she is marvellous/the bosom, the nose **Michèle Roberts.** in the bar.

She is shameless, despicable, vile **Zinaida Gippius.** She.

She is too young to eat/chocolates **Colleen J. McElroy.** Defining it for Vanessa.

She is very beautiful **Anonymous.** untitled.

She kept finding arrowheads **Paula Gunn Allen.** Madonna of the hills.

She knows, being woman, that for him she holds **Lizette Woodworth Reese.** The second wife.

She leaned her head upon her hand **Frances Ellen Watkins Harper.** Vashti.

she lives alone/normally **Michèle Roberts.** busy Lizzie.

She looked out the window at some inward greying door. **Roberta Hill.** Leap in the dark.

she looks at me/and i see the knife **Marnie Walsh.** Vickie Loans-Arrow 1972.

She looks at me still/scathing me still **Barbara Gravelle.** The new Joan come out of the fire.

She made no sound/but held her body as/a driveling wind **Wendy Brooks Wieber.** The other. (One, The other, And).

She neglects her work. **Becky Birtha.** The woman in Buffalo is given to waiting.

she never wanted/no never once/did she wanna/be white/to pass **mary hope lee.** on not bein.

she opens her sweet gullible cunt **Judith Kazantzis.** shout.

She placed cotton soaked in oil/on her arms **Helen Wong Huie.** My mother's arms.

She ran with her ball in her light dress floating and free **Eleanor Farjeon.** The girl with the ball.

She reigns in the tarred cottage in the corn, **Ruth Pitter.** The old woman.

She rose to his Requirement—dropt **Emily Dickinson.** 732.

she runs coatless/colder than winter **Akua Lezli Hope.** No one comes home to lonely women.

she said:/he told me that he loved me **Fay Chiang.** choreopoem IV; 1935/chinatown.

She said disowning is the only treason. **Stephanie Strickland.** Love that gives us ourselves.

She said, If tomorrow my world were torn in two, **Phyllis McGinley.** The 5:32.

She said the Jehovah Witness man/gave her the cane to walk with. **Gayl Jones.** 3-31-70. (Journal).

She said to one: 'How glows **Elizabeth Daryush.** Subalterns.

She sank however into my soul A weight of sadness **Adrienne Rich.** For Ethel Rosenberg.

She saw it like a shape, like a joy **Gayl Jones.** Salvation.

she say goddam you/charlene them kids of yours **Marnie Walsh.** Vickie Loans-Arrow 1972.

She says 'How was you?' Kissing. 'Come on in, **Anna Adams.** Unrecorded speech.

She says these words,   made this remark: **Anonymous.** untitled.

She shakes in the take-off lounge. **Judith Kazantzis.** The frightened flier goes north.

She showed me her real hair **Shirley Kaufman.** Meron.

She sighed, but soon it mixed with common air, **Anne Finch, Countess of Winchilsea.** The loss.

She sits in the house for days on end. **Dahlia Ravikovitch.** Portrait.

She sleeps on a cot in the living room. **Lynn Emanuel.** Silence. She is six years old.

She smelled him right away: the woodsy twang of cologne he wore: the **Alexis De Veaux.** French doors: a vignette.

"She speaks in a slight accent about her wild seas **Gabriela Mistral.** Stranger.

She stands as pale as Parian statues stand; **Christina Rossetti.** A soul.

she stood there like a Inca statue, African earrings—hanging **Amina Baraka.** Sortin-out.

she strolls in the valley, alone **Michèle Roberts.** madwoman at Rodmell.

She tells you she is beautiful. **Beverly Tanenhaus.** untitled.

She thought she woke up. **Joy Harjo.** The black room.

She turns and calls him by name, **Rachel.** His wife.

she waited on the 7th floor **Ntozake Shange.** Frank Albert & Viola Benzena Owens.

She wakes first./Goes to her basket where the spools sit **Susan MacDonald.** Seamstress.

She walketh veiled and sleeping,/For she knoweth not her power; **Charlotte Perkins Gilman.** She walketh veiled and sleeping.

She wanted to arrive in heaven with beautiful hair, **Joan Swift.** My grandmother's hair.

She was there before Ceasar's day **Edith Lovejoy Pierce.** Pattern.

She was unloaded and delivered to us, glory be! **Anonymous.** untitled.

She was wearing the coral taffeta trousers **Victoria Sackville-West.** Full moon.

She went out making hats when she was young **Jean Pedrick.** Hats.

She who carries/in her heart a love **Yosano Akiko.** untitled.

She who continues./She Who has a being **Judy Grahn.** untitled.

she who has no love for women/married and housekeeping **Elaine Feinstein.** Calliope in the labour ward.

She wouldn't like Agnes to be/like some types today. **Kathleen Fraser.** Agnes.

She'd be sitting by the fire, **Kathleen Fraser.** Agnes.

the sheets are damp/where i lay **Felice Newman.** Rites of spring.

She's a copperheaded waitress, **Judy Grahn.** Ella, in a square apron, along Highway 80. (The common woman).

she's going, the nice girl who smiled **Michèle Roberts.** poem on the day of the autumn equinox.

She's going to the Negev/he's going to study medicine in Italy **Miriam Oren.** About her & about him.

she's so fine/she's so bad/foxy lady **Fay Chiang.** choreopoem I.

She's the figure skater you've always hated, **Sandra M. Gilbert.** The one he loves. (The love sequence).

She's walking all alone in the jungle **Victoria Theodorou.** Nuyen Ti Soy.

A shine and shock/Are scarlet lilies **Anne Welsh.** Sight.

Shining pins that dart and click **Jessie Pope.** Socks.

The ship will never tame **May Miller.** The trip back. (Not that far).

ships in deep water **Barbara Moraff.** untitled.

Shirley Aphrodite! I'm with you still in Lockland **Roberta Lefkowitz.** Scrawl.

shit i hate those hospitals **Carol Bergé.** tessa's song.

Shiva/is dancing/in the fire **Carol Tinker.** untitled.

Shivering, cold, I run/Blindly into the city. **Adrianne Marcus.** Alone, we dream as gods.

The shopkeeper hands you/a key. It is to a box **Virginia Gilbert.** Outside the Kampsongs, at the market, waiting.

Should I know this room, **Penelope Shuttle.** Locale.

Should you ask me whence those stories, **Maida Stanier.** Hiawatha's pancake.

Shout, shout, up with your song! **Cicely Hamilton.** The march of the women.

Showfare cost a lot/but we ran the/movies every chance **Sherley Anne Williams.** The iconography of childhood.

Shuttle-cock and battle-door/A little pink-love **Mina Loy.** Love songs. (V).

sick folks/n spells that so n so's **Ntozake Shange.** sassafrass.

Sick I am and tired of this everyone **Ann Dunn.** untitled.

sideman/how many edges fill? **Alice Karle.** untitled.

Sighing, sleeping alone all night, **Mother of Michitsuna.** untitled.

the sign of blessing/from the Mother **Miriam Dyak.** Three.

A silence slipping around like death, **Angelina Weld Grimké.** A winter twilight.

Silent is the House—all are laid asleep; **Emily Brontë.** Silent is the House.

Silent, scuffing the grass/The gulls circled the pond, **Frances Gill.** Gulls.

Silent, submissive, still,/on antiseptic slabs **Rita Peck.** Fish market.

the silent world i guard/builds with its dream **Reina María Rodríguez.** From my guard post watching the world.

Silently/time passes. **Hatsui Shizue.** untitled.

A silken transfer waking from sleep **May Miller.** Place in the morning.

Silver dust/lifted from the earth, **Hilda Doolittle.** The pear tree.

Since I don't know my mother, **Baba Akiko.** untitled.

Since I've felt this pain **Ono no Komachi.** untitled.

Since Naturally Black is Naturally Beautiful **Audre Lorde.** Naturally.

Since our relations/are like the crumbling **Sei Shōnagon.** untitled.

Since the images you demand/cling to me **Nishi Junko.** Revolution.

Since "the pillow knows all" **Lady Ise.** untitled.

Since they have died to give us gentleness, **May Wedderburn Cannan.** 'Since they have died.'

Since you walked out on me **Nina Cassian.** Lady of miracles.

Sing a song of War-time, **Nina Macdonald.** Sing a song of War-time.

Sing! Let us sing out, **Hien Luong.** Songs that cannot be silenced.

singing a prolonged hymn of expectation **Michele Murray.** At sixteen.

Singing and shouting they swept to the treacherous forest **Margery Lawrence.** The lost army.

A single post, a point of rusting/tin in the sky **Marina Tsvetayeva.** Poem of the end.

Sister,/do not marry/to forget **Toi Derricotte.** For a god-child, Regina, on the occasion of her first love.

Sister, don't scold me. **Mririda n'Ait Attik.** Sister.

Sister Maureen Murphy, a teaching nun in **Toi Derricotte.** The testimony of Sister Maureen.

Sisters/git yr/blk/asses/out of that/re/volution/ary's/bed. **Sonia Sanchez.** rev pimps. (Memorial).

Sisters!/I love you./Because you love you. **Gwendolyn Brooks.** To those of my sisters who kept their naturals.

Sitting in the maid's room asking her about her daughter, who is some- **Michelle Cliff.** Obsolete geography.

Sitting there on the/assembly line piecing **Carolyn M. Rodgers.** Aunt Dolly.

6 percent of the world's population **Miriam Dyak.** Forbidden sweets.

The skin like burnt glass or **Eeva-Liisa Manner.** untitled.

The sky is covered with darkness, **Anonymous.** untitled.

The sky over Cyprus is blue **Carol Muske.** Special delivery to Curtis: the future of the world.

The sky was blue, so blue that day **Angelina Weld Grimké.** For the candle light.

The sky was gold in those days **Valerie Sinason.** In the beginning.

slapping open handed/transparent boy **Anna Lee Walters.** A teacher taught me.

Sleds were sticking. Wagons/screeched and the small forest **Bella Akhmadulina.** Snowless February.

sleep/the shy girl **Carol Bergé.** tessa's song.

Sleep, darling/I have a small/daughter called/Cleis, who is **Sappho.** Sleep, darling.

Slender bamboos grow by the window. **Pao Ling-hui.** After one of the 19 famous Han poems.

Slender, delicate, soft jade, **Chao Luan-luan.** Slender fingers.

Slender reeds/Cadenced waterfalls **Lucha Corpi.** Rain.

The slender, shy, and sensitive young girl/is woman now, **Margaret Walker.** For Gwen—1969.

Slender, unrepenting women/harvesting shells by the sea **Victoria Theodorou.** Picnic.

Slim sentinels/Stretching lacy arms **Helene Johnson.** Trees at night.

Slow wand'ring came the sightless sire and she, **Henrietta Cordelia Ray.** Antigone and Oedipus.

Small cherries sip delicately **Chao Luan-luan.** Red sandalwood mouth.

Small paths go straggling over the heath **Henriette Roland-Holst.** Small paths.

A small rain falls on lovers **Patricia Henley.** To grave, to cradle.

The smell, smell/of your cigar, **Marina Tsvetayeva.** The smell, smell.

Smile, Death, see I smile as I come to you **Charlotte Mew.** Smile, death.

Smile lie rockets/opens his arms of an aquatic **Iris Zavala.** Smile lie rockets . . .

Smiles of the world/wrapped in rancid air **Lucha Corpi.** Our worlds.

Smoke./A mud brown haze/of barbeques, trucks coughing, **Kate Ellen Braverman.** Weekend man.

The smoke traces its figure over the papers. **Soleida Ríos.** Difficult hour.

Snakes bears those animals/with death in their bellies **Shirley Kaufman.** Jerusalem notebook.

The snow dances and the frost flies. **Chu Shu-chên.** Plum blossoms.

snow in a strange city/hungry in the morning **Jan Clausen.** dialectics.

Snow in the winter, **Shirley Kaufman.** Claims.

The snowdeer licking salt/anticipates the frozen river. **Pamela Victorine.** untitled.

Snowmountains/way to Aspen **Alice Karle.** untitled.

A snowy morning/Everywhere II, II, II (two, two, two) **Den Sute-Jo.** untitled.

so a book didn't fall on you/out of the sky like a bomb, **Jan Clausen.** Poem on the occasion of not receiving The Academy of American Poets' Walt Whitman Award for an outstanding first manuscript of poetry.

So cold the air freezes, dropping in scales **Adelaide Blomfield.** Attics.

So did my poor hurt Solitude accuse me. **Naomi Replansky.** I met my Solitude.

So easy to stir up a feast **Lisel Mueller.** Stone soup.

So he opes a vaster knowledge to the view, **Elizabeth Wolstenholme-Elmy.** Woman free. (LVI).

So he that saileth in this world of pleasure, **Anne Bradstreet.** Contemplations.

So, it's a gorgeous afternoon in the park **Donna Kate Rushin.** The tired poem: last letter from a typical un-employed black professional woman.

So just as that wild animal, the sea, **Wendy Battin.** The lives we invite to flower among us flower beyond us.

So, kneeling by the river bank **Margaret Walker.** Prophets for a new day.

So laying the armour aside/I do not appeal the judgement **Barbara Gravelle.** The new Joan come out of the fire.

So many years between my love/and your absence. **Claudia Lars.** Letters written when night grows.

So Miss Myrtle is going to marry? **Helen Selina (Lady Dufferin).** The charming woman.

So much she caused she cannot not account for **Elizabeth Jennings.** Old woman.

So now I have this will to make: **Etel Adnan.** The enemy's testament.

So then we came to the Island, **Vera Brittain.** We shall come no more.

So they don't expect/letters.   So they wait for— **Marina Tsvetayeva.** A letter.

so to tell the truth/we must make fiction **Janet Dubé.** So to tell the truth.

so today finally I was no longer waiting **Miriam Dyak.** Dying.

So warm I may melt. **Christina Jenkins.** Sunday morning.

So we were reading poems/About people dying **Lynda Efros.** untitled.

so what life is hard, bitter & sad **Ellen Marie Bissert.** Farewell.

So you are all contradiction, **Elizabeth Dixon.** Ranmore.

So you have swept me back, **Hilda Doolittle.** Eurydice. (I).

So you're home from the wars, **Martha Collins.** Homecoming.

soap/toilet paper/a grocery list begins **Margaret Porter.** when i rite.

A soft grey mist,/Poppies flamed brilliant where the woodlands bend **Aimee Byng Scott.** July 1st, 1916.

Soft hangs the opiate in the brain, **Maria White Lowell.** An opium fantasy.

Soft lamp shinin/and me alone in the night. **Sherley Anne Williams.** Any woman's blues.

A solemn discourse is not necessary **Ann Lauterbach.** The yellow linen dress: a sequence.

Solemnly swearing, to swear as an oath to you **Judy Grahn.** Vera, from my childhood. (The common woman).

A solo full of quivering flesh flying **Jayne Cortez.** Solo.

Some come in the window **Alice Karle.** untitled.

Some covenant is broken. **Joan LaBombard.** The covenant.

Some keep the Sabbath going to Church— **Emily Dickinson.** 324.

Some people see only you **Ana Blandiana.** The couple.

Some there are who say that the fairest thing seen **Sappho.** untitled.

Some white men came to Acoma and Laguna a hundred years ago **Leslie Marmon Silko.** Toe'osh: a Laguna coyote story.

Some words, seldom spoken/and then whispered only, I **Sherley Anne Williams.** What is love if it is only known through words saying it would be hard for me to leave you? (The house of desire).

somebody almost walked off wid alla my stuff **Ntozake Shange.** untitled.

Someday when I'm even more tired **Gabriela Mistral.** Death sonnets.

Someone/clinks/a ring of keys/relentlessly **Veronica Porumbacu.** With a ring.

Someone said/to/me/that/if the South/rises/again **Alice Walker.** Once.

Someone squeezed the juice/of a black fruit in my soul: **Dulce María Loynaz.** Premonition.

Someone's lost and someone turns on the light. **Barbara Anderson.** There and here.

Something hums in the mind's ear. **Sara Miles.** Through the weather.

Something in her holds a little back, **Cory Wade.** Enough.

Something keeps me from screaming **Michele Murray.** The woman who lives inside the world. (7).

Something once bloomed/That lit the walls **May Miller.** Rhodes. (Not that far).

Sometime during the third expedition, **Robin Becker.** The landing.

sometimes/someone/quite blond/and black **Ruth Weiss.** There is no evil only restlessness!

sometimes at night/i hear snatches **Felice Newman.** Rites of spring.

Sometimes I feel so bad/I ask myself **Alice Walker.** FAMILY OF.

Sometimes I see reflections on bits of glass on sidewalks **Genny Lim.** Wonder woman.

Sometimes in the over-heated house, but not for long, **Charlotte Mew.** Fame.

Sometimes she forgets that her oldest daughter is a little girl. **Suzanne Juhasz.** Shimmering threads like hair.

Sometimes the rumor of a death/just beginning in someone **Ellen Wittlinger.** Someone you love.

sometimes we could feel the impending close **Johari M. Kunjufu.** Story for the remainder.

Sometimes we get up/Get up as for a resurrection **Marie Luise Kaschnitz.** Resurrection.

Sometimes you do it to the children **Judith Kazantzis.** Playing water polo in Angola in the words of an ex-South African mercenary, 32 Battalion, reported Feb '81.

sometimes you look like lady day/the smokiness of yr silence **Jessica Tarahata Hagedorn.** Sometimes you look like lady day.

sometimes you look like lady day/the way you hang yr head **Jessica Tarahata Hagedorn.** Sometimes you look like lady day.

sometimes you look like lady day/the way your eyes are colorless with pain **Jessica Tarahata Hagedorn.** Sometimes you look like lady day.

Somewhere/under my sleep/I am awake, **Virginia Gilbert.** untitled.

Son, of great fortune have I none **Christine de Pisan.** Christine to her son.

The son replied,"For all your good advice, **Parvin E'Tesami.** To his father on praising the honest life of the peasant.

the song starts when you know/how to hold one note **Susan North.** Poem for her thirty-fifth birthday.

A song to your blood./Your heart, magnificent inexorable pump. **Molly Myerowitz Levine.** A song to your blood.

Soon I shall cease to be. **Izumi Shikibu.** untitled.

Soon I will climb the hill to the sunlight, **Desirée Flynn.** From the rain forest.

Sorrows play at the edge of these willow leaf curves. **Chao Luan-luan.** Willow eyebrows.

Soulfolk, think a minute **Margaret Goss Burroughs.** To soulfolk.

A sound like a small wind **Alice Walker.** Part II: The Child. (Early losses: a requiem).

sound rising/acquires a/musical structure **Carol Tinker.** a smart & final iris.

Soweto/when i hear your name **Jayne Cortez.** For the brave young students in Soweto.

Spaghetti in a big kettle, an apron on, I am cooking spaghetti. **Phyllis Koestenbaum.** Blood journey.

Sparkling glass/seeing eyes/glossiness blinds **Rota Silverstrini.** The fish tank.

Spastic man/I love you/I want to take you **Susan Kennedy Calhoun.** Mission Street bus.

Speak earth and bless me with what is richest **Audre Lorde.** Love poem.

Speak, heralds of our honored dead **Margaret Walker.** THIS IS MY CENTURY . . . black synthesis of time.

Speak the truth to the people **Mari Evans.** Speak the truth to the people.

Speak to me. Take my hand. What are you now? **Muriel Rukeyser.** Effort at speech between two people.

speaking of marriage/the particulars **Jill Gernand.** girl talk.

Spent is the torch of Love, broken his dart, **Barbara Torelli-Strozzi.** On the murder of her husband.

Spicier. The best thing would be snow, and soon. **Jane Miller** 5 a.m.

The Spiker holds a Silver Ball **Emily Dickinson.** 605.

Spires of Grace Church, **Lola Ridge.** Spires.

Spirit flowers are our lives, **Della Burt.** Spirit flowers.

The spirits of children are remote and wise, **Frances Cornford.** Ode on the whole duty of parents.

Spirits of the abnormally born/live on in water **Audre Lorde.** October.

Spittle washes my face, **Teru Kanazawa.** untitled.

Splendid song of red swan **Cleva Solís.** January moon.

Sprays of frost flowers form **Ping Hsin (Hsieh Wan-ying).** (Multitudinous stars and spring waters).

spring comes late to these/upthrust slabs **Jan Clausen.** (the road). (dialectics).

Spring comes slowly—/after/stormy winters and **Rosemari Mealy.** untitled.

Spring comes: the flowers learn their coloured shapes. **Maria Konopnicka.** A vision.

Spring has come to the women's quarters. **Li Ch'ing-chao.** To the tune "A hilly garden."

Spring has passed/and it seems as if summer had come, **Empress Jitō.** The sudden appearance of cherry blossoms.

spring is reverent **Felice Newman.** Rites of spring.

Spring trees grow heavy **Alice Karle.** untitled.

The sprouting grass waiting for spring, **Gio.** untitled.

I spy butterfly/In quietly still waters **Paula Yup.** Peace.

Squeeze not my hands/for eternity will come, **Gabriela Mistral.** Intimate.

Stairs arise out of a village **Olga Broumas.** Mornings remembering last nights.

Standing in the 14th st snack place **Fran Winant.** Dyke jacket.

Stars are shining/the eyes of men are closed **Rabi'a al-Adawiyya.** Two prayers.

The stars have not yet retired, and the sky is still dark. **Anonymous.** Women Transport Corps.

The stars pass./The moon passes. **Empress Jitō.** untitled.

Start with the bounds. What's to go out or stay. **Ann Stanford.** Composing the garden.

the starter hunched/at the blocks quivers with the whole race **Barbara Szerlip.** The crossing.

Statuary used to fill the gardens of rich **Linda Gregg.** Lilith.

Stay, shade of my shy treasure! Oh, remain, **Juana de Asbaje.** untitled.

Stay with my work./I decided not to answer; **Rosalie Moore.** The phone.

Steer me my splendid ship/Of memory, your sails unfurled **Erica Marx.** Speeding ship.

(Steingeroll) new signs putting/short putting new signs **Anonymous.** The dance of the greased women.

Steps   Steps/Spaces   inbetween   steps **Alice Karle.** untitled.

Still are there wonders of the dark and day; **Angelina Weld Grimké.** To keep the memory of Charlotte Forten Grimké.

Still falls the Rain— **Edith Sitwell.** Still falls the Rain.

still I walk the perimeter/of her house: **Mary Patten.** Mother.

Still, it's *how* we negotiate **Akua Lezli Hope.** Getting to know, or stepping out in an entirely different way.

Still the walls do not fall, **Hilda Doolittle.** The walls do not fall. (XLIII).

Still they burn on, the wind-sown poppies, **Barbara Noel Scott.** The wild poppies.

Stir up your warm waves within her **Margriet Schaye.** An old witch's warning to a young man in love.

Stone for stone/No questions **May Miller.** Egypt. (Not that far).

Stone of embittered particles, **Maya Islas.** untitled.

Stoplights edged the licorice street with ribbon, **Roberta Hill.** Leap in the dark.

The straight flagged road breaks into dust, into a thin white **May Sinclair.** Field ambulance in retreat.

A straight flagged road, laid on the rough earth, **May Sinclair.** Field ambulance in retreat.

The straight in a curve/is what Matisse is after **Diana Chang.** What Matisse is after.

Strange that the self's continuum should outlast **Kathleen Raine.** The transit of the gods.

Stream sorrow, eyes:/wailing-weary **Tumadir al-Khansa.** Elegy for her brother, Sakhr.

Stridor! Trucks hurl themselves **Barbara Howes.** Shunpike.

Struggle of class/etched across the richness/of my flesh— **Rashidah Ismaili.** Struggle of class.

stuck and calm/i want what you want **Carol Tinker.** untitled.

Stuck in old Oedipal dreams/I will have a king or no one, **Elizabeth Keeler.** Of generations and being woman.

Such is the force of each created thing **Anne Collins.** The soul's home.

Sucked by the tongue and the lips **June Jordan.** From sea to shining sea.

The sudden warning has arrived! **Concha Michel.** In the vital process (1964).

Suddenly/she is sitting/by the river **Kristina McGrath.** The afternoon in May. (Sequence from blue to blue).

Suddenly in the square by Onofrio's Small Fountain **Joan LaBombard.** In the old city: Dubrovnik.

Suddenly nothing is coming right. **Joan Larkin.** Song.

Suddenly, willessly, within/a comfortably rainy hour, I thought: **Bella Akhmadulina.** Bartholomew's night.

Suicides & spinsters—/all our kind! **Erica Jong.** Dear Colette.

A sultry wind blows hot. **Anna Akhmatova.** Deception.

Summer comes./The ziczac hovers **Helene Johnson.** Magalu.

The summer countryside, with the round hills patchy **Lyn Hejinian.** We are not forgetting the patience of the mad, their love of detail.

The summer day suffocates, smothers, pants **Anna de Noailles.** Poem on azure.

The summer heat dries the partitions of the fallen honey-comb **Sandra McPherson.** Utanikki, August 1978.

Summer matures. Brilliant Scorpion/Appears. **Helene Johnson.** Summer matures.

Summer mornings we/rose early to go/and rob the trees **Sherley Anne Williams.** The iconography of childhood.

The summer that I was ten— **May Swenson.** The centaur.

The sun falls/in a blood-soaked ditch **Katerina Anghelaki-Rooke.** My mama and satan.

The sun fits eyes in bluemountain **Alice Karle.** ''Darkness.''

The sun is setting, dear people. The slight **Jean Symons.** Elegy.

sun on the green plants, your prattle **Diane di Prima.** Brass furnace going out: song, after an abortion.

The sun sets. The wind moans. **Ts'ai Yen.** Eighteen verses sung to a Tatar reed whistle. (VII).

sundays have an ungentle/habit of hanging around **Pat Nottingham.** Entries: 15.

Sunken murmurs rise from the sea bottom **Takiguchi Masako.** Blue horse.

Sunlight in the house/and the rooms **Penelope Shuttle.** Maritimes.

The sunlight that pulls itself over the roof-tops looks vacant, **Kirti Chaudhari.** Inertia.

the supremes done gone/and sold their soul **Sonia Sanchez.** The supremes-cuz they dead. (Memorial).

Sure as the brakes on a Buick, **Nancy Sullivan.** For my Aunt Florence who when praying gives God not only her friends' names but also their addresses.

susie was assigned to die. **Alta.** susie.

suspended/in pastel silence **Pat Crutchfield Exum.** 3 serendipitous poems.

The swallows pass in restless companies. **Mary Webb.** Swallows.

swaying in the summer breeze/a piece of rope   two bales of hay to stand on **Judith McDaniel.** November passage.

Sweat begins to ooze from Compass's/forehead **Inoue Michiko.** Get angry, Compass.

Sweet and sad/like love overwhelmed **Yosano Akiko.** untitled.

Sweet Anne of Winchilsea, you were no hellion **Dilys Laing.** Sonnet to a sister in error.

Sweet Ethel was a roaming gal **Linda Piper.** Sweet Ethel.

Sweef soft face/Bloated and defiled **Jessica Tarahata Hagedorn.** Fillmore Street poems: August, 1967.

Swirling spring/Blossoming tree **Ricarda Huch.** Young girl.

Swish, swash, went Fatima's shoes **Judith Kazantzis.** Fatima.

swiss memories/carve a scree/in my mind **Michelene Wandor.** dream.

A sword/flexible, supple and strong **Karin Boye.** A sword.

Takamura Kotaro/speaks/of fireplaces **Geraldine Kudaka.** On writing Asian-American poetry.

Take back that Heart, you with such Caution give, **Aphra Behn.** To Lysander, on some verses he writ, and asking more for his heart than 'twas worth.

Take calendars./Take a morning, waking **Barbara Szerlip.** How to determine your birthday upon waking in a strange place which is more than likely your own bed.

Take care, he said, your poems are almost **Jane Augustine.** After Yeats.

Take it as you will, not violently **Georgina Herrera.** Introduction and apology.

Take this rose and share with me **Rosemari Mealy.** New chapters for our history.

Taking one poem to make another **Elise Passavant.** Thoughts on the unicorn.

Talk to me. Talk to me. **Chedva Harakavy.** Talk to me, talk to me.

talking proletariat talks/over instant coffee **Ana Castillo.** 1975. (Napa, California).

talking up a storm/in your camel nose **Michelene Wandor.** people, on a bad day.

The Tall prince/leans from the roan mare **Maureen Owen.** Silk-screen.

The tall, tall and handsome man **Denise Salfeld.** Ballad of the handsome man.

Tania died/with the fever of the task still waiting. **Yolanda Ulloa.** Ita.

A Tatar chief forced me to become his wife, **Ts'ai Yen.** Eighteen verses sung to a Tatar reed whistle. (II).

Teach the kings sonne, who king hym selfe shall be, **Mary Sidney Herbert, Countess of Pembroke.** Psalm lxxii.

The teacher has the flowers on her desk, **Marjorie Baldwin.** The nature lesson.

The teacher talks to Pima children. **Rita Garitano.** Morning at Salt River Day School.

a teacher taught me/more than she knew **Anna Lee Walters.** A teacher taught me.

The teachers of my child have forgotten memory **Sarah Appleton.** Book of my hunger, book of the earth.

Teaching physics back in North Dakota, my brother never writes, **Alison Zier.** Postage due.

A tear interrupts/and no lamp is left in the sky. **Eunice Odio.** Portraits of the heart.

Tear it out of the history books! **Pauli Murray.** Dark testament.

The tears gush from my eyes, **Anonymous.** untitled.

Tears in your eyes/You ask for sympathy; **Yosano Akiko.** Tangled hair.

the telephone keeps ringing **Gayl Jones.** Tripart.

Tell everyone/Now, today, I shall **Sappho.** untitled.

Tell me,/Was Venus more beautiful **Amy Lowell.** Venus Transiens.

"Tell me a story, father, please," **Ann Plato.** The natives of America.

tell me if i turn black **Emily Katherine Harris.** Inform me.

Tell me something **Adrienne Rich.** Mother-in-law.

Tell this story of the deer's skull **Susan Griffin.** Deer skull.

Tell your son, my son,/what we endured: **Renata Pallottini.** Message.

Teller of tales sat on a beehive **Jeanne Sirotkin.** Tarantella.

Tempered, annealed, the hard essence of autumn **Pan Chao.** Needle and thread.

The temptation is to shred it, **Ann Lauterbach.** The yellow linen dress: a sequence.

Ten dancers glide/across a mirror floor. **Cecília Meireles.** Ballad of the ten casino dancers.

Ten months I've been/a prisoner of her/iridescent light **Elizabeth Gross.** Sea shell.

Ten more minutes!—Say yer prayers, **Sybil Bristowe.** Over the top.

Ten thousand bees in the backyard. **Laura Chester.** Bees inside me.

Tender he was, perplexed and jealous; yet **Anna Akhmatova.** The white bird.

Tenderness for my mother/who is too old, **Elizabeth Keeler.** Inheritance.

tending palpa/bility, **Rochelle Owens.** Penobscot bird.

A tent with rustling breezes cool **Lady Maisun.** She scorns her husband the Caliph.

Tentacled for food,/You range your underwater neighbourhood. **Naomi Replansky.** In the sea of tears.

The terrible black quarrels, **Joanne de Longchamps.** The glassblower.

Terror of knowing/just so many . . . **Janet Sternburg.** Vitalie.

Than *Cloris* her fair hand withdrew, **Aphra Behn.** The disappointment.

Thanksgiving we talk long distance. **Patricia Henley.** Poem for Charley.

that anger bone mal mamma/that rattle painted red, painted fresh blood, slaughtered enemy **Chrystos.** Give me back.

That boy in the seventh row at the secondary modern **Carla Lanyon Lanyon.** The dunce.

That day during lunch hour/at Alamo which-had-to-be-its-name **Ines Hernandez Tovar.** Para Teresa.

That man over there say/a woman needs to be helped into carriages **Sojourner Truth.** Ain't I a woman?

That nigger is . . . . *Cold* **Akua Lezli Hope.** His own maniac self.

That night, I was a clockwork doll, **Dahlia Ravikovitch.** Clockwork doll.

That "old last act"!/And yet sometimes/all seems post coitum triste **Adrienne Rich.** Two songs.

. . . That our earth mother may wrap herself **Anonymous.** Song to earth mother.

That pink curtain, she says,/reminds her that when she **Dona Stein.** visiting M. at the Happy Valley Nursing Home.

That poem I didn't write/when I wrote poems— **Leah Goldberg.** That poem I didn't write.

That sound like the scratch/scratch of an old recording **Wendy Brooks Wieber.** One. (One, The other, And).

That spring night I spent *See* Pillowed on your arm/only for the dream of a spring night,

That sweet sinewy green nymph **Marge Piercy.** Laocoon is the name of the figure.

That the war would be over before they got to you; **Gwendolyn Brooks.** When you have forgotten Sunday: the love story.

That was the summer you stopped answering the phone, **Sara Miles.** for Nancy.

That was when the war was on, the one we felt good **Linda Gregerson.** How love, when it has been acquired, may be kept. (De arte honeste amandi).

That's what they ordered for the old man **Shirley Kaufman.** Abishag.

Their bodies lined up against the walls **Susan Griffin.** Waiting for truth.

Their hair, pomaded, faces jaded **Maya Angelou.** Sepia fashion show.

Their hands should minister unto the flame of life, **Mary Gabrielle Collins.** Women at munition making.

Their origin and their history patriarchal poetry their **Gertrude Stein.** Patriarchal poetry.

Then a shiver ran down every spine **Bella Akhmadulina.** Rain.

Then laziness like an illness unfolded me **Bella Akhmadulina.** Rain.

then marriage, the baby and making him so mad in that N.Y. apartment **Judith Hemschemeyer.** Indulgence and accidents.

Then. . . . she (Ninmah) made into a woman who **Anonymous.** untitled.

Then the moment slips away from you, **Jan Heller Levi.** My father's wedding. (A sequence for my mother).

then there/was/the charming/half-wit **Alice Walker.** Once.

then there was/the/picture of/the bleak-eyed/little black/girl **Alice Walker.** Once.

Then there was a difference. *See* The First Separation.

there, again you are/fine ladies, fine lips, **Michelene Wandor.** two poetry readings.

There are five people in this room **Alice Walker.** Representing the universe.

There are gargoyles on the ceiling **Irene Friis.** No walls.

There are magpies on the South hill. **Lady Ho.** A song of magpies.

There are many men like you, perhaps **Dorothy Livesay.** One way conversation.

There are many people returning from the market **Anonymous.** Waiting for mother.

there are sixty-five miles/of telephone wire **Joy Harjo.** "Are you still there."

there are some poems that you just don't want to write **Mae Jackson.** My last feeling this way poem.

There are women./The rhythm of their hips **Barbara Szerlip.** Sweet revenge.

There came to me assistance, **Anonymous.** Bride the aid-woman.

There had been death There had been fire **June Jordan.** Poem about a night out: Michael: good-bye for awhile.

there had been no sound: **Irena Klepfisz.** The monkey house and other cages.

There had to have been a wolf that night, **Adrien Stoutenburg.** Riding Hood, updated.

There have been years now **Sukey Durham.** The crossing.

There is a black dog in my painting. **Kathleen Fraser.** Joan Brown, about her painting.

There is a deep brooding/in Arkansas. **Maya Angelou.** My Arkansas.

There is a fish/whose anus is his mouth. **Dilys Laing.** Ocean fable.

There is a peaceful little community **Mitsui Futabako.** Grazing.

There is a place.   There is a miracle. **Muriel Rukeyser.** Nine poems for the unborn child.

There is a poem on the way, **Kathleen Raine.** Invocation.

There is a problem of number. **Judith McCombs.** Advice to the photographers of atrocities.

There is a tree, by day,/That, at night,/Has a shadow, **Angelina Weld Grimké.** Tenebris.

There is a wine shop by the shore of West Lake. **Chu Chung-hsien.** To the tune "A branch of bamboo."

there is a woman/with a mountain/of stones **Mariah Britton Howard.** reports.

there is a woman in this town **Pat Parker.** There is a woman in this town.

There is a woman walks as I walk, carrying packages over her hip as we **Felice Newman.** Sister.

"There is always/the possibility of joy . . ." **Susan North.** Ascent.

There is an aggressive ring at my door **Barbro Backberger.** I'm taking off . . .

There is fifth whiteness/Called   Reality. The brush **Adrianne Marcus.** Alone, we dream as gods.

There is in human closeness a sacred boundary **Anna Akhmatova.** In intimacy there's a secret place.

There is no need now to rush about my life, **Susan Saxe.** Patience. (Notes from the first year).

There is no night/when the lightning does not flash, **Lady Sagami.** untitled.

There is no place we can/look for you, not in the bones of your twin, **Dona Stein.** Map (for Matthew).

there is no reason/for our ecstasy- **Miriam Dyak.** Three.

There is no solitude/like the death of a sinner. **Adrienne Ingrum.** Loomit.

There is no welcome sign. No number **Adrianne Marcus.** Grey: the madness.

There is nothing like the cool/of the wind in this place **Tagami Kikusha-Ni.** The wind from Mt. Fuji.

There is reason for disrespect. **Rashidah Ismaili.** Dialogue.

There is snow in the air, as there is about my heart, **Muriel Grainger.** The scattering.

There is so much blossom and naked dawn **Rafaela Chacón Nardi.** Mountain girl.

There is this edge where shadows **Joy Harjo.** Call it fear.

There is this old man, wistful, hungry, peaked, **Josephine Miles.** Afternoon walk.

There is unfeminine (but oh, so Female) **Susan Saxe.** Questionnaire. (Notes from the first year).

'There it is!—/You play beside a death-bed like a child, **Elizabeth Barrett Browning.** Aurora Leigh.

There let thy bleeding branch atone **Emily Brontë.** There let thy bleeding branch atone.

There lives in/my childhood street/an old woman **Tove Ditlevsen.** Self portrait 4.

there must have been a battle somewhere **Rachel Maines.** 2-15-43/2-15-76.

there shall come clouds of darkness/unto the land— **Sister Bernadine.** The sermon. (Revelations).

There they go marching all in step so gay! **Katharine Tynan.** Joining the colours.

There used to be a second dark bag **Merrill Oliver.** The birthmark.

There was a man,—don't mind his name, **Winifred M. Letts.** The deserter.

There was a man who married a maid. She laughed as/he led her home. **Helen Adam.** I love my love.

There was a Shadow on the moon; I saw it poise and tilt, and go **Rose Macaulay.** The shadow.

There was a small woman called G. **Anonymous.** untitled.

There was always a murder within another murder. **Muriel Rukeyser.** Reading the Kieu. (Searching/not searching).

There was no sound at all, no crying in the village, **Margaret Sackville.** A memory.

There was of course/my father. My old man. **Frankie Hucklenbroich.** Genealogy.

There   was the mountain **Diane Wakoski.** My Chinese fairy tales for La Monte, who dislikes the obvious.

There wasn't a chill even underneath the pines. **Roberta Hill.** Conversation overheard on Tamalpais Road.

There wasn't time between the way/you placed my hands around you **Sara Miles**. More.

There were bizarre beginnings in old lands for the making **Margaret Walker**. Dark blood.

There were only three mystics **Alice Karle**. An epic (with renaissance flute).

There were the clerks of the zenith and the figures, **Josephine Miles**. Nadirs.

There where the rose is harsh and waxen, **Rafaela Chacón Nardi**. Words South.

there will be no husband, no children, **Evelyn Posamentier**. Immigration.

There will come soft rains and the smell of the ground, **Sara Teasdale**. 'There will come soft rains.'

There'll be no war/I tell myself, looking at the sky **Judith Kazantzis**. No war.

There's a rim/to the universe Abba draws **Shirley Kaufman**. Jerusalem notebook.

There's a strange sort of college, **Edith Aubrey Wingrove**. untitled.

There's a warm slap at your back **Carol Simone**. I come up smiling.

There's an illness, of the sort that's named for a man **Linda Gregerson**. Indications that one's love has returned. (De arte honeste amandi).

There's been a Death, in the Opposite House, **Emily Dickinson**. 389.

There's in my mind a woman/of innocence, unadorned but **Denise Levertov**. In mind.

There's little joy in life for me, **Charlotte Brontë**. On the death of Anne Bronte.

there's my heart again/ready for its late night cure **Lina de Feria**. Papers for a man's retirement.

There's no call for the caress that leaves my fingers, **Alfonsina Storni**. The lost caress.

There's no Xmas leave for us scullions, **M. Winifred Wedgwood**. Christmas, 1916.

There's the girl who clips your ticket for the train, **Jessie Pope**. War girls.

These/are the buses of/the century running **Sherley Anne Williams**. the wishon line.

These acres breathe my family, **Anne Wilkinson**. Summer acres.

these are her rooms,/her way of bringing you **Susan Efros**. Her rooms.

These are tales told in darkness **Sherley Anne Williams**. The iconography of childhood.

These are women locked in my joints **Chrystos**. I walk in the history of my people.

These ashes lie still. **Teru Kanazawa**. Revolution.

These be/Three silent things: **Adelaide Crapsey**. Triad.

These fragmented verses/Are only drops of spray **Ping Hsin (Hsieh Wan-ying)**. Multitudinous stars and spring waters.

These hills at sunset/turning copper **Shirley Kaufman**. Jerusalem notebook.

These I have never touched but only looked at. **Elizabeth Jennings**. Greek statues.

these slates of history/are my only friends. **Pat Nottingham**. Carnevale.

These snapshots taken by ghetto children **Adrienne Rich**. Photographs of an unmade bed.

these women at thirty-five/have moved into the faces **Suzanne Juhasz**. These women at thirty-five.

They are busy in the moon/whispering, laughing **Dona Stein**. Night garden, with ladies.

They are cutting down the great plane-trees at the end **Charlotte Mew**. The trees are down.

They are dreaming of children. Torrential **Maria Beneyto**. Nocturne in the women's prison.

They are gone, those light gallants of times long ago! **Rosalie Jonas**. Envoy-The convent, New Orleans 1840–1850.

They are holding his arms, bringing him off the plane, **Sharon Olds**. Pilot captured by the Japanese, 1942.

They are not for us any more: green fields where corn stands high; **Margaret Walker**. FANFARE, CODA, AND FINALE.

They are ours/fighting mothers with **Geraldine L. Wilson**. OUR CHILDREN ARE OUR CHILDREN.

They are pouring the city: **Muriel Rukeyser**. Concrete. (Searching/not searching).

They are the sequences of an imagined love **Nancy Bacelo**. It's still early.

they bring no flowers/no candy **Nikki Grimes**. The takers.

They buried me in gold, stopped up my mouth in copper, **Diana Ó Hehir**. Breaking the lid of night.

they called/Grateful meetings/did/Grateful dances **Mari Evans**. The great Civil Rights Law (A.D. 1964).

they called the 'jump-up'/or the mambo/ **Ntozake Shange**. sassafrass.

They came for you at daybreak **Anna Akhmatova**. Requiem 1935–1940.

They came in ships/from a distant land **Pat Parker**. untitled.

They came to me and said, ''There is a child.'' **Muriel Rukeyser**. Nine poems for the unborn child.

they clapped when we landed/thinking africa was just an extension **Nikki Giovanni**. They clapped.

They climb the mountains on their knees **Mary Crow**. Montserrate.

they come/to knead my flesh **Nikki Grimes**. The takers.

they come dressed in bones/in feathers **Colleen J. McElroy**. When poets dream.

They couldn't see the future **Heather McHugh**. On faith.

they did not build wings for them/the unmarried aunts; instead they **Irena Klepfisz**. they did not build wings for them.

They don't have to lynch the women anymore **Judy Grahn**. A woman is talking to death.

They don't wait for letters. **Marina Tsvetayeva**. A letter.

They dug at the small mound, pushing **Robin Becker**. The landing.

They eat beans mostly, this old yellow pair. **Gwendolyn Brooks**. The bean eaters.

They go along the graveled walks, **Constance Carrier**. Seminary.

They go by, go by, love, the days and the hours **Teresa de Jesús.** They go by, go by, love, the days and the hours.

They got me out of my lair **Etel Adnan.** The enemy's testament.

They had it together/and they laid it out **Mari Evans.** The people gather.

They had never had one in the house before. **Gwendolyn Brooks.** Bronzeville woman in a red hat.

they hadn't known/of the gardens **Wendy Brooks Wieber.** And. (One, The other, And).

They have asked me to speak in public **Muriel Rukeyser.** The artist as social critic. (Searching/not searching).

They have fenced in the dirt road/that once led to Wards Chapel. **Alice Walker.** Burial.

they have reached/me their eyes are bright **Carol Tinker.** Hannya.

They heard the South wind sighing **Frances Ellen Watkins Harper.** The crocuses.

They lie up in the darkened bedroom **Sherley Anne Williams.** fourth life. (Driving wheel).

They lived out in a women's house **Stephanie Markman.** The rime of the ancient feminist. (VII).

They looked at me all ghosts/and silent observers **Harriet Rose.** Mellisandra.

They made her of the softest clay **Lucha Corpi.** Marina mother. (Marina).

They more than we are what we are, **Kathleen Raine.** Statues.

They moved like rivers in their mended stockings, **Mary Oliver.** The grandmothers.

They never thought/you would live, get up from the snow. **Anna Akhmatova.** They never thought.

They nicknamed me Mririda. **Mririda n'Ait Attik.** Mririda.

They put the screens around his bed; **Winifred M. Letts.** Screens.

They say Ideal beauty cannot enter **Elizabeth Barrett Browning.** Hiram Powers' "Greek Slave."

They say La Jac Brite Pink Skin Bleach avails not, **Josephine Miles.** Government injunction restraining Harlem Cosmetic Co.

They say that the plants do not speak, nor the brooks, nor **Rosalía de Castro.** They say that the plants do not speak.

They shut me up in Prose— **Emily Dickinson.** 613.

They sit in a glass egg, **Judit Tóth.** Dead embryos.

They stand in the sun by the pool, **Constance Carrier.** Two, remembered.

They stay as drops/of sap/on a leaf. **Elizabeth Keeler.** The couple.

They still woo me there, and none miss me; **Lilian Bowes Lyon.** Helen meditates before her portrait as a woman.

They stroked me with white dust, **Chase Twichell.** Franz, the world is abstract.

They swing across the screen in brave array, **Florence Ripley Mastin.** At the movies.

they take/stations/in the broken doorways **Mari Evans.** The Friday ladies of the pay envelope.

They taught me things all wrong, **Rosario Castellanos.** Learning about things.

They threw her body on a stretcher **Victoria Theodorou.** Old song.

They told me/I smile prettier with my mouth closed. **Jean Tepperman.** Witch.

They told us/Our mothers told us/They told us. **Ama Ata Aidoo.** Cornfields in Accra.

they want me to settle down/when I have not yet lived **Frances C. Chung.** untitled.

They were after the picnic food **Leslie Marmon Silko.** Toe'osh: a Laguna coyote story.

They were coming across the prairie, they were gallop- **Tekahionwake.** The cattle thief.

they were just meant as covers/in winter **Teresa Palma Acosta.** My mother pieced quilts.

they were nebulous visitors **Christina Meneghetti.** untitled.

They were women then/My mamma's generation **Alice Walker.** Women.

They weren't the kind who loved deeply. **Magaly Sánchez.** Confusion.

They will come—/posterity—/and analyze: **Grace Butcher.** Images.

they're always curious about what you eat as if you were **Irena Klepfisz.** they're always curious.

They're dancing. two step. They let go grab on snap apart **Cynthia Kraman Genser.** Club 82: Lisa.

They're making a girl for the times, **Belkis Cuza Malé.** They're making a girl for the age.

They've left a loaf of bread/out on the table—half-burnt, half-white, **Gabriela Mistral.** Bread.

They've left you in a corner. And there you stand . . . **Ana Ilce.** Table.

they've taken my house. **Lina de Feria.** Kinfolk.

thick ice   you/rib me **Michelene Wandor.** untitled.

Thin,/long mustard weed; **Jana Harris.** Poem for a stranger.

Thine is a strain to read amongst the hills, **Felicia Hemans.** To the poet Wordsworth.

things begin again/on homeland/this time **Johari M. Kunjufu.** Return.

Things can get so easily out of hand. **Ann Stanford.** Composing the garden.

things quietly violent/into the sun **Alexandra Grilikhes.** Feeling the goddess II.

Things that live here: star apple, pineapple, custard apple, south sea apple; **Michelle Cliff.** Obsolete geography.

Think of sweet and chocolate,/Left to folly or to fate, **Gwendolyn Brooks.** The Anniad.

Thinking of you, and all that was, and all **Christina Rossetti.** Monna Innominata: a sonnet of sonnets.

Thinking we were safe—insanity! **Rosemary Tonks.** Story of a hotel room.

a third woman receives foreign/signals thru her breast. **Susan Efros.** Kaiser Hospital trilogy: three women at the mercy of unknown gods.

Thirteen's no age at all. Thirteen is nothing. **Phyllis McGinley.** Portrait of girl with comic book.

This August evening I've been driving **Adrienne Rich.** Transcendental etude.

This crust of bread we try to share **Adrienne Rich.** Photographs of an unmade bed.

this dark of which I am the face **Judith Kazantzis.** the bath.

This dense body with which I close all exists, **Olga Orozco.** Jonah's lament.

This divine October afternoon I would like **Alfonsina Storni.** Pain.

This endless beginning/nothing will move forward **Miriam Dyak.** April 6.

This evening/the night protecting me **Nadia Tuéni.** untitled.

This flutter that comes with me everywhere **Chana Bloch.** Magnificat.

This girlchild was born as usual **Marge Piercy.** Barbie doll.

This great hunger for chocolate seizes me. **Elizabeth Keeler.** Again, flowering.

This I am: fretful as wind, perverse, **Virginia Moore.** Not an apology.

This institution,/perhaps one should say enterprise **Marianne Moore.** Marriage.

This is a give-away poem/You have come gathering **Chrystos.** Ceremony for completing a poetry reading.

This is a poem for me/and women like me **Sandra Maria Esteves.** For Tulani.

This is dedicated to Merry Clayton, Cissy Houston, Vonetta **Donna Kate Rushin.** The Black back-ups.

this is how it is./or can be. **Carolyn M. Rodgers.** Touch. Poem 5.

This is how they sharpen knives on a stone. **Marina Tsvetayeva.** Poem of the end.

This is my century/I saw it grow **Margaret Walker.** THIS IS MY CENTURY . . . black synthesis of time.

This is my curse on thee. God send thou love **Rábi'a bint Ka'b.** A curse.

This is my letter to the World **Emily Dickinson.** 441.

This is no country for old women, **Ellen Gilchrist.** Clanking to Byzantium.

This is not such a hot/time for you or for me. **June Jordan.** From sea to shining sea.

This is really the story of a/sista who was very too-ga-tha **Sherley Anne Williams.** The house of desire.

This is St. Michael and all angels weather, **Rumer Godden.** Michaelmas daisies.

This is the image: the forsaken street **Karen Gershon.** Scene at evening.

This is the landscape of the Cambrian age: **Elaine Feinstein.** Coastline.

this is the last battleground **Michèle Roberts.** Irish prisoners of war.

This is the light of the mind, cold and planetary. **Sylvia Plath.** The moon and the yew tree.

This is the mountain/where ben Yochai walked. **Shirley Kaufman.** Meron.

This is the story of the day in the life of a woman trying **Susan Griffin.** This is the story of the day in the life of a woman trying.

This is the sword/That you shall wield for me (says the world-lord) **Elizabeth Daryush.** This is the sword.

This is the truth, my lover: **Anonymous.** untitled.

This is to be told in the manner of a Borscht Belt comedian—another true **Charlotte Carter.** This is to be told in the manner of . . .

This is what is important/A first birthday picture **Colleen J. McElroy.** Where iguanas still live.

This is what they mean when they say/shack. **Julia Fields.** Big momma.

This is your dream./We are masked in white. **Adrianne Marcus.** Alone, we dream as gods.

This July air swells and swells. You may as well be taking **Molly Vaux.** Farmer's news.

This life of ours would not cause you sorrow **Murasaki Shikibu.** untitled.

this menopause of mine/pauses too frequently **Astra.** Bloody pause.

The moment cannot bear its own fullness **Raquel Chalfi.** A witch cracking up.

this morning/me and my cousin/charlene lost-nation **Marnie Walsh.** Vickie Loans-Arrow 1972.

This morning I wanted to bring you roses **Marceline Desbordes-Valmore.** The roses of Saadi.

this morning, the memory of you/dissolves like breath on glass **Vivienne Finch.** Inertia.

This one I won't tell you about, since you ought not to know **Linda Gregerson.** The love of nuns (De arte honeste amandi).

this place/this dream/place/once left will be gone **Barbara Szerlip.** zocalo.

This ragged sunflower face glows from the brush **Madeline DeFrees.** Gold ring triad.

This road I'm taking is long and bright **Rita Boumi-Pappas.** Artemis.

This room in which I lie sick **Anna Akhmatova.** This room in which I lie sick.

This script is a weapon: **Anne Blackford.** Family script.

This silence I've nurtured **Jenny Mastoraki.** untitled.

This story of our wanderings, is true. **Carol Lee Sanchez.** The emergence no. 1.

This story was told to me by another traveller, just passing **Margaret Atwood.** Circe - Mud poems.

This summer I dreamed that Emma Goldman **Clare Coss.** Emma.

This sun touched Benin/blew away shackles **Malkia M'buzi.** Lament.

This then be for real: **Joan Gibbs.** Internal geography - Part One.

This time I am going to tell the truth about what happened **Jeanne Murray Walker.** Northern liberties.

This to the Crown, and blessing of my life, **Anne Finch, Countess of Winchilsea.** A letter to Dafnis April: 2d 1685.

This trickery of paint which you perceive **Juana Inés de la Cruz (Sister).** To her portrait.

This trip was unplanned. Nothing like Europe **Adrianne Marcus.** Letter from an exile.

This useless lace stitched around my moon blue sleeve. **Rachel Loden.** What the sirens sang.

This was not a good time to be gay **June Jordan.** From sea to shining sea.

This was the surplus childhood, held as cheap! **Alice Meynell.** The Sunderland children.

This way, that way/I do not know **Sappho.** untitled.

This woman breathes burning air/with a clear mind. **Shlomit Cohen.** Drawing of a woman.

This woman didn't faint **Digdora Alonso.** Radio photo.

This woman is a lesbian be careful **Judy Grahn.** A woman is talking to death.

This woman is Black/so her blood is shed into silence **Audre Lorde.** NEED: a chorale of Black women's voices.

This woman vomiting her/hunger over the world **Sonia Sanchez.** Present.

those/where our mouths/clasp and we're **Alexandra Grilikhes.** The vanguard artist dreams her work.

Those Black bitches tore it up! Yakkety **June Jordan.** From sea to shining sea.

Those old tunes take me back. I used to go **Anna Adams.** Her dancing days.

Those that go down into silence . . . **Ada M. Harrison.** New Year, 1916.

Those white New England winters— **Kathleen Lignell.** To say whose side you're on.

Thou famished grave, I will not fill thee yet, **Edna St. Vincent Millay.** Sonnet. (cxxvi).

Thou hast no grave. What is it that bereaves, **Michael Field.** Possession.

Thou large-brained woman and large-hearted man, **Elizabeth Barrett Browning.** A desire (To George Sand).

Though she lives there as the wood's **Marie Ponsot.** On the country sleep of Susanne K. Langer.

Though you are a continent and two seasons away, **Jo Ann Hall-Evans.** Cape Coast Castle revisited.

Thought nest where secrets bubble **Barbara Guest.** ''Couch of space.'' (Quilts).

The thought urges connecting/does one feel? someone between the lines? **Amanda Berenguer.** Communications.

A thousand companions in jail. **Teresinha Pereira.** News from my town.

A thousand martyrs I have made, **Aphra Behn.** Song: a thousand martyrs I have made.

a thousand miles not a single **Carol Tinker.** untitled.

(''thousands - killed in action'') **Gwendolyn Brooks** Appendix to the Anniad: leaves from a loose-leaf war diary.

A thread of silver marks along the sand **Jenny Joseph.** The lost continent.

three mouths/kiss/like fish **Miriam Dyak.** Three.

Three summers since I chose a maid, **Charlotte Mew.** The farmer's bride.

Three women—sisters, my second cousins; unmarried; middle-aged—live **Michelle Cliff.** Obsolete geography.

Through all hopes that keep us brave, **Elizabeth Barrett Browning.** A man's requirements.

Through random doors we wandered **Naomi Long Madgett.** Exits and entrances.

Through the long ward the gramophone **Eva Dobell.** Gramophone tunes.

Through the summer windows of afternoon **Phyllis Gotlieb.** Paradigm.

Through the window screen I can see an angle of grey roof **Minnie Bruce Pratt.** The sound of one fork.

Through the woods the fields,/enmeshed in the machinery of my breathing, **Grace Butcher.** The runner wonders.

Through these pines/The breeze equally **Yosano Akiko.** Tangled hair.

Thru fat crowds/her face ketch de light. **Celia Watson Strome.** Nr. 10.

thru the kaleidoscope/you become **Rota Silverstrini.** Kaleidoscope.

The thrust of life within into the world, gathering the world **Sarah Appleton.** Book of my hunger, book of the earth.

thumb/poet of misfortune **Barbara Szerlip.** untitled.

Thus, if thou wilt prove me, Dear, **Elizabeth Barrett Browning.** A man's requirements.

Thy anger erst in field/Our scatt'red squadrons broke; **Mary Sidney Herbert, Countess of Pembroke.** Psalm lx.

Thy body is no more thy house, **Mary Elizabeth Coleridge.** Horror.

Thy flapping shade and flying strings **Eliza Cook.** My old straw hat.

Thy mercie Lord, Lord now thy mercie show, **Mary Sidney Herbert, Countess of Pembroke.** Psalm lvii.

Thy mother is the Great Wild Cow, living in Nekheb, **Anonymous.** untitled.

Tied-dyed woman wrapped/in Ife Blues—Songhai smiles **Fatimah Afif.** Tanka.

Time after time in dreams you rise/reproachful **Adrienne Rich.** A woman dead in her forties.

Time and its ally, Dark Disarmament, **Tekahionwake.** ''And he said, fight on.''

Time: counted by hunting, killing **Armitage Hargreaves.** Present tense.

Time flies, hope flags, life plies a wearied wing; **Christina Rossetti.** Monna Innominata: a sonnet of sonnets.

the time i dropped your almost body down **Lucille Clifton.** The lost baby poem.

Time is engraved on the pale green faces **Hsiung Hung.** Written in the sunset.

Time returned-in an instant- **Claudia Lars.** Letters written when night grows.

Time that is always gone stays still **Rosemary Dobson.** The mirror.

Time to tend/the fields again **Wendy Rose.** Lost copper.

Time to wipe away the slime/from inner rooms of thinking, **Margaret Walker.** Now.

Time was/When we traded bunkbeds **Eugenie Eersel.** For my number one younger sister.

Time was I had a tender heart, **Ruth Pitter.** Maternal love triumphant or, song of the virtuous female spider.

Time was we stoned the Prophets. Age on age, **Charlotte Perkins Gilman.** The prophets.

Time . . . What is time? **Claudia Lars.** Letters written when night grows.

time's frown in the loneliness of a very high tower **Lina de Feria.** Kinfolk.

Tiny lady/dweller in the heart of a bird **Alejandra Pizarnik.** Clock.

tired, soft/and full of blood **Carol Tinker.** How can we end human suffering.

'Tis not enough for one that is a wife **Elizabeth Tanfield Carey, Lady.** Chorus. (The Tragedie of Mariam, the Faire Queene of Jewry).

'Tis strange, this Heart within my breast, **Anne Finch, Countess of Winchilsea.** A song.

"'Tis the Octoroon ball! And the halls are alight! **Rosalie Jonas.** Ballade des Belles Milatraisses, The Octoroon ball, New Orleans, 1840–1850.

'Tis true I write and tell me by what Rule **Anne Finch, Countess of Winchilsea.** The apology.

the tissue sent with/vision the integrity of **Carol Tinker.** untitled.

Title Divine—is mine!/The Wife—without the Sign! **Emily Dickinson.** 1072.

Tlazolteotle/the woman/who swallows shit **Gloria Anzaldúa.** The servant goddess. (Three women in the closet).

To a man eating a pear/you pose a question **Tomioka Taeko.** Please say something.

To all that is brief and fragile **María Eugenia Vaz Ferreira.** A furtive glass.

To be a marionette. **Dahlia Ravikovitch.** The marionette.

to be an outcast an outlaw **Susan Sherman.** Lilith of the Wildwood, of the Fair Places.

to begin/to continue to begin **Fran Winant.** To begin.

to choose a side/is only the half of it **Jan Clausen.** dialectics.

To confirm a Thing and give thanks **May Swenson.** To confirm a thing.

To eye the dark woodland of your bequest **Marie Ponsot.** Late.

To fear you/is to fear myself **Susan Sherman.** Lilith of the Wildwood, of the Fair Places.

To get things straight/must your eyes see what my eyes see? **Elizabeth Cook-Lynn.** Some of my best friends.

To illustrate . . . two-in-the-morning **Virginia de Araújo.** Letter to Connie in the Maine woods.

To kill love so as not to commit suicide, that is self defense **Yoshihara Sachiko.** Resurrection.

To leave the world/serve God **Compiuta Donzella.** untitled.

To lie at the edge of the forest/with your face in the earth is miraculous **Yunna Moritz.** In memory of Francois Rabelais.

To lose everything at once—/nothing neater! **Marina Tsvetayeva.** Poem of the end.

To love somebody/Who doesn't love you **Kasa no Iratsume.** untitled.

To me, today, somehow/everyone appears retarded **Magdalena Gomez.** Dream medley.

To put it mildly, the mistress of that house would **Bella Akhmadulina.** Rain.

to resort/to the bastard medium of words **Barbara Szerlip.** Note to a hitchhiker who stayed for one day for Fernando.

To root for the you I have not betrayed **Marie Ponsot.** Late.

to say I failed, that is walked out **Diane di Prima.** Brass furnace going out: song, after an abortion.

To show the lab'ring bosom's deep intent, **Phillis Wheatley.** To S. M. a young African painter, on seeing his work.

To sing of wars, of captains, and of kings, **Anne Bradstreet.** The prologue.

To soften the terror of living **Cheryl Clarke.** Palm-reading.

to state each horror/would be redundant. the objects **Irena Klepfisz.** The monkey house and other cages.

To the BEGINNING I give my name, **Concha Michel.** Genesis.

To the white-mantled maidens **Corinna.** untitled.

To the wife of my bosom/All happiness from everything **Gertrude Stein.** A sonnet. (Patriarchal poetry).

To this, to this, after my hope was lost, **Sara Teasdale.** Strange victory.

To you/Who peek across restaurant tables at flushed angels **Summer Brenner.** Childless mothers.

Today/I'm making for my friends/a rich dark dough, **Barbara Smith.** The bowl.

Today, as I rode by, **Margaret Postgate Cole.** The falling leaves.

Today, because I couldn't find the shortcut through, **Jorie Graham.** To a friend going blind.

Today I am modest like an animal, **Esther Raab.** Today I am modest.

Today I bring my own child here; **Alice Walker.** Burial.

Today I cleared out the kitchen with Dougie so Hedley/could sand the kitchen floor. **Stef Pixner.** A day in the life . . .

Today I saw a thing of arresting poignant beauty: **Alice Ruth Moore Dunbar-Nelson.** Snow in October.

Today I saw a woman plowing a furrow. Her hips are **Gabriela Mistral.** Sister.

Today I was irresponsible. **Julia Fields.** Seizin.

Today i went downtown and signed away/another dream. i watched the other women **Ana Castillo.** A Christmas carol: c.1976.

Today is the anniversary of our parting **Ise Tayū.** untitled.

Today is the third Sunday/since the equinox. **Sandra M. Gilbert.** Winterpoem.

Today my mother and sisters/have come to see me. **Alfonsina Storni.** They've come.

Today we walked into the forest **Kathy Engel.** In my father's cabin.

today, you came upstairs breaking/the news of al's death **Susan Efros.** Not quite making it.

Today you told me/you kicked the first lady/you lived with/out **Diane Wakoski.** To an autocrat.

A toe/With amorphous mountain/On its back **Jessica Tarahata Hagedorn.** Love poem from an unfaithful lady.

Together our hands find no indifferent touch. **Helene Davis.** Affair.

Tonight a stranger followed me home. **Nancy Willard.** The poet invites the moon for supper.

Tonight as I sleep alone **Anonymous.** untitled.

Tonight I have a date/with two tall poplars **Esther Raab.** A serenade for two poplars.

Tonight I jerk astart in a dark **Adrienne Rich.** Her waking. (Night-pieces: for a child).

Tonight I regret/the peace **Lili Bita.** The barbarian.

Tonight I understand for the first time **Linda Pastan.** In the middle of a life.

Tonight let reeds be growing/Along your veins' **Lan Ling.** Beyond silence.

Tonight you have hung my room with nets. **Natasha Morgan.** The nets.

Too bold to sin, too weak to die; **Elizabeth Barrett Browning.** Bianca among the nightingales.

Too many of the dead, some I knew well, **Frances Cornford.** In the backs.

too much energy she tried to show with/her hands moving outward **Kathleen Fraser.** The fault.

Too tough **Sara Miles.** Doing time.

Torn coat/dusty shoes/thin white hair **Lourdes Casal.** Conversation at the Bridgeport train station with an old man who speaks Spanish.

Toss your gay heads,/Brown girl trees; **Angelina Weld Grimké.** At April.

Toughest gal I ever did see **Margaret Walker.** Kissie Lee.

The Toulouse-Lautrec woman/Lolls with open mouth **Sylvia Read.** Pictures.

Towards the starry sky,/apples go flooding **Hashimoto Takako.** untitled.

towering rocks sound in the evening **Anonymous.** Song of a woman in labor.

The track is slippery, where water drips, **Desirée Flynn.** From the rain forest.

Trade a king's freedom for a barrel of molasses, **Pauli Murray.** Dark testament.

The traffic drones, where drones is a noun. Whereas **Lyn Hejinian.** The coffee drinkers answered ecstatically.

The traffic halted/and for a moment **Helen Dunmore.** The Polish husband.

The trail climbs in zig-zags **Sun Yün-fêng.** The trail up Wu Gorge.

The train tunnels dry clutter/from Paris to Vienna **Kate Ellen Braverman.** Tracks.

trains cut the tracks, old women scream. **Evelyn Posamentier.** Immigration.

The Trans-Western pipeline vice president came **Leslie Marmon Silko.** Toe'osh: a Laguna coyote story.

Traveling for days to reach you, **Diane Wakoski.** Journey.

Travelling homesick with the West wind, **Sun Yün-fêng.** Travelling in the mountains.

The tree was a gift for your tears. **Minerva Salado.** Old woman in the park.

Tree women quest for sun thru/threaded rains in this **Malkia M'buzi.** Tree women quest for sun . . .

Trees are minimal in winter **Jeanne Murray Walker.** Necessity.

A trellis of sticks/Crowned with chrysanthemums— **Ping Hsin (Hsieh Wan-ying).** Multitudinous stars and spring waters.

Trembling November winds,/steam whistling in tenement pipes **Kattie M. Cumbo.** Nocturnal sounds.

Tremors, and yet my daughter **Lynne McMahon.** Asthma.

The tricolor badge sings audacity/on her hat **Magaly Sánchez.** End of the first act: ovation for Théroigne de Mericourt.

The triumph of Art compels few womenkind; **Rachel Annand Taylor.** Art and women.

The troubled waters/are frozen fast. **Murasaki Shikibu.** The tale of the Genji.

A troubling thought/held my soul in her palm **Zelda.** Sound out your voices, morning prayers.

The trout, speckled and brown and spotted, **Marion Marlowe.** The trout.

True genius, but true woman! dost deny **Elizabeth Barrett Browning.** A recognition. (To George Sand).

Trust in love lost to the dark of your disguise, **Marie Ponsot.** Late.

Trust me, I have not earned your dear rebuke,— **Christina Rossetti.** Monna Innominata: a sonnet of sonnets.

Truth has been concealed, like 15th-century meat **Cynthia Macdonald.** The river Honey Queen Bess.

Trying to make sense in the new island paradise **Lois Elaine Griffith.** Lena Lime observes Ash Wednesday in New York City '77.

The tulips are too excitable, it is winter here. **Sylvia Plath.** Tulips.

Turn your head/Look down **Michele Murray.** The woman who lives inside the world. (10).

Turning back, he found no face, **Shiraishi Kazuko.** A Chinese Ulysses.

turning into my own/turning on in **Lucille Clifton.** Turning.

'Twas mercy brought me from my Pagan land, **Phillis Wheatley.** On being brought from Africa to America.

The twenties are too much sung; the nine years **Jean Overton Fuller.** To a young man on his thirtieth birthday.

Twenty, jealous,/Wilting this summer **Yosano** Tangled hair.

26° below zero The cats fly/up walls burn **Miriam Dyak.** Winter solstice 1975.

Twice forty months of wedlock I did stay, **Katherine Philips.** Orinda upon little Hector Philips.

Twisting her conscience in a coil of words **Phoebe Hesketh.** The serpent.

two babies sitting in the doorway of the hotel **Frances C. Chung.** Guatemala.

2 broken cups:/do not forget. **Jessica Tarahata Hagedorn.** 2.

2 pm: two degrees **Michelene Wandor.** Christmas, 1978.

Two rooms and a hallway/separate our bodies/our bodies separate us **Lynda Koolish.** Joseph's coat.

Tyrant, why swelst thou thus, **Mary Sidney Herbert, Countess of Pembroke.** Psalm lii.

Unable to sleep,/I gaze at the flowers of the bush clover, **Ise Tayū.** untitled.

Uncertain as rain the future lies submerged **Rosemary Joseph.** Going north for Christmas.

Under a ceiling high Christmas tree/I pose **Jessica Tarahata Hagedorn.** Filipino boogie.

Under a hat of sky/I shake the snakes out. **Laura Beausoleil.** Dance mad.

Under noon sun she rides the white mare **Jane Augustine.** After Yeats.

Under the dusty print of hobnailed boot, **Rosemary Dobson.** Country press.

Under the edge of february/in hawk of a throat **Jayne Cortez.** Under the edge of february.

Under the waning moon/In the dawn— **Sun Yün-fêng.** Starting at dawn.

Underclothes soak in cold water in garage and bathroom basins. **Phyllis Koestenbaum.** Blood journey.

(unfinished/in progress/in-the-building **Carole Bergé.** scene.

The unfurling of bark/by my voice **Francisca Ossandón.** untitled.

The unicorn flies/over my head **Jessica Tarahata Hagedorn.** Birthday poem for Gregory Reeves.

Unless you can dance through a common bar **Mahsati.** untitled.

Up from the bronze, I saw/Water without a flaw **Louise Bogan.** Roman fountain.

Up on the fourth floor of Lincoln Hospital **Janet Sternburg.** The facts of life.

Up the broad southern stair/I climbed, as always, in dream **Barbara Howes.** A point of view.

Upon a sudden, as I gazing stood, **Rachel Speght.** The dream.

Upon an old estate from ancient sires descended **Anna Marie Lenngren.** The portraits.

Upon closing the dream,/when I folded the letter, **Elsie Alvarado de Ricord.** As required by law.

Upon her soothing breast/She lulled her little child; **Emily Brontë.** Upon her soothing breast.

Upon his dull ear fell the stern command; **Carrie Williams Clifford.** The black draftee from Dixie.

Upon the angle of its shade **Elizabeth Barrett Browning.** Bianca among the nightingales.

Upon this marble bust that is not I **Edna St. Vincent Millay.** Sonnet. (LXVII).

Upstairs on the third floor **Helene Johnson.** Bottled.

Use to be/Ya could learn/a whole lot of stuff **Willie M. Coleman.** Among the things that use to be.

the utter form of giving form to thought **Cristina Meneghetti.** untitled.

Vagabond was I,/without wine, **Carilda Oliver Labra.** Naked and forever.

Vaginas of women, all the clusters **Ellen Bass.** untitled.

Vague, submarine, my giant twin **Dilys Laing.** Ego.

Vanessa asks me what a beggar is **Digdora Alonso.** Two poems for my granddaughter.

The various works, imperial queen, we see, **Phillis Wheatley.** On imagination.

a very friendly/prison/this is— **Gayl Jones.** Tripart.

Very soon the Yankee teachers/Came down and set up school; **Frances Ellen Watkins Harper.** Learning to read.

Victoria, Carlota, and Eugénie, **Elizabeth Coatsworth.** The empresses.

Violet twilights I carry with me from my/primeval times, **Edith Södergran.** Violet twilights.

Virginity O my virginity! **Sappho.** Bridesmaids' carol.

A voice from the dark is calling me. **Anna Wickham.** Divorce.

Void only—/Take away your veil of stars **Ping Hsin (Hsieh Wan-ying).** Multitudinous stars and spring waters.

Wait till the darkness is deep; **Wallada.** To Ibn Zaidun.

Waiting for you now/I imagine your hair in the wind **Zaida del Río.** untitled.

Wake up, dear boy that holds the flute! **Mira Bai.** untitled.

"Wake up!" sez God. **Celia Watson Strome.** Nr. 12.

waking/at the bottom of the dark **Jan Clausen.** Waking at the bottom of the dark.

Waking. Another white dream./In the hospital room someone **Adrianne Marcus.** Alone, we dream as gods.

Waking to darkness; eawrly silence broken **Nora Bomford.** Drafts.

Walk in the day . . . Walk in the night **Judy Lucero.** Jail-life walk.

Walking along the Bowery, can't/help but think of the saddest **Frances C. Chung.** untitled.

Walking down to the shop by the railway crossing, saying good morning, **Michelle Cliff.** Obsolete geography.

Walking through the water and over the rocks, I am exploring the river- **Michelle Cliff.** Obsolete geography.

"Want a boat?" ask God. **Celia Watson Strome.** Nr. 6.

want to/really touch you/become **Mariah Britton Howard.** solution #9 "to touch you."

Wanting to stomp down Eighth Avenue snow **June Jordan.** Poem for inaugural rose.

War is Eldridge's next/reincarnation **Sherley Anne Williams.** a record for my friends.

War or peace, the border is never empty, **Kinereth Gensler.** The border.

The warm rain and pure wind/For the first time have broken **Li Ch'ing-chao.** The sorrow of departure, to the tune "Butterflies love flowers."

The warm rain falls unfeeling/Like scattered silk threads. **Ho Shuang-ch'ing.** To the tune "Washing silk in the stream."

Warning!/There are only three mystics here **Alice Karle.** An epic (with renaissance flute).

War's wasted era is a desert shore, **Elizabeth Daryush.** For a survivor of the Mesopotamian Campaign.

Wartime. We sit on warm/weathered, softening grey boards **Adrienne Rich.** A woman dead in her forties.

was it moments like these/that made you think of her? Hunger. **Alexandra Grilikhes.** Our lady, solitude.

Was it shown to you, scoffing child, **Anna Akhmatova.** Requiem 1935–1940.

Wash man out of the earth, shear off/The human shell. **Eilean ni Chuilleanain.** Wash.

Washing the floors to send you to college **June Jordan.** Oughta be a woman.

Washing up the dishes;/Washing up the plates; **M. Winifred Wedgwood.** The V.A.D. scullery-maid's song.

WASP liberationist/you invited me/token minority **Marcela Christine Lucero-Trujillo.** No more cookies, please.

Watch out for that man coming in the door. **Belkis Cuza Malé.** Faust.

watching my enemy's corpse/passing before my door. **Georgina Herrera.** Reflections.

Watching the black hours through to morning **Jan Clausen.** SESTINA, WINCHELL'S DONUT HOUSE.

Water flooded everywhere/dripping over the edges of the plate of the world. **Catriona Stamp.** Rebirth.

The water from the little fall doth shine **Anonymous.** untitled.

The water games shine in the moonlight **Dulce María Loynaz.** Water games.

The water's song/uses all the mysteries **Chelly Lima.** Reservoir at night.

A wave of blond fog/like a gauzy flounce. **Marina Tsvetayeva.** Poem of the end.

A wave of coldness/Passes between us, **Yosano Akiko.** untitled.

waves are hard/the swimmers arms and mouth **Mary Winfrey.** Gertrude Ederle swims the Channel (August 6, 1926).

Waves rise. The sidewalk talks. **Paula Gunn Allen.** Riding the thunder.

The way I die is strange . . . It's not life **Delmira Augustini.** Unspeakable.

the way I hear tell aunt jennie **Colleen J. McElroy.** Caledonia.

We all have our faults. Mine is trying to write poems. **Carolyn Kizer.** Singing aloud.

We all have these lapses, the jar **Susan Fromberg Schaeffer.** For Judy Garland.

We all wanted to go to you, **Marge Piercy.** Homage to Lucille, Dr. Lord-Heinstein.

We are/ready for the night **Sherley Anne Williams.** the peacock poem. (The house of desire).

We are a meadow where the bees hum, **Denise Levertov.** Bedtime.

We are connected further back than time allows. **Georgette Cerrutti.** Raining the water.

We are in her kitchen;/we have one enormous/pot and all the spices **Dona Stein.** Putting Mother by.

We are moving from state to state, **Wendy Battin.** Letters from three women.

We are sailing. Already/we see the Hellespont **Eeva-Liisa Manner.** And so the oracles. (Cambrian).

We are the aliens of this world, **Adrianne Marcus.** In defense of circuses.

We are the dead/ones the slow/fast suicides **Sonia Sanchez.** Old words.

We are the stepsisters. **Belkis Cuza Malé.** The stepsisters.

We are things of dry hours and the involuntary plan, **Gwendolyn Brooks.** kitchenette building.

We are tied to Mars' tail. The previous days **Blanca Varela.** The captain.

we are two women/we live on this farm   without men **Judith McDaniel.** November passage.

We boogied when I was eight **Jessica Tarahata Hagedorn.** Autobiography part two: rock and roll.

We bought from Laotian refugees a cloth **Maxine Hong Kingston.** Absorption of rock.

We buried of our dead the dearest one— **Elinor Jenkins.** Dulce et decorum?

We came upon him sitting in the sun, **Margaret Postgate Cole.** The veteran.

We cannot approach her direct, so abstract, so cold, so beautiful. **Hilda Doolittle.** Helios and Athene.

We can't be sure what/their meaning was, but we **Virginia Gilbert.** The ritual.

We come to uncrate the newness of this world, **Lucienne Desnoues.** First things.

We cook on a woodstove in a kitchen behind the house. Our water is taken **Michelle Cliff.** Obsolete geography.

We didn't know we had a third parent **Judith Kazantzis.** Progenitor.

We do not tell ourselves all the things we **Sherley Anne Williams.** first fable. (Driving wheel).

We don't escape any lessons/learned   lived   through **Grace Wade.** Lessons.

We don't lack people here on the Northern coast, **Carolyn Kizer.** Amusing our daughters.

We dressed each other/Hurrying to say farewell **Empress Eifuku.** untitled.

we drink and she pulls/her face up tight **Marnie Walsh.** Vickie Loans-Arrow 1972.

We enter each other as we enter/closed houses, slowly at first, **Adelaide Blomfield.** Attics.

We exist on the edge of death death gives us our names **Gladys Zaldívar.** Hector floating in the night.

We fell like leaves in love, accountable **Adelaide Blomfield.** Attics.

We flicker/the same way we flame **Sherley Anne Williams.** a record for my friends.

We followed her unto the chamber-door, **Anonymous.** The assembly of ladies.

We forgot to water the plaintain shoots **Audre Lorde.** Solstice.

We had forgotten You, or very nearly— **Lucy Whitmell.** Christ in Flanders.

We have drunk wine and discussed literature. **Ch'iu chin.** To the tune ''The Narcissus by the river.''

We have forgotten Paris, and his fate. **Janet Lewis.** Helen grown old.

We have hung this house with roses **Joan LaBombard.** August.

We have not forgotten the market square— **Pauli Murray.** Dark testament.

We have reached the age/of light meals . . . **Isabelle Vuckovic.** Maturity.

We held no future. **Judith Kazantzis.** Progenitor.

we know the hard heavy pull of/weights riveted to our dreams **Gloria Gayles.** Sometimes as women only.

We know the story./She turns/back to find her trail/devoured by birds. **Rae Armantrout.** Generation.

We lay and ate sweet hurt-berries **Rose Macaulay.** Picnic.

We leave our homes in the morning, **Ella May Wiggins.** The mill mother's lament.

we lived next to the tank field **Jeanne Sirotkin.** Untitled.

We love with great difficulty/spinning in one place **Janice Mirikitani.** Sing with your body.

we made love/prologue to deeper rivers **Nikki Grimes.** The takers.

We mazed through the purple velvet ladies **Alice Karle.** An epic (with renaissance flute).

We meant while we were together to create **Marie Ponsot.** Late.

We must say it all, and as clearly **Alice Walker.** Each one, pull one.

We paled with love, we shook with love, **Elizabeth Barrett Browning.** Bianca among the nightingales.

We passed each other, turned and stopped for half an hour, then went our way, **Charlotte Mew.** On the road to the sea.

We pick/the bittersweet grapes/at harvest **Ana Castillo.** Dedicado al Sr. Chavez, Sept. 1975. (Napa, California).

we pioneer/this life. like/pulling teeth. **Jan Clausen.** The kitchen window.

We planned to shake the world together, you and I **May Wedderburn Cannan.** Lamplight.

We play by the rules of winter. **Bella Akhmadulina.** December.

We push our raft out on the river **Sonya Dorman.** Two poets on the way to the palace.

We put the shoe on him the first time this morning, **Máire Mhac an tSaoi.** The first shoe.

We reach for destinies beyond/what we have come to know **Alice Walker.** Beyond what.

we rented a house not knowing/it was a branch of hell on reina street **Lina de Feria.** Kinfolk.

we returned to the place we lived **Lina de Feria.** Kinfolk.

We rise from the snow where we've **Carolyn Forché.** Selective service.

We rose from the bed and sat at the table. **Susan Wood.** Your story.

We shall enjoy it/As for him who finds **Sappho.** untitled.

We shall not escape Hell, my passionate **Marina Tsvetayeva.** We shall not escape hell.

We sit together./The morning air/pure as water **Molly Myerowitz Levine.** First tooth.

We sleep in meadows together/mother and child. I stroke **Cherríe Moraga.** Like I am to no one.

We sleep naked on rocks together **Cherríe Moraga.** Like I am to no one.

We stand naked behind the line. **Judith Herzberg.** On the death of Sylvia Plath.

We stare and shout—/Smash together, **Diana Chang.** Still life.

We started from a station in the city, **Josephine Miles.** Trip.

we stay awake until the wee hours of the night because we are free ameri- **Osa Hidalgo-de la Riva.** She's.

We, that are held of you in narrow chains, **Julia Ward Howe.** Furthermore.

We, the rescued,/From whose hollow bones death had begun to whittle **Nelly Sachs.** Chorus of the rescued.

We, the women still left, the survivors, **Anonymous.** Poem for Jacqueline Hill.

We think of her hidden in a white dress **Linda Pastan.** Emily Dickinson.

We thought—we thought/we could/like everyone, **Patricia Cumming.** Further notes for the alumni bulletin.

We tie up the world around you **Miriam Dyak.** Dying.

We touched land/White gulls flew on **May Miller.** Canary Islands. (Not that far).

We went and we had spice apple ale together **Sherry Hollingsworth.** untitled.

We went in the Green Grasshopper **Alice Karle.** An epic (with renaissance flute).

We were a woman family:/Grandma, our innocent Queen; **Lorna Dee Cervantes.** Beneath the shadow of the freeway.

We were black, we were black, **Elizabeth Barrett Browning.** The runaway slave at Pilgrim's Point.

We were hundreds of thousands, **Judith Kazantzis.** Progenitor.

We were Mayans./We were also Jews. **Georgette Cerrutti.** Raining the water.

We were not raised to look in **Sherley Anne Williams.** you were never miss brown to me.

We were six women. My lover **Marilyn Hacker.** Up from D.C.

we were talking about proletarian internationalism **Reina María Rodríguez.** Now, at the hour of our life.

we will never meet again face to face. **Yosami, Wife of Hitomaro.** untitled.

We will watch him with meaningful looks, **Sharon Barba.** Siblings.

We women, we are so near the brown earth. **Edith Soder-gran.** We women.

we would have perished in the sea **Wilmette Brown.** Voices from the diaspora home.

we would rather lie alone **Alta.** untitled.

Wealth covers sin—the poor **Kassia.** untitled.

The weeks fly lightly **Anna Akhmatova.** Requiem 1935–1940.

Weeps out of Western Country something new. **Gwendolyn Brooks.** The birth in a narrow room.

Well and/If day on day/Follows, and weary year **Adelaide Crapsey.** Trapped.

Well, death's been here/for a long time— **Anne Sexton.** Live.

well me and bobby simon/drink some more **Marnie Walsh.** Vickie Loans-Arrow 1972.

Well then, it's all over. The case **Rita Boumi-Pappas.** Maria R.

Well, they are breathing in and out **Susan Fromberg Schaeffer.** The hills.

Well, we will do that rigid thing **Katherine Philips.** Parting with Lucasia: a song.

Well, well, I know the wise ones talk and talk; **Augusta Webster.** A castaway.

We're hoping to be arrested/And hoping to go to jail **Margaret Walker.** Street demonstration.

We're married, they say, and you think you have won me,— **Alice Cary.** The bridal veil.

West Side—corn tortillas for a penny each **Carmen Tafolla.** Allí por La Calle San Luís.

wet your fingers warm me a little **Lina de Feria.** Wet your fingers.

We've billiards, bowls an' tennis courts, we've teas an' motor-rides; **Cicily Fox Smith.** The convalescent.

What a little girl had on her mind was: **Ibaragi Noriko.** What a little girl had on her mind.

What a loveliness to hold. **Judit Tóth.** To the newborn.

What are we? I know not. **Anna Hempstead Branch.** The monk in the kitchen.

what are ye?/I know not./Brazen pan and iron pot, **Anna Hempstead Branch.** The monk in the kitchen.

What are ye/I know not;/Nor what I really do **Anna Hempstead Branch.** The monk in the kitchen.

What are you doing/with your red eyes, your bulging belly, **Rachel Loden.** Mother.

What can be wrong/That some days I hug this house **Susan Fromberg Schaeffer.** Housewife.

What can you expect/from a woman with seventy-seven years, **Maryam bint Abi Ya'qub al-Ansari.** untitled.

What did I miss as I went searching? **Muriel Rukeyser.** Not searching. (Searching/not searching).

What difference does it make/What other people say **Anonymous.** untitled.

What do I want out of life? **Helen Wong Huie.** untitled.

What do these men really want **Jana Harris.** Glitter box.

What do we know of the road **Cleva Solís.** The traveller.

What do you do at the moment of dying? Do you **Rosario Castellanos.** Dawn.

What do you see as you vaguely watch the wall **Anna Akhmatova.** Memory's voice.

What do you think, old woman,/Who neither smiles nor uncurls her fingers **Helen Aoki Kaneko.** Enigma.

What do you want/Coming to this 'ere 'ell? **Madeline Ida Bedford.** The parson's job.

what do you want/gimme a little something before i start **Colette Inez.** Reading da leaves.

What does she dream of, lingering all alone **Charlotte Brontë.** What does she dream of?

What God of exactitude and trash knocked open their hulls **Roberta Lefkowitz.** Scrawl.

What guilt was there, apportion it aright **Elizabeth Wolstensholme-Elmy.** Woman free. (XIII).

What happened when the lieutenant/came over to you? **Virginia Gilbert.** Leaving, the sepulcre city.

What has poor Woman done, that she must be **Aphra Behn.** Sir Patient Fancy.

'What has your country done for you, **Emily Orr.** A recruit from the slums.

What I have of wisdom/is yours **Barbara Szerlip.** Icarus to his father.

what I think when I see/a she with fantastic legs **Jill Gernand.** untitled.

(What if tomorrow/we were dead **Jessica Tarahata Hagedorn.** Epic eulogy for boy and girl who almost killed each other with aspirin for love and homosexuality and pregnancy's sake.

What is an angel?/An angel/is a poet who hasn't **Nellie Hill.** The poet learns to fly like an angel but gets nothing to eat.

What is around me is/this huge shape I can't visualize **Anne Waldman.** Mother country.

What is green in me darkens, muscadine. **Denise Levertov.** Stepping westward.

What is here for me: where do these things lead: **Michelle Cliff.** Obsolete geography.

What is hidden in the fruit of summer? **Teresa Torres.** Poem.

What is it? Something sought by everyone? **Atsumi Ikuko.** Different dimensions.

what is it that I cannot bear to say? **Diane di Prima.** Brass furnace going out: song after an abortion.

What is it with these people-swallowing streets **Teresa de Jesús.** All of a sudden.

What is our innocence,/what is our guilt? All are **Marianne Moore.** What are years?

what is want sometimes is specifically/what is need. **Carolyn M. Rodgers.** Touch. Poem 4.

''What kind of a god inhabits a stone?'' **Judith Ivaloo Volborth.** Black-coat meets coyote (Three conversations of the absurd).

What kind of well is the newborn's dreams? **Judit Tóth.** To the newborn.

What kind of woman goes searching and searching? **Muriel Rukeyser.** Searching/not searching.

What lutes, what notes, what waterfalls of music, **Rosemary Dobson.** Azay-le-rideau.

What new responsibilities are we hatching now **Vivienne Finch.** Green ice.

What one menagerie could house you both? **Judith McCombs.** Games mammals play.

What! Run from the bits of flying paper, **Michele Murray.** The woman who lives inside the world. (5).

What shall I give my children? who are poor, **Gwendolyn Brooks.** What shall I give my children?

what song shall i sing you/amid epidemic prophecies **Sonia Sanchez.** A poem for Sterling Brown.

what started out as a simple adventure **Michèle Roberts.** after seeing *Walkabout*.

What terror embossed my face onto your hatred **Audre Lorde.** NEED: a chorale of Black women's voices.

What was Inez supposed to do for/the man who declared war on her body **Jayne Cortez.** Rape.

What was it? What was it?/Flashing beside me, lightning in daylight at the orange **Muriel Rukeyser.** Woman as market.

what will we do/when there is nobody left **June Jordan.** Poem for Nana.

What witchlike spell weaves here its deep design, **Anna Hempstead Branch.** Sonnets from a lock box. (XIV).

What words/Are left thee then **Adelaide Crapsey.** To an unfaithful lover.

What would it be like/for the landscape of the moon **Fran Winant.** A sacred grove.

What you Americans call a boycott of the junta? **June Jordan.** Problems of translation: problems of language.

What you need is/a compliment to plump you up **Kathleen Fraser.** What you need.

What you said/keeps bothering me **Gloria T. Hull.** Poem.

Whatever I find if I search will be wrong. **Ruth Fainlight.** The other.

Whatever this is, you have only this moment to do **Ann Stanford.** Crisis.

what's haunting me is not a shadow **Eugenie Eersel.** The plantation.

When a fly wounds the water the wound **Jane Kenyon.** The pond at dusk.

When a person has died the men bring their little drums. **Anonymous.** untitled.

When all is fulfilled/in another life, because it's too late here— **Claudia Lars.** Letters written when night grows.

'When all this is over,' said the swineherd, **Eilean ni Chuilleanain.** Swineherd.

When Byna came from Scotland to Barbados **Lois Elaine Griffith.** A Barbadian true to life fantasy.

When dead you will lie forever forgotten, **Sappho.** To an uneducated woman.

When evening comes/sorrow overwhelms my mind. **Kasa no Iratsume.** untitled.

When Genêt came with the Panthers/To raise defense funds, **Josephine Miles.** Fund raising.

When Gilbert's birthday came *last* spring, **Jessie Pope.** The Nut's birthday.

When God was/folding up the sky **Mariana Sanson.** untitled.

When he was a prince and I was a frog **Ann Dunn.** untitled.

When he went down to the square, the pavilions now **Ágnes Nemes Nagy.** Ikhnaton's night.

When hit comes ter de question er de female vote, **Rosalie Jonas.** Brother Baptis' on woman suffrage.

When I am dead, my dearest,/Sing no sad songs for me; **Christina Rossetti.** Song.

when i awake/i wonder/if the color **Yoshihara Sachiko.** I forget.

when i came to new york/used to work at a factory on twenty-second street **Brenda Connor-Bey.** Martha.

When I die/passing to another nature/the invisible Carmel— **Zelda.** The invisible Carmel.

When I first opened my eyes **Janet Dubé.** Autobiography.

When I found my father that night, the blood **Sharon Olds.** History: 13.

When I grew up I went away to work **Margaret Walker.** Whores.

When I lift my arms and poise the balancing rod, **Diane Wakoski.** The tightrope walker.

When i make love to you/i try **Pat Parker.** For Willyce.

When I married/it was a tiny chapel. **Vidaluz Meneses.** When I married.

When I meet the skier she is always **Adrienne Rich.** Transit.

When I pour sake/for the man I love **Anonymous.** untitled.

When I put myself out on a saucer/in the sun **Diana Chang.** Cannibalism.

When I see numbers/in their forearms' flesh **Shirley Kaufman.** Jerusalem notebook.

When I sensed the slow/satisfaction in his late **Margriet Schaye.** Recollected in tranquility.

When I set out for Lowell, **Anonymous.** The Lowell factory girl.

When I stop at home/I see the windows **Laura Beausoleil.** Living where you are.

When I was a child I knew red miners **Margaret Walker.** Childhood.

When I was a girl by Nilus stram **Adelaide Crapsey.** The witch.

When I was a young girl, I entered the room with authority. **Cheri Fein.** Rock bottom nourishment.

When I was fair and young, and favor graced me, **Elizabeth I, Queen of England.** When I was fair and young.

When I was forty, and two feathers sprung **Elinor Wylie.** False prophet.

When I was once familiar/with the family faces, **Jane Katz.** The palm-reading.

When I watch you wrapped up like garbage **Lucille Clifton.** Miss Rosie.

When I wrote of the women in their dances and wildness, it was a mask, **Muriel Rukeyser.** The poem as mask.

when it falls from the air/our death will be less **Michèle Roberts.** levelling with death.

When it gets towards Christmas **Sarah Kirsch.** Brief landing.

when it is over/your vital signs cease **Susan North.** There is a point.

When it's the man I love/he goes by and doesn't come in **Anonymous.** untitled.

When I've got the blues **Anonymous.** untitled.

When just a touch of orange/just barely gold **Chelly Lima.** Reservoir at night.

When love is a shimmering curtain **Maya Angelou.** On diverse deviations.

When maidens are young, and in their spring, **Aphra Behn.** When maidens are young.

When men are old, and their friends die, **Margaret Postgate Cole.** Praematuri.

When mother died, rows of cans/lined her basement shelves, defense **Judith McDaniel.** When mother died.

When my last visit, I to London made, **Anne Finch, Countess of Winchilsea.** Ardelia's answer to Ephelia.

When our two souls stand up erect and strong, **Elizabeth Barrett Browning.** Sonnets from the Portuguese. (XXII).

When people ask who you are/say you are Africa **Donna Allegra.** When people ask.

When she cannot be sure/which of two lovers it was with whom she felt **Denise Levertov.** Woman alone.

when she died i mourned/a silent mourning. **Irena Klepfisz.** The monkey house and other cages.

When she died, lightning struck in the north, **Lucha Corpi.** The devil's daughter.

When she died no face turned pale, no lips trembled **Nazik al-Mala'ikah.** Elegy for a woman of no importance.

When she was no longer matter/he began to create her. A dimple on her cheek **Miriam Oren.** When she was no longer.

When spring escapes/freed from being huddled in winter's sleep, **Princess Nukada.** When the Emperor Tenji ordered Fujiwara Kamatari to judge between the beauty of cherry blossoms and the red autumn leaves on the hills, Princess Nukada gave judgment with this poem.

When the African Arts,/home again, **Margaret Danner.** At home in Dakar.

When the bell rings or you hear the knocking at the door **June Jordan.** Blue ribbons for the baby girl.

When the bumble bees ride their black motor cycles down to the **Diane Wakoski.** Black leather, because bumble bees look like it.

When the child in your womb **Anonymous.** untitled.

When the Cretan maidens/Dancing up the full moon. **Sappho.** untitled.

When the daughters came for me **Tess Gallagher.** In that time when it was not the fashion.

when the enemy comes/the men run to the mountains **Olga Broumas.** the knife & the bread.

when the Greek sea/was exceptionally calm **Olga Broumas.** Sometimes, as a child.

When the hours are only being filled **Mireya Robles.** untitled.

When the Indian steps/across old rock **Mei-Mei Berssenbrugge.** Ghost.

When the Life-Giver hid from the night, **Marnie Walsh.** Thomas Iron-Eyes. Born circa 1840. Died 1919, Rosebud Agency, S.D.

When the loneliness of the tomb went down into the market-place **Mona Sa'udi.** untitled.

When the moon floats like a hunk of Russian melon **Anna Akhmatova.** When the moon floats.

When the Orient is lit by the great light **Vittoria Colonna.** untitled.

When the rain is raining,/I am under the eave; **Anonymous.** untitled.

When the sheep are in the fauld, and the kye at hame, **Anne Lindsay Barnard, Lady.** Auld Robin Gray.

When the sun opened clouds and walked into her mongrel soul, **Roberta Hill.** Leap in the dark.

When the thunder came I swore I would be good. **Phyllis Koestenbaum.** Blood journey.

When the whale spat me out on this beach **Victoria Theodorou.** Picnic.

when they checked me in, i was thinking: **Toi Derricotte.** Maternity. (Natural birth).

when they first come/they screech with wildness **Irena Klepfisz.** The monkey house and other cages.

When they offered me the glass/I turned it down. **Martha Shelley.** The tree of begats.

when they took us   to the shower   i saw **Irena Klepfisz.** death camp.

when tokens were thirty cents and **Esther Louise.** tokens for ''t.''

When Viera was buried we knew it had come to an end. **Carolyn Forché.** Because one is always forgotten.

When War's red banner trailed along the sky, **Henrietta Cordelia Ray.** Robert G. Shaw.

When we are going toward someone we say **Marge Piercy.** Simple-song.

When we are separated,/not by choice or circumstance, **Myrtle Bates.** There should be time.

When we come up/from our own dregs **Grace Butcher.** After the quarrel.

When we were children old Nurse used to say **Charlotte Mew.** The quiet house.

When weary with the long day's care, **Emily Brontë.** To imagination.

When Winter's royal robes of white **Charlotte L. Forten.** A parting hymn.

When, with breaking heart, **Anryū Suharu.** untitled.

When yesterday I went to see my friends— **Alys Fane Trotter.** The hospital visitor.

''when you and me and mommy/live together,'' **Jan Clausen.** the kitchen window.

When you came, you were like red wine and honey, **Amy Lowell.** A decade.

When you guess why the eyelid falls **Silvia Barros.** untitled.

When you have/once had/a great joy **Tove Ditlevsen.** Self portrait 2.

when you were dying/I turned my eyes away **Eleni Fourtouni.** Lament.

When your mouth said goodbye **Elsie Alvarado de Ricord.** When your mouth said goodbye.

Whenever the snakes come/to die in caves, **Chedva Harakavy.** Whenever the snakes come.

Whenever the wind blows/I try to question it, **Mother of Michitsuna.** untitled.

where are we now where is the hope **Barbara Szerlip.** Ambassador's daughter.

Where did that Bedouin woman/get all her strength— **Shulamit Apfel.** Bedouin woman.

Where do these steps lead? **Gavriela Elisha.** Where do these steps lead?

Where dwell the lovely, wild white womenfolk, **Mary Elizabeth Coleridge.** The white women.

Where have you gone/with your confident/walk with **Mari Evans.** Where have you gone.

Where have you soared so still tonight? **Anna Rydstedt-Dannstedt.** This thing only.

Where I crouch there is massive quiet **Michele Murray.** The woman who lives inside the world. (6).

Where is my body falling, quick, catch it! Shadow like **Sarah Appleton.** Book of my hunger, book of the earth.

Where is the love that might have been **Georgia Douglas Johnson.** Celibacy.

Where sunless rivers weep/Their waves into the deep, **Christina Rossetti.** Dream-land.

Where the mountain crosses/On top of the mountain **Anonymous.** Dream song of a woman.

where the mushrooms grow/large and bulbous **Diane Wakoski.** W. Rings on her fingers & bells on her toes she shall have music wherever she goes.

where there's smoke/where there's blue-grey curlings **Michelene Wandor.** office party 1981.

Whereas the outrageous violation of human rights **June Jordan.** A last dialog on the left.

Wherever/we walk/we will make **Muriel Rukeyser.** Wherever.

Whether I sit or lie **Ukihashi.** untitled.

While fighting for his country, he lost an arm **Nina Cassian.** A man.

While I bent your way/Listening with gray in my hair **Emily Katherine Harris.** Cabal.

While I recline on an emerald velvet divan **Carol Simone.** At thirty.

"While I sit at the door,/Sick to gaze within, **Christina Rossetti.** Eve.

While I'm gone, white mother, kill the fattened oxen **Caroline N. M. Khaketla.** The white and the black.

While my hair was still cut straight across my forehead **Rihaku.** The river-merchant's wife: a letter.

while she was berrying/she bore that child **Anonymous.** the choice.

While some "rap" over this turmoil **Margaret Danner.** The rhetoric of Langston Hughes.

While the astronomer/from his Mount Palomar telescope **Digdora Alonso.** untitled.

While the untroubled snows were maintaining **Bella Akhmadulina.** A bad spring.

While you read I am/winding up the round hours **Molly Vaux.** January.

Whilst like a Glimering Taper still *I* burn, **Aphra Behn.** To Lysander, on some verses he writ, and asking more for his heart than 'twas worth.

Whilst with his falling wings, the courtly Dove **Anne Finch, Countess of Winchilsea.** Jealousie is the rage of a man.

Whips, curses; these must answer those! **Elizabeth Barrett Browning.** The runaway slave at Pilgrim's Point.

White blood of apple on the plate **Molly Vaux.** April.

White butterflies settle on blue grass. **Celia Gilbert.** The stone maiden.

White faces,/Like helpless petals on the stream, **Helen Dircks.** London in war.

White flash—as the whole of it **Carol Bergé.** Another view into love.

The white horse of death came steadily **Rita Spurr.** The white horse.

White Painted Woman has reached middle age by means of it, **Anonymous.** untitled.

White Painted Woman's power emerges, **Anonymous.** untitled.

The white roses I tried to braid in my hair **Yamakawa Tomiko.** untitled.

white sand-dollars flash from our sea: **Carol Bergé.** letter from point lobos.

The white winter light/hastens the day through the panes, **Malka Heifetz Tussman.** Spoil.

The white women/are talking about/their poets. **Barbara Smith.** Theft.

Whiteness   the whiteness of these skies **Yunna Moritz.** Poems for her sick mother.

who/years after/the discipline   the concerts **Mary Winfrey.** thoughts about Clara Schumann.

Who are you?/I grew up in the schoolrooms of the Dakotas, **Nancy Willard.** The graffiti poet.

Who can sleep soundly, dying through the dark? **Shirley Bridges.** So few sleep soundly.

Who could know in advance **Shindō Chie.** Space.

Who decided what is useful in its beauty **Marge Piercy.** Looking at quilts.

who forged this night, what steel **Diane di Prima.** Brass furnace going out: song, after an abortion.

Who goes?/Not the leaders of the people **Mitsuye Yamada.** On the bus. (Camp notes).

Who has lifted the pen! **Sarah Appleton.** Book of my hunger, book of the earth.

Who has strangled the tired voice/of my forest sister? **Noémia da Sousa.** Appeal.

Who in one lifetime sees all causes lost, **Muriel Rukeyser.** Who in one lifetime.

Who is going to Rai Ratanpur and who is going to Drug? **Anonymous.** untitled.

who is it wants me/who makes the animal noise **Janet Hamill.** Belladonna.

who is that cigar mouthed man **Margaret Porter.** Sugarman.

Who is this child, alone **Jean Kenward.** An old snapshot.

Who knows/that in the depth of the ravine **Abutsu-Ni.** untitled.

First Line Index 169

Who knows/What disillusionments await, **Femi Sisay.** Yon pastures green.

Who plays the rain's harp? **Dulce María Loynaz.** The harp.

Who sees the stranger/Grasp/To maintain his balance **Jessica Tarahata Hagedorn.** The fundamental man.

who swallowed/Tonatiuh/rains/oceans of blood **Gloria Anzaldúa.** The woman. (Three women in the closet.)

Who thinks of June's first rose today? **Charlotte Mew.** June, 1915.

Who told you where I am **Paula Ludwig.** To the dark god.

Who took the mind's natural image/and rubbed it clean? Who said, Begin **Virginia de Araújo.** Letter to Connie in the Maine woods.

Who was it that took away my voice? **Bella Akhmadulina.** Silence.

Who was so strong and shrewd! **Bella Akhmadulina.** Muteness.

who will finally say/I am all heaven and hell **Barbara Szerlip.** Who will finally say.

The whole city is iced over. **Anna Akhmatova.** Voronezh.

Who's for the trench— **Jessie Pope.** The call.

Whose dog am I?/The time clock's dog. **Naomi Replansky.** A good day's work.

Why am I distracted all day, dreaming of the twelve **Sandra M. Gilbert.** The twelve dancing princesses.

Why did he tell me:/I'm afraid/to go. **Shirley Kaufman.** Jerusalem notebook.

Why did no-one say it/was like this? **Marguerite Wood.** Rouen.

"Why do/You thus devise/Evil against her?" **Adelaide Crapsey.** Susanna and the elders.

Why do I even want to call her up **Adrienne Rich.** For Ethel Rosenberg.

Why do you always live upstairs? she asks, showing the same **Marlene Leamon.** Upstairs.

"Why do your People dance like that," **Judith Ivaloo Volborth.** Black-Coat meets coyote (Three conversations of the absurd).

Why don't I write in the language of air? master a new **Mona Sa'udi.** untitled.

Why hast thou left me? Whither fled, **Sappho.** untitled.

Why, in that single glance I had/Of my child's face . . . I tell you all, **Elizabeth Barrett Browning.** The runaway slave at Pilgrim's Point.

Why should/I, even I/be jealous **Anonymous.** Why should I be jealous.

why the call/for elaborate ritual **Barbara Szerlip.** The end of something.

Why utter the names of gods or stars **Rosario Castellanos.** Someone else.

Why will people/have no mercy on me? **Anonymous.** The widow's song.

Wide are the streets, and driven clean **Carola Oman.** Brussels, 1919.

Wife and servant are the same, **Mary Lee (Lady Chudleigh).** To the ladies.

Wife of Kohelet, the fish in the pond are dead. **Shlomit Cohen.** Wife of Kohelet.

Wild nights—Wild nights! **Emily Dickinson.** 249.

A wild patience has taken me this far **Adrienne Rich.** Integrity.

the wild wind whoops birds/shoots bulls of milk whoops **Barbara Moraff.** untitled.

Will the lady with locker key 43/please come out of the water. **Valerie Sinason.** Will you come out now?

Wind/Gives speech/to trees. **Helen Aoki Kaneko.** Wind.

The wind blows through/the little hut in the rice field **Shunzei's daughter.** untitled.

The wind is a blackbird. **Diane Wakoski.** The blackbird.

Wind shakes the grass. **Lan Ling.** A melody.

The wind stops./Nothing is left of Spring but fragrant dust. **Li Ch'ing-chao.** Spring ends, to the tune "Spring in Wu-ling."

Winds that drift over the desert, **Dorothy S. Obi.** Winds of Africa.

wine rages in my blood **Michèle Roberts.** hangover.

The winter being over,/In order comes the Spring, **Anne Collins.** Song (I).

The winter birds/are flying from the North **Pinkie Gordon Lane.** Migration.

the winter enters her/so silent, it/slants in and **Michèle Roberts.** poem on the day of the spring equinox.

Winter, to me your gestures are/cold and careful; yes, in **Bella Akhmadulina.** Winter.

The winter you were five/you ate a hundred apples **Judith Goren.** The planting.

Winter's gesture to me is/chilly and persistent. **Bella Akhmadulina.** Winter.

Wisdom has broken my arms, shattered my bones— **Anne Hébert.** Wisdom has broken my arms.

"Witch!/Witch!/Cursed black heart, **Amy Lowell.** Witchwoman.

Witchcraft was hung, in History, **Emily Dickinson.** 1583.

With a dagger in my hand/with a lilac at my breast **Magdalena Gomez.** For my lover, the artist.

With a hole in my stomach with four grey hairs with a **Susan Sherman.** Love poem/for a capricorn.

With dusty beams/Of light magnifying/Fantasies **Jessica Tarahata Hagedorn.** A plaster and plexiglas creation.

With each pain/She screams at God. Through the door **Adrianne Marcus.** The woman in the next room.

With flowers for teeth, a hairnet of dew, **Alfonsina Storni.** I'm going to sleep.

With frowning brows and pouting lips she sate, **Sylvia Pankhurst.** In lofty scorn.

With hate and misery/my sleeves are never dry. **Lady Sagami.** untitled.

With heavy instruments of mind I mine **Elizabeth Keeler.** The mountain in my head, its periodic loss.

With her head swinging like a white lily, **Shiraishi Kazuko.** The anniversary of Samansa's death.

With how intense a fire the celibate **Dilys Laing.** Except ye become. . . .

With my breath I cut my way through the six forests **Lalleswari (Lalla).** untitled.

With no other identify than the/letters of V.C. **Etel Adnan.** The enemy's testament.

With sails full set, the ship her anchor weighs, **Helen Hunt Jackson.** Emigravit.

With the clear/plastic speculum, transparent **Olga Broumas.** untitled.

With what a childish and short-sighted sense **Helen Hunt Jackson.** Danger.

with your apartment/reeking of dirty diapers **Frances C. Chung.** Chinese dentist.

Withering, shrivelling, dancing,/The wet cold boulevard **Tuo Ssu.** Night street.

Within my bosom stirs once more tonight **Zeb-un-Nissa.** Lament.

Within my casement came one night **Henrietta Cordelia Ray.** The dawn of love.

Within my heart a stab I felt— **Teresa of Ávila.** In the inmost recesses.

Within, your eyes are windows **Ingeborg Bachmann.** Songs in flight.

Without a prayer in the wind's direction, **Shlomit Cohen.** So abruptly.

Without a word/Without a demand **Yosano Akiko.** untitled.

Without changing color/in the emptiness **Ono no Komachi.** untitled.

Without Controul she gazes on that Face, **Aphra Behn.** To Lysander, on some verses he writ, and asking more for his heart than 'twas worth.

Without expectation/there is no end **Audre Lorde.** Summer oracle.

Without warning their nest/Has become dangerous to the swallows. **Ch'iu Chin.** A call to action.

Woke up this mornin' when chickens was crowin' for days **Bessie Smith.** Young woman's blues.

The woman/who swallowed/Tonatiuh/rains/oceans of blood **Gloria Anzaldúa.** The woman. (Three women in the closet).

the woman/who wrinkles/the flesh of the lakes **Gloria Anzaldúa.** Contemporary goddess. (Three women in the closet).

Woman as gates, saying:/"The process is after all like music, **Muriel Rukeyser.** Kathe Kollwitz.

A woman comes to my door and asks for bread. **Linda Gregg.** Lilith.

The woman downstairs/who is my mother **Genny Lim.** The only language she knows.

Woman fears for man, he goes **Denise Levertov.** Abel's bride.

A woman grew, with waiting, over-quiet. **Elisabeth Eybers.** Narrative.

A woman in a tobacco factory wrote/a poem to death. Between the smoke **Nancy Morejón.** Woman in a tobacco factory.

The woman in my notebook/has escaped. **Lorna Dee Cervantes.** The woman in my notebook.

A woman in the shape of a monster **Adrienne Rich.** Planetarium.

The woman in white lies on the lawn **Jeanne Sirotkin.** Debutante.

The woman is getting on her last bus **Anonymous.** Poem for Jacqueline Hill.

A woman is on fire. **Minerva Salado.** Special report for International Women's Day.

a woman is slicing meat; **Susan Efros.** Kaiser Hospital trilogy: three women at the mercy of unknown gods.

A woman leads me in, **Toi Derricotte.** The testimony of Sister Maureen.

A woman making advances publicly **Judith Kazantzis.** A woman making advances publicly.

A woman on a park bench, fall in the park, **Phyllis Koestenbaum.** Blood journey.

The woman took a train/away away from herself. **Dilys Laing.** The double goer.

woman who cradled me, and made me rise **Michele Roberts.** lament for my grandmother on the day of the winter solstice.

A woman who languidly breaks/a dry twig, leaning out of the high **Siti Nuraini.** A woman.

The woman who swims in her tears **Susan Griffin.** The woman who swims in her tears.

The woman who walks with her cane every afternoon unless it rains, **Phyllis Koestenbaum.** Blood journey.

A woman who writes feels too much, **Anne Sexton.** The black art.

A woman who's arrived at a ripe old age **Zelda.** A woman who's arrived at a ripe old age.

the woman whose head is on fire **Judy Grahn.** untitled.

A woman with a burning flame **Georgia Douglas Johnson.** Smothered fires.

Woman with broad, rough hands **Magda Portal.** Woman.

Woman with the body of a lesbian **Lili Bita.** Portrait.

A woman working hard and wisely **Kassia.** untitled.

Woman's own soul must seek and find that fay, **Elizabeth Wolstenholme-Elmy.** Woman free. (LVIII).

The womb/Rattles its pod, the moon **Sylvia Plath.** Childless woman.

Women by the thousands were walled-in **Victoria Theodorou.** Picnic.

Women, disdainful, uncaring/bridegrooms waiting **Victoria Theodorou.** Picnic.

the women gather/because it is not unusual/to seek comfort in our hours of stress **Nikki Giovanni.** The women gather.

Women have loved before as I love now; **Edna St. Vincent Millay.** Sonnet. (XCV).

Women much loved, who never had enough, **Anna Margolin.** Years.

Women receive/the insults of men/with tolerance, **Dilys Laing.** Veterans.

Women should be pedestals **May Swenson.** Women.

Women's or men's hair waltzed with the wind like/streamers **Chung Ling.** Dusk on the veranda by Lake Mendota Summer 1968.

Wonder of the trolley,/memory's unexpected actor **Mirta Yañez.** The visits.

Won't you be my chauffeur **Memphis Minnie.** Me and my chauffeur blues.

Wood smoke/has become a bird **Albis Torres.** Wood smoke.

Wooden stairs scrubbed with red brick **Luisah Teish.** Hoodoo Moma.

woolen and secure/you are walking in Brooklyn **Rachel Maines.** Finders keepers.

The word is out that I am your enemy **Julia de Burgos.** To Julia de Burgos.

World,/it was long time ago that I first saw you **Nishi Junko.** Remorse came slowly.

the world container: delicate blue egg **Michèle Roberts.** whose death at easter (on the train between London and Leeds).

The world is/not with us enough. **Denise Levertov.** O taste and see.

The world will stare at those who wear **Eliza Cook.** My old straw hat.

World, you destroy yourself **Concha Michel.** Genesis.

The world's love runs thin. **T'ang Wan.** To the tune "The Phoenix hairpin."

A worthless woman; mere cold clay **Elizabeth Barrett Browning.** Bianca among the nightingales.

Would I be more than a bubble breaking? **Angelina Weld Grimké.** A Mona Lisa.

Would I might go far over sea, **Marie de France.** Would I might go far over sea.

Wrapped in a shawl you lay in your basket, **Judit Tóth.** To the newborn.

Wrapped in anger/Like a filthy coat **Anne Hébert.** Land-scape.

Wrapped up in myself:/most of what I believe **Myra Glazer.** Recognition.

The wretched Flavia on her couch reclined, **Mary Wortley Montague, Lady.** Saturday: the small pox.

wrist/aerial moroe took her into **Ntozake Shange.** cypress.

Write it down. Write it. In ordinary ink, **Wisława Szymborska.** Starvation camp near Jaslo.

Writing a poem is trying to catch a fluff of cloud **Naomi Long Madgett.** Writing a poem.

Wrong, followed by a deeper wrong! **Elizabeth Barrett Browning.** The runaway slave at Pilgrim's Point.

Ye shall watch while kings conspire **Elizabeth Barrett Browning.** The curse. (A curse for a nation).

Ye stolid, homely, visible things, **Anna Hempstead Branch.** The monk in the kitchen.

The year of my mother's divorce **Joan Swift.** Pneumonia.

a year since i came here/and tomorrow christmas **Jan Clausen.** A Christmas letter.

years will fall through our fingers **Nzadi Zimele-Keita (Michelle McMichael).** what we know.

Yellow birds flutter through the red maples **Hsüeh Ch'iung.** A song of Chin Men District.

A yellow flag on the west peninsula **Victoria Theodorou.** Picnic.

Yellow lilies,/White malamute straining **Sheila Nickerson.** In the alley: June.

Yes, I remember that pain precisely, **Nina Cassian.** The blood.

Yes, it is getting harder. **Ann Stanford.** Composing the garden.

Yes my child come do the birth dance **Anonymous.** untitled.

yes, sam johnson, **Carol Tinker.** untitled.

Yes, she'd seen it all before/the boozed up dreams **Okoyo Loving.** Ritual.

Yes, Tadeusz Rozewicz, I too/prefer old women. **Marya Fiamengo.** In praise of old women.

yesterday,/had lunch with my Grandmother. **Kitty Tsui.** the words of a woman who breathes fire: one.

yesterday a lovely day/we traveled to the country **Fran Winant.** Yesterday.

Yesterday Andreas came here and I showed him my quilt **Barbara Guest.** Revered quilts. (The mushroom quilt from water mill).

Yesterday evening I saw your corpse **Joyce Mansour.** untitled.

Yesterday you were kind, a new breed **Beverly Tanenhaus.** My hair is black.

Yet, as hetaira,—comrade, chamber-mate,— **Elizabeth Wolstenholme-Elmy.** Woman free. (XII).

Yet I must go: we will submit, **Katherine Philips.** Parting with Lucasia: a song.

Yet when it was all done aright,— **Elizabeth Barrett Browning.** The runaway slave at Pilgrim's Point.

Yin and yang, they say,/female and male but the real **Marge Piercy.** Night fight.

Yonder you weep **Nāzik al-Malā'ikah.** Jamila.

you/offer me pecan pie/and a fair skin **Michelene Wandor.** American Margaret.

You./We have never met/yet/we know each other **Ann Castillo.** Our tongue was Nahuatl.

You and I/Have so much love, **Kuan Tao-shêng.** Married love.

You and me/we live inside an egg **Anonymous.** untitled.

You are a mildewed painting. **Tuo Ssu.** Sprout.

You are a troll/you hobble towards us **Miriam Dyak.** Dying.

You are always new and always hidden; **Anna Akhmatova.** You are always new.

you are becoming/many heads **Rota Silverstrini.** Kaleidoscope.

you are becoming free **Rota Silverstrini.** Kaleidoscope.

you are bored with the waiting **Barbara Szerlip.** 59: Huan/dispersion.

you are doing/an egyptian thing **Rota Silverstrini.** Kaleidoscope.

You are every woman I ever loved/and disavowed **Adrienne Rich.** A woman dead in her forties.

You are fortunate, dear friends, that you can tell **Vidya (Vijjika).** untitled.

You are growing yourself/out of nothing: there's **Chana Bloch.** Magnificat.

You are horizontal./I am vertical. **Lin Ling.** Footpaths cross in the rice field.

You are my stick, my prop **Felicity Napier.** Houseplant.

You are sitting/in a room/preparing for something **Kristina McGrath.** The hour in April. (Sequence from blue to blue).

. . . You are stolen kisses in my unsuspecting sleep **Marté Jones.** You are stolen kisses in my unsuspecting sleep.

You, being grown and little pleased by growth, **Dilys Laing.** Lot's daughter.

You block the zenith sun/and hold stars in your palm! **Marina Tsvetayeva.** Akhmatova.

You bring me silver and turquoise **Willyce Kim.** Keeping still, mountain.

You by the village street **Anonymous.** The abortion.

You can call me Herbie Jr. or Ashamah **June Jordan.** Unemployment/monologue.

You can only go down so far **Jeanne Sirotkin.** A love poem.

You can sigh o'er the sad-eyed Armenian **Frances Ellen Watkins Harper.** An appeal to my countrywomen.

you can swim in tampax/you can ride **Frances Landsman.** Tampax.

You can't control anger,/and you can't control us, **Julia Vinograd.** Deal.

You can't kill a young woman **Marilyn Bobes.** War dispatch.

You coil like strips of a clay bowl **Gerda S. Norvig.** Even before the mirror Myra.

You danced a magnetic dance **Jayne Cortez.** So many feathers.

You day-sun, circling around, **Anonymous.** Song for bringing a child into the world.

You do not know the breaking through **Ellen Bass.** You do not know the breaking through.

You don't/know/who I am **Rosmarie Waldrop.** Confession to settle a curse.

You don't understand, my friend, you don't understand. **Mirta Aguirre.** Poem of profound truth.

You empress of the stars, the heavens' worthy crown, **Catharina Regina von Greiffenberg.** Spring-joy praising God. Praise of the Sun.

You feed and feed/me like a fool I eat until **Olga Broumas.** Fools. (Of fruit whose black seed fire).

You fell like silk slipping through itself **Alice Karle.** Suicide.

You gathered incredible strength/in order to die **Blaga Dmitrova.** To my father.

You gave me everything **María Eugenia Vaz Ferreira.** Posthumous story.

You gave me this skull in the woods **Susan Griffin.** Deer skull.

You gave your life, boy, **Winifred M. Letts.** What reward?

You have left me to linger in hopeless longing, **Anonymous.** The weaver's lamentation.

You have started out on the good earth; **Anonymous.** untitled.

You have taught me how to dress without **Mae Jackson.** On learning.

You have watched me   and know. **Diane Wakoski.** The statue. (Largely because of coincidence and partly because of chance, I have taken up a new address at 47th Street and Avenue F).

You held my lotus blossom/In your lips and played with the **Huang O.** To the tune "Soaring clouds."

you, in yr levi jacket,/standing in the hall, **Alta.** untitled.

You keep me waiting in a truck **Ai.** Twenty-year marriage.

You know/I sure would like to write a blues **Jayne Cortez.** You know.

"You know," Black-Coat went on,/"Our Shepherd loves all lambs." **Judith Ivaloo Volborth.** Black-Coat meets coyote. (Three conversations of the absurd).

You know I have a husband. **Chang Chi.** A faithful wife.

You know, she said, they made you/a dress of fire. **Dahlia Ravikovitch.** The dress.

You know the lark/will not abandon me **Cleva Solís.** The road.

You know the problem:/Change and move **Lynn Suruma.** Turning corners.

You leaped from the white horses **Erinna.** The distaff.

You leave in anger,/confusion, love **Olga Broumas.** Separation. (Of fruit whose black seed fire).

You lie on the sofa all day, washed in fog, **Sandra M. Gilbert.** The love sickness. (The love sequence).

You little know the heart that you advise; **Mary Wortley Montague, Lady.** In answer to a lady who advised retirement.

You look for her/someone you could crack **Marina Rivera.** Even.

You "made a virtue of necessity" **Alice Meynell.** To conscripts.

You made it rain, Lady **Fareedah Allah.** You made it rain.

You may go on the warpath; **Anonymous.** You may go on the warpath.

You may write me down in history **Maya Angelou.** Still I rise.

You mix flesh. your first time with his paintbox: **Joan Larkin.** Blood.

You must break through old thought **Elizabeth Daryush.** You must break through old thought.

You must get back to the plan **Ann Stanford.** Composing the garden.

You must remember never to offend the gods **Ann Stanford.** The fountain.

You need the untranslatable ice to watch. **Gwendolyn Brooks.** Appendix to the Anniad: leaves from a loose-leaf war diary.

You never heard her name. **Olga Orozco.** Noica.

you never understood my reasons for leaving **Barbara Szerlip.** The crossing.

You no longer cared to know us **Eleni Fourtouni.** Pappouli.

You of the eternal truths   O great queen of queens **Enheduanna.** Inanna exalted.

You often went to breathe a timeless air **Frances Cornford.** The scholar.

you opened me like a silent rose in a holocaust of your tongue **Jan Zaleski.** With my velvet gun.

you, other there, dark/as a church, insular **Olga Broumas.** the knife & the bread.

"You ought to do a book, Miss Me; **Judy Dothard Simmons.** Equal opportunity.

You overhear conversations in the street. **Beverly Tanenhaus.** Quasi-liberation in Upstate New York.

You paced naked in my room like another cage, **Julia Vinograd.** Summer murder.

You played heroic, necessary/games with death **Adrienne Rich.** A woman dead in her forties.

You raise the ax,/the block of wood screams in half, **Ai.** The anniversary.

You refuse to own/yourself, you permit **Margaret Atwood.** You refuse to own.

you return to your poems **Susan North.** Poem for her thirty-fifth birthday.

You said it over the top of the book, **Carol Muske.** Chapter one.

You said: *My father didn't cry.* **Alfonsina Storni.** Ancestral weight.

You said you were/Life,/not its master. **Fina García Marruz.** You too.

you say/colour is clear: **Michèle Roberts.** to a male intellectual.

You say I am mysterious. **Elsa Gidlow.** untitled.

You say I lay for years/in the fleshy web of your shoulder **Kate Ellen Braverman.** Lies.

You say, "I will come." **Otomo no Sakanoe.** untitled.

"You say that you believe in Democracy for everybody, **Margaret Goss Burroughs.** Everybody but me.

You say, That's no gift to bring them: Death? **Virginia de Araujo.** Letter to Connie in the Maine woods.

You say there is a little Tom/in all us old niggers, **Myrtle Bates.** From the sidelines.

you, saying/'wherever you go, **Carol Bergé.** letter from point lobos.

you see, my whole life/is tied up/to happiness **Nikki Giovanni.** Woman poem.

You see them walking along the yellowed corners of the album, **Belkis Cuza Malé.** The photogenic ones.

You send me back to share/my own scars   first of all **Adrienne Rich.** A woman dead in her forties.

You show me the poems of some woman/my age, or younger **Adrienne Rich.** Translations.

you show me the ring,/the date incised in gold, **Jan Clausen.** the kitchen window.

You slapped me—/no one had ever slapped me— **Leila Djabali.** For my torturer, Lieutenant _____ .

You sleeping I bend to cover. **Adrienne Rich.** The crib. (Night-pieces: for a child).

"You smell good/you smell/as a woman should" **Dorothy Livesay.** Breathing.

You sowed in me, not a child/but yourself. **Celia Dropkin.** Poem.

You speak of art/and your soul is like snow, **Lorna Dee Cervantes.** para un revolucionario.

You stand and hold the post of my small house, **Auvaiyar.** untitled.

You stand over it/Without sadness. It is **Hsiung Hung.** The pitcher.

You strange old ghouls, **Helen Hamilton.** The ghouls.

You stretch out/flat on your back **Ann Stanford.** Going to sleep.

You swing of necessity into male rhythms **Lola Ridge.** Russian women.

You tell me not to long for you. **Yosami, Wife of Hitomaro.** untitled.

You thatched the roof with leaf and branch **Anonymous.** untitled.

You think I am like your grandmother **Judith Minty.** Meditation on friendship: getting lost in the woods with Deena—Jamesville, NY.

You think I shrieked then? Not a sound. **Elizabeth Barrett Browning.** The runaway slave at Pilgrim's Point.

you think you/need me. think/that i **Carolyn M. Rodgers.** Masquerade.

You thought, He must be pale, he must be silent, **Sandra M. Gilbert.** You discover you're in love with the dead prince. (The love sequence).

You thought I had the strength of men, **Mary Elizabeth Coleridge.** A clever woman.

You, walking past me,/not toward my dubious witchcraft— **Marina Tsvetayeva.** You, walking past me.

You wanted to compare, and there/we were, eyes on each eye, the lower **Olga Broumas.** Amazon twins.

You went back. There pain is real. **Virginia de Araújo.** Letter to Connie in the Maine woods.

You were a sophist,/Pale and quite remote, **Gwendolyn B. Bennett.** Advice.

You were sleeping, today, while I was looking about us **Bella Akhmadulina.** You were sleeping.

You were standing in the garden/your garden **Eleni Fourtouni.** In a dream.

You were tall and beautiful. **Mary Dorcey.** First love.

You were the proud one, the kid in the secret room **Sandra M. Gilbert.** You fall. (The love sequence).

You, when your body, life shall leave **Anne Finch, Countess of Winchilsea.** Melinda on an insippid beauty.

You who accept the voices of the stars **Ada Negri.** Tonight.

You who ask where I find the courage **Vesna Parun.** A return to the tree of time.

You who sat safe at home/And let us die **Margery Lawrence.** Transport of wounded in Mesopotamia, 1917.

You will be South/What more than South and South and above all South, **Milagros González.** I am America's child . . .

You will begin to be alone **Rosario Murillo.** On account of the picture.

You will enter the world where death by fear and explosion **Muriel Rukeyser.** Nine poems for the unborn child.

you will know her presence/in the half-light **Alexandra Grilikhes.** Mistress of the animals.

You with the salt-blue eyes **Mary Barnard.** The Rock of Levkas.

You woke, your body a stream **Georgette Cerrutti.** Raining the water.

You won't fall behind. I'm the convict, **Marina Tsvetayeva.** Akhmatova.

you write again/I fold your letter into my pocket **Susan North.** For Michael.

You Ye; The bee's jail, Puck workhouse **Rochelle Owens.** Hera Hera Hera.

You'd know her/when you look down the block **Sharon Henderson.** Blue jean wearin women???

You'll make tea/I'll make toast **Tomioka Taeko.** Living together.

You'll soon know your name is Vanessa **Digdora Alonso.** Two poems for my grandmother.

young black woman knocks at my door **Eve Triem.** Breaking a voodoo.

A young girl moves like an ear of grain **Sophia de Mello Breyner Andresen.** The young girl and the beach.

Young love in her virginity/Burns up a list of loves **Charlotte Mitchell.** May Day.

Young men there are in plenty, **Anonymous.** untitled.

The young queen was Elizabeth **Alice Karle.** An epic (with renaissance flute).

Young women don't open windows. **Marilyn Bobes.** Old ideas speaking.

Your battle-wounds are scars upon my heart, **Vera Brittain.** To my brother.

your body is a wasteland **Barbara Szerlip.** untitled.

Your breasts/ sliced-off The scars **Adrienne Rich.** A woman dead in her forties.

Your elbow at the window, cloistered woman, **Shlomit Cohen.** Wife of Kohelet.

Your elephant adolescence in sandlots Brooklyn: **Marge Piercy.** 16/53.

your face dissolving in water, like wet clay **Diane di Prima.** Brass furnace going out: song, after an abortion.

your friends are sympathetic/solicitous at first **Susan North.** When your husband goes to prison.

your goddamned belly rotten, a home for flies. **Diane di Prima.** Brass furnace going out: song, after an abortion.

Your hand moves/a parallel cut of air, **Elaine Dallman.** A parallel cut of air.

Your hands like that The grass The sun **Susan Sherman.** Because words do not suffice.

Your heart faltered, attacking **Dona Stein.** For F. J. L. (May 7, 1919 - May 2, 1972).

Your hideaway barely picked up/rumors of the mechanized city: **Claudia Lars.** Evocation of Gabriela Mistral.

Your honey? Who remembers your honey? **Leah Goldberg.** A look at a bee.

YOUR HOUSEPLANT IS A DELICATE THING. **Susan Wallbank.** Why so many of them die.

Your husband's grandfather labors over history, **Shlomit Cohen.** Wife of Kohelet.

your ivory teeth bare in the half-light **Diane de Prima.** Brass furnace going out: song, after an abortion.

Your laughter is like a burst pomegranate **Ingrid Jonker.** When you laugh.

Your light is not yet broken: **Anne Ridler.** The gaze.

Your mother flies from Boston to Phoenix. **Susan North.** After ten years.

Your name is a bird in my hand, **Marina Tsvetayeva.** Verses to Blok.

your olive face appears before me **Lorraine Sutton.** Your olive face.

Your pain sleeps like a lioness. **Rachel Nahem.** Elegy for my mad mother.

Your small hands, precisely equal to my own— **Adrienne Rich.** Your small hands.

Your smile, delicate/rumor of peace. **Maya Angelou.** Woman me.

Your thighs your belly;/their sweep and strength, **Mary Dorcey.** Sea flower.

Your turn came, and you chose to take it, **Asphodel.** Winter solstice—for Frank.

Your voices sprayed over the walls **Carolyn Forché.** Message.

Your window is on the eastern side, **Bella Akhmadulina.** Your window is on the eastern side.

Your words are frost on speargrass, **Lola Ridge.** Amy Lowell.

You're still missed. Remember the day **Virginia de Araujo.** Letter to Connie in the Maine woods.

''Your're too soft . . . always were. You'll get nothing but shit. **Lorna Dee Cervantes.** Beneath the shadow of the freeway.

Youth gone, and beauty gone if ever there **Christina Rossetti.** Monna Innominata: a sonnet of sonnets.

Youth of my heart, my beloved one, **Kubatum.** Love song to King Shu-Suen.

zimbabwe/and we/are one **Safiya Henderson.** harlem/soweto.

Zuni ring knocks/against steel **Carol Tinker.** untitled.